D0945150

THE ENGLISH CHURCHES IN A SECULAR SOCIETY

The English Churches in a Secular Society

Lambeth, 1870-1930

Jeffrey Cox

New York   Oxford
OXFORD UNIVERSITY PRESS
1982

Copyright © 1982 by Oxford University Press, Inc.

Library of Congress Cataloging in Publication Data

Cox, Jeffrey.
   The English churches in a secular society.

   Bibliography: p.
   Includes index.
   1. Church of England—History.   2. Sociology,
Christian—England.   3. England—Church history.
4. Church of England—England—Lambeth (London)—
History.   5. Sociology, Christian—England—
Lambeth (London).   6. Lambeth (London, England)—
Church history.   7. London (England)—Church
history.   8. Dissenters, Religious—England—History.   I. Title.
BX5101.C64   283′.42165   82-2157
ISBN 0-19-503019-2   AACR2

Acknowledgment is due to the following for permission to reprint:

Charles Chaplin, *My Autobiography*. Copyright © 1964 by Charles
Chaplin. Reprinted by permission of Simon & Schuster,
a Division of Gulf & Western.

Photographs on pages 52 and 54, copyright Greater London Council,
reproduced by permission.

Cartoon on page 208 from the *Brixton Free Press*, copyright British
Library, reproduced by permission.

Cartoons on pages 189 and 213 from *Punch*, reproduced by permission.

Printing (last digit): 9 8 7 6 5 4 3 2 1

Printed in the United States of America

To Lois

Acknowledgments

This book evolved from a doctoral dissertation submitted to the Department of History at Harvard University. I owe special thanks to my supervisor, Professor John Clive, and to my other teachers at Harvard, particularly Professor H. J. Hanham, who first encouraged me to take a sceptical look at the existing literature on the English churches. Professor Wallace MacCaffrey read the dissertation and offered a number of helpful suggestions. Another teacher, Professor Charles Garside of Rice University, stimulated and encouraged my interest in the history of religion. My good friend and fellow historian Roger Draper spent many hours arguing with me about some of the ideas which found their way into the book.

I would not have been able to write this book at all without the friendly cooperation of numerous South London clergymen, ministers, elders, and church secretaries who helped me to gain access to a variety of church and chapel records, showed me around many of Lambeth's church and chapel buildings, served tea, and in some cases took an interest in my spiritual condition. I owe a particular debt of gratitude to the Rev. Alan Argent, Yvonne Evans, and other members of Trinity Congregational Church in

Brixton. Equally helpful were archivists and librarians at the Minet Library in Lambeth, the British Library of Political and Economic Science, the Greater London Record Office, the British Library, and Dr. Williams's Library. I received additional help, while living in England, from the late Rev. E. A. Payne, the Rev. G. R. Dunstan, and the staff of the Institute of Historical Research.

Versions of my argument were presented to a meeting of the 1662 Society in London, to the late Professor H. J. Dyos's Urban History Seminar at Leicester University, to the annual meeting of the American Historical Association, and to the History Colloquium at the University of Iowa. My research was financed, in part, with a Danforth Fellowship from the Danforth Foundation, a Sheldon Traveling Fellowship from Harvard University, a Fulbright Travel Grant, and a University of Iowa Old Gold Summer Fellowship.

In the final stages of my research I had the benefit of comments about my argument from Professor W. O. Aydelotte and Dr. James Obelkevich. The final manuscript received a useful critical reading from Professor R. K. Webb. I also want to thank Nancy Lane and Curtis Church, my editors at Oxford University Press. Walter Bell and Paul Heer assisted with proofreading. The map on page 29 is based on the map which appeared in Janet Roebuck's *Urban Development in Nineteenth Century London: Lambeth, Battersea, and Wandsworth* (Phillimore and Co. Ltd., London, 1979).

My parents, Dr. and Mrs. Jack R. Cox of Teague, Texas, supported and encouraged my research in a great variety of ways. My greatest debt of gratitude goes to my wife, Lois, who helped and encouraged me in so many ways that it would be useless to attempt to enumerate them in print.

J.C.

Iowa City, Iowa
February 1982

Contents

LIST OF TABLES

Note: for the reader's convenience, all the numbered tables may be found together at the end of the text, on pages 277–309.

ABBREVIATIONS

The following abbreviations have been used in the notes or in the text.

BFP: Brixton Free Press
C.O.S.: Charity Organization Society
GLRO: Greater London Record Office
H.C.: House of Commons
L.C.C.: London County Council
SLP: South London Press

Notations A and B refer to notebooks in the Booth Collection, British Library of Economic and Political Science, London School of Economics. The place of publication of works cited in the notes is London unless otherwise noted.

THE ENGLISH CHURCHES IN A SECULAR SOCIETY

I

The Problem of Decline

The churches of England are now almost empty on an ordinary Sunday morning. The Church of England remains a significant institution, of course, despite the tiny numbers of regular church-goers. The press faithfully reports the pronouncements of the Archbishop of Canterbury, and the kindly parson is embraced, not without some irony, as an essential part of the social land-scape in some parts of the countryside. But religion is not supposed to be important, at least not in England. Books about recent English history usually fail to mention it altogether, and the subject of religion often provokes boredom. The churches are regarded as quaint and harmless but peripheral institutions, and curiosity about their workings and fate as a species of anti-quarianism.

The religious indifference of the twentieth century resembles in some respects that of the eighteenth century. But eighteenth-century apathy was reversed in the late eighteenth and the early nineteenth century, when the English people either endured or entered into a succession of religious crusades conducted by men and women who were convinced that England should be Christianized—or re-Christianized. At first largely evangelical, this movement broadened into a general revival of almost all forms of Church and Dissent until it was dissipated in the various movements for "social Christianity" in the very late nineteenth century.

Historians have often judged the success or failure of this revival according to one standard: did the churches persuade the emerging urban working class to attend Sunday services *en masse*? By the mid-nineteenth century it was already becoming clear that the answer to that question was no (although there were, of course, working-class churchgoers). Since the goal of the ecclesiastical troops and their officers was the creation of a churchgoing nation, their campaign has often been pronounced a failure.[1] But there is another way of looking at the Victorian churches. When compared to the last third of the twentieth century, the mid-Victorian period appears to swarm with religious activity. It followed a century of religious revival which animated all but the coldest, most rationalistic denominations, and generated new ones throughout the industrial areas. Dissenters and Methodists appealed effectively to England's growing numbers of shopkeepers and artisans, and the challenges of Nonconformity and urban infidelity summoned an energetic response by the established church.

The Church of England was reinvigorated in spite of enormous difficulties, for it had been closely identified with a rural landowning elite throughout the early modern period. When landowning influence receded in the eighteenth and nineteenth centuries, little popular affection for the church remained.[2] Burdened with the most inflexible structure of any western European church, the Church of England labored among an alien urban working class which felt no sense of popular loyalty. But the church found new and significant social functions at both parochial and national levels. Its achievements, like those

1. This is usually taken to be the point of K. S. Inglis's *Churches and the Working Classes in Victorian England* (1963).

2. See Alan Everitt, *The Pattern of Rural Dissent: The Nineteenth Century* (Leicester, 1972), on the association between rural landownership and Anglican religious practice; also D. M. Thompson, "The Churches and Society in Nineteenth Century England: A Rural Perspective," in G. J. Cuming and Derek Baker, eds., *Popular Belief and Practice,* Studies in Church History, 8 (Cambridge, 1972), pp. 267–76.

of the other denominations, have been obscured by an unjustified sense of failure, engendered by unrealistic expectations. Even its greatest success is sometimes regarded as a failure. The Church of England succeeded in capturing or maintaining the allegiance of new urban as well as old rural elites—in many cases no doubt the same families and one class. These elites regarded the Church of England as a useful social institution, financed its parochial activities, and upheld churchgoing as a model of social respectability for the deferential farther down the social scale.

Although failing to achieve their stated goal of attracting the entire nation to public worship, the churches succeeded in making public deference to religious values—and public acknowledgment of the importance of religion—almost universal among the upper and middle classes. The famous 1851 census of church attendance was conducted in such a way as to make it impossible to compute the actual number of churchgoing individuals, but the accuracy of the registrar general's summary is not in dispute: "The middle classes have augmented rather than diminished that devotional sentiment and strictness of attention to religious services by which for several centuries they have been so distinguished. With the upper classes, too, the subject of religion has obtained of late a marked degree of notice, and regular church attendance is now ranked amongst the recognized proprieties of life."[3] Would any other voluntary institution which attracted several million people to an ordinary weekly meeting be judged a failure?

It is also time to reexamine the institutional relationship between all of the churches and the English working class, as well as the character of "popular belief" among the unchurched, heathen masses. The Church of England succeeded in placing a parish church with a clergyman within reach of every Englishman, using only voluntary funds for purposes of expansion after 1818, and these parochial clergymen concerned themselves with far more than public worship. Through the sacramental rites of passage and through an enormous network of social welfare institutions—rural and urban—the church stayed in touch with the working class in ways which a concentration upon public

---

3. Census of Great Britain, 1851. *Religious Worship, England and Wales: Reports and Tables* (1690), House of Commons (1852–53), vol. 89, p. clviii.

worship alone obscures. No institution could rival the Church of England in geographical comprehension. Secular social reformers looked with envy at the network of thousands of clergymen placed in every neighborhood in the land, from the dark corners of the urban slums to remote villages abandoned by every other civilizing influence. After 1850 Nonconformists emulated them with thousands of "mission halls," preaching stations which evolved sometimes into autonomous chapels and sometimes into social welfare auxiliaries of the mother chapels. In the mid-nineteenth century only a rudimentary national bureaucracy, the local magistrates, and the often corrupt vestries were available to cope with rapid social change at the local level. Outside the spheres of public health, education, and the poor law, the state began moving decisively in the areas we would now label social services well after the turn of the century. As late as 1900 only the Guardians of the Poor, with their strictly limited responsibilities, could compete in their national distribution with the clergyman, the "man whose ministerial services each [person] claims as a right by day or night . . . only a national church provides this."[4]

The churches did not intend for things to turn out in precisely this way. But the consequences of collective social action are rarely the intended ones. The churches intended to persuade the entire nation to attend Sunday services, and there indoctrinate churchgoers with Anglican or Nonconformist values. Instead they persuaded only a portion of the upper and middle classes to attend church, and created a vast parochial and philanthropic network which provided the sacraments and social services to the working classes and the poor. In the second half of the nineteenth century the churches usually portrayed themselves as in a kind of giant settlement house, blanketing the entire nation with good works and providing England's best hope of bridging the gap between the classes. Complaints of working-class non-churchgoing have often been misunderstood as confessions of failure when they were in fact appeals for support. Like modern social workers who depend upon the existence of the poor for their livelihood, Victorian clergymen depended upon the existence of the unchurched. This was not cynical

4. A. C. Cooper-Marsdin, *Church or Sect*, 2nd, enlarged ed. (1918), p. 181.

opportunism. Anglican parishes in particular were not designed merely to produce regular churchgoers. Anglican clergymen, as they pondered the parable of the Good Samaritan and the Church of England's role as a "national church," felt both a religious obligation and a historical obligation to provide their services to all who wanted them. Those services included more than public worship; they embraced the entire range of religious philanthropy. Nonconformists, responding to the same social conditions and intellectual environment, found it similarly difficult to separate the tasks of converting a person and providing for his material welfare. The Victorian churches were hardly a failure. They were arguably Victorian England's most important voluntary social institution.

Sometime after 1850 this great religious crusade faltered. First came the "ethical revolt against Christian orthodoxy" and the Darwinian revolution in thought, which made agnosticism respectable if not universal by the turn of the century. Then religious institutions began to wither away. Whether this institutional decline began as early as 1850 or as late as World War I is a matter of dispute. Some Nonconformist denominations ceased to grow in real terms around 1850, others in the 1880s. Nonconformity continued to grow in absolute numbers until 1906 and 1907 when, with stunning unanimity, each denomination began to shrink.[5] Church attendance may have been holding its own in real terms between 1850 and 1880, but was almost certainly in decline by the 1880s.[6] Anglican baptisms, confirmations, and Easter communion statistics grew mysteriously in both real and absolute terms until the 1920s.[7] But by the end of that decade virtually all Protestant statistics (except of church closures) were

5. See the indispensable statistical compilation in Robert Currie, *Methodism Divided: A Study in the Sociology of Ecumenicalism* (1968); also Alan D. Gilbert, *Religion and Society in Industrial England: Church, Chapel and Social Change, 1740–1914* (1976); Robert Currie, Alan Gilbert, and Lee Horsley, *Churches and Churchgoers: Patterns of Church Growth in the British Isles since 1700* (1977).

6. See D. H. McLeod, "Class, Community and Religion: The Religious Geography of Nineteenth Century England," *Sociological Yearbook of Religion in Britain*, 6, 1973, pp. 29–73; E. R. Wickham, *Church and People in an Industrial City* (1957), pp. 109, 148.

7. Church Information Office, *Facts and Figures about the Church of England*, no. 2 (1962), p. 52; no. 3 (1965), pp. 54, 60.

plunging inexorably. This downward trend produced a mood of gloomy defeatism interrupted only by an ephemeral "revival" of the 1950s which generated illusory hopes. Arnold Bennett's comments of the 1920s could have been written in any subsequent decade: "I never hear discussion about religious faith now. Nobody in my acquaintance openly expresses the least concern about it. Churches are getting emptier. . . . The intelligentsia has sat back, shrugged its shoulders, given a sigh of relief, and decreed tacitly or by plain statement: 'The affair is over and done with.' "[8]

There are two generally accepted explanations for this decline of religious ideas and institutions during the last century, and almost everyone who has thought about the problem has found some form of one or the other persuasive. According to the first, the Victorian intellectual revolution itself caused the decline of the churches. Behind this explanation lies a more general model of social change. Intellectuals are thought to act as the vanguard of popular beliefs and values, and the "advanced" or "progressive" values filter down through the social scale over a few decades or centuries (in sociological jargon, "stratified diffusion").[9] This is a simplistic model of social change, now largely confined to textbooks. Not all "advanced" ideas become popular attitudes as a matter of course. Furthermore, ideas take on meaning from their social context. An idea may be incoherent in one society or decade, irrefutable in another. Victorian doubters raised no fundamentally new objections to Christianity. The problem of evil was underlined by the theory of natural selection, but the author of the Book of Job wrestled with similar difficulties. The real question has been well stated by Alasdair MacIntyre: "Why [could] incoherences which only presented problems to an Occam . . . present insuperable obstacles to a T. H. Huxley or a Russell?"[10]

8. *The Religious Interregnum* (1929), pp. 8, 10.

9. A more sophisticated version of this approach may be found in Hugh McLeod, *Class and Religion in the Late Victorian City* (1974), ch. 8. A formless intellectual chaos, accompanied by a "new hedonism," spreads to a middle class newly freed from the fear of Hell.

10. "Is Understanding Religion Compatible with Believing?" in Bryan Wilson, ed., *Rationality* (Oxford, 1970), p. 75; on objections to Christianity see H. R. Murphy, "The Ethical Revolt against Christian Orthodoxy in Early

MacIntyre has an answer which he shares with the great
majority of social theorists, sociologists, and social historians
along with many others who are unaware of their allegiance to
any formal theory of social change: the sociological theory of
secularization. Those scholars who have challenged its usefulness
have yet to discover a coherent alternative, and even find their
doubts rejected as unintelligible. Unable to conceive of alternative theories, social theorists regularly cite evidence of the
existence of a decline of religion in Britain as if it were conclusive
evidence in support of their particular theory of the causes of
this decline.[11]

Bits and pieces of the theory of secularization may be found
scattered about in the writings of Max Weber. He argued that
Western society was increasingly organized according to the
principles of instrumental rationality, of means/ends rationality
which placed the greatest value upon the adaptation of means to

---

Victorian England," *American Historical Review*, July 1955, pp. 800–817;
McLeod, *Class and Religion*, pp. 227ff.

11. Two attempts to sidestep the theory both involve nothing more than a
redefinition of terms. Talcott Parsons defines secularization as a diffusion of
Christian values throughout society in "Christianity in Modern Industrial
Society," in Edward A. Tiryakian, *Sociological Theory, Values, and Socio-
cultural Change* (New York, 1963), pp. 38ff.; Daniel Bell removes religion
from society altogether and places it within an autonomous realm called "culture" in "The Return of the Sacred? The Argument on the Future of Religion," *British Journal of Sociology*, vol. 28, no. 4, Dec. 1977, pp. 419–49. Peter
Berger and Thomas Luckmann limit secularization to orthodox religious
ideas and institutions, but leave the fundamental theory intact, in "Sociology
of Religion and Sociology of Knowledge," *Sociology and Social Research* 47
(4), July 1963, an argument extended in Peter Berger, *The Sacred Canopy:
Elements of a Sociological Theory of Religion* (New York, 1967), and Thomas
Luckman, *The Invisible Religion: The Problem of Religion in Modern Society* (New York, 1967). David Martin simply argues that the theory of secularization may be wrong in "Towards Eliminating the Concept of Secularization,"
in Julius Gould, ed., *Penguin Survey of the Social Sciences* (1965), reprinted
and elaborated upon in *The Religious and the Secular: Studies in Secularization* (New York, 1969). This suggestion met with a remarkable response in
Currie, *et al.*, *Churches and Churchgoers*, pp. 99ff., where statistics of the
decline of churchgoing and ecclesiastical marriage in Britain are confidently
cited as evidence for the theory of secularization, as if the fact of decline is
itself evidence in support of a particular theory of decline. Bryan Wilson re-
sponds similarly in *Contemporary Transformations of Religion* (1976), pp. 13–
15; Cf. Alasdair MacIntyre, *Secularization and Moral Change* (1967), p. 8.

ends without reference to any particular hierarchy of values.[12] The crisis of modern society, Weber argued, emerged from the conflict between instrumental rationality and value-oriented or substantive rationality. Instrumental rationality, both as an intellectual principle and as a principle of social organization, undermines all substantive rationality, all hierarchies of value.[13] Among those hierarchies of value are the great world religions, which are mankind's most systematic attempt to explain the meaning of life. Although instrumental rationality undermines all values, not merely religious values, religion is particularly vulnerable because of its comprehensive attempt to establish meaning. The practical manifestation of instrumental rationality —technology—gives mankind a sense of understanding at the same time as it undermines other attempts to supply meaning. Consequently, modern industrial bureaucratic society produces a "demystification" or "disenchantment" of the world,[14] and the rise of this rational bureaucratic and industrial society explains the decline of both religious values and religious institutions everywhere.

The theory of secularization is the religious counterpart of the theory of modernization, and it has been refined and elaborated upon by Weberian sociologists who argue that the rational organization of social life along instrumental lines strips ecclesiastical institutions of their social functions. Furthermore, the competition of rival value systems—pluralism—causes a general religious crisis in society which leads to indifference and unbelief. These theorists specifically and dogmatically state that

12. Max Weber, *Economy and Society: An Outline of Interpretive Sociology*, trans. by Ephraim Fischoff, *et al.*, ed. by Guenther Roth and Claus Wittich (New York, 1968), vol. 1, pp. 24–26, 85; vol. 2, pp. 809–31; "The Social Psychology of World Religions," in *From Max Weber: Essays in Sociology* trans. and ed. by H. H. Gerth and C. Wright Mills (New York, 1946), pp. 293–94.

13. "The Social Psychology of World Religions," pp. 281–82, and "Science as a Vocation," pp. 152–56, both in *From Max Weber*.

14. "The fate of our times is characterized by rationalization and intellectualization and, above all, by the 'disenchantment of the world.' Precisely the ultimate and most sublime values have retreated from public life either into the transcendental realm of mystic life or into the brotherliness of direct and personal human relations"; in *From Max Weber*, p. 155. Cf. *Economy and Society*, vol. 1, pp. 476–80, and *From Max Weber*, p. 284.

religion is, or soon will be, a *merely* marginal phenomenon in *all* advanced industrial societies.[15]

Weber stood in awe of the juggernaut of Western rationality, and his pessimism about the consequences of its universal triumph may have led him to misjudge the direction of historical change. Secularization theorists have great difficulty in interpreting examples of the vitality or growth of religious institutions in a modern or modernizing society. For example, British sociologists of religion, in particular Bryan Wilson and Alasdair MacIntyre, have gone to extraordinary lengths to describe American religion as uniquely superficial, materialistic, and meaningless.[16] This difficulty becomes acute in the discussion of religion during the English industrial revolution. Historians have professed to see a massive loss of faith in almost every period of modern English history, but social historians generally identify the industrial revolution as the primary "cause" of secularization. But why were the industrial revolution and the subsequent modernization of English society accompanied by a revival of almost all forms of religion as well as the creation of new and unique forms in the evangelical revival of the eighteenth and nineteenth centuries? According to Harold Perkin, religion became both more and less important during the industrial revolution, and other social historians have been forced to resort to convoluted and some-times unintelligible metaphors. Eric Hobsbawm argues that, despite the quantitative growth of religious bodies during the industrial revolution, religion mysteriously became "recessive" rather than "dominant" during that period. Alan Gilbert identi-fies "latent" secularization in the "manifest" growth of religious bodies during the industrial revolution.[17]

15. See Bryan Wilson, *Religion in a Secular Society: A Sociological Comment* (1966), ch. 3; Berger, *The Sacred Canopy*, chaps. 6, 7; MacIntyre, *Seculariza-tion and Moral Change*, pp. 44ff.; W. G. Runciman, "The Social Explanation of Religious Beliefs," *Archives Européennes de Sociologie (European Journal of Sociology)* 10 (2) 1969, p. 184; also in this tradition is Alan Gilbert, *The Making of Post-Christian Britain* (1980).

16. Wilson, *Religion in a Secular Society*, ch. 6; MacIntyre, *Secularization and Moral Change*, p. 32, and more emphatically in "Secularization," *The Listener*, February 15, 1968, p. 194.

17. Harold Perkin, *The Origin of Modern English Society 1780–1880* (1969), p. 203; Eric Hobsbawm, *The Age of Revolution 1789–1848* (1962), p. 261;

The origin of these difficulties lies in the description of the "modern world" as one in which all religion is, or soon will be, "merely marginal." Religious men and women are not invariably found among "marginal" or "archaic" sectors of modern society. On the contrary, there is a positive association between religious practice and social status in most Western democracies. Modern industrial societies—even the totalitarian ones—are not monolithically secular or irreligious. The pluralistic democracies are not completely and utterly devoted to utilitarian technocratic values to the exclusion of all others. Nor is it true, as Peter Berger argues, that those accepting supernatural beliefs are an isolated "cognitive minority" in the modern word, sharing the dilemma of a "witch doctor cast among logical positivists."[18] Repeated surveys of popular beliefs in the industrial democracies lead to the same conclusion: those who disavow any form of belief whatsoever in the supernatural are a decided minority in the Western industrial nations.[19]

Although far from "secular" in the Weberian sense, modern societies can hardly be described as Christian. They are a mosaic of belief and unbelief, devotion and apathy, faith and agnosticism, individualistic and corporate religion, and confusion. It is pluralism which most clearly distinguishes the present from the past in matters of religion. The last two centuries have seen the imperfect victory of that most admirable of seventeenth-century Baptist doctrines: "The magistrate is not by virtue of his office to meddle with religion, or matters of conscience, to force or compel men by this or that form of religion or doctrine."[20] The watershed separating the religious past from the religious present is not the advent of the industrial revolution, but the emergence of the secular state. Cast out among a multitude of private interests, the churches must compete.

Gilbert, *Religion and Society,* pp. viii, 205; cf. Gilbert, *The Making of Post-Christian Britain,* pp. 76–80.

18. *A Rumor of Angels: Modern Society and the Rediscovery of the Supernatural* (New York, 1969), pp. 18, 21.

19. Summaries for various nations in Hans Mol, ed., *Western Religion: A Country by Country Sociological Inquiry* (The Hague, 1972); also see Gallup Polls and surveys cited by Berger himself, *A Rumor,* pp. 39, 40.

20. Cited in A. C. Underwood, *A History of the English Baptists* (1947), p. 42.

Clergymen have long feared that the churches would wither and die unless buttressed by the state, and secular intellectuals have hoped that religious ideas would be unable to withstand the rigors of a free market in ideas. These hopes and fears have been transformed into sociological theory: Peter Berger argues that the churches dig their own graves in the very process of adapting to modern society. The modern form of religious organization, the denomination, itself promotes the great enemy of religious faith, pluralism. Faced with competing belief systems, most people prefer to believe nothing at all.[21] But Berger's theory demands a general social rejection of the supernatural or sacred which he assumes but does not demonstrate. Even very conservative denominations and institutionalized sects which have long recognized the existence of 'true Christians' in other denominations may extend legitimacy to other religious groups without abandoning their own views. Furthermore, there is some evidence that denominational competition stimulates religious practice without eroding religious faith. Both the Netherlands and the United States of America, with fragmented denominational structures and relatively large minorities with no religious affiliation, have higher levels of religious orthodoxy in popular belief as well as higher levels of religious practice than Sweden, where there is a numerically dominant national church and a low percentage of the population renounces its religious affiliation. (The best explanation of why the emergence of the secular state has not led to the automatic secularization of civil society may be found in Karl Marx's *Essay on the Jewish Question.*)

There are important religious differences between modern societies which have as much to do with their own unique religious histories as they do with universal processes of social change. "Pluralism" may have different consequences in two industrial nations. Or, to take another example, "structural differentiation" simply cannot be correlated successfully with low levels of religious belief or practice.[22] In a country where the church has sole responsibility for education, the assumption of that function by the state will naturally reduce the social importance of the church, although not necessarily of religious

---

21. *The Sacred Canopy*, pp. 147ff.
22. Mol, *Western Religion*, pp. 16–17.

beliefs. Where the primary function of a religious group is the justification and legitimation of nationalistic or ethnic or class or regional sentiment, structural differentiation may leave it unscathed.

In an attempt to solve some of these problems, particularly the seeming anomaly of a persistence of supernatural views in modern industrial societies, both Daniel Bell and Thomas Luckmann have argued that religious beliefs are wholly divorced from religious institutions in the modern world.[23] Bell argues that religion exists, along with art and literature, in an autonomous sphere called "culture." Luckmann argues that we should search for the "invisible religion" of modern society, shared "structures of legitimation" held in common in secular societies. It makes sense to assume, with Luckmann, that popular beliefs will drift away from institutional orthodoxy in a free market in religion (although it is by no means clear to what degree early modern or medieval "popular belief" resembled Christian orthodoxy). But how much of a drift? Once again, global theories of social change have triumphed over readily available facts. Luckmann greatly overestimates the chasm between existing popular religious views and traditional church-oriented Christianity, and he assumes the universal irrelevance of religious institutions in modern societies. Modern countries are not all alike. Some of them display relatively high levels of Christian orthodoxy, others do not. Religious institutions thrive in some countries and regions, and dwindle away in others. Furthermore, in the Western democracies there is a very rough correlation between the level of religious practice and the orthodoxy of popular beliefs. Churches are not wholly incompetent at the task of indoctrination, and denominations with high levels of church attendance generally have a more orthodox church membership than those with low levels of church attendance.[24] It defies common sense merely to assume, in the absence of evidence, that the fate of certain ideas is wholly unrelated to the fate of institutions specifically devoted to the promulgation of those ideas. It is at least possible that the decline of church attendance

23. Bell, "The Return of the Sacred"; Luckmann, *Invisible Religion*.

24. See Charles Y. Glock and Rodney Stark, *Religion and Society in Tension* (Chicago, 1965), pp. 119–22, on the relationship between belief and practice in American churches.

in England proceeded simultaneously with a decline in the orthodoxy of popular belief, although any observations about the relationship between the two are, to say the least, mainly speculative. This is not a simple problem, and it makes no sense at all to solve it by fiat, with a declaration that religious faith and religious institutions are permanently divorced everywhere in the modern world.

A more ambitious attempt to face up to, rather than evade, the anomalies and contradictions in the theory of secularization may be found in David Martin's *A General Theory of Secularization* (1978), which is all the more interesting in the light of Martin's earlier criticism of the theory (see note 11). His "general theory" resembles the Weberian theories of Bryan Wilson, Peter Berger, and others, although it is in some ways even more sweeping and correspondingly less useful.[25] But Martin fully recognizes that the general trends which he outlines might be nullified or altered out of all recognition by the particular cultural and historical circumstances of a particular country or culture or religious tradition.[26] Sensitive to the complexity of history, he outlines a number of "patterns" of secularization which incorporate growth and revival as well as decline and decay, and which are useful and stimulating.

But Martin leaves us with a logical difficulty. His general theory only explains decline. Growth or revival is explained by "something else," usually "history," and it is telling that his discussions of the exceptions to the general rule of decline in the modern world are more interesting than his discussions of patterns which conform to the general theory. We are not allowed to entertain the possibility that decline and decay might be explained by something other than the general trends which are incorporated into the general theory. If "history" or "historical

25. See David Martin, *A General Theory of Secularization* (1978), p. 160, where he links the future prospects of Christianity to the level of home-ownership and the prevalence of small-scale work environments. The spread of homeownership in twentieth-century Britain has done nothing for the churches. There is a similar contrast between a sensitive examination of the variety of patterns of religious change on the one hand, and a determination to fit them all into an overall explanatory pattern on the other, in Hugh McLeod, "The De-Christianization of the Working Class in Western Europe, 1850–1900," *Social Compass,* vol. 27, 1980, 2/3, pp. 191–214.

26. *Ibid.*, pp. 3, 13.

and cultural circumstances" can explain growth, can they not, in some cases, explain decline as well? Martin's theory, like other theories of secularization, diverts our attention from possible explanations of the decline of religion in modern Britain. The general theory serves as a substitute for serious scholarly inquiry. In that respect, it obscures as much as it illuminates.

I am not arguing that a secularization of thought has not occurred, or that pluralism may not, in some cases, cause the decay of religious faith and religious institutions, or that the social consequences of the industrial revolution were unimportant for religion. I am simply arguing that groups of men and women, as well as isolated individuals, continue to adopt religious views of the world. These groups are not doomed to an inevitable failure to grow or successfully propagate their views, and they may in some circumstances significantly influence the life of a modern nation. Furthermore, their views are not necessarily epiphenomenal or meaningless or empty, but may be genuinely "religious" by any reasonable definition of the word (although it is true that religion rarely exists in a "pure" form and is almost always intermixed with something else).[27] We should use greater caution in linking "decline" with broad general theories of secularization. If specific historical circumstances may be used to explain the growth or revival or persistence of religion, they might also be used to explain decline, decay, or indifference. And if these arguments are correct, it is necessary to reexamine the decline of religion in England during the last century, since most explanations are based upon a different set of assumptions.

England stands out among modern nations in the degree to which its people are "unchurched." It shares with the Scandinavian countries a pattern of high levels of "purely nominal" participation in the ecclesiastical rites of passage combined with extraordinarily low levels of regular religious practice, lower than most continental nations and the other English speaking nations, including Scotland. The English are not "secular" in Berger's sense of the word, for they are just as willing as other peoples to embrace some unverifiable notion of God or reincarnation or

27. The nearest approach to a satisfactory sociological definition of religion may be found in Clifford Geertz, "Religion as a Cultural System," in Michael Banton, ed., *Anthropological Approaches to the Study of Religion* (1966), p. 4.

private prayer or other evidence of a willingness to countenance the existence of a world beyond our own. But popular belief is less likely to take a recognizably Christian form in England than in America and other nations with higher levels of church attendance.[28]

Only Roman Catholicism, strengthened by the proscription of mixed marriages and a continuing immigration, has shown any signs of vitality in twentieth-century Britain. The Irish character of English popular Catholicism remains strong in obvious ways, such as the availability of Irish newspapers in church literature stalls. As Catholics became more widely distributed both geographically and socially, Roman Catholic churches sprang up in formerly all-Protestant suburbs, small towns, and villages. Most neighborhoods contain a small pool of potential recruits in addition to the Catholics already resident—Protestants attracted to the liturgy, or to a flourishing church; children rebelling against strongly Protestant or strongly agnostic parents.[29] But neither the appeal of authoritarianism in an age of catastrophe nor the appeal of the liturgy itself accounts for Catholic growth, for conversions have been a negligible component of expansion. An expanding social base has coincided with the appropriation of religious symbols as a means of maintaining ethnic identity.

But what of the two languishing traditions, the Anglican and the Nonconformist, whose followers accounted for most of the Victorian churchgoing nation? Both traditions entered a period of decline between 1870 and 1930 which has not been reversed.

28. David Martin, "Great Britain: England," in Mol, ed., *Western Religion,* pp. 229–47; and *A Sociology of English Religion* (1967), pp. 52–58. Martin assumes that "churchgoers are more 'orthodox' than non-churchgoers," pp. 53–54. Levels of church attendance and of religious "orthodoxy" both are lower in Britain than in America and France. See George H. Gallup, *The Gallup International Public Opinion Polls: Great Britain 1937–1975,* 2 vols. (New York, 1976), pp. 3, 13, 166, 403–07, 995, 1250–51, 1417–18; *The Gallup International Public Opinion Polls: France, 1944–75,* 2 vols. (New York, 1976), pp. 106–7, 233–37, 310, 523, 619, 661–63, 703–5, 828, 838, 962; *Public Opinion 1972–77* 2 vols. (Wilmington, Del., 1978), pp. 392ff., 627, 859.

29. These comments are based largely upon Anthony E. C. W. Spencer, "The Demography and Sociography of the Roman Catholic Community in England and Wales," in Laurence Bright and Simon Clements, eds., *The Committed Church* (1966), pp. 60–84.

Why? This question can only be answered by examining the ideas and activities of men and women active in the churches and relating them to their social environment. What were clergymen saying? What were their attitudes? What were the attitudes of churchgoers to the churches? of non-churchgoers? How was "popular religion" related to religious institutions? The churches had to compete both socially and intellectually, and clergymen and ministers knew it. Unless it wishes to remain a tiny sect, a church in a pluralistic society must address the public or a section of the public in terms which relate to their everyday concerns. To say that is not to be cynical. It is merely to recognize the dual nature of all religious institutions, which must witness to the transcendent while establishing themselves as social institutions. Both the churches and civil society have long recognized that only a small percentage of the population can afford to forsake the world and adhere strictly to theological principle. That is why monasticism and world-rejecting sectarianism have played such prominent roles in the history of the West. That is why individuals who take the Sermon on the Mount literally have often been labelled demon-possessed or insane. Attitudes toward religion in general and the churches in particular were shaped by perceptions of the churches' relationship to society and other social institutions in a "free market in ideas." What did the churches have to offer? Why should anyone believe what they were saying? How did that change?

Although the decline of religion is a national phenomenon, these are questions which must first be answered through a local study.[30] The decline of the churches happened at the parochial and congregational level. It is impossible to study every individual church and chapel in England, and a sample of parishes and congregations scattered about the country could not be

30. Other local studies of this period either ignore the problem of decline or take it for granted. See McLeod, *Class and Religion,* on social class and "mentalité"; Robert Moore, *Pit-men, Preachers and Politics: The Effects of Methodism in a Durham Mining Community* (1974), on politics. Stephen Yeo's study of Reading, on the other hand, points the way to the answers to some of these questions, and I am indebted to him for many suggestions: *Religion and Voluntary Organizations in Crisis* (1976); also "Religion in Society: A View from a Provincial Town in the Late Nineteenth and early Twentieth Centuries," Sussex D.Phil., 1971.

related to its social environment. My own choice for study is South London, and particularly the Borough of Lambeth. With a population of about 300,000 at the turn of the present century, Lambeth was the second largest of the newly created metropolitan boroughs—Islington was larger and Stepney almost as large—and larger than many substantial provincial cities. London was sorting itself into concentric bands of internally homogeneous social status, each of which crossed Lambeth. Because it was a borough of such unusual shape—roughly six miles long and one mile wide—it was a statistically compact urban corridor encompassing great social diversity: the slums around Waterloo Station and Lambeth Palace; the more or less respectable working-class housing of Vauxhall, Kennington, Stockwell, and West Dulwich; terraces of commuters, mostly clerks, who made a daily exodus to the City from Loughborough Park and West Norwood. The deteriorating upper-middle-class respectability of Brixton Hill, a neighborhood which was still compared with Hampstead in the 1880s, stood in contrast to the more well-to-do hills and rises slightly farther out—Tulse Hill and Denmark Hill, Streatham and Upper Norwood. Because of this heterogeneity Lambeth hovered near the median on lists of the London boroughs ranked according to social status by some index such as overcrowding, ratio of domestic servants to separate occupier, or percentage of professionals. Many London neighborhoods were transformed socially with each new generation, but Lambeth, because of its shape and social diversity, allows some control over the ever-present social deterioration which affected almost all of the older areas of England's cities.

Most of the pecularities of London—the ethnic diversity of the East End and the concentration of wealth, power, affluence, and influence in the City and the West End—were entirely absent across the bridges. With its own labor market and economic life, South London had an exclusively residential and industrial character which appalled Sir Walter Besant: "It is a city without a municipality, without a centre, without a civic history. It has no university. It has no colleges apart from medicine. Its residents have no local patriotism or enthusiasm. It has no clubs. It has no public buildings. It has no West End." Another writer complained that "She [South London] has not even achieved the unhappy eminence of East London, happy hunting ground of the philanthropist."[31]

Lambeth's ethnic homogeneity matched its diversity of social classes. Everyone agreed that Lambeth was extraordinarily English for an urban area, with none of the continental flavor of the East End, the overwhelming Irish presence of western Lancashire, or the Welsh and Scottish enclaves which characterized most English cities: "A city of manageable size," according to one writer, "which has never had any very great foreign immigration to affect the constant, age long influx of young countrymen and women; a microcosm, as I take it of all England."[32] Although a few Irish lived between Kennington Lane and Lambeth Road, Lambeth was even more English than other South London boroughs, for the South London Irish were concentrated in Southwark and Rotherhite.

Every area of England, urban and rural, experienced a decline of religious institutions. The pattern has been different in Lancashire and other areas of Irish settlement, but ethnicity was a sideshow for most of the English people between 1870 and 1930. Most of them had little experience with the wealth and power of the West End, or the ethnic diversity of the East End, or the Protestant-Catholic hatreds of western Lancashire, and much experience with a conurbation of slum, deteriorating suburb, and new suburban growth.

31. Besant cited in *Church Times*, May 26, 1899; Oliver Madox Hueffer, *Some of the English: A Study towards a Study* (1930), p. 23; see E. J. Hobshawm, "The Nineteenth Century London Labour Market," in Centre for Urban Studies, ed., *London: Aspects of Change* (1964), pp. 3–28.

32. Hueffer, *Some of the English*, p. 15; general information about Lambeth is available in the extraordinary volumes of the *Survey of London,* nos. 22 (1951) and 26 (1956), and in H. J. Dyos, "The Suburban Development of London South of the Thames," London Ph.D., 1952; Dyos's later book, *Victorian Suburb: A Study of the Growth of Camberwell* (Leicester, 1961), contains additional information about a similar South London borough.

2

Public Worship

Upon arriving in Edwardian Lambeth to observe the manners and morals of its inhabitants, a social anthropologist would notice the churches very quickly, along with houses, warehouses, pubs, shops, and schools, and he would soon associate certain obvious social activities with these buildings. Private houses were for eating, sleeping, and raising children. Shops and warehouses were for buying, selling, and storing goods which were, on the whole, produced elsewhere. Schools housed classes in various subjects. But what happened in church buildings? Would he conclude that churches and chapels were primarily used for public worship?

Not from simple observation. Worship was only one of dozens of activities which occurred on the premises of churches and church halls. Most of the larger Edwardian church buildings were in use daily, and it would have been difficult to discover a common denominator for the typical succession of events. Only upon talking to various people would he discover that church buildings were regarded as houses of worship, that the Sunday morning and Sunday night assemblies were accorded a special significance denied to all other activities, and that the essential meaning of the buildings was inextricably bound up with those meetings. Others would paint a different picture, arguing that a church was more generally the site of various ceremonial rites of passage. But the former view would prevail among the men and women who were most closely associated with the churches and chapels, as well as in "public opinion" as expressed in books and newspapers, and these are reasons enough to examine the meaning and importance of worship more closely.

On a wet December Sunday in 1902, 26,375 individuals performed the ritual of public worship in the morning in Lambeth, and 33,550 in the evening (see Table 1): slightly under 9 percent of the population in the morning, almost exactly 11 percent in the evening. It is impossible to discover the number of separate individuals who attended church once or more on that Sunday, but it is possible to make a rough estimate. The census-takers of the *Daily News,* greatly concerned with accuracy, were aware of the problem, and conducted a semi-scientific census of the number of "twicers" who attended church both morning and evening in a sample of London churches and chapels (see Table 2). After an estimate for the number of "twicers" is deducted, roughly 50,000 Lambeth churchgoers remain (see Table 2A).

Although 50,000 sounds like a large number of people, public opinion at the time was dominated by all sorts of inherited notions about the "normal" level of churchgoing and this was regarded as a depressingly low figure. It was lower than previous years, for morning church attendance had fallen from 17.2 percent of the population in 1851 to 11.7 percent in 1886–88 and 8.7 percent in 1902; evening attendance rose from 13.5 percent in 1851 to 14.4 percent in 1886–88, falling to 11 percent in 1902 (see Table 1). These figures almost certainly overstate the real decline in the number of churchgoers. The 1851 figures are estimates by clergymen and consequently overstated.[1] The practice of attending twice on Sunday was apparently in decline, further distorting the figures. Finally, Lambeth experienced rapid social deterioration in some neighborhoods after 1886,

1. In 1899 Charles Booth's interviewers recorded estimates of "average" attendance by every Lambeth incumbent. Their estimates were higher, in virtually every case, than the actual attendance recorded three years later by the Daily News census. See Booth Collection, B-269, 271, 272, 304, 309, 312, 392; British Library of Economic and Political Science, London School of Economics.

and some churchgoers simply left, to continue their churchgoing elsewhere. Nevertheless, churchgoing was declining. No one claimed that it was becoming more popular. And the fact of decline, combined with an exaggerated notion of the piety of the past, obscured the social importance of public worship both for the Edwardians and for subsequent historians.

These 50,000 churchgoers accounted for roughly 17 percent of Lambeth's population, and it is not unusual to find the word "only" placed before a figure like 17 percent in discussions of churchgoing. Furthermore, historians often imply, perhaps unconsciously, that a declining institution like the church is, by definition, unimportant.[2] But that is illogical, and other institutions are not treated in that manner. The pub was "in decline" throughout the first half of the twentieth century, but no historian has labelled it "unimportant." In the 1930s Mass Observation discovered a regular pubgoing population of 9 to 10 percent of the population in Bolton, 6 percent in Fulham. But they never described the pub as unimportant or referred to "only" 10 percent.[3]

The family, work, and school were more or less compulsory, but it is difficult to discover a voluntary institution in Edwardian Lambeth which rivalled the churches in social importance. These 50,000 churchgoers do not even represent Lambeth's regular churchgoing population, if "regular" is defined as once a month or more, and public worship was only one of a great number of church-related activities which enrolled thousands more. If public worship had been the only dimension of religion in Lambeth and 50,000 the sum total of all churchgoers, it would have remained a voluntary social ritual of enormous interest and importance. Leaders of the small Lambeth chapter of either the Social Democratic Federation or the Independent Labour Party would have been astonished to find 50,000 at a run-of-the-mill weekly meeting on a rainy day. In the general election of 1900 only 11,476 adult males voted in Lambeth, compared to 16,268 adult males at both worship services on a Sunday in 1902 (probably about 14,000

2. This appears to be the assumption behind many of the comments on early twentieth-century religion which appear in textbooks on recent British history.

3. Mass Observation, *The Pub and the People: A Worktown Study* (c. 1943), p. 111.

individual worshippers). But two of Lambeth's four seats were uncontested in 1900, and in 1906 the number of voters in four contests rose to 31,671.[4] Perhaps the occasional general election vote is more strictly comparable to the act of attending church only at Christmas and Easter, whereas voting in the more frequent local government, school board (until 1903), and Board of Guardians elections is comparable to weekly church attendance. Voters in local elections could sometimes be numbered in the hundreds. Although very difficult to calculate, friendly society enrollments may have rivaled churchgoing. Twenty-two secular friendly societies without branches enrolled 4624 members in 1899, and the Foresters alone, the largest of the multi-local friendly societies, had 3654 members.[5] The twenty-four trade unions belonging to Lambeth's two trade councils enrolled 5343 members in 1901.[6] The small Edwardian cinematographs, still using a hazardous, inflammable film, provided no challenge to the churches. Nor did theaters and music halls, for despite Lambeth's reputation as a site of low entertainment there were only two in Lambeth in 1905 with an additional seven licenses granted for "concert halls and dining rooms" including two in Anglican parochial halls.[7]

Few Lambeth streets lacked some sort of church or chapel, but even fewer lacked a pub, and Lambeth's 172 churches, chapels, and mission halls competed with 430 pubs and beerhouses (1905).[8] The large pubs rivaled the old parish churches in territoriality, defining a neighborhood or a fare stage on the tram, and all of the larger pubs hosted banquets and business meetings for cyclist clubs, friendly societies, and trade unions. The onslaughts of the licensing magistrate and the cinema were only beginning in 1902,

4. Figures from F. H. McCalmont, *The Parliamentary Poll Book of all Elections* (7th ed., 1910).

5. Reports of the Chief Registrar of Friendly Societies for 1900. H.C. 1901 (35), vol. 72, pp. 82–95.

6. Report by the Chief Labour Correspondent of the Board of Trade on Trade Unions in 1901. H.C. 1902 cd. 1348, vol. 97, p. 150. This figure does not include all union members in Lambeth or members of the various cooperative societies.

7. London County Council, Local Government and Statistical Dept., *London Statistics,* vol. 16, 1905–6, p. 187.

8. *Ibid.,* p. 209.

and the Edwardian pub certainly surpassed the church in weekly attendance and probably in Sunday attendance also. Upset at that prospect, a group of Walworth Primitive Methodists conducted a "census of Sunday pub attendance" in early 1900. Anxious pubwatchers counted those entering fifteen neighborhood pubs, classifying them as men, women, children with jugs or bottles, or, ominously, children without such containers.[9] Their fears were amply confirmed, for the total number of pubgoers exceeded the entire population of their ecclesiastical parish. The pub was one Edwardian social institution which was indisputably more popular than church or chapel.

Lambeth's churchgoers, like Lambeth's pubgoers, were not evenly distributed according to age or sex or social class, and their social distribution is significant. Although at least nominally Christian, churchgoers were divided into warring sects with divergent views upon the nature of the universe and the character of English society. Roman Catholicism was relatively insignificant in Lambeth, accounting for less than 0.5 percent of morning and 0.2 percent of evening attendance (see Table 1). The remaining houses of worship may be classified conveniently as: 1. church; 2. chapel; or 3. mission hall. A parish church was distinguished by the presence of an Anglican incumbent, a chapel by the presence of a self-supporting Nonconformist congregation. The mission hall was sustained *for* the congregation by outsiders, and no one expected a mission hall—Anglican or Nonconformist—to pay its own way. Mission halls sprang into existence in the mid-nineteenth century and had virtually disappeared by the mid-twentieth. They accounted for 26 percent of Nonconformist and only 9 percent of Anglican aggregate attendance in 1902. Consequently, Nonconformists outnumbered Anglicans at both the morning and evening service (see Table 1).

There were more women than men in Edwardian Lambeth, but women outnumbered men in the pews by an even greater margin. The churches attracted 7 percent of the adult male population in the morning and 9.5 percent in the evening compared to 8.4 percent and 14.6 percent respectively of women (see Table 11). For many people the real mid-day festival on Sunday was dinner,

9. B-273, p. 83. The South East London Mission, Old Kent Road: 8511 men, 4107 women with 547 babies, 3305 boys and girls "under 13." Population of the ecclesiastical parish, 13,953. Walworth abuts Lambeth.

not church, and wives and servants responsible for that ceremony could not attend the 11 A.M. service. Children accounted for a larger percentage of the morning than the evening congregation: accompanying their servant-keeping parents to a "family service," or going with father if the wife remained at home, or being shuttled from morning Sunday School directly to the service if both parents remained at home (afternoon Sunday School was more popular, however). At one riverside Baptist chapel in Bermondsey "An old lady who lived facing the chapel came to services on the condition that she could go out during the hymn before the sermon to see that her fire was all right, and that the dinner was cooking properly, and return just as the text was being announced. She did that regularly for five or six years."[10] Few women went to such pains, waiting instead for the evening service which was 50 percent adult female. Servants were customarily free on Sunday evening as well. Some employers apparently expected servants to attend church or chapel with the family, and even paid for their pews, but servants evidently preferred to worship on their own. "We get a number of servants, mostly those of church people," a Congregational minister claimed. "Servants are independent and usually prefer to go to a different church to their employers."[11]

The chapel attracted more men than the parish church, and men actually outnumbered women at morning Nonconformist services in one district in the borough (North Lambeth) where women greatly outnumbered men in the overall population (see Table 10). Many Nonconformists argued that this was the natural result of competition between an enervating and feminine Anglo-Catholicism and a robust, masculine Nonconformist Protestantism. However, among Anglicans the evangelical parishes showed no less of a marked feminine presence than their Anglo-Catholic counterparts (see Table 4), and the most evangelical of the Nonconformist denominations, the Baptists, attracted a larger proportion of females than the more liberal and liturgical Nonconformist denominations. Others suggested that church organization rather than formal theology accounted for the difference.

10. J. C. Carlile, *My Life's Little Day* (1935), p. 72.

11. B-303, p. 57; cf. Booth, *Life and Labour*, ser. 3, vol. 6, p. 101; vol. 3, pp. 103-4, 110-14, 147-49, 186, on similar patterns in the West End.

The democratic polity of Dissent attracted men, who were given real responsibility for running chapel affairs, while women accepted clerical authority in parish affairs just as they accepted a subordinate position at home. There may be something to that, although the most democratic denomination, the Baptists, had the highest ratio of women to men among the Nonconformists. The Wesleyans, on the other hand, placed far more authority in the hands of the minister but came much nearer than the Baptists to achieving an even ratio of men to women (see Table 3). Nonconformist congregations generally included a larger proportion of children as well as men, which supplies a partial explanation for the contrast between Anglican and Nonconformist. Nonconformity was a minority tradition which required a greater commitment than Anglicanism. It became a family as well as an individual tradition, and family churchgoing became a means of reinforcing family loyalty and cohesion among Nonconformists. The percentage of children in each denomination also varied roughly with the proportion of its overall attendance accounted for by mission halls (see Table 3). Many mission halls were entirely for children, and 63 percent of all morning worshippers at Nonconformist mission halls were children, only 33 percent at Nonconformist chapels (36 percent and 18 percent respectively in the evening). But when mission halls are excluded altogether, the contrast between Anglican and Nonconformist sex ratios remains, with 1.2 adult women for every adult man in the Nonconformist morning service compared to 1.7 among the Anglicans, and 1.6 Nonconformist women per man in the evening compared to 2.0 Anglican women per man (see Table 3).

It was well known throughout the nineteenth century that religious beliefs and practices varied dramatically from one neighborhood to another, and Lambeth was no exception. Its population grew from 27,985 in 1801 to 301,895 in 1901, when its physical development was almost complete. Until 1824, Lambeth was served by the ancient parish church of St. Mary, Lambeth, two chapels of ease, one Wesleyan and a handful of Dissenting chapels. The first new Anglican parishes within the ancient parish were created in 1824: one on Waterloo Road near the river, the other three in Kennington, Brixton, and Norwood. In each of these new parishes an imposing Greek revival structure was erected. The Waterloo Road was already developed, but the

Kennington, Brixton, and Norwood churches, situated on open ground at important road junctions, provided an architectural focus for their neighborhoods. Around them spread rows of houses for clerks, shopkeepers, and skilled artisans, constructed in routine fashion by small-scale commercial speculators, each new development luring away the most respectable from the neighborhoods nearer the river and causing the older communities to decay. New ecclesiastical parishes were carved out of the original five until, by 1900, there were more than thirty. In 1885 Lambeth was divided into four parliamentary divisions (North Lambeth, Kennington, Brixton, and Norwood) which varied roughly in social status according to their distance from the river (see note, Table 5).

In 1900 the upper part of the North Lambeth district was, according to Charles Booth, "a maze of small streets and courts crowded in many parts with a low living population. These streets, set at every conceivable angle to each other, appear on our map like stitches of embroidery filling in the groundwork of a pattern made by the crossing of the main thoroughfares. And a terrible embroidery it proves to be, as we look closer and closer into it: of poverty, dirt and sin."[12] The number of families in the more respectable houses could be identified by the different curtain patterns in the several windows, for even those houses had, it was said, "a family in each corner and one in the middle of the floor." The riverside, Waterloo Station, and the street markets of the New Cut and Lower Marsh were the focuses of this area and provided employment for wharf and riverside laborers, a colony of dustmen picking through riverside refuse, cabmen, prostitutes, and costers. South of Waterloo Station, in the vicinity of Lambeth Palace, was a neighborhood which had suffered both physical and social deterioration. Unlike the Waterloo Road area it had recently included some of the "better sort" of working men, but the expansion of the London and Southwestern Railway yard had driven them out, to Stockwell or Brixton. At Doulton's potteries and warehouses, for instance, the skilled employees lived away from the area, riding trams to work, while the laborers still lived near the river.

In the next district, Kennington, the ground rose from the

12. Booth, *Life and Labour*, ser. 3. vol. 4, p. 7.

Lambeth with major roads, districts, and neighboring districts

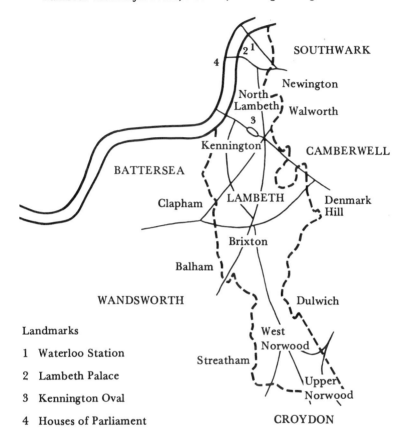

Landmarks

1 Waterloo Station

2 Lambeth Palace

3 Kennington Oval

4 Houses of Parliament

marshy riverside to a flat central plain displaying "shabbiness but not squalor." On one side of Kennington Park lived the employees of the railway, gas works, vinegar works, and potteries, on the other a higher proportion of respectable clerks and retired tradesmen. The spots of concentrated poverty became less frequent. South London's broad thoroughfares still displayed large, respectable houses with gardens near Kennington Park: "The division is much brighter and in general more cheerful—the women look much less care-worn."[13]

13. B-326, p. 43.

Charles Booth complained that the next district, Brixton, was "a little oppressive on account of its extreme respectability," a respectability which coexisted with rapid social deterioration. "Street after street testifies to the virtue of the shopkeepers," Booth continued, "who are found here in large numbers."[14] Brixton in fact had a very mixed population. One parish was described as consisting of "doctors, shopkeepers, theatrical and musical people, much shabby gentility and many lodgers; medical students, clerks, artisans and some labourers." Another was said to be one-fourth professional people, civil servants, solicitors, and merchants, one-fourth clerks, one-half small shopkeepers and artisans.[15] Printers and meat market employees rode the all-night train service from Loughborough Junction to the City. The upper middle and servant-keeping classes lived on the broad thoroughfares lined with Georgian and early Victorian houses set back from the roadway with broad gardens in front, which gave Brixton an air of spaciousness and even elegance. The occasional garden was built over by a shop, portent of the middle-class evacuation of the next generation. At Brixton Hill the central plain ended: "the ground rises and falls successively, with gardens and large houses on the upper slopes, while in the valleys cluster streets occupied by clerks and artisans, with a certain number of poor on the lowest ground."[16] Climbing past a few remaining mansions of the very wealthy, the Brixton Hill Road reached the Church of Holy Trinity, Tulse Hill, whose vicar longed for a socially mixed parish like his previous one in Sheffield: "We used to have a nice lot of poor. It provides work for the district visitors and gives vent generally for a practical Christianity."[17]

In the farthest district from the river, Norwood, the ground fell again, to less gentility but also to a smaller proportion of the working class proper. Norwood was the characteristic home of the commuting clerk, solidly lower middle-class, fiercely Tory at every election between 1885 and 1945, socially as remote from the London of politics, journalism, and finance as a clerk in any provincial suburb. Although West Norwood had open spaces and

14. B-326, p. 51.
15. Booth, *Life and Labour,* ser. 3, vol. 6, p. 43; B-305, p. 129.
16. Booth, *Life and Labour,* ser. 3, vol. 6, p. 61.
17. B-305, p. 229.

no overcrowding, property values were depressed in 1900 as large estates came onto the market and the houses were pulled down to make way for rows of "workmen's dwellings" or "artisans' " tenements. As the ground rose again toward the Crystal Palace at Upper Norwood, detached houses appeared and the vicar wrote in the parish magazine: "The deep tides of poverty and consequent sin do not reach up to us."[18] These outer neighborhoods—West and Upper Norwood with neighboring Dulwich and Streatham—were not socially homogeneous by mid-twentieth-century standards, for pockets of poverty were scattered throughout them. Only a handful of ecclesiastical parishes literally contained no poor inhabitants, unlike those created in the suburban housing tracts of the twenties and thirties which carried the physical separation of the classes to new extremes. But to a family moving from inner London, the Edwardian suburbs were a new world. "To a boy coming out of Battersea," Richard Church wrote, Dulwich "was half-way to paradise. I could not believe our good fortune; our own small garden had three chestnut trees in it. . . . I was no longer molested by fear of gangs of urchins; the aspect of the street no longer threatened me with the sullen gloom of poverty, bareness, and the negative picturesqueness of squalor and brutality. I began to feel more confidence in life. How could I do otherwise, after being transplanted into paradise?"[19]

Lambeth church attendance, morning and evening, varied predictably with social status, growing as one moved away from the river (see Table 6). Apparent exceptions to this rule occur when Anglican and Nonconformist statistics are considered in isolation, but those exceptions merely reflect the presence of large, prosperous churches in the poorer districts which attracted middle-class worshippers from a wide area (Christ Church, Westminster Bridge Road, a Congregational church in North Lambeth, and St. Mark's, Christ Church, and St. John the Divine in Kennington).

Both Anglican and Nonconformist attendances were higher in the wealthier than in the poorer districts, although the Noncon-

18. Christ Church, Gipsy Hill, *Parish Magazine,* Aug. 1906.

19. Richard Church, *Over the Bridge* (1955), pp. 182, 191; cf. Louis Heren, *Growing Up Poor in London* (1973), p. 182.

formists were more successful than Anglicans in the poorer neighborhoods. Nonconformists in fact attracted more worshippers than the Anglicans in all four of Lambeth's districts if mission halls are included. The gap between Anglican and Nonconformist levels of attendance narrows in the wealthier districts and disappears altogether even farther into the suburbs, in the neighboring district of Croydon. The morning service was fashionable, the evening service popular. Morning rivaled evening attendance only in Norwood, and there only among Anglicans. The implications of this well-known association between middle-class status and enthusiastic churchgoing have not been fully assimilated, in part because general theories of secularization often relegate religion to the margins of modern society, to doomed or anachronistic occupational groups such as artisans or farmers. The fact that "the working classes did not attend" is sometimes cited as evidence of the unimportance of religion. Victorian and Edwardian urban religion was important precisely because the churches were better able to attract those with wealth and power than those without, those who could make decisions affecting the lives of others rather than those who could not, those in the center of society rather than on the margins, those in the sectors of society most resembling the modern, associational *Gesellschaft* rather than the pre-modern communal *Gemeinschaft*.

By the turn of the century most clergymen had become fully accustomed to the overwhelming influence of social class upon patterns of churchgoing, but their responses to that fact varied considerably. Some were fatalistic while others were still determined to "reach the workers." Others were positively complacent, arguing that the church exerted other forms of influence in working-class households and that the working classes were religious in their own way despite their indifference to the middle-class ritual of church attendance. Earlier in the nineteenth century many people had assumed that churchgoing was in some way "natural" and non-churchgoing an aberration, or merely the result of a faulty deployment of resources. This argument produced an obsession with "accommodation," which in turn rested upon the assumption that pews which could be built would eventually be filled. And the Church of England did face frustrating legal barriers when attempting to supply adequate num-

bers of urban parishes and clergymen, for the rural pattern of
clerical deployment was protected by the parson's freehold and
its accompanying system of patronage.[20] In the long run this
inflexibility probably forestalled a disastrous rationalization of
small country parishes, but the system produced urban parishes
of daunting size. In the face of these very real problems, however,
the Church of England managed to blanket England's cities with
new parishes in the nineteenth century. In Lambeth more than
eighty clergymen were at work in over thirty parishes by 1900,
and clergymen in large parishes were no less effective than those
in small parishes. There is no discernable statistical relationship
between small parishes and higher levels of church attendance in
Lambeth's working-class neighborhoods in 1902 (see Table 7).
Smaller parishes attracted a larger percentage of the parochial
population to Sunday worship only in churchgoing Norwood.

Furthermore, church attendance was unrelated to clerical
deployment as well as to parochial size. Much of the discussion
in the Paul Report of 1964 on the deployment of the clergy was
based on the premise that more clergymen would produce more
worshippers, that "the urban activities of 7,000 additional parochial clergy . . . would produce 700,000 [additional] Christmas
communicants."[21] Lambeth provides an excellent test for this
theory, for in 1902 the Church of England deployed more clergymen per capita in working-class than in suburban Lambeth (see
Table 8). There were two "High" parishes in North Lambeth
with four curates each and two Evangelical parishes with three
each. Those parishes almost certainly received funds from the
national parochial aid organizations of their respective church
parties. In one parish with three curates the incumbent was a man
of considerable wealth who subsidized at least one curate. The
deployment of the clergy in the areas of greatest "need" reflected
Victorian anxiety about working-class non-churchgoing and the
class divisions which it mirrored. But when the number of persons
per clergyman in each of Lambeth's ecclesiastical parishes is
correlated with the sum of morning and evening Anglican attendance as a percentage of the population in each parish, the

20. See the discussion in Leslie Paul, *The Deployment and Payment of the
Clergy* (1964), passim.
21. Paul, *Deployment*, p. 166; cf. n. 34 below.

relationship is statistically insignificant. The Church of England's attempts to increase church attendance by supplying more clergymen to working-class neighborhoods were largely if not entirely ineffective in Lambeth. Clerical effectiveness depended entirely upon the social composition of the parish. In North Lambeth the parochial mean of total Anglican attendances for each Anglican clergyman was 156, in Kennington 342, in Brixton 540, and in Norwood 737 (see Table 9). Both strategies—creating new parishes and placing more clergymen in existing parishes—produced results which were insignificant in working-class North Lambeth and Kennington, barely perceptible in mixed Brixton, and clearly discernible only in suburban, churchgoing Norwood.

The sex ratios and the age structure of Lambeth's congregations varied from district to district, but these ratios do not adequately reflect variations in the composition of the population (see Table 10; for a comparison of Lambeth with other boroughs see Tables 11 and 11A). However, concern over the female character of the working-class parishes was strong among Lambeth clergymen, and it was not misplaced. Men rarely attended Sunday Anglican services in working-class neighborhoods. Church was for women, and there was a general assumption, which historians have not entirely avoided, that women were unimportant, religion was for women, and religion was therefore unimportant. A Lambeth Vicar retorted: "I have never been in any way affected by the silly jibes one sometimes sees and hears about religion being an occupation for women and children. Influence for good or bad is the property of the woman far more than the man, and so the bringing up of women 'in the fear and nurture of the Lord' is infinitely the most important of the Church's duties to her children."[22] Although he obviously was affected by the silly jibes, he did have a point. Working-class women were arguably responsible for more culturally significant decisions than either working-class men or more affluent women. The working-class husband generally worked (if employed), went to the pub, mended his rabbit hutches and pigeon lofts, and demanded conservatism in certain details of family life. Women assumed responsibility for more contacts with representatives of institutions outside the family such as teachers, education authorities,

22. B-305, p. 27. Vicar of St. John the Divine, Kennington.

rent collectors, local pawnbrokers, relieving officers from the
Board of Guardians, Sunday School teachers, district visitors, and
the local vicar. It would be possible to make too much of this—
many working-class men were active in politics, trade unions, and
the chapel—but it is impossible not to be impressed with the
crucial role of working-class mothers in keeping a family together
and successfully raising many children against daunting odds.[23]
For those who went to church, religion was just one more aspect
of household management.

One other point should be made about sex ratios in working-
class neighborhoods. The proportion of men attracted to church
services was higher in middle-class districts, but so was the proportion of men involved in all social institutions. For instance,
the electorate was larger and the percentage of the electorate
voting was generally larger as well in the suburbs. Over 10,000
voted in Norwood in 1906, under 5000 in North Lambeth. But
total male church attendance—morning and evening—in 1902 was
58 percent of all voters in working-class North Lambeth, only 33
percent in suburban Norwood. The opportunity for a dispropor-
tionate Nonconformist influence was even greater in working-
class neighborhoods, for their percentage of the electorate varied
inversely with social class. Nonconformist male attendance (1902)
was 40 percent of the number of voters (1906) in working-class
North Lambeth, under 20 percent in suburban Norwood. Even
after deducting twicers and those not qualified to vote, Nonconformist worshippers probably accounted for one-third of North
Lambeth's electorate.

How were patterns of church attendance changing? The earlier
censuses of 1851 and 1886–88 are not strictly comparable to the
exhaustive and reliable *Daily News* census of 1902, but the practice of churchgoing was clearly in decline (see Table 12). The
rate of decline was almost certainly magnified artificially by the
declining number of twicers and by Lambeth's social deteriora-

23. See Alexander Paterson, *Across the Bridges* (1911), pp. 32, 38, 211; Charles
Chaplin, *My Autobiography* (New York, 1964), passim; Jack Dash, *Good Morn-
ing, Brothers* (1969), p. 13; C. F. Garbett, *In the Heart of South London*
(1931), p. 61, all on South London; cf. A. S. Jasper, *A Hoxton Childhood*
(1969), passim, on North London; Robert Roberts, *The Classic Slum: Salford
Life in the First Quarter of the Century* (1973), pp. 2, 27, 42–43, 46ff., on
Lancashire; Robert Moore, *Pit-men, Preachers and Politics* (1974), p. 147, on
Durham.

tion. Between 1886 and 1902 an unknown number of Lambeth churchgoers escaped to suburban Croydon, to continue the practice there. The churchgoing proportion of the population in 1902 in Lambeth and Croydon, taken together, is roughly equal to that of Lambeth alone in 1886–88 (see Table 12A). Lambeth's decline was disproportionately Anglican and concentrated in the morning service. The relative resilience of the evening service reflects the churches' attempts to attract worshippers to the more "popular" evening service as more affluent Sunday morning churchgoers left the borough, and as the churches faced intensified competition from bicycling and commercialized Sunday amusement.

Nonconformity accounted for 36 percent of total attendance in 1851, 46 percent in 1886, and 53 percent in 1902. (see Tables 1 and 12; total attendance refers to separate attendances, not individuals). The 1851 census recorded no mission halls—some probably existed but the movement was in its infancy and its impact negligible—but by 1886 19 percent of Nonconformist attendances were in mission halls, by 1902 35 percent. Despite the mission halls Nonconformity had declined by about 13 percent in real terms (i.e., as percentage of population) from 1886. This was the late Victorian dilemma everywhere. As their chapels filled with worshippers their percentage of the population slowly waned. But absolute growth (in numbers) mattered more than real (percentage) growth in practical, everyday terms. Lambeth's population virtually doubled between 1851 and 1886, and in order to grow by 10 percent in real terms the Nonconformists had to more than double their numbers. The evening service in 1851 attracted 7282 Nonconformists, in 1886 18,288: a religious boom. Even after declining 13 percent between 1886 and 1902 in real terms, Nonconformity still had a larger evening attendance in 1902 than in 1886, and more than twice as many total attendances as in 1851.

Lambeth's two outer districts showed a more marked decline in attendance—both morning and evening—than the poorer inner districts, confirming the theory that the decline in church attendance was strongest among the more affluent classes (see Table 6). But an analysis of this sort tells us little about the behavior of individuals or families. Furthermore, neither Anglican nor Nonconformist figures, taken alone, confirm that pattern. The Anglican decline was least severe, for instance, in still suburban Norwood, and most dramatic in the intermediate districts of Kennington and Brixton which were deteriorating most rapidly. The Nonconformist decline was virtually confined to Brixton and Norwood, the wealthiest districts, and in Kennington Nonconformist overall attendance rose by 23 percent between 1886–88 and 1902. The rate of Nonconformist decline was greatest in suburban areas, the rate of Anglican decline in rapidly deteriorating areas.

The mean number of persons per Anglican clergyman in Lambeth's parishes grew from 2938 to 4576 between 1886 and 1902, and average parochial population from 8356 to 9204. But deployment was not the root of Anglican difficulties. In 1886, as in 1902, there is no apparent relationship between the number of persons per clergyman in a parish and total attendance in working-class or mixed neighborhoods. Nor is there any relationship between small parishes and larger attendances in the same neighborhoods. But in suburban Norwood there is a nearly perfect statistical relationship between persons per clergyman and overall attendance in 1886. Clergymen were becoming less effective in Lambeth but this trend is noticeable only in areas of high churchgoing (see Tables 7 and 13). In 1902 effective deployment still mattered, but only within a churchgoing neighborhood, and it mattered less than in 1886.

Six Lambeth parishes can be identified as ritualistic in 1906, and two others were widely regarded as "high" (see Table 14). Clergy and congregation were locked into guerrilla warfare over liturgical issues for decades in two of these parishes. The vicar of St. Andrew's, Stockwell, for instance, introduced sung worship and weekly Holy Communion in the early 1890s (along with one of the first democratically elected parochial church councils in the Church of England). His successor was still struggling to introduce the sanctus gong, stations of the cross, and incense in the 1920s, patiently declaring that he had gone without incense for twenty years and was willing to go without for another twenty.[24] Despite controversies, the five parishes which definitely maintained a ritualistic emphasis for the entire period 1886–1902 increased their morning church attendance as a percentage of

24. St. Andrew's, Stockwell, *Parochial Magazine*, 1892, passim; St. Andrew's, Stockwell, Parochial Church Council, Minutes, 23 Oct. 1923; *Brixton Free Press*, 13 April 1923, p. 11.

the population by 5 percent while overall Anglican attendance was falling by nearly 40 percent (see Table 14). The increase in ritualistic morning attendance was one bright spot in the bleak Anglican situation. The bulk of the increase occurred in two entirely working-class parishes, St. Peter, Vauxhall, and St. John the Divine, Kennington.

In twenty-nine Lambeth parishes, total Anglican church attendance as a percentage of parochial population in 1886–88 may be compared directly with that of 1902, and the parishes ranked according to their success in resisting the general decline in church attendance—number one having the least real decline and number twenty-nine the most (see Table 15). Four of the "top ten" churches in Lambeth's parochial "league table" were ritualistic, but four of them including the top three were extremely evangelical, a contrast further complicated by the presence of three distinctly evangelical churches among numbers nineteen to twenty-nine. The terms "low church" and "evangelical" are often used interchangeably, but there were a number of Lambeth parishes, referred to as "low church" in 1902, which were not emphatically evangelical. They were "low and dry." Their incumbents probably leaned more toward the evangelical than the Anglo-Catholic side in matters of formal theology, but the characteristic evangelical code words were missing from their sermons. These "low church" clergymen believed in matins, evensong, and "no enthusiasm." They expected middle-class families to attend church as a matter of course, detested both Nonconformists and Roman Catholics, and generally carried on with a very old-fashioned parochial structure of Sunday Schools and soup kitchens. The vicar of St. Michael's, Stockwell, was almost an ideal type. "Churchgoing is almost entirely a matter of social standing," he explained. "A certain class will come to church unless you positively repel them while another class cannot be induced to come at all. You have only to go further south to find them filling the churches at a place such as Sydenham." Although non-churchgoing did not disturb him, the abolition of a redundant parochial soup kitchen did: "So much sentiment has always clung to the soup kitchen at St. Michael's."[25] De-

25. St. Michael's Stockwell, *Annual Report*, 1899; B-305, p. 115. The Vicar of St. Michael's is quoted with some embellishment in Booth, *Life and Labour*, ser. 3, vol. 6, p. 44.

pendent upon a dying social custom, "low church" clergymen
seemed to throw up their hands unanimously in despair.
"Church-going, as a family custom, was now a thing of the past,"
Canon Allen Edwards of All Saints, South Lambeth, told the
Kennington ruri-decanal conference in 1899, and the vicar of
St. James, Camberwell, told Charles Booth's interviewer that
"The habit of church-going is dying; families used to come; now
the younger ones are off bicycling."[26] His parish had no clubs,
no societies, and no nurse. The vicar had no curate and hoped
never to have one, and more parochial funds went toward wind-
ing the church clock and tuning the organ than toward philanthropy. Parochial church attendance declined 76 percent in fifteen years, and each of these three "low" parishes stood near
the bottom of Lambeth's parochial league table.

Along with these three "low and dry" parishes in the bottom
ten were four parishes which were theologically evangelical.
Their evangelical clergymen were more likely than their "low
and dry" colleagues to emphasize the Protestant nature of the
church, to mention the need for conversion in their sermons, to
discuss sanctification and justification and the nature of grace,
and to cooperate with evangelical Nonconformists. They also
whined and complained incessantly: "From all of these Evangelical churches," Charles Booth wrote, "arises a wail against cycling
and other forms of Sabbath breaking and unrest; found, as one
of the clergy pathetically says, 'where you would least expect it.'
The Sunday playing of the L.C.C. [London County Council]
band is very much objected to. The bandstand is within ear shot
of St. Jude's church, and is said to increase the difficulty of keeping the boys in Sunday School." The vicar complained: "Imagine
the position when we have been singing 'When I Survey the
Wondrous Cross' to hear them playing 'Wait 'til the Clouds Roll
By.'" Booth's usually tolerant interviewer noted that "his views
on social questions have but little value and his bases of comparison are slender." Another evangelical clergyman admitted to
driving people away because he "could not move with the
times."[27] Despite differences in theology, these "low evangelical"

26. B-272, p. 67; B-305, p. 103.

27. Booth, *Life and Labour*, ser. 3, vol. 6, p. 63; B-272, p. 165; B-305, p. 191.
The parishes both evangelical and "low" were St. Stephen's, South Lambeth;
St. Jude's, East Brixton; St. Paul's, West Brixton; St. Saviour's, Herne Hill.

clergymen conducted their parishes very much like their "low and dry" neighbors. What distinguished "low church" clergymen—evangelical or not—was an obsession with certain outward manifestations of social change, an eccentric social analysis inviting ridicule, and a helpless devotion to the most old-fashioned forms of parochial organization. And parochial organization, unlike clerical deployment, was important.

The "Sunday amusements" argument was often heard in the late nineteenth century, and there is no doubt about the fact that the churches faced more competition from bicycling and Sunday concerts. But as an explanation for the decline of churchgoing, it is insufficient. The American churches have accommodated themselves to a public even more devoted to mechanized Sunday entertainment. And some Lambeth parishes, even some evangelical parishes, were flourishing in 1900 despite the ominous presence of bicyclers in the streets.

Of the "top ten" churches, four were ritualistic, one was mildly evangelical with a prosperous and well-financed parochial organization, one was of the "low evangelical" type discussed above but placed in a parish of continuing suburban growth, and four were evangelical but of a rather different type from the "low church" parishes. These evangelical incumbents were "activist evangelicals" who ran their parishes very differently from their "low evangelical" colleagues. Appalled by the state of British society, these clergymen were optimistic about the prospects for their own parishes; although conservative in theology they were innovators in parochial organization; although in fact often dependent upon conventional churchgoing, they had never been theoretically reconciled to it. They knew that people were sinful and had to be coerced or lured into the pew, and were not surprised to find it difficult. Cordial with the Nonconformists, they sent away large sums to foreign missions. St. Andrew's, Lambeth, for instance, was an entirely working-class and extremely poor parish where the neighborhood aristocracy lived in the housing blocks erected by the Peabody philanthropy. The parish held its own in part through "Pleasant Sunday Afternoon" services for men, advertised as "Happy Services for Men. Happy! Helpful! Homely!" In an area where parishes usually had trouble keeping the parish church in repair, St. Andrew's raised £48 for the Church Missionary Society and £11 for the Church Pastoral Aid Society through offertories and boxes in Sunday School classes during 1899.[28] In another of the successful evangelical parishes, Christ Church, North Brixton, the vicar was a famous preacher, but "his parish management is no less successful, and to ensure this he has had to regard much as 'a business depending upon personal attention.' He has under him a great staff of workers and much is done to reach the people. Whether they come to church or not the whole parish is evangelized."[29]

At the far end of Lambeth, in a middle-class churchgoing suburb, members of the congregation at the activist evangelical parish of Christ Church, Gipsy Hill, complained of so many parochial organizations that "one really grows bewildered among them." In 1902 alone Christ Church sent funds to the South American Missionary Society, St. Mary's Southwark Aid Fund, Religious Tract Society, Moravian Missions, Mission to Seamen, Mission to Lepers, Mission to Deep Sea Fishermen, London Jewish Society, London City Mission, Italian Church Reform Association, Irish Society, Irish Church Missions, the Industrial Society, Dr. Barnardo's Homes, Colonial and Continental Church Society, Church Pastoral Aid Society, Church of England Waifs and Strays Society, Zenana Mission Society, Church Missionary Society, and the Bishop of Sierra Leone's Fund. Organizations devoted to the conversion of French and Irish Roman Catholic priests received enthusiastic support. Locally, the parish maintained a mission hall, district visitors, a provident society, a temperance society, and the Church Lads' Brigade.[30] A separate member of the congregation bore the responsibility for soliciting funds within the parish for each of these causes and organizations.

It is instructive to compare these "activist evangelical" parishes with the ritualistic parish of St. John the Divine, Kennington, which encompassed the Sultan Street area of Camberwell, a neighborhood "without counterpart in London" according to Charles Booth. "There are places more squalid and there may

28. B-269, pp. 141, 157. The activist evangelical parishes were Christ Church, Gipsy Hill; Christ Church, North Brixton; St. Phillip's, Kennington; St. Andrew's, Lambeth.

29. Booth, *Life and Labour*, ser. 3, vol. 6, pp. 40–41.

30. Christ Church, Gipsy Hill, *Parish Magazine*, Aug. 1901 and May 1902.

be people more debased, but there are none whereon the word
'outcast' is so deeply branded."[31] Its vicar, the Rev. C. E. Brooke,
was the son of a wealthy, evangelical cloth manufacturer in Hud-
dersfield and had been converted to Anglo-Catholicism at Oxford.
He "loved bricks and mortar," and while still a curate in 1871
he donated £10,000 to allow the nave of the new church to be
included in its original construction. He also saw that the patronage of the parish was placed in the hands of Anglo-Catholic
trustees. By 1900 St. John's was positively overweighted with
organizations staffed by 10 curates, 25 district visitors, 150 Sunday School visitors, 170 other volunteer workers, 1 paid and 9
voluntary bell-ringers, 2 lay readers, 1 paid nurse, and 8 voluntary sisters. Twenty-five hundred students received "definite
religious teaching," with warnings against Dissent, in the day
schools and 1500 more were taught in Sunday School. There
were 1500 communicants, 1200 guild members, and 500 in clubs
as well as a hostel "for the dying," a burial guild, a day nursery,
a penny savings bank, a benefit society, a sanitary committee, a
men's institute, and a registry office for servants. To attract men,
"even Socialistic meetings with real live Socialists were tried."[32]
Overall church attendance rose from 1455 in 1886–88 to 1802 in
1902, although population continued to grow so rapidly that
there was a slight decrease in the percentage of parochial population attending church. A number of outsiders were attracted to
this extraordinary parish, but almost all of the members of
the various parochial organizations and many of the worshippers
came from within their wholly working-class and poor neighborhood. The neighboring parish of St. James was wholly middle-
class and "low church" evangelical. It had "no clubs, no societies,
and no nurse" as well as a 76 percent decline in church attendance in fifteen years.

What mattered, then, was not ideology, but effort; not a rational deployment of the clergy so much as a highly motivated
and well-financed clergy. Only one of the ten parishes at the bottom of the list in Table 15 had a large parochial organization

31. Booth, *Life and Labour*, ser. 3, vol. 6, p. 15.
32. A. G. Deedes, ed., *Charles Edward Brooke: A Memoir* (1913), p. 101; and
The Church of St. John the Divine, Kennington: A Short History (1969), passim; B-305, pp. 21ff.; Booth, *Life and Labour*, ser. 3, vol. 6, pp. 41–42.

(All Saints, South Lambeth).[33] Only two of the top ten obviously depended largely upon conventional middle-class churchgoing (St. Matthews, Brixton Hill; Holy Trinity, Tulse Hill). The church parties supplied what the low church clergymen lacked: a motive for strenuous effort. Parishes which emphasized public worship and nothing else were unable to attract worshippers. Parishes which had the money and energy to sponsor a range of parochial activities and enroll a large number of lay volunteers succeeded in attracting more worshippers, even in working-class neighborhoods.[34]

The overall decline in Nonconformist attendance was less severe because the bright spots were brighter. Mission halls flourished, some of the more plebeian Nonconformist bodies such as the Free Methodists and the Primitive Methodists grew, and the Baptists grew in some neighborhoods (see Tables 6 and 16). The resilience of plebeian Nonconformity was most evident in Kennington, where three Free Methodist, one Primitive Methodist, one Baptist, and one Congregational chapel increased their total attendances by nearly 60 percent between 1886–88 and 1902. A new Primitive Methodist chapel was opened, and a flourishing Congregational mission hall made a rather unusual transition to the status of "chapel" (see Table 6). These shabby, isolated "little Bethels" combined truculence with feebleness, conservative theology with Progressive politics, enthusiasm for temperance with hostility to socialism; their "meddling" ministers suffered constant public abuse from both Tory and Socialist local politicians as well as from the handful of secularist radicals within the local Liberal party. Chapel members were described as "artisans, mechanics, the lower middle class and some unskilled"; "lower middle and working class—mainly the

33. All Saints, South Lambeth, was "low and dry" but sponsored a highly successful Sunday School which enrolled thousands, using the Board Schools in the parish to house their Sunday classes. But the rest of their parochial activities appear to have been moribund, with the possible exception of some mothers' meetings.

34. The Paul Report argued that lay agency was highly effective in increasing church attendance (pp. 268–69). It is impossible to measure precisely the parochial distribution of Lambeth's deaconesses, scripture readers, Bible women, Sunday School teachers, and district visitors. I suspect that their energy and morale mattered more than their mere presence.

latter"; "middle class and working people but not the labouring class." They were lower middle-class with a much larger admixture of the skilled working-class than most Lambeth chapels.[35]

The Congregational mission hall turned chapel in Kennington, Wheatsheaf Hall, had been established in 1884 by W. S. Caine, a temperance reformer and M.P. Much influenced by Mearns's *Bitter Cry of Outcast London* in the eighties, Caine believed that "anyone could start a similar work in almost any district in London." He built and maintained the building but contributed no cash—"The idea is to give every one something to do. Money will come in from the people—there is no need to ask."[36] Wheatsheaf Hall grew from 17 to 250 members between 1884 and 1894, and by the turn of the century its members contributed to foreign missions and the usual Nonconformist charities. Wheatsheaf Hall resembled, in some respects, a nearby Wesleyan effort, Springfield Hall, which attracted an evening attendance of nearly 1500 in 1902. Like Wheatsheaf Hall, it had been established as a result of anxiety about non-churchgoing in the 1880s during the Wesleyan Forward Movement, but it continued to be run for rather than by its congregation.

Of the three major Nonconformist denominations—Baptist, Congregationalist, and Wesleyan—the Baptist attendance held up best, but only in one district, Norwood. "The Baptist churches here," Booth wrote, "have been subject to splits, a not unnatural result, perhaps, of strong and conscientious Protestantism, but may even prosper by division."[37] Schism certainly led

35. The chapels were Fentiman Road United Methodist Free Church, Paradise Road United Methodist Free Church, Southville United Methodist Free Church, Warham Street Primitive Methodist Chapel, Claylands Congregational Chapel, Wynne Road Baptist Chapel, Dorset Road Primitive Methodist Chapel (new), Wheatsheaf Hall (Congregational, new). Their total attendance grew from 1503 in 1886 to 2383 in 1902, from 1.8 percent of the population of the district of Kennington to 2.5 percent. B-271, pp. 17, 157, 201; B-303, p. 133. These figures would be even more impressive with the addition of the 1500 attendances at the Wesleyan Springfield Hall, a dependent mission hall which attracted the same sort of person.

36. John Newton, *W. S. Caine, M.P.* (1907); on Hughes see B-271, p. 15, and *The Life of Hugh Price Hughes, by his daughter, Dorothea Price Hughes* (1904).

37. Booth, *Life and Labour*, ser. 3, vol. 6, p. 119.

to growth. A census at Chatsworth Road Baptist Chapel in 1886 counted 1008 chapelgoers at both services; after losing most of their servant-keepers to the newly established Landsdowne Hall (open to evangelical non-Baptists as well), it drew 1938 in 1902 and Landsdowne Hall 849. These were middle-class churches: at Lansdowne Hall one-half of the congregation kept servants (but only two families had coachmen); managers and merchants in the City attended Chatsworth Road, comfortable and even prosperous but not wealthy. At about the same time, a faction of Norwood's Gipsy Road Baptist Chapel seceded to form the Gipsy Road Tabernacle, and both causes flourished.[38]

There is no obvious reason for the growth of Kennington's autonomous "little Bethels" at a time when other chapels— large and small—were languishing. Wheatsheaf Hall is an exception, however, for it originated as a mission hall and mission halls were still growing, not only in Kennington but in other parts of Lambeth, and continued to be the sites of extraordinary efforts to attract worshippers. Patrons of the mission hall movement such as W. S. Caine and the Wesleyan Hugh Price Hughes (who was a minister in Lambeth when he concocted plans for the Forward Movement) were concerned about the "Condition of England." Their anxiety combined both material and spiritual fears. They had stumbled onto a technique—the mission hall—which worked when well financed, and they had access to the necessary funds, either personal or denominational. Their success was recapitulated on a smaller scale by a number of Lambeth's chapels and independent religious entrepreneurs.

The fissiparous Norwood Baptists, on the other hand, were members of a movement which resembled the Evangelical Party of the Church of England—followers of C. H. Spurgeon. Spurgeon had been a father figure to students of his Pastor's College in South London, many of whom needed training in elementary English, and exercised an almost episcopal oversight over them after they graduated. He counted on wealthy friends for funds to establish new chapels in outlying suburbs. The wealthy builder William Higgs, for instance, was pleased to construct any chapel he was allowed to design. He designated Spurgeon "the

38. B-315, p. 149; B-313, p. 5; *Chatsworth Road Baptist Church* (1959), at Minet Library, Lambeth; J. B. Wilson, *The Story of Norwood,* prepared by H. A. Wilson (1973), p. 21.

only minister who keeps bricks and mortar out of my head during public worship."[39] Although Spurgeon died in 1892, his influence remained, and his followers were distinguished by their high morale. "Whatever this master workman put his hand to," Booth wrote, "seems to have been well and solidly accomplished, and to have been endowed with lasting life. Not only does an immense congregation gather round his son and successor, but the numerous independent organizations which he initiated and assisted during his lifetime, still retain their vigour. . . . Such was the power he exercised that, as one admirer phrases it, 'you could not hear him without saying, 'What can I do for Jesus?' "[40]

C. F. G. Masterman proposed an explanation for Spurgeon's success and for the success of other large Nonconformist preaching centers: "the manifest tendency of the Nonconformist worshippers to collect together into strong centres—that centralising system which is inevitable where preaching is so emphasized and the stimulus and guidance of the pulpit so much desired." He assumed a fixed churchgoing population; the success of one chapel damaged "the smaller chapels round, which are emptied to swell the great congregations . . . the congregation slowly melts away, as the old faithful depart and the younger members are drawn to more obvious attractions."[41] It is easy to juxtapose a flourishing chapel with a number of dilapidated, decaying causes nearby, but misleading to imply that many of the worshippers at Spurgeon's Tabernacle would even consider attending a "little Bethel." The churchgoing population was not constant, and many of the semi-churched attended a large and flourishing church or chapel precisely because it conducted its services on a grand scale. At age fourteen, Herbert Morrison spent his Sunday nights visiting churches which featured a famous preacher, and remembered in particular F. B. Meyer, T. H.

39. William Higgs, *A History of the Higgs or Higges Family*, with manuscript notes and letters, n.d., p. 139. Someone should write an academic biography of Spurgeon. In the meantime see his *Autobiography*, 4 vols. (1898–1900), compiled by his wife; W. Y. Fullerton, *C. H. Spurgeon: A Biography* (1920); J. C. Carlile, *C. H. Spurgeon: An Interpretive Biography* (1933); Ernest W. Bacon, *Spurgeon: Heir of the Puritans* (1967); Patricia S. Kruppa, review of Spurgeon and Moody literature, *Victorian Studies* 7 (June 1964).

40. Booth, *Life and Labour*, ser. 3, vol. 4, p. 74.

41. Richard Mudie-Smith, ed., *Religious Life of London*, pp. 203–4.

Spurgeon (C. H. Spurgeon's son and successor), A. J. Waldron of
St. Matthew's, Brixton, R. J. Campbell, and John Clifford—the
first three of them in or near Lambeth.[42] V. S. Pritchett's father
made the rounds to hear famous preachers: "He wanted religion
to smarten up and get snappy. . . . He did not really distinguish
between the big shopkeepers and the popular Nonconformist
preachers."[43] The large centers probably drew worshippers from
small chapels—there is no reason why they should be immune
to such attractions—but that sort of leakage was not the root of
their problems. Small, ailing chapels could be found as easily in
neighborhoods with no large preaching center nearby (such as
parts of Battersea and Wandsworth where the leading Nonconformist chapels were only of moderate size). The closing of Spurgeon's Tabernacle would hardly have sent Herbert Morrison
rushing to join the faithful few huddling in a small chapel
nearby.

Churchgoing in Lambeth was both important and declining
in 1902. Its importance was magnified by the social distribution
of churchgoers. Its decline was most noticeable among the middle classes, in the suburbs, in the more prosperous denominations, and in those Anglican parishes which emphasized Sunday
worship and little else. Exceptional effort could withstand the
decline, but exceptional effort is by definition limited to a few.
Even Baptist attendance declined by 6 percent in real terms,
and patrons like W. S. Caine were clearly struggling against
long odds, not because their efforts were unsuccessful, but because so few joined them. But why a general decline of conventional Anglican churchgoing? Why a similar decline among the
most prosperous Nonconformist denominations, the Congregationalists and the Wesleyans? Church attendance cannot be
considered in isolation. It was only one dimension of Lambeth's
religious institutions, and those institutions were only one dimension of religion. A closer look at the whole structure of
religious organization may supply clues to the social meaning of
church attendance and the causes of its decay.

42. *Herbert Morrison: An Autobiography by Lord Morrison of Lambeth*
(1960), p. 22.
43. V. S. Pritchett, *A Cab at the Door* (1971 ed.), p. 21.

3
The Churches
and Urban Society

In the twentieth century we often assume that the churches are primarily concerned with something narrowly defined as "religion," something which can be distinguished readily from other things which are "really social" or "really political" or "really a question of social class." The Church of England has always defied such distinctions and assumed responsibility for much more than the maintenance of public worship and the encouragement of private devotion. The character of the church's social functions and social responsibilities has changed considerably over the centuries, however, and in the nineteenth century churchmen faced two unfamiliar problems: the virtual triumph of the principle of voluntary consent in matters of religion, and the separation of the social classes in the large cities. In the Victorian countryside patterns of Anglican church attendance still reflected the various forms of influence wielded by squire and parson, and Anglicans naturally continued to use their considerable social influence in the city as well as the countryside. Lambeth Nonconformists complained of difficulties in procuring leases from Anglican landlords for new chapels, and at least three Lambeth incumbents attempted to purge their parishes of Dissent in the 1890s by purchasing the solitary, representative chapel outright.[1]

But churchmen knew that rearguard actions of this sort would neither secure popular allegiance to the church nor maintain the social status of the clergy. The Church of England was forced to compete in a free market in religion, and to contend with the strange world of the city. Anglicans were agreed upon a strategy of providing the great cities with a network of parishes, but even as they succeeded at that enormous task many churchmen complained that the parishes were not working. They found the traditional functions of the rural parish threatened in single-class parishes of any kind, especially but not exclusively those where only the poor lived. "There was nothing left behind but a residue of powerless poverty," the Christian Socialist Canon Scott Holland complained. "There were no people on the spot who had leisure enough to take up ordinary civic duties. There were no people of education enough to be able to put the resources of civilization into action. A wholly unnatural condition had been produced."[2]

The separation of the classes did not merely lead to alienation from the church, they argued. It also led to a more general social malaise which threatened the well-being of English society. The evil consequences of this wholly unnatural condition were never precisely described. An overzealous fund raiser for the South London Church Fund put it bluntly when he claimed that only his agency restrained the masses from their natural desire to loot and destroy the mansions of Park Lane, but hysterical appeals of this sort were made only infrequently and to audiences immune to subtle language.[3] Clergymen generally appealed to a much more diffuse and general. fear of unspecified social disorders

1. B-272, pp. 7 and 67; B-303, pp. 7–127. The chapels were Vauxhall Baptist Chapel in the parish of St. Peter's, Vauxhall; Reheboth Strict Baptist Chapel in Epiphany, Stockwell; Lothian Road Congregational Chapel in St. John the Divine, Kennington. The Vicar of All Saints, S. Lambeth, purchased an abandoned chapel in his parish in order to "keep other people out." On leaseholds for chapels see Booth, *Life and Labour*, ser. 3, vol. 6, pp. 118, 123; cf. F. M. L. Thompson, *Hampstead: Building a Borough, 1850–1914* (1974), p. 387.

2. Henry Scott Holland, *A Bundle of Memories* (1915), p. 90.

3. See the complaint, perhaps exaggerated, in the *Brixton Free Press*, 5 April 1912, p. 5.

emanating from the city. They never claimed that the social problem could be solved simply by persuading the masses to attend church, but they did identify their own private interests with the public interest in a more subtle manner. They defined church attendance, not merely as an act of individual choice, but as the outward and visible sign of the healthy social relationships which the church nurtured through its parochial activities. In attempting to solve its own institutional problem—to make its urban parishes work—the Church of England was addressing a broader social problem. Piety became intertwined with anxiety, and the very problems which threatened to swamp the church provided opportunities for an appeal to the middle classes for support. The church was constructing a comprehensive network of urban parishes which could be used to combat the unnatural condition of society. The clergy's task was to decide precisely how this was to be done, and then sell their solution to the public.

In the 1850s Charles Kemble of Wadham College, Oxford, moved to Lambeth as incumbent of St. Michael's, Stockwell, a new urban parish with no parochial structure or financial resources, "pronounced by the highest authorities on such subjects as unmanageable."[4] In 1859 he published a solution to the church's problems in *Suggestive Hints on Parochial Machinery*, a paper originally read at a meeting of the rural deanery. A clergyman's first task, he argued, was to conduct the services of his church without upsetting his parishioners. But his general object in all parochial activities was "to diffuse Christian influence through all classes; to present Christianity under its practical aspect; to gather out God's people; to effect a moral improvement in society; to edify God's church." To these ends it was "most desirable to obtain, at the earliest possible period, female visitors, and those from an upper grade of society . . . one great benefit arises from the bringing of classes into mutual intercourse. The visitor is better as a married woman, being in the world, one who knows the world and its trials." The clergyman assigned the poor streets of his parish to these ladies, who were to distribute tracts and books, invite children to Sunday School, persuade adults to attend public worship, provide hospital letters for the ill, and distribute "meat, bread, coals, wine, beer, arrowroot, rice,

4. *Suggestive Hints on Parochial Machinery* (1859).

tea, or money." They were to collect deposits to the provident fund and return them with interest in coals or clothing in June or December, lend blankets in the winter, and supply each prospective mother with "a Bible, a Prayer Book, a quart of oatmeal, a pound of sugar, and a pound of soap."[5]

Drawing naturally upon the paternalistic traditions of rural Anglicanism, clergymen searched for new social functions for their ill-defined institution. Social services of this sort were in demand by needy parishioners, and there was a ready supply of anxious middle-class philanthropists, eager to donate both time and money. "There are happily many springs of Christian benevolence open," Kemble observed. "The columns of *The Times* are open to advertisements; the purses of a liberal public are open too."[6]

Although the vicar of St. Michael's would never have admitted it, other Christians were active in his neighborhood—Baptists, Congregationalists, various forms of Methodist—and they were drawing upon very different traditions to justify similar activities. On the defensive throughout most of the nineteenth century, the Anglicans were attempting to regain lost ground, or so they thought. But Victorian Nonconformists believed that history was on their side. Gradually their grievances were remedied, their numbers grew, their chapels attained a new dignity: they began calling them churches. These late Victorian chapels, now stranded on nearly all English thoroughfares, physically manifested God's favor. Looking back on their old meeting houses, middle and late Victorian Nonconformists could remember the unpretentious boxes erected meekly on back streets, inadequately supplied with light by guttering candles, the hymns accompanied not by organ, but by fiddle, bass-viol, sackbut, and dulcimer. That had been

5. *Suggestive Hints*, pp. 10, 24–25; a more extensive clerical social analysis and plea for parochial extension, so that the "soothing and elevating power of the Church" might be applied to social evils, may be found in Frederick Meyrick, M.A., *The Outcast and the Poor of London; or, our present duties toward the poor; a course of sermons preached at the Chapel Royal, Whitehall* (1858). The practical outcome of such exhortations may be surveyed in almost any Victorian parish magazine. That of St. Clement Danes, Strand, has been reprinted: *St. Clement Danes Parish Magazine for 1874: A record of parish social work one hundred years ago*, Colin Harvey, ed., History of Social Work Reprint no. 113 (Heatherbank Press, Milngavie, Dunbartonshire, 1974).

6. *Suggestive Hints*, p. 9.

St. Michael's, Stockwell Park Road.

the heroic age. They had only to look around to see the fruits of their ancestors' endurance. Most prominent, from the pews, was the organ, dominating the front of the church and providing a suitable backdrop for the preacher within the spacious Gothic building. The minister himself perhaps served on the local vestry, board of guardians, or school board and often cut a figure in the local newspaper. Adjacent to the church sanctuary stood a well-equipped church hall with Sunday School rooms and a kitchen for tea, suitable for religious, political, and social gatherings and for philanthropic activities to benefit the poor.

But prosperity made many Nonconformists uneasy. In 1870 the congregation of Claylands Congregational Chapel moved from their Georgian building on a Kennington side street into a new red brick neo-Gothic church building boldly fronting a major thoroughfare in then-suburban Brixton. Shedding the label "chapel," the congregation adopted the title of Brixton Independent Church. But their minister only agreed to the move from Kennington to Brixton on the condition that the old chapel be maintained as an integral part of the church's work. "Unless those who live in healthy and pleasant suburbs," he argued, "are prepared to make some sacrifice to care for those who are compelled to live in crowded and to say the least unlovely neighborhoods, the condition of the poor will grow sadder year by year."[7] District visitors also began regular philanthropic work at several sites in Kennington and North Lambeth. A pamphlet published by Brixton Independent Church in 1896 spoke smugly of the mid-Victorian years as "the twilight time of modern civilization . . . before the renascence of active church work; when the poor were not 'considered' but regarded as a nuisance, and spoken of as the dangerous classes."[8]

Although Brixton Independent Church was unique in the degree of its theological liberalism, it was typical of late Victorian Nonconformist chapels in its response to urban social conditions. The heterogeneity of Victorian Nonconformity makes generalizations hazardous, but in general it is fair to say that both Old Dissent—mainly Baptists and Congregationalists—and Methodism had traditionally shared a view of their responsibilities toward

7. *The Wandering Polyzoon: A Story of the Moffatt Institute* (1896), p. 50.
8. *Ibid.*, p. 8.

Brixton Independent Church, Brixton Road.

society which was very different from the Anglican view. At the chapel level, Nonconformists were obliged to look after their own members in distress, usually through some sort of communion fund. Furthermore, all Christians were obliged to engage in acts of charity toward outsiders in obedience to Christ's commands and in response to His love. But Nonconformists felt no general social obligation, as Nonconformists, to engage in philanthropy or social reform simply in order to improve the social conditions around them. Yet that was precisely what the minister of Brixton Independent Church urged upon his congregation.

The theory of the evangelical revival had always been a theory of social change. As each person in England was persuaded to accept genuine, rather than formal, Christianity, England would become a Christian nation, that is, a nation of Christian individuals. Whatever social problems might be regarded as critical, they either would be resolved in this process or could not be resolved until after the nation was Christianized. This theory had to be revised, but not openly repudiated, as circumstances changed. As Nonconformists became more thoroughly integrated into English society, and as the institutions which emerged from the evangelical revival began to grow and require more care and attention, this individualistic conversionism began to give way to the notion that there was more than one way to effect changes in English society (a notion which Anglican evangelicals had, on the whole, always recognized). Two quotations will illustrate my point, the first from a sermon by a provincial minister to the East Kent Baptist Association in 1837. He contrasted the present with a future when:

> The sublime realities of our faith will produce an elevation of character, a loftier spiritual bearing, diffusing its effects over the whole. Stern principles will pervade all dealings between man and man. The precepts of Christianity will be applied to all the concerns of life. Religion will be completely amalgamated with the business of the world, infusing into it the healthy spirit of holiness. . . . The mild and pure spirit of the gospel will exert a salutary influence even over those who refuse to yield personal subjection to its authority. . . . Christians will acquire a marked predominance among their fellow citizens.[9]

Instead of individual conversion, he saw diffusion, infusion, amalgamation, and influence. A Christian society could be recognized by the "marked predominance" which Christians would acquire.

The reaction against the conversionist tradition sometimes reached the point of conscious complaints of the "excessive individualism" of the evangelical revival, especially in the influential sermons of R. W. Dale. But usually obeisance was made to the evangelical tradition and the contradictions ignored as Nonconformists called for a new corporate activism, for action as a group to create a Christian nation in which Christians (i.e., Dissenters) would exercise crucial forms of influence. Edward Miall's

9. *East Kent Baptist Association Circular Letter for 1837*, p. 7.

The British Churches in Relation to the British People (1849) was
a sort of handbook for a particular variety of corporate activism.
Although believing firmly in a free market in religious ideas,
Miall differed from utilitarian social theorists in having a very
clear idea of what the truth was. He realized that simple persuasion would hardly insure the triumph of the Gospel in the
English nation's hierarchy of values. Obstacles must be cleared
from the path of truth:

> As a rule, and speaking of classes rather than of every individual of
> which the class may consist, we are bold to say that people huddled
> promiscuously together, and crowded, as are our lowest poor, into filthy
> domiciles, confined, close, pestiferous, *cannot* be made religious. . . .
> Physical obstacles must be overcome by physical means, political ob-
> stacles by political means. . . . The hindrances in our way are of as
> irremovable a character by direct religious agency, as if they were geo-
> graphical. We must, therefore, set ourselves to attack, not depravity by
> promulgation of the gospel, but crowded dwelling houses, filthy habits,
> utter domiciliary discomfort, by appropriate remedial methods.[10]

Miall was ostracized by other Nonconformists when he first
began to publish the *Nonconformist* (whose strident motto so offended Matthew Arnold) in the 1840s, and his corporate activism
was often associated with a group labeled "political Nonconformist." But many Nonconformists, including some Wesleyans,
who bitterly disagreed with Miall shared his more general notion
that Nonconformity should be a "power in the land." The precise character of this diffusion, infusion, amalgamation, and influence was the subject of bitter dispute. A great deal of energy
was dispersed in politics and in the construction and maintenance
of new church buildings which were designed to establish a visual
Nonconformist "presence" on the High Street. Others merely
wanted to eliminate various Nonconformist grievances. Miall
himself recommended concerted action to solve the social problem, and set the stage for the growth of late Victorian social
radicalism, another variant of corporate activism. By the 1870s
the leading Congregational ministers—R. W. Dale, James Guin-

10. *The British Churches in Relation to the British People* (2nd ed., 1850),
p. 268.

ness Rogers, Newman Hall, Thomas Binney—would have agreed with Miall on general principles if not on precise tactics. Although meeting persistent resistance from many Wesleyans[11] and some Baptists, the theory of corporate activism was widely accepted by the most influential Nonconformist leaders of the eighties, and completely dominated the Free Church Council from 1895 until World War I.

The philanthropic entrepreneurs of Brixton Independent Church should be seen, then, in the light of two changes in Victorian Nonconformity. The chapel, like the parish, was becoming a focal point for middle-class Christians who wished to do something about "the social problem." At the same time, some but not all Victorian Nonconformists were redefining their obligations toward society. The mission hall played an important and sometimes misunderstood role in these changes. Miall recommended a direct assault upon the social problem through the agency of the mission halls, which began to proliferate in the railway arches, garrets, cellars, and hired rooms of the Victorian city about mid-century. The *British Weekly* identified 873 of them in London alone in 1888—173 Anglican, 233 sponsored by the leading Nonconformist denominations, 467 others sponsored by individual patrons and inter-denominational agencies such as the London City Mission and the Salvation Army.[12] The Anglican missions were largely integrated into the parochial system, and although Anglican evangelicals cooperated in the London City Mission and other interdenominational agencies, most of those in the miscellaneous category were in fact Nonconformist (clergymen almost always identified London City Missionaries as

11. The Wesleyans are a partial exception to almost every generalization about Victorian Nonconformity, including this one. However, social radicals like H. P. Hughes on the one hand, and influential Wesleyan laymen like H. H. Fowler and R. W. Perks on the other, were interested in advancing the interests of Nonconformity as a corporate body. John Kent argues that Hughes was in some sense a tool of these powerful laymen: "Hugh Price Hughes and the Nonconformist Conscience," in G. V. Bennett and J. D. Walsh, eds., *Essays in Modern English Church History* (1966), p. 204. Both the social radicals like Hughes and the imperialistic laymen like Perks and Fowler were "corporate activists" and cooperated on many issues, but they had very different visions of what was to be achieved in politics.

12. *British Weekly*, 13 Jan. 1888, no. 63, vol. 3, supp.; 20 Jan. 1888, pp. 238–39.

Dissenters, even if they claimed to be Anglican).[13] Strict evangelicals regarded the mission halls as nothing more than preaching
stations, but other Nonconformists regarded them as a base for
an attack upon urban social evils. Miall loosely associated mission halls with a system of "clubs, friendly and benefit societies . . .
whereby our churches may usefully and very legitimately increase
their moral influence."[14] For Miall, and for the members of the
Brixton Independent Church, the mission hall was the Nonconformist answer to the Anglican parochial system.

By the 1880s both Anglicans and Nonconformists, drawing
upon different ideological traditions but responding to similar
urban problems, were deeply involved in the provision of charity and social services. To an outside observer, it appears to be
their major enterprise. Only the erection of church buildings
received more time and attention. In 1899 and 1900 churches and
chapels in Lambeth alone sponsored *at least* 58 thrift, slate, and
friendly societies, 57 mothers' meetings, 36 temperance societies
for children, 36 literary or debating societies for young men, 27
Bible classes, 27 girls' or young women's clubs, 25 cricket, tennis,
or other sports clubs, 25 savings banks or penny banks, 24 Christian Endeavour societies, 21 boot, coal, blanket, or clothing clubs,
19 adult temperance societies, 17 branches of the Boys' Brigade
or Church Lads' Brigade, 13 vocational or adult classes, 13 men's
clubs, 10 gymnasiums (usually devoted to recreational classes of
some sort), and 10 maternity societies. There were 16 nurses and
two part-time doctors as well as a part-time dentist in addition to
those sponsored by the provident dispensaries which were closely
linked to the churches. Furthermore there were two "servants'
registries," two lodgings registries, two "industrial societies"
which employed women at needlework, one burial guild, one
convalescent home, one hostel for the dying, one invalid kitchen,

13. See J. M. Weylland, *These Fifty Years, Being the Jubilee Volume of the
L.C.M.* (1884), passim, on this problem. L.C.M. *Annual Reports* for the Edwardian decade show that nonconformist chapels far outnumbered Anglican
parishes in lists of contributing congregations, although the Anglican gifts
were naturally larger. Those Anglicans who participated in the L.C.M. were
in many cases on the ideological fringes, not merely of Anglicanism, but of
Anglican Evangelicalism. See John Kent, *Holding the Fort: Studies in Victorian Revivalism.* (1978), on this interesting subculture.

14. *The British Churches,* p. 292.

cripples' classes, a children's playtime, a day nursery, a "prostitutes' institute," several libraries, and dozens of Sunday Schools
in addition to the extensive work of extraparochial and trans-
denominational organizations (see Table 17).

The chapels continued to sponsor many more auxiliaries designed for members of the congregation, especially young members, than for outsiders. Lambeth Nonconformists sponsored at
least 61 young men's literary or debating societies, Christian Endeavour societies, and cricket, tennis, or football clubs; the
Church of England only 24. The Church of England, on the other
hand, maintained its claim to philanthropic predominance by
establishing 108 mothers' meetings, maternity societies, thrift,
slate or friendly societies, boot, coal, or clothing clubs, and savings or penny banks to the Nonconformists' 63. Furthermore,
every single Anglican parish claimed to provide relief—in money
or in kind—to the poor of their parish. Only thirty of the fifty-
five Nonconformist chapels and mission halls surveyed by Booth
made such a claim. Twenty of the chapels either helped only
their own members (usually the elderly) or objected to relief altogether—60 percent of all Baptist, 33 percent of the Congregationalist, and only 20 percent of the Wesleyan and other
Methodist chapels. The Tooting Baptist Chapel returned its
questionnaire about relief with the single sentence: "The Established Church should dispense charities."[15] Some of the smaller
Baptist chapels gave no general relief because they were chapels
of the poor, mutual aid societies for their own members.

The majority of Nonconformists who admitted to participation in religious philanthropy were seriously divided over its
meaning. Was it a portent of the coming millenium of social
harmony, merely a preface to personal conversion, or simply an
act of love by a Christian for his neighbors? By the turn of the
century some Nonconformists had become so involved with philanthropy that outsiders searched in vain for the "religious"
aspects of their work. The minister of the Murphy Memorial
Hall in Southwark claimed that his "sole object was to do good.
We avoid the 'come to Jesus style' and emphasize morality,
cleanliness and temperance."[16] But such men insisted on the

15. A-54, p. 17. Five chapels gave no answer.
16. B-278, p. 127.

religious character of their work. F. H. Stead objected bitterly when Charles Booth published this description of his influential Congregational settlement in South London: "In regarding, as it does, everything as religious which is not irreligious, it only follows the lines of all the great Congregational churches, but whereas with them we find a great social structure rising from a religious base, here the order is reversed. The social effort is the base, and so far nothing that can be called a church has risen from it."[17] Booth was one of those social observers who distinguish the "religious" from the "merely social" on the basis of nothing more than "good common sense," but his wife wrote some sensible words of advice to him about this controversy: "You will have to modify about the non-religious basis of Mr. Stead's work. When a man says he does it all from religious motives and to a religious end, one must believe him."[18]

At the other extreme from Stead and Murphy stood the Rev. Archibald Brown, minister of the East London Tabernacle in the 1890s and of Lambeth's Chatsworth Road Baptist Chapel after 1900. He represented the evangelical Baptists associated with C. H. Spurgeon's party who condemned philanthropic work as a diversion from the church's true mission. But on closer inspection we find that, although social radicals like Stead and evangelicals like Brown preached very different messages, their practical activities among the poor can hardly be distinguished. The East London Tabernacle distributed 6000 garments and the sum of £2580 to the poor in 1890, maintained a soup kitchen, a friendly society, a Boys' Home at Bow Road, a Girls' Home at Sheering, and housing for the poor at the Hawthorne Model Dwellings on Bow Common, where "Christian people" were preferred at two shillings a week.[19] This tradition continued at Chatsworth Road, although Brown lamented the absence of poor people in Norwood.

Spurgeon's Metropolitan Tabernacle itself proudly omitted the usual chapel yearbook on the grounds that "there are no social agencies," and one of its elders criticized some Baptist

17. *Life and Labour*, ser. 3, vol. 4, p. 86.

18. Belinda Norman-Butler, *Victorian Aspirations: The Life and Labours of Charles and Mary Booth* (1972), p. 133.

19. G. H. Pike, *The Life and Work of Archibald G. Brown, Preacher and Philanthropist* (1892), pp. 19, 113.

missions for "emphasizing social efforts."[20] But the Metropolitan Tabernacle sponsored three mothers' meetings with 150 to 200 members in 1900, paid the salary of a district nurse who cooperated with a neighboring vicar in providing unsectarian medical care, and supplied around £100 to the neighborhood poor.[21] One of the Tabernacle's South London mission halls, managed by a man who claimed that "we have no social agencies," sponsored a 400-member mothers' meeting, a district visiting society which distributed £130 from a benevolent fund, a program of summer holidays for local children, and a convalescent home for invalids.[22]

Evangelical Baptists objected, not to philanthropy or even to social work as such, but to the exaggerated significance bestowed upon it by the Nonconformist social radicals. The social radicals, unlike both evangelicals and socialists, did not distinguish clearly between philanthropy and social reform. One was an extension of the other; both were attempts to create a society more closely resembling the Kingdom of God. Although they sometimes condemned "mere philanthropy," their activities were variations upon older philanthropic themes, pursued with a new urgency and a new sense of meaning. "Almost all accept social work of various kinds as intermediary to higher things," Charles Booth wrote. "How similar these social efforts are, by whomsoever undertaken, is very remarkable."[23] The similarity of the Anglican, liberal Nonconformist, and evangelical Nonconformist responses to the social problem reflects a common anxiety about the condition of England and a shared adaptation of ecclesiastical structures to the city.

I am tempted to describe the structure of religion in Lambeth as a churchgoing middle class building churches and providing social services for the non-churchgoing working class and poor, but that would be a considerable oversimplification. Lambeth's bewildering variety of class and status distinctions defy tidy analysis, and the boundaries between churchgoer and non-churchgoer, middle and working class, comfortable and poor, respectable and rough, shifted from one district and one parish to

20. B-277, pp. 2–3.
21. *Ibid.*, pp. 7, 135.
22. B-274, pp. 19, 21.
23. *Life and Labour*, ser. 3, vol. 1, p. 31.

another. The churchgoing women in one poor Anglican parish might find themselves consigned to the parochial mission hall in a wealthy suburban parish. Nonconformist sports and social clubs intended for the children of the chapel often attracted the children of non-churchgoers. Non-churchgoers in some cases "captured" ecclesiastical philanthropic organizations and used them for their own purposes.

At one extreme stood a parish where, in theory, all activities were carried out for the poor. The congregation of St. Mary's, Lambeth, was divided into two groups, according to the Rector: the poor on the one hand and the Archbishop of Canterbury on the other, who "comes in and takes his seat like any miserable layman."[24] But these parishioners remade the parochial clubs in their own image. The 130 members of the Hercules Club for working lads aged fourteen to twenty had a gymnasium and two club rooms with billiards, but the "better sort" belonged only to the Young Men's Friendly Society. The Friendly Society members graduated to the adult Baroda Club. "It appears to be a point of honour with the governing majority of the club," the Rector claimed, "not to have anything to do with the church."[25] In this case non-churchgoing was a badge of respectability, and there was little overlap between the Baroda Club and the Church Brotherhood, a men's organization which attended special services in the church on Sunday afternoon.

By way of contrast, the parish of St. Peter's, Leigham Court Road, was predominantly suburban (although it sponsored a mission hall on the parish's one poor street), and status distinctions developed within the churchgoing middle-class constituency. The Vicar's Discretionary Fund was established in 1896, not for the poor, but for crises in the lives of those "of a parish like this, so largely inhabited by people who pay rates and taxes, must live in moderately good houses, must dress fairly well, yet live on an income which will just allow both ends to meet."[26] Ten years later this "respectability fund" was regarded as a great success, and the new vicar urged his parishioners to "turn a beggar from the door" since "a bare one percent of these stray cases are

24. B-272, pp. 73, 75.

25. B-272, p. 75.

26. St. Peter's, Streatham, *Annual Report for 1896*, pp. 13–14.

genuine." "Only the parson knows," he confided, "what real distress exists in the most unexpected quarters among people who have to hide their poverty."[27]

Between these two extremes—one entirely working-class and the other largely suburban—stood most of Lambeth's churches and chapels, arayed upon a complicated spectrum of status. In the highest class of chapel the minister referred to the percentage of "carriage folk" in his congregation. The next category of chapel was divided between those who kept two or three servants and those who kept only one, followed by congregations in which "servant-keeper" and "non-servant-keeper" were the relevant distinctions. Below that were various combinations of clerk, shopkeeper, artisan, "comfortable working man," and the poor. These fundamental categories were then overlaid with secondary distinctions based upon church and chapel auxiliaries, in particular those for children. The Lambeth Wesleyan Mission maintained a regular Sunday School for members' children and a "rough" Sunday School which gradually trained children for the regular school, but the Sunday School at suburban Roupell Park Wesleyan Chapel was entirely working-class: "Nothing is done for the better class children. The theory is that they are instructed at home."[28] At Brixton Hill Wesleyan Chapel most of the congregation kept servants and the Sunday School was reserved for "a rather lower though still comfortable class"; the day schools also served a class which did not attend this chapel—parents with at least £150 a year but no servant.[29] At St. Phillip's Kennington, the parents of the fee-paying day school children made up most of the active congregation. "The fee paying children will not mix with those of the free schools, either in Sunday School or anywhere else," the vicar complained. "In fact they appear to be a most exclusive set."[30] The minister of the Waterloo Road Bible Christian Chapel echoed his complaint: "The children won't mix though the parents do."[31] Brixton Independent Church could not attract the working classes to some organizations, according

27. St. Peter's, Streatham, *Annual Report for 1906,* unpaged.

28. B-271, p. 111; B-313, p. 25.

29. B-304, p. 113.

30. B-272, p. 161.

31. B-270, p. 33.

to its minister, because "I can't get my own people to stay away."[32]

It is impossible to classify accurately all church auxiliaries according to social class, or even separate in every case those for non-churchgoers from those of the churchgoers. The distinction existed in many cases although it is blurred in others. The documents are inadequate in any event, and it is therefore necessary to classify them functionally into seven categories: 1. those providing direct relief to the poor in money or in kind; 2. channels for indirect relief such as mothers' meetings, boot, coal, blanket and clothing clubs; 3. thrift organizations, penny banks, savings banks, "slate" clubs; 4. direct medical services; 5. day schools and Sunday schools 6. social clubs; 7. organizations for popular recreation and entertainment.

1. Direct Poor Relief

The district visitors handled much of the regular distribution of money, food, and clothing. Most Lambeth parishes, despite the recurrent alarm about the segregation of the classes, in fact contained some streets inhabited by servant-keepers (colored red on Booth's maps) and some very poor streets. The vicar usually had little trouble gathering a band of middle-class ladies into the District Visiting Society, and each visitor was assigned a group of fifteen or twenty families or a section of a poor street to visit during the day while her husband was away in the City. In theory the visitors were married women, but in fact the unmarried— both older unmarried women and daughters accompanying their mothers—easily outnumbered the married. I have been unable to estimate the number of district visitors active in Lambeth in 1899, but they worked in almost every parish—coming from the suburbs into working-class parishes when necessary—and there were few complaints of difficulty in recruiting district visitors except in a few parishes which had suffered a complete middle-class exodus. (Sunday School teachers, on the other hand, were generally in short supply.) Lady visitors at All Saints, West Dulwich, visited every house in the parish regularly and poor households weekly. "My people wish there was more to do," the vicar observed, and clergymen generally believed the district visitors

32. B-303, p. 71.

indispensable.[33] "Take away our visitors and other organizations for three months," the vicar of All Saints, South Lambeth, predicted, "and the church would be almost empty."[34] An outside observer claimed that in the parish of St. John the Divine, "no one is left untouched," and that the visitors of St. Mark's, Kennington, "know everyone in every house."[35] St. Saviour's, Herne Hill, had three distinct sets of visitors: "Those who go round to all, distributing the magazine and selling over 700 copies a month; those who visit the sick, and on that errand can enter houses of some pretensions of comfort; and lastly, the Provident Fund Collectors, who visit only the poor streets."[36]

The social importance of district visiting can hardly be overestimated. It was the major spare-time activity for large numbers of ordinary suburban women, many of whom had strictly limited opportunities for any significant community involvement in social services. Visitation obviously reflected a continuing desire among the middle classes to aid the poor or engage in some form of community service, and the original theory of visitation, the "bringing of different classes into mutual intercourse," remained remarkably unchanged between 1860 and 1900. It was the most notable Victorian response to the anxiety produced by the physical separation of the classes—more important than the familiar Charity Organization Society and the much discussed settlement movement because far more extensive, less visible to historians because decentralized (and because the social significance of religious institutions has been ignored). It kept the church in direct contact with thousands of non-churchgoers in Lambeth, millions in the nation. How "the poor" responded is difficult to say, although they clearly did not display the gratitude which the visitor expected. The visitor's condescension inevitably engendered hostility and the corresponding middle-class resentment so brilliantly described by Gareth Stedman Jones as "the deformation of the gift."[37] Others must have looked upon the visitors as simply part of the social landscape, as yet another incompre-

33. B-312, p. 207.
34. B-272, p. 61.
35. B-273, p. 117.
36. Booth, *Life and Labour,* ser. 3, vol. 6, p. 51.
37. Gareth Stedman Jones, *Outcast London: A Study in the Relationship Between Classes in Victorian Society* (1971), ch. 13.

hensible but familiar figure of authority like the vicar, the relieving officer, or the school attendance officer.

Clergymen and district visitors braved a torrent of monotonous
criticism throughout the late nineteenth century. The relief
associated with visitation, the critics argued, was indiscriminate
and demoralizing. Criticism often came from people deeply involved in giving relief, demonstrating the mixed motives and
confusion surrounding the middle-class response to "the poor"—
guilt over ignoring them combined with a fear of pampering and
thus "pauperizing" them. District visitors did adjust their methods
somewhat in response to criticism after 1880, in particular by
substituting "mendicity tickets" for money and gifts. The tickets,
usually worth a shilling and redeemable at local shops, supposedly
discouraged outright bribery, prevented relief money from flowing
into the pub, and allowed a closer inspection of the recipient so
that the "undeserving" might be eliminated. Associated with this
reform was a sustained attempt by the Charity Organization
Society to eliminate soup kitchens where food was distributed
without personal inquiries into the recipient's need. By 1900 soup
kitchens were rare, although eliminating them had been a
struggle. The vicar of St. Mark's, Kennington, complained that
the soup kitchen "had been far and away the most popular object
of yearly subscription—mostly from parishioners in large houses
on Kennington and Clapham Roads." After it was discontinued
in 1897, yearly subscriptions to St. Mark's district visitors fell
from £181 to £67.[38]

These complaints did not impress, and minor reforms did not
satisfy, the Charity Organization Society. Their Southwark, North
Lambeth, and Vauxhall committees labored heroically, with a
devotion matched only by that of extreme religious zealots, to
stem the flood of relief. Although it is generally thought that the
C.O.S. became more and more irrelevant after the 1880s because
of its rigid opposition to any measure which smacked of "col-
lectivism," it still succeeded in marshaling significant support for
its local committees in the 1890s. The upsurge of concern over
poverty in the last two decades of the nineteenth century pro-

38. B-272, pp. 122ff.; cf. a similar experience at St. Michael's, Stockwell: *St.
Michael's Annual Report*, 1899.

duced many new theories about poverty and its cure, but on the local level it merely caused a further proliferation of private and religious philanthropy which intensified public anxiety about "pauperisation" even further. Many people who did not share the C.O.S. dogma that indiscriminate charity was itself the major cause of poverty were nevertheless upset about the chaotic and uncoordinated distribution of money and tickets and the attendant dangers of bribery, and the C.O.S. proposals were the only obvious means of control.

The C.O.S. worked closely with the Church of England both locally and nationally.[39] At the local level Anglican parishes provided a framework within which the C.O.S. attempted to establish its network of urban villages with a sort of voluntary poor-law system enforcing sound principles upon religious philanthropists. Anglican philanthropy might, in theory, be placed under some control. The real enemies of the C.O.S. were not the often exasperating Anglican clergymen so much as the philanthropic anarchists of the Nonconformist societies and mission halls who alarmed the C.O.S. and others with their extravagant claims. In 1899 in one section of South London, for instance, the Wesleyans claimed to have fed 2500 children during the winter, the Kent Street Sunday School 800 every Friday. The Lansdowne Place Ragged School boasted 12,818 free breakfasts, 2235 free dinners, and 4772 half-penny dinners.[40] The Poor Children's Society "Children's Dinner and Orphans Aid Fund" supplied 3000 Christmas and New Year's Roast Beef Dinners at no fewer than fifteen schoolrooms and mission halls in Southwark and Lambeth in 1899.[41] It is little wonder that people began to fantasize about vast amounts of relief going to the poor. "A continuous vast river of charitable help," C. F. G. Masterman wrote, "pours through the channels of these missions into every corner and crevice of their homes; bread, clothing, boots, vegetable soup, grocery tickets, monetary assistance, fall sometimes, like the rain of

39. In 1900 its patron was the Queen, its president the Archbishop of Canterbury, and its list of vice presidents included two dukes, two marquesses, four earls, four other peers, and six bishops: C. L. Mowat, *The Charity Organization Society 1869–1913* (1961), p. 82.

40. *Life and Labour*, ser. 3, vol. 4, p. 115.

41. B-273, flyer inserted in bound manuscript volume.

heaven, upon the just and unjust."[42] The amounts spent on feeding children in particular do not seem to have been that high, but the Nonconformist mission halls were beyond the control of the C.O.S. or indeed of anyone. Anglican clergymen, on the other hand, might be trusted under some circumstances to distribute relief properly. Nonconformists were understandably alienated by the C.O.S.'s evident Anglican bias, and criticized it more readily on principle. The Browning Settlement in Walworth opposed any investigation of relief recipients on the grounds that it destroyed their self-respect. The Congregationalist director of the Lambeth Ragged School refused to cooperate with the C.O.S. because "you should trust the poor," an attitude shared by his minister at the Brixton Independent Church who asserted in a sermon that "Christianity is concerned with the survival of the unfit."[43]

The C.O.S. organized local registries of relief recipients and encouraged each Anglican parish to set up a relief committee run "along C.O.S. lines," but they found the church frustrating. Clergymen readily agreed to cooperate with the C.O.S. and steadfastly refused to introduce its rigor, which conflicted with the Anglican tradition as they saw it, with their own sentimental response to the everyday suffering of the poor, and with their middle-class parishioners' desire to give away food, money, and clothing. "I am one who can't naturally refuse," a Brixton vicar confessed, and the vicar of St. Peter's, Leigham Court Road, proudly announced in 1894 that no request for help from the poor was ever turned down.[44] Not every clergyman agreed, and some were genuine charity organizers themselves, but with remarkable consistency clergymen behaved one way at C.O.S. meetings and another way when confronted with requests for help. St. Anne's, South Lambeth, operated a relief committee "on C.O.S. lines," but the vicar asserted that the church cannot be too strict and must "act sometimes on the off chance."[45] Of the

42. Richard Mudie-Smith, ed., *Religious Life of London* (1904), p. 191.

43. B-272, p. 57; *Brixton Free Press*, 14 June 1912, p. 5.

44. B-305, p. 219; *St. Peter's Annual Report for 1894* (his successor followed a radically different policy).

45. B-272, p. 149.

eight parishes assigned to the North Lambeth C.O.S., only three were described by the committee's chairman as cooperative. According to him, the rector of Lambeth's idea of charity was "to give half crowns," and three of the parishes professed cooperation in theory and refused in practice while two were positively hostile.[46] Harry Toynbee of the Southwark C.O.S. (brother of one of the famous historians and father of the other) described the most persistent obstacles to the spread of sound principles of relief as "the desire to yield to the kindly impulse, the ease with which it can be thoughtlessly gratified, the unpleasantness of repressing it."[47]

The eight Lambeth parishes supervised by the C.O.S. distributed roughly 30 percent of the direct relief flowing through all of Lambeth's Anglican parishes. But even when all of Lambeth's parishes are taken into account, the flow of money was unlikely to pauperize very many of the poor. According to the estimates of the clergymen of thirty of Lambeth's thirty-three parishes, £4088 was allocated to "direct relief" in 1899 (see Table 17). It is impossible to estimate accurately the amount of Nonconformist relief, which was largely handled by philanthropic societies, but twenty-five Lambeth chapels reported giving £850 to outsiders in 1899. This figure includes the contributions of most of Lambeth's large chapels but not of Christ Church, Westminster Bridge Road, which reportedly gave lavishly. Congregationalists were responsible for over half of the Nonconformist sum. A figure of £5000 can be considered a reasonable minimum figure for the amount of direct relief distributed directly through the churches and chapels, although not through other religious philanthropies, in 1899.

Compared with the needs of the people of Lambeth the amount was small, although no doubt very significant in individual cases. It was, as the critics claimed, distributed chaotically. As an item of church expenditure, relief ranked well behind clerical salaries, ordinary parochial expenditure on building maintenance, and capital expenditure, although crude statistics do not tell us what percentage of the clergyman's time was expected to be devoted

46. B-272, pp. 39–43.
47. B-273, p. 21.

to philanthropic and charitable work, nor do they tell us what percentage of the activities in the church buildings was devoted to the improvement of social conditions.[48] But of the institutions addressing one pressing aspect of the social problem, poverty, only the Board of Guardians surpassed, and no other rivalled, the importance of the churches. During the year beginning at Michaelmas, 1899, the nine relieving officers of the Lambeth Board of Guardians distributed £14,203 in money and in kind for the out-relief of paupers.[49] The churches and chapels of Lambeth supplied a minimum of roughly £5000—at least one-quarter of the entire relief burden of the district.

48. St. Michael's, Stockwell, devoted 75 percent of its total expenditure of £2715 in 1892 to church expenses, clerical salaries, and day schools although that included the purchase of a freehold; *48th Annual Report*, 1894. Brixton Independent Church paid its pastor a salary of £870 in 1895—33 percent of total expenditure—while all religious and philanthropic societies (including national societies, denominational societies, missions and local philanthropy) received £662—25 percent of expenditure; *Yearbook*, 1895. St. Aubyn's Congregational Chapel, Upper Norwood (in Croydon but with members in Lambeth) devoted 17 percent of all subscriptions to the Boot Club, Visitation Society, Infant's Friend and Clothing Society, and Blanket Society in 1899, and the neighboring Presbyterian Church spent from 2 to 11 percent of its budget (both offertories and subscriptions) for "religious and benevolent" purposes between 1874 and 1903; *St. Aubyn's Annual Report for 1899*; M. D. Carruthers, *The Candlestick: A Record of St. Andrew's Presbyterian Church, Upper Norwood 1874–1924* (1925), appendix. Three Anglican parishes in Lambeth devoted 6, 11 and 17 percent of their yearly offertories to the "poor and needy"; St. Peter's, Leigham Court Road, *Annual Report*, 1899; St. John the Evangelist, Angell Town, *Annual Report*, 1896; St. Andrew's, Stockwell, *Yearbook*, 1906. After 1900 parishes began reporting their patterns of expenditure much more regularly to the church commissioners and by 1908 the *Church Yearbook* was able to report that 8.8 percent of parochial expenditure in English was devoted to "general charitable objects" (£501,776); *Facts and Figures about the Church of England* (1961), pp. 82–83.

49. H.C. 1900 (137) vol. 73, p. 754; 1900 (137–I) vol. 73, p. 782. This figure excludes £301 spent on children's board, but includes all expenses associated with out-relief except officers' salaries and the cost of relief stations. The Lambeth Guardians supervised London's second largest district. In addition to the nine relieving officers who had wide discretionary powers in cases of emergency, they employed a full-time collector to collect from relatives. One representative of the Lambeth Charity Organization Society was on the Board, which heard all new cases. Another COS representative was allowed to hear out-relief cases, although she was allowed no say in the decision. B-383, interview with Mr. Thurnall, clerk to the Guardians, 5 April 900.

2. Indirect Relief

These calculations still underestimate the voluntary transfer of wealth in Edwardian Lambeth, for they exclude much Nonconformist relief, almost all of the relief distributed by the religious philanthropic societies, and a great deal of indirect relief distributed by churches and chapels through clubs and "self-help" organizations. The most prominent of the latter was the mothers' meeting. There were fifty-seven of them in Lambeth—thirty-four Anglican and twenty-three Nonconformist. Sixteen of these meetings averaged sixty-three members each. They were usually run directly by a clergyman or minister and were attended readily by a deferential class of working-class women (and sometimes very poor women) 'who could not leave their families in order to attend Sunday worship. The mothers usually contributed a small amount each week which was then augmented by funds from the church or chapel and returned as coal, clothing, or a Christmas bonus. This led to accusations of hypocrisy and outright bribery from many people including, as usual, some of the most active promoters of the mothers' meetings. Members were reportedly subject to jibes and sneers from their neighbors for "going for what they can get." They tolerated this unpleasantness, not merely for the Christmas bonus, but for the opportunity of having tea with the curate and hearing a short homily. The meeting was a symbol of respectability rather like churchgoing for someone higher in the social scale. In 1910 a Brixton journalist described the importance of the weekly mothers' meeting on a poverty-stricken street near his own home:

The cleansed roadway and paths appeal to me as a prelude to a sort of domestic early closing which takes place about 2:45 on Mondays. It is about that hour that a proportion of the adult femininity of ——— Street leaves their homes with mixed feelings for the mission room of St. ——— Church for their weekly mothers' meeting. The procession grows in volume as Christmas approaches. But neglect to wear "something black" on such occasions would apparently savour of desecration. A general interest is awakened in the stream of mothers carrying parcels, bags and an air of virtue that belongs not to other times and to other clothes. Which probably accounts for the complacent manner in which the ladies who will shortly be in converse with the curate and district visitors accept sarcastic taunts from a few neighbours whose apparel necessarily shows signs of the necessity of being "done up."[50]

A "maternity society" for pregnant women was sometimes associated with the mothers' meeting (at least ten of them in 1899). The thirty members of the St. Saviour's, Brixton Hill, maternity society each received a box containing one-half pound of tea, one pound of sugar, one-half pound of soap, a quart of oatmeal, and some clothing; they were given a half-crown when the box was returned and the baby baptized. The Brixton Unitarian Chapel sponsored a day nursery with two nurses in the 1880s, and St. John the Divine, Kennington, supported a day nursery as well.[51] But day care was assumed to be the mother's responsibility. These nurseries were associated with medical facilities and designed to preserve the health of the infant, not allow the mother to work. The other major activity for women was loosely styled "rescue work"—the equivalent of missionary work among derelict and homeless men. This was usually done, not through the parish or chapel, but through voluntary societies such as the "Mission to Women Criminals." St. Mary's, Lambeth, did sponsor a special weekly service for prostitutes, and Lambeth's "Association for the Care of Friendless Girls" was a precursor of the Southwark Diocesan Moral Welfare Association, whose activities expanded dramatically after 1900 in cooperation both with the local parishes and the Borough of Lambeth.

The various boot, coal, clothing, and blanket clubs in Lambeth (at least seventeen Anglican and four Nonconformist) were not always associated with the mothers' meetings, although they were almost always managed by the district visitors. Children were occasionally enrolled in a "boot club" through their Sunday School and expected to contribute a small sum each week. Both the mothers' meeting and the relief club were increasingly regarded as old fashioned by 1900, in part because they never achieved the goal of eliminating bribery and competition between the denominations. Bribery was not simply an anxious fantasty of the charity organizer, although its extent was certainly exag-

50. *Brixton Free Press*, 2 Dec. 1910.

51. B-305, p. 211; R. K. Spedding, *Resurgam! Being the Book of the Effra Road Unitarian Christian Church, Brixton* (1941), pp. 16–19; A. G. Deedes, ed. *Charles Edward Brooke: A Memoir* (1913), p. 52.

gerated. Complaints were concentrated in a few neighborhoods, and some clergymen freely admitted the necessity of bribing children with treats and excursions in order to keep them in Sunday School.

Bribery seems to have run amuck in West Southwark and two or three neighboring parishes in North Lambeth, where Anglicans complained as bitterly as Nonconformists about the legacy of Father A. B. Goulden of St. Alphege's. At his death in 1896 the parochial relief fund had a balance of £2528.[52] Everyone admitted that the Anglican sisters of the parish used bribery, and a London City Missionary claimed that the men in St. Alphege's Bible class received a suit for regular attendance, the women a dress, and each family so many pounds of meat. The nearby Hope Street Mission responded to this real or imagined philanthropic aggression by giving women a blanket for regular attendance and an apron for occasional attendance, and rumors flew around the neighborhood of women who supported themselves entirely by attending as many as ten different mothers' meetings.[53] That was gossip, but the director of Fegan's Homes (an orphanage and mission) admitted that he lured away members of other mothers' meetings by such tactics, and the rector of Christ Church, Southwark, put a stop to his predecessor's practice of leaving relief tickets in prayer books.[54] Some women would leave the worship service after finding them. Christ Church and the Surrey Chapel (Primitive Methodist) cooperated in Mr. Vaughan's Charity, an almshouse newly constructed on the site of the old manor house of Southwark, and women hoping to be elected attended the place of worship which possessed the right of nomination to the next vacancy.[55]

3. Thrift Societies

Roman Catholics scorned Protestant bribery and claimed that "so far from giving we go round and collect money even from the poorest."[56] And by 1900 both Anglicans and Nonconformists,

52. *St. Alphege's Parochial Report,* 1896, inserted in B-269.

53. B-270, pp. 133–35.

54. B-273, p. 77; B-269, p. 75.

55. B-269, p. 123.

56. B-271, p. 175.

embarrassed by tales of bribery, were attempting to replace the various relief clubs with "thrift clubs" which collected money from the poor—although unlike the Catholics the Protestants returned the money rather than keeping it. The popularity of these slate clubs, provident and friendly societies, and penny banks reflected a genuine demand for small-scale savings institutions. There were fifty Anglican societies in 1899 (including fifteen penny banks for children), and the thirty-three Nonconformist thrift societies reported over 4000 members (see Table 17, columns 5 and 8). The oldest of Lambeth's thrift institutions, the Lambeth Savings Bank, had been founded on Lambeth Green in 1818 as a "bank for the poor" with the Rector of Lambeth serving as *ex officio* trustee.[57] The popularity of savings institutions continued to grow after 1900. Lloyd George addressed the opening meeting of the Christ Church, North Brixton, Slate and Loan Club in 1900 when its deposits were £479, an amount which tripled by 1905.[58] The Christ Church, Westminister Bridge Road, Benefit Club, founded in 1902, was dividing £1200 yearly later in the decade.[59]

These church-related friendly societies and thrift clubs should be considered in the context of the entire range of Victorian provision for the unpredictability of the economy and the life cycle. A middle-class association such as the Lambeth District Teacher's Association provided a benevolent fund for temporary relief of members, a provident society for sick pay, life assurance and deposits, and an orphanage fund.[60] The "better sort" of working men might belong to one of Lambeth's twenty-two secular Friendly Societies without branches (4624 members excluding those societies affiliated with a church or chapel in any obvious way) which registered with the Chief Registrar for Friendly Societies and Trade Unions in 1899.[61] The largest and most successful were occupational or associated with a union, such as the London and Southwestern Friendly Society (a regional rather

57. *South London Press,* 11 April 1903.

58. Christ Church North Brixton Slate and Loan Club, Notes by J. Avery, Esq., 30 January 1963, Greater London Record Office A/CB5/107.

59. *The Christ Church Jubilee Souvenir Book* (1926), p. 28.

60. *Lambeth District Teacher's Association Yearbook,* 1895.

61. H.C. 1901 (35), vol. 72, pp. 82–95.

than local society holding £33,000 for railwaymen), the Music Hall Friendly Society, and the Southwest Cabdrivers' Friendly Society. The Ancient Order of Foresters, the dominant national lodge in the south of England, had twenty-four clubs with 3654 members, and Lambeth was world headquarters for both the united Order of Comical Fellows and the Ancient Society of Comical Fellows A.D. 1790. Partly overlapping and partly serving a slightly lower social class, an indeterminate number of slate clubs (very informal insurance or savings clubs) were organized around the local pub with the publican sometimes serving as treasurer. Each December the newspapers featured several stories of slate club treasurers who disappeared with the funds just before payout time at Christmas.

The churches and chapels filled in gaps left by the occupational friendly societies and lodges and at the same time reached those not included in any organized group. Some of the ostensibly secular lodges, such as the Loyal Stockwell Lodge in St. Andrew's parish and the Temperance Hope Branch of the Foresters in St. Mary-the-Less, simply fitted into the Anglican parochial structure. The Lambeth Pension Society had been active since 1826 and, like the Lambeth Savings Bank, was informally associated with the Church of England. Other clubs were simply mutual benefit societies identical to those associated with the Lambeth District Teacher's Association: the Surrey Tabernacle Benevolent Society with 1083 members and £18615 in deposits was an insurance society for Strict and Particular Baptists. In other cases the chapels or mission halls served as informal mutual aid societies without benefit of a separate, formal club. The 180 members of the Railway Mission Hall—almost all railway employees and their families—immediately raised £16 for the family of a member killed in a railway accident, and another chapel attended by railwaymen, Wheatsheaf Hall, sponsored three slate clubs with over 500 members, a penny bank with 1500 members, and an organization called the Friends of Labour Loan Society.[62]

Church- and chapel-related societies were usually far more informal than the registered friendly societies—house to house collections were made by district visitors in many cases—and presumably reached more women since the regular friendly societies

62. B-271, pp. 7, 211.

were generally for men. In 1905 conflict between the two forms
of friendly society (the registered and the informal) led to a
"Conference on Permanent Benefit Societies and Slate Clubs" in
South London, during which the latter defended themselves
against charges of irresponsibility by claiming greater accessibility
at lesser expense to members.[63] Below the level of the slate clubs
respectable enough to defend themselves were more disreputable
financial agencies, in particular pawnbrokers and those always
referred to as "women moneylenders." The pawn shops varied
greatly in respectability, but clergymen claimed that small-time
moneylenders who lent at $1d$ in the shilling per week to those
who could be watched were disliked and feared.[64] The extent of
this sort of activity can never be quantified, but it is worth comparing the combined Lambeth membership of forty-six registered
secular friendly societies (the independent societies without
branches and branches of the Foresters)—8278 in 1899—with the
number of members affiliated with twenty-one of the twenty-three
Nonconformist Friendly Societies and slate clubs for adults—4159.
The Nonconformists had fewer societies than the Anglicans (with
thirty-five), whose membership figures are impossible to calculate.

4. Medical Services

Lambeth's churches and chapels directly sponsored at least
sixteen nurses in 1899. Six Anglican parishes sponsored a nurse
for their own parish only (one was shared with a neighboring
parish in Wandsworth), but medical care for the South London
poor was generally organized around district dispensaries and
nursing associations closely associated with the churches. The
vicar of St. Matthew's, Brixton, was *ex officio* director of the
Brixton dispensary and responsible for public appeals for funds,
and ten clergymen were among the forty officers of the Camberwell Provident Dispensary (4445 regular members, 11,306
persons eligible for benefits in return for $4d$ to $10d$ a month de-

63. *South London Press*, 1 April 1905; many of the informal slate clubs run
by publicans are unrecorded—the "Jolly Boys" Musical and Benevolent Society was founded in 1900 by Charles Muddle, proprietor of the Crown, New
Cut, "for rendering financial aid to the poor and needy of the populous districts of Lambeth." *South London Press,* 15 December 1900.

64. B-270, p. 167; cf. C. S. Garbett, *In the Heart of South London* (1931) p. 61.

pending upon family size).[65] The Bishop of Rochester was patron of the Southwark, Newington, and Walworth District Nursing Association, which covered twenty-three parishes including some in Lambeth.[66] Their two nurses and three probationers saw those patients who could procure a reference from a clergyman or a doctor. Parishes in North Lambeth participated in the South London and District Nursing Association. Although an occasional Nonconformist minister appeared among the directors of these associations, they were greatly outnumbered by clergymen. The patients themselves were naturally excluded from any voice in their management.

Among the Nonconformists, the Metropolitan Tabernacle sponsored a Baptist nurse in Kennington and the Brixton Independent Church assigned two nurses to its Moffatt Institute in North Lambeth and supported a convalescent home at Herne Bay.[67] The independent London Medical Mission opened a dispensary in a shop in North Lambeth in 1898 with two doctors and eight nurses, including some in training for medical mission work. Patients preferred it to a hospital because the wait was not so long. Admitted with queue tickets at 9:30 A.M., those with high numbers could go home after a compulsory religious service at 10. The dispensary was open Wednesday night for factory girls and Monday night for working men, their nurses visited the sick at home, and patients were eligible for a convalescent home at Folkestone and a "Holiday House" at Sevenoaks.[68] Similar operations elsewhere in South London included the dispensary at Fegan's Orphanage at Southwark, and the Anglican Evangelical Oxford Medical Mission in Bermondsey where tickets for medical help had first to be obtained from the parish church.[69] Most clergymen and some Nonconformist ministers distributed "hospital letters," supplied by the hospital or a wealthy patron, which

65. B-312, p. 1; Camberwell Provident Dispensary, *Annual Report,* 1899.

66. Southwark, Newington and Walworth District Nursing Association, *Annual Report,* 1898; Sixteen of forty-one on its "council" were clergymen.

67. B-272, p. 135; *Brixton Independent Yearbooks,* 1890–1905.

68. B-276, pp. 93ff.; the main dispensary of the London Medical Mission was at St. Giles; in 1975 that building was headquarters for a London City Missionary attempting to evangelize the theatrical people of the West End. The Lambeth Branch handled 15,532 cases in 1898.

69. B-273, p. 59; B-278, p. 105.

allowed the bearer entrance to a hospital, and even people who would not otherwise seek help willingly applied for "surgical aid letters" in order to obtain "expensive appliances" such as trusses or braces.

5. Education

Churches and chapels felt a special responsibility for education as well as for medical care and managed to retain and even extend their control over the former as well as the latter. Anglican day schools fitted into the parochial structure, and many clergymen regarded the schools as their most important work. Most Anglicans expected both the schools and the parish to inculcate a very general piety among the students along with a mild allegiance to the Church of England, and were satisfied that the schools contributed to upholding the "tone, manners, and morals of the district." This was to be achieved through a short daily worship service which probably succeeded in promulgating a very general sort of assent to some mangled version of the Christian faith among the students along with a life-long aversion to church services. Herbert Morrison recalled attending the Lingham Street Church of England School: "Every afternoon . . . in the sullen twilight of a winter's afternoon, we would intone the somewhat dreary hymn, 'The Day Thou Givest, Lord, is Ended.' Something about the atmosphere of that final five minutes has left a memory of perpetual wintry gloom about my school hours, just as release from class brings a memory of sunny streets once we were through the playground gates."[70] Anglo-Catholics (and Roman Catholics) did not hesitate to proselytize in their schools: at St. Peter's, Vauxhall (Church of England), students were taught that it was sinful to attend the Board School. The doctrines of the Real Presence and Confession were taught in class, and the children prepared for confirmation. "Through the children we get the parents," the vicar claimed.[71]

70. Herbert Morrison, *An Autobiography, by Lord Morrison of Lambeth* (1960), p. 18.

71. B-272, p. 7; also B-271, p. 175, interview with the Rev. Father Brown of St. Anne's Roman Catholic Church, Harleyford Road: "Nearly all the Roman Catholics and some Protestants who live nearby like the school— from them come poorer Protestant converts."

The more prestigious church schools were thought to attract a higher class of student. According to one clergyman "the better off don't like their children sitting next to the poor." The churches could exercise some selectivity if they wished through fees and other devices.[72] But their competitive advantage derived from snobbery could not compensate for lack of money, and the Church of England schools received increasingly keen competition from the Board Schools. This led to pressure for government funds, and the 1902 Education Act was a significant Anglican victory in educational policy, one which did not stop the relative decline of Church Schools but significantly altered its rate. After the reorganization of 1903 there were twenty-four L.C.C. schools in Lambeth and thirty-seven denominational schools of various sorts including three Anglican grammar schools (giving them a monopoly in secondary education), one Swedenborgian, three Wesleyan, and three Roman Catholic primary schools.[73]

The Board Schools, as they were still called for a number of years after 1902, provided 60 percent of the accommodation. The Wesleyans displayed a remarkable devotion to their schools in an area where they were not very strong (the Wesleyan day school in West Norwood remained open through World War II). But other Nonconformist denominations provided no schools directly, and it was often said, especially by clergymen, that Dissenters felt no responsibility for education. Recent Anglican historians have simply repeated this accusation without making an attempt to understand the Nonconformist position or the religious significance of state education.[74] The logic of the Nonconformist ideological heritage combined with their changing social status drove them, not merely to accept state intervention, but to look upon some manifestations of it as particularly blessed by God (a

72. B-305, p. 155. St. Saviour's, Herne Hill Road, charged 9d a week for secondary school; the Wesleyan Elementary School on Brixton Hill charged 25 shillings a term; B-272, p. 161; B-305, p. 57.

73. London County Council, *London Statistics*, vol. 16, 1905–6, pp. 263ff. For the history of a Lambeth church school see Pamela and Harold Silver, *The Education of the Poor: The History of a National School 1824–1974* (1974).

74. E. R. Norman, *Church and Society in England, 1770–1970: A Historical Study* (Oxford, 1976), p. 203; cf. G. S. R. Kitson Clark, *The Making of Victorian England* (New York, 1969), pp. 175–76, on an earlier period.

position confused by the persistence of mid-Victorian antistatist rhetoric). Many Nonconformists supported the voluntary
British and Foreign School Society before 1870 and most "British"
schools were absorbed by the school boards between 1870 and
1900 along with more sectarian Baptist and Congregational
Schools. Despite what some Anglo-Catholic clergymen said about
them, the Board Schools were not pagan institutions. Most social
observers agreed that they were more efficient at inculcating religious knowledge than the Sunday Schools, and state-school
scripture teachers were often dedicated Nonconformist laymen.
The intensity of Nonconformist hostility to the 1902 Education
Act surprised almost everyone. Nonconformists regarded the
school boards and Board Schools as their own by 1900, a fact
which the Anglicans and Fabians who designed the act ignored.
The act combined a subsidy for their enemies (the Anglicans)
with the destruction of their own institutions (the school boards).

Few Lambeth children escaped some exposure to Sunday
School. C. F. G. Masterman wrote of South London Sunday
Schools:

> The Sunday Schools and the Sunday attendance of children at church
> in all the poorer districts serve a purpose quite distinct from that of
> religious instruction. Children go whose parents are of all religions and
> none; streets containing not a single adult worshipper will contribute
> their swarms of clean and intelligent infants. The selection of a school
> . . . seems entirely haphazard—nearness, excellence of the annual treat,
> the lateness of assembling, and the laxity of discipline being apparently
> the chief attractive elements. Certainly the last thing thought of is the
> nature of the religion taught. I have no doubt that Sunday Schools con-
> ducted by mild-mannered and generous Buddhists in South London
> (provided they were white in colour—we have an aversion to foreigners)
> would draw large and appreciative audiences.[75]

Church services in 1902 attracted 18 percent of those aged five
to fourteen in the morning and 14 percent in the evening, but in
1905 the Lambeth auxiliary of the Sunday School Union reported 28,317 scholars on the rolls.[76] This Nonconformist society

75. "The Problem of South London," in Mudie-Smith, ed., *Religious Life of London*, pp. 189–90.

76. *South London Press*, 8 April 1905. In a 1957 Gallup survey 73 percent of
a national sample of adults claimed to have attended Sunday School regularly

alone enrolled nearly 50 percent of all eligible children in Lambeth (students were not enrolled unless they attended at least once). Christ Church, Westminster Bridge Road (Congregationalist), conducted nine Sunday Schools in the morning and afternoon and six in the evening with 5000 students and 400 teachers.[77] There were no Buddhist Sunday Schools in Lambeth to test Masterman's theory, but Unitarians, Swedenborgians, and the South London Ethical Society easily collected neighborhood children into their Sunday Schools. I have discovered only one chapel—a small group of Strict and Particular Baptists near Clapham—which tried to start a Sunday School and failed. Unlike some of the Sunday Schools in Lancashire which succeeded in enrolling adults, Lambeth's Sunday Schools were entirely for children. "Like most children, I went to Sunday School," Herbert Morrison wrote, "until I got my first job and became a man."[78] Parents used the Sunday Schools to get the children out of the house on Sunday. Chapel members enjoyed seeing all the scholars assemble in the chapel for the yearly Sunday School anniversary, although this event was not nearly so important in Lambeth as in the north of England. Children attended for "treats" and excursions. "We are obliged to have treats because of our Dissenting brethren," a West Dulwich clergyman complained. When he began his work all the children went to a Nonconformist Sunday School, but "gradually they all came over to me; the other school had to close."[79]

6. Clubs

Edwardian Nonconformists in particular continued to display great optimism about the prospects for producing a new, sober generation through indoctrination in one of the thirty-six children's temperance organizations in Lambeth, especially the Band of Hope. But the Band of Hope enrolled only very young chil-

---

as a child, 17 percent sometimes, 10 percent never. Gallup, *The Gallup International Public Opinion Polls. Great Britain 1937–1975,* vol. 1, 1937–1964, p. 405.

77. Booth, *Life and Labour,* ser. 3, vol. 4, p. 34.

78. Morrison, *Autobiography,* p. 22.

79. B-312, p. 205.

dren, and older children were not interested in further indoctrination about the evils of drink. The chapels found it necessary to
lure older children, particularly males, into one of the relatively
new and very popular uniformed organizations. The Boy Scouts
had not been founded by 1900, but the Anglicans had the Church
Lads' Brigade and the Nonconformists the Boys' Brigade. The
preponderance of the Church Lads' Brigade over the Boys'
Brigade (twelve chapters to five) was temporary, for the former
had been founded in South London in 1891 as an Anglican
equivalent to the rapidly growing Boys' Brigade which was spread-
ing south from Glasgow.[80] The spread of the Boys' Brigade
among London Nonconformists may have been delayed by controversies about militarism during the Boer War. A chapel in
Upper Norwood withdrew its unit from the Boys' Brigade and
established a "Boys' Life Saving Society" with swimming drill,
fire brigade, and ambulance class. According to the minister,
chapel workers "were attracted by the idea of a society which has
the idea of saving life as its root motive, rather than by a brigade
that teaches youngsters how to fight and perhaps to take life."[81]
But both the Boys' Brigade and the national Boys' Life Brigade,
which omitted the military drill, spread rapidly within South
London Nonconformity after 1900; both were eclipsed by the
Boy Scouts, which included churches, chapels, and secular organizations among its local sponsors, after 1907.

The Anglicans generally established more clubs (such as the
Girls' Friendly Society) and "institutes" designed for working-
class adolescents than the Nonconformists, who concentrated on
their own chapel members. The eight "working lads' institutes"
in Lambeth usually met in an improvised club room with billiards, and five of them offered gymnasium classes. They continued to grow in popularity after the turn of the century, for they
catered to a lower social class than the uniformed organizations
and cost nothing. Girls' clubs emphasized education and sewing.
The rector of Lambeth, generally bemused by all the goodness

80. Church Lads' Brigade, *Annual Report*, 1898; *St. Mary's Lewisham, Church
Lads' Brigade, 1892–1924*, (1925), p. 11; Boys' Brigade, *Annual Reports*, 1890–
91; Austin E. Birch, *The Story of the Boys' Brigade* (2nd ed., 1965).

81. B-315, pp. 98–99. The Boys' Brigade and the Boys' Life Brigade merged
in 1926.

he found among the working classes, reported that the "Daisy Club for Working and Factory Girls" had 330 members, a drawing room, a garden, and some accommodation for respectable working girls. The girls sponsored dances and had begun to take part in sanitary work: "I went down the other evening and found them hard at work, talking out their cases, drains and smells, defective flushings and all the rest of it."[82]

Anglican clergymen were not notably successful as sponsors of working men's clubs, for they often closed clubs when gambling was discovered. But at least twelve were open for a number of evenings a week for coffee, tea, billiards, and a short devotional talk of some kind. These clubs operated at a ludicrous disadvantage when competing with other working men's clubs such as the London and South Western Railway Institute, the North Brixton Gladstone Club, and the West Norwood Reform Club, for the latter served beer (in the Liberal clubs, over the objections of the temperance wing of the party).

Clergymen hoped that all of these clubs would in some way produce large numbers of regular, communicant churchgoers, but they did not. And clergymen did not cease establishing them when churchgoers failed to appear, for they were satisfied with a general moral influence upon society. If they could not create regular churchgoers, they would produce good citizens. That was equally part of the church's civilizing mission. Nonconformist ministers wished to produce good citizens also, but the problem of producing active church members was more pressing for them and the most obvious potential recruits were their own children. The critical age for a Nonconformist was adolescence, when he or she had normally quit the Sunday School but had not settled down to a regular family life with its associated chapel membership. The normal life of the chapel, dominated by parents and their friends, was not likely to appeal to young Nonconformists. Consequently the chapels established dozens of literary and debating societies for adolescents, young men's clubs, and Christian Endeavour societies (forty-three to the Anglicans' sixteen).

Lambeth's twenty-four Christian Endeavour societies belonged to a national federation. The movement had been imported from

82. B-272, p. 79.

America in 1887 by a minister at Crewe, and claimed over six thousand societies in 1900—mostly Baptist and Congregationalist. It claimed to be a comprehensive young persons' organization eliminating the need for separate societies for "literary work, athletics, civic studies, charities and social pleasures which split the young into a lot of sundered cliques."[83] Christian Endeavour societies had their own hymnbooks and supplied members with pocket notebooks with a scripture verse for each day. Each society promoted temperance, daily Bible reading, prayer, purity, and the conversion of the young, although its theological tone reflected that of the sponsoring chapel.

Literary or debating societies for young men (at least nineteen in Lambeth) were enormously popular, for regular secondary education was in short supply for intelligent but poor lower middle class students, and there was little competition from the scattered secular, socialist and ethical society equivalents before the turn of the century. The chapel societies often discussed things which had only a remote connection with what is ordinarily called religion—the *Daily News* prompted debate as often as the Bible—but few young Nonconformists had clear ideas of precisely where to locate the boundary between religious concerns and other sorts of concerns.[84] A recent critic described Nonconformity in the 1890s as a "religious community that had lost its bearings and reneged on its inheritance,"[85] and the character of these debating societies supplies some evidence in support of his assertion. But it is important to remember that questions of the proper role of the House of Lords, the ownership of land, and the propriety of temperance legislation were as much a part of the Nonconformist inheritance as questions of the nature of the church and the ethical consequences of the atonement. Young Dissenters debated all of these questions while trying to decide what it meant, if anything, to be a Dissenter in 1900. It was not

83. *Christian Endeavour Yearbook*, 1900.

84. On literary and debating societies see William Margrie, *My Eighty Years in Camberwell* (1957); William Kent, *Testament of a Victorian Youth* (1938), chaps. 4, 5; Morrison, *Autobiography*, pp. 30ff.; William Sanders, *Early Socialist Days* (1927), passim.

85. Donald Davie, "Dissent in the Present Century," *TLS*, 3 December 1976, p. 1519.

an easy question to answer and perhaps they failed to answer it, but they cannot be accused of wholly ignoring their own religious tradition any more than they can be accused of grasping it blindly.

7. Popular Recreation and Entertainment

Nonconformists contradicted all stereotypes by providing sports and entertainment for the general community more readily than the Anglicans. Of the forty-three amateur teams in the Lambeth auxiliary of the South London Cricket League, twenty-six had names which clearly identified them with a chapel; the Lambeth auxiliary of the Sunday School Union sponsored forty cricket teams in January 1900.[86] These clubs, originally intended for the young people of the chapel, seem to have attracted others— outsiders from the natural Nonconformist constituency of pros-perous artisans, clerks, shopkeepers, and minor bureaucrats. For working men the Nonconformists offered popular entertainments, a Pleasant Sunday Afternoon or Pleasant Saturday Evening program in the tradition of earlier "temperance entertainment" and loosely associated at this time with some sort of men's "brotherhood."

The popular image of Nonconformists as mean, small-minded bigots was fueled by a continuing addiction to sabbatarianism even by liberal Nonconformists, and by a renewed puritanicalism among more extreme evangelicals. Nonconformists on the Lam-beth Borough Council responded to charges of mindless puri-tanicalism by pointing to Lambeth's largely Nonconformist cricket league, but to no avail as long as they opposed Sunday entertainments in the park. No longer generally opposed to pleasure for its own sake, liberal Nonconformists insisted on opposing cricket on Sunday as a sort of symbol of their ability to influence public conduct, to be a "power in the land."

The puritanical image was exacerbated by acrimonious debates within Nonconformity over the propriety of certain kinds of entertainment in the chapel. The pastor of Chatsworth Road Baptist Chapel, Archibald Brown, continued to circulate his

86. *South London Press*, 20 Jan. 1900, 12 May 1900.

pamphlet called *The Devil's Mission of Amusement,* which had
led to accusations in the liberal Nonconformist press that he was
a kill-joy, a sour bigot, and a victim of religious melancholia.
(The *Daily Telegraph* entered the debate by predicting future
volumes entitled "Is Seven Hours of Sleep Satanic?," "The Sin-
fulness of a Country Walk," and "Lawn Tennis a Short Cut to
Perdition.")[87] Unrepentant, the author claimed that the members
of Chatsworth Road Chapel find their recreation in Christ, and
have discovered that the Book of Deuteronomy is not really dry
when you get into it.[88]

An ardent fisherman, Brown was not really opposed to all
amusement, only to Baptist chapels going into competition with
music halls. But the contrary view—that everything is religious
which is not clearly irreligious—generally prevailed among the
ministers and active laymen of the Congregationalists and
Wesleyans and even among some groups of Baptists. Each day in
the winter the York Road Congregational Chapel sponsored
"Dinner Hour Concerts" between 1 and 2 P.M. which attracted
between two and three hundred men (from works along the
river) who had their meal and a smoke while listening to some
sort of entertainment and an occasional "speaker on social subjects."[89] The nearby Waterloo Road Bible Christian Chapel held
both afternoon and evening services on Sunday at the Old Vic,
with a mixture of lantern slides and hymns from Sankey's *Sacred
Songs and Solos* interspersed with the distribution of temperance
pledges.[90] Chapel entertainments became so common that in 1900
the Lambeth Board of Guardians heard complaints from an out-
raged ratepayer about the exemption of mission halls from the
rate: "No one will make me believe that such a thing as an entertainment with singers in Highland costume rendering patriotic
songs is for religious purposes. In another instance a concert was
given in aid of a cricket club." The subject was then dropped,
tacit recognition by the Guardians of the impossibility of isolat-
ing the "religious" aspects of Lambeth's church work.[91]

87. G. H. Pike, *Archibald G. Brown,* p. 100.

88. B-313, p. 11.

89. B-270, pp. 60–61.

90. Pamphlet inserted in B-273.

91. *South London Press,* 12 May 1900.

.   .   .

This catalog of ecclesiastical social services is far from exhaustive, for a great deal of individual effort through churches and chapels went unrecorded. Furthermore, a snapshot of activity during the years 1899-1900 fails to demonstrate how rapidly the social functions of an institution could change in response to changing social conditions. Although not formally associated with any church or chapel, the Old Vic (built as a theater) evolved in the same manner as Lambeth's ecclesiastical institutions (built for public worship). In the 1870s Miss Emma Cons, who came from the Anglican "Christian Socialist" milieu, moved to Lambeth, formed the South London Dwellings Co., and purchased the Surrey Lodge near Waterloo Station as an experiment in philanthropic housing for the poor. Caroline Martineau, of the prominent Unitarian family, helped her to purchase the Old Vic in order to provide "purified" entertainments for the working classes. After a series of crises it was put on a sound financial basis by Samuel Morley, an evangelical Congregationalist, who seems to have been converted to the cause of popular entertainment while viewing a performance at the Old Vic. In 1888 the Charity Commissioners, partly through the intervention of the Duke of Westminister, diverted some ancient charitable bequests, purchased the freehold, and vested it in the Royal Victoria Hall Foundation. A Christian Socialist, a Unitarian, an evangelical Congregationalist manufacturer, and an Anglican peer cooperated in the provision of improving concerts, clean "tableaux vivants," and opera excerpts at the Old Vic, undeterred by George Bernard Shaw's complaint that music was being used as "a handmaid in the cause of religion and sobriety."[92]

The Old Vic generated other activities almost immediately. One of the chain of temperance eating houses established by John Pearce occupied the front of the building. In 1884 a Unitarian minister presented a series of lectures on electricity at the hall, and within a year some sixty students were attending classes in rooms formed out of dressing rooms behind the stage. In 1889 Morley Memorial College for Working Men and Women form-

92. B-273, pp. 145, 153 (interview with Miss Cons); cf. Cicely Hamilton and Lillian Baylis, *The Old Vic* (1926); Richard Findlater, *Lillian Baylis, the Lady of the Old Vic* (1975), chaps. 1, 2.

ally opened, and in 1892, 640 students (208 clerks and the rest assorted artisans) attended its classes in elementary science, modern languages, elocution, and shorthand. After the Bible Christians began Sunday services, the Old Vic, with its temperance lectures, improving concerts, temperance cafe, adult vocational classes, gymnasium and library, was distinguishable only in its scale from any number of church- and chapel-related institutions which had grown out of settlement and parochial and mission hall activity—prompted by precisely the same improving motives which had led Miss Cons to Lambeth in the first place.[93]

Even tiny missions, sometimes evangelical in inspiration, used the same methods. At St. Winifred's near Southwark Park the founder and president and inspiring force was a Mr. Morriss, who earned his living as a clerk in the City. "It began as a botany class, became a boys' school, and has expanded into a mission," and Mr. Morriss claimed to have placed more than one hundred boys as clerks and office boys in the City.[94] Several miles away in what was then suburban Balham, a Mr. C. H. Baker founded the Church Institute in 1868 for the "promotion of education, recreation, and religion." By 1899 more than four thousand students were enrolled in technical education classes, including "a large number of clerks, artisans, and labourers, and about one thousand boys who have just left school."[95]

A person concerned about the condition of the people of Lambeth naturally turned to the churches and their progeny. Their motives were mixed, and it is important to avoid the claim that all of this activity was not "really religious." Like all religion, it was religious and something else as well. It was "middle-class" only in a highly qualified sense of the phrase, for social concern motivated recruits to church work from a variety of occupations: ladies who served all the churches as district visitors, builders and clerks and artisans who volunteered to teach Sunday Schools and preach in mission halls, working men who became London City Missionaries. The minister of Roupell Park Wesleyan Chapel claimed that guilt was the motive: "You can get any money you want for relief, but it is much harder for church expenses. A lot

93. B-273, p. 153.
94. Booth, *Life and Labour*, ser. 3, vol. 4, pp. 154–55.
95. Booth, *Life and Labour*, ser. 3, vol. 6, p. 102.

of people think that in giving they are doing something for their soul's salvation."[96] Perhaps because church expenses were threatened, other ministers echoed his complaint. "The people on the hill have a morbid conscience," a West Norwood Congregationalist complained, "and give to relieve it."[97]

It is impossible to identify one motive which outweighs the other motives for collective action in this case. There was guilt, certainly, and fear and compassion, but also piety. Late Victorian churchgoers heard a lot about the Parable of the Good Samaritan. Evangelicals wanted to save souls, but almost all of Lambeth's Christians wanted to do something for their fellow man. Large numbers of ordinary people in churches and chapels rejected the theory behind the Victorian Poor Law—that those who cannot make it go to the workhouse—and those who did not reject it were repeatedly told that they should. Social control was one, but not the only, function of religious philanthropy. The advocacy of philanthropy and liberal out-relief by the Guardians did not usually entail the rejection of the need to distinguish, as a matter of policy, between the deserving and undeserving poor. But by 1900 some religious philanthropists, usually liberal Nonconformists, were strenuously urging upon their hearers the evil consequences of that distinction. Both Christian compassion and Christian universalism combined to produce the attitude behind much of Britain's welfare state legislation of the twentieth century—that everyone should be taken care of in dignity.

The Rev. Bernard Snell, minister of Brixton Independent Church, contrasted Christianity with paganism in precisely those terms in a Hospital Sunday sermon to his congregation in 1912. Nature, he said, encouraged the survival of the fittest by killing the weak in order to strengthen the physical stock. Christianity, on the other hand, concerned the survival of the unfit. Paganism was the worship of strength, Christianity the protection of the weak—the spirit of kindness and pity which does not "break the bruised reed."[98]

96. B-313, p. 31.
97. B-315, p. 147.
98. *Brixton Free Press*, 14 June 1912, p. 9.

4

Diffusive Christianity and the Churchgoing Nation

1. Popular Religion and the Churches

Although historians have recently shown some skill in reconstructing the popular religious beliefs of early modern and Victorian England using ecclesiastical court records, sermons, and diaries, and the research of folklorists,[1] the religious views of early nineteenth-century villagers may be easier to retrieve than those of late nineteenth-century city-dwellers. Folklorists in search of quaint customs have shown no interest in the daily habits and customary views of the suburban grocer of the 1890s, who is beyond the reach of the polls and surveys which are so useful for more recent decades.[2] The most abundant sources of evidence about the late nineteenth century are the books and articles of middle-class social observers—clergymen, ministers, philanthropists, and journalists—who took an interest in the religion of the people. Their views are badly flawed, for they

1. Keith Thomas, *Religion and the Decline of Magic* (1971); James Obelkevich, *Religion and Rural Society: South Lindsey 1825–1875* (1976).

2. Oral history might be of some use. See Paul Thompson, *The Edwardians: The Remaking of British Society* (Bloomington, Indiana, 1975), pp. 203–14.

projected their own preconceptions onto the minds of ordinary people as often as they faithfully reported the facts, but their opinions are nonetheless useful and do not have to be taken at face value. They disagreed with each other often. Their conclusions betray a variety of class biases and professional interests rather than a consistent, monolithic class bias, and they can be sorted and sifted and corroborated with other sorts of evidence.

One view was that South London at the turn of the century was pagan (or heathen, a milder word for some reason). Assertions of this sort sometimes reflected the genuine frustration of devoted clergymen faced with public indifference, and sometimes represented no more than an attempt to alarm potential middle-class donors and patrons. In one sense it was in the interests of churchmen to identity non-churchgoing with irreligion or paganism, since it was widely believed in South London, indeed generally accepted, that religion was a good thing and paganism a bad thing. Atheism in public was wholly unacceptable, even illegal in some circumstances, and the *Brixton Free Press* expressed a common assumption in claiming that "every man must have a religion of some sort."[3] If clergymen could have identified non-churchgoing with irreligion, churghgoing might have become more popular. But non-churchgoers, who outnumbered regular churchgoers, naturally resisted clerical attempts to link regular churchgoing and true religion, and often did so by turning Protestant doctrine against the clergy in a wholly logical manner. The tenuous link between true religion and churchgoing was something of a popular cliché, and clergymen faced occasional taunts from both of Lambeth's newspapers, the *South London Press* observing that "mere churchgoing" did not always make men better, and the *Brixton Free Press* declaring: "The nearer to church, the farther from God."[4] But when a group of South London's most prominent clergymen described South London as "pagan" in 1900, largely in an attempt to stir

3. BFP, 18 Oct. 1907; in 1906 a Liberal candidate for the Lambeth Borough Council "retired on account of the hindrances his atheistic tendencies would prove to getting ladies to vote the ticket"; in 1909 a Hoxton tailor received a 13-day sentence for public blasphemy on Clapham Common and apologized to the court for "outraging the feelings of the public." BFP, 26 Oct. 1906, 25 June 1909.

4. SLP, 19 Dec. 1900; BFP, 17 June 1904.

up financial support from readers of *The Times,* the *South London Press* received numerous angry letters denouncing this insult to the character of South Londoners and unjustified slur against the working man.[5] The people of Lambeth thought of themselves as Christians, but insisted upon defining their own religious beliefs rather than taking them from clergymen.

Anglo-Catholics and Roman Catholics, who regarded churchgoing as an essential act of piety rather than a good habit, naturally took a dim view of this conventional religion. The word "pagan" sprang readily to the lips of Anglo-Catholic clergymen, and they meant it (a Kennington vicar described his parishioners as "being, take them all in all, a criminal and immoral set").[6] But popular religion was not, by any reasonable definition of the word, paganism, and other church parties took a different view of it. Instead of raising the specter of paganism and irreligion, both Anglican and Nonconformist evangelicals complained instead of religious saturation. A Baptist minister complained that Norwood was "sodden by the gospel, and not saved by it."[7] He meant that South Londoners were so devoted to their own version of Christianity, to their belief in a God who would be fair to them in the next world if not this one, that they were unreceptive to the unrealistically demanding faith of the evangelicals. The public, inoculated with a little religion, was immune to the true faith. A London City Missionary complained of complacency on the deathbed:

I called on a man, old and knowing that he was ill, not expecting to recover. I asked him if he believed in the Bible, and got an affirmative reply. Did he know that he was a sinner? "Yes." Did he know that those who died as sinners went to Hell? "Yes." Did he know that those who died repentant went to Heaven? "Yes." Had he repented? "No." Did he know that he was dying? An acquiescent silence. Was he going to die like that? No reply. The next day he died, but as though he went to sleep. Utter indifference! That's like many of them.[8]

Religion is one way of dealing with death; clergymen complained that stoicism was more common.

5. April and May 1900.

6. B-305, p. 9; St. John the Divine, Kennington.

7. B-313, p. 15.

8. B-278, p. 133.

Other clergymen were more tolerant of popular religion and its indifference to the official version of organized Christianity. In 1903 the bishop of Rochester (whose diocese included Lambeth at that time) warned his clergymen not to dismiss what he called "diffusive Christianity," which he described as the penumbra of the "embodied" Christianity of the church. Compared with the doctrines of the church, he admitted, "the diffusive has never been so strong, or wielded such versatile and ready instruments." It was often capricious, shallow, and unbalanced, and liable to shade off into what is not Christian at all. Nevertheless, God worked through the diffusive as well as the embodied forms of Christianity, using the former to correct "ecclesiasticism." He warned the clergy that much that they might assume to be antagonistic was Christian in its own way, and that they might be fighting against God when they thought themselves staunch in His cause.[9]

Many ordinary clergymen in working-class parishes and the more liberal Nonconformist ministers shared his assessment of diffusive Christianity. They insisted that indifference to church attendance did not represent unbelief or even dislike, and that outright hostility, atheism, and unbelief were more rarely encountered than in the 1880s. "Nobody goes to church," a veteran Lambeth clergyman admitted. "It has always been so; a very small percentage goes. You can work up a connection with relative ease, but attendance at church is not the natural sequel . . . it is not dislike, it is not unbelief. All the mothers bring their children to be christened, and I myself feel like a grandfather to the parish . . . the attitude of the people is remarkably friendly."[10] A canon of St. Saviour's Southwark, found the poor almost without exception "with a strong sense of religion at the core. They are quite uninstructed but in a general way they believe in Jesus Christ the Good Shepherd and in the Trinity; they wish their children to be baptized and receive religious instruction; they wish to be married in the church." Even more remarkable was "their wonderful resignation in the hour of death. They always seem ready to go and quite satisfied with a few simple religious phrases to comfort them. Vague as their religion is,

9. Gwendolen Stephenson, *Edward Stuart Talbot, 1844–1934* (1936), pp. 157–59.
10. B-272, p. 103. St. Mary-the-Less.

they have not been troubled with doubt and are able at the end to accept religious comfort quite simply and childlikely."[11] A London City Missionary who wandered the streets and pubs commented upon the friendly reception he received for his very different ministrations: "The gospel is a great power with the people at the time. They will thank you for speaking to them and mean well, but soon forget."[12]

These comments might be dismissed as wishful thinking, and these men certainly ignore the hostility which the churches could still encounter. Nonconformist missioners were physically ejected from some slum streets, and clergymen rebuffed even in respectable households. Fredrick Willis records an occasion when his working-class mother, who considered herself a good Anglican even though a non-churchgoer, hinted to a visiting clergyman that "she could transact her business with God in the future without an intermediary."[13] But whatever major problems the churches faced, outright unbelief was not one of them. Direct evidence is virtually non-existent, but a variety of religious professionals, describing what they were up against, sketched the outlines of a "diffusive Christianity" which comprised a general belief in God, a conviction that this God was both just and benevolent although remote from everyday concerns, a certain confidence that "good people" would be taken care of in the life to come, and a belief that the Bible was a uniquely worthwhile book and that children in particular should be exposed to its teachings. The argument that the poor believe in the Trinity "in their own way" should be discounted altogether unless an extremely generous latitude be given to definitions of the Trinity. It is quite likely that an Edwardian opinion poll would have turned up a hilarious variety of views upon the nature of Christ, but Jesus Christ seems to have played a minor role in Lambeth's "diffusive Christianity." He was not altogether absent, and popular religion may have been pre-orthodox rather than Unitarian or unorthodox on this issue. People appear to have been willing to say good things about Jesus Christ when they got around to

11. A-54, p. 107. St. Saviour's became the cathedral church of the Diocese of Southwark in 1905.

12. B-270, p. 151.

13. Frederick Willis, *Peace and Dripping Toast* (1950), p. 41.

it. Politicians in working-class neighborhoods, for instance, regarded Jesus as a useful person to have on their side. Labour politicians claimed Jesus for socialism, and handbills distributed by a Congregational settlement house urged the local electors to join with Jesus in voting Progressive in the L.C.C. elections: "If Jesus were a Walworth carpenter living in the blocks off East St., how would he vote next Tuesday?"[14] But even if a social survey had turned up orthodox popular views about the person of Christ, it would have meant very little, for Christ played little visible role in popular religion.

"Diffusive Christianity" contained no hints of the intensely supernatural (but often heterodox) popular piety found among the actively Roman Catholic populations of nineteenth-century Europe. Nor is there much evidence of survivals of the semi-pagan magic and superstition which historians have discovered among English villagers in the early nineteenth century and before. The rise of a class society, the spread of scientific ideas, and the emergence of an urban working-class culture had finished the job begun by the Protestant Reformation, and purged diffusive Christianity of centuries old non-Christian accretions. Semi-pagan superstition had subsided into "luck."[15] It is natural to assume that this "diffusive Christianity" was a debasement of a formerly pure popular orthodoxy, and that is possible. But it is equally possible that it was simply the most that a millenium of indoctrination had achieved in implanting Christian ideas in the popular mind. With its veneration of the ethical teachings of "scripture" and a God obviously borrowed from the Christian tradition, diffusive Christianity was something more than simple theism, although not much more. Clerical complacency about diffusive Christianity, when it was not mere fatalism, may have reflected a dim recognition that popular Christianity was nearer to orthodoxy in 1900 than it ever had been.

Compulsory primary education greatly strengthened diffusive Christianity, and was much more effective at Christian education than the Sunday Schools which absorbed an enormous percentage of the churches' time and effort. Although virtually

14. B-277, p. 163; cf. Obelkevich, *Religion and Rural Society*, p. 302; Hugh McLeod, *Class and Religion in the late Victorian City* (1974), pp. 49–66.
15. Obelkevich, *Religion and Rural Society*, p. 312.

universal, the Sunday Schools were notoriously undisciplined, and Board School teachers of the eighties and nineties looked upon them, not as a civilizing agency, but as an irritating source of indiscipline. Sunday School "treats" often took the form of an excurson which prompted a general holiday spirit among the children. If neighboring Sunday Schools staggered their treats, successive groups of children infected the Board School with their merriment. If several treats occurred simultaneously, it caused a dip in school attendance matched only during the hopping and measles seasons. The Webber Street Board School, Westminster Bridge Road, matched the Sunday School with its own treats in order to maintain attendance.[16] William Margrie complained of the ineffectiveness of the Maze Pond Baptist Sunday School in Peckham: "Big boys used to stand at the entrance and stick pins into the arms of the girls as they came out. Inside the 'students' spent the afternoon in turning their handkerchiefs into 'bunnies' and throwing them at one another. One cannot imagine a greater contrast than that between my Sunday School and my day Board School. In the former there was no discipline at all, in the latter there was too much. The old Board School was like a prison."[17]

In the Board Schools and their successors, the L.C.C. schools, religious teaching was carried on by trained teachers in a disciplined atmosphere. Nonconformist ministers encouraged devout young Dissenters to become religion teachers. William Kent recalled his scripture teacher at the Gaskell Street School as a Wesleyan local preacher and Bible class leader who was especially good at a vivid retelling of accounts of the crucifixion. One of his Sunday Schools teachers at the Clifton Street Methodist Chapel was a semiliterate stonemason who read only the Bible, the *Daily News,* and the *Methodist Recorder.*[18] Compulsory religious education by the state was not intended to produce "born-again" Christians, and was generally limited to scripture lessons with moral overtones. But it is difficult to believe that it did not aid the diffusion of religious knowledge and increase the number of persons to whom Christian symbols and

16. B-273, pp. 187ff.

17. William Margrie, *My Eighty Years in Camberwell* (1957), p. 5.

18. William Kent, *Testament of a Victorian Youth,* pp. 35, 62.

language were meaningful. The schools were better at that task than the Sunday Schools, which were in turn superior to what preceded them (i.e., nothing at all). The churches made rather frantic attempts to upgrade the quality of the Sunday Schools in the late nineteenth and the early twentieth century, but an Edwardian Anglican observer of South London sadly admitted that the schools must be given the major responsibility for religious education. Sunday Schools were haphazard, he argued, but in the schools "at the end of nine years the intelligent boy will, under a good teacher, have gained a knowledge of scripture history and Gospel narrative."[19] Parents approved of the scripture classes, which relieved them of the obligation to provide religious training, and those classes may well have been the primary source of Lambeth's demystified popular Christianity. Between 40 and 50 percent of Lambeth school accommodation was supplied by church-related elementary schools which taught more church doctrine. Except in Anglo-Catholic and Roman Catholic schools, however, there was a similar emphasis upon practical, everyday moral advice.

The schools supplied one set of links between popular religion and the churches, although a very indirect one. The Church of England's sacramental rites of passage supplied another one which, although direct, was in some ways more frustrating to the church, for in the popular mind the Christian sacraments were associated with "luck" more than with anything resembling Christian devotion in the minds of the clergy. Baptism was lucky for the child, a church marriage lucky for the couple, churching lucky for the mother. In these matters as in everything else associated with popular religion, evidence is scanty and motives were almost certainly mixed. Respectability may have played as large a role as "luck" along with the notion that God as well as one's neighbor was in some way pleased with the performance of sacramental rites of passage. The sacraments may have also supplied a ritual dimension for the more clearly Christian end of the spectrum of beliefs encompassed by diffusive Christianity.

There are no acceptable statistics of the ratio of baptisms to births in Lambeth, but this sacrament was clearly very common

19. Alexander Paterson, *Across the Bridges*, p. 79.

even in families of the lowest status. Women were almost always responsible for a family's practice of these rites of passage, which were part of an attempt to maintain a minimum level of respectability for the family. A. S. Jaspers grew up in Hoxton, not Lambeth, but his autobiography is one of the few which record details of family life among the very poor. His sister "decided to have her baby Christened. . . . On the Sunday she gave a party. It was the usual beer up."[20] A character in Ted Child's semi-autobiographical novel of life in Brixton later in the twentieth century claims that "Religion had always run a very slow third in our house. Mum got him [father] to church on time to make it legal and for me and Sally to get splashed, but that was it—at least as far as pop was concerned."[21] Respectability was as important to a working-class as to a middle-class mother, and for the former more was at stake when children were beset by crime and drunkeness. Consequently working-class mothers resolutely insisted upon Anglican rites of passage. In the middle-class parish of Christ Church, Gipsy Hill, the one poverty stricken street supplied 10 percent of the infants christened in 1895–96: the child of an ostler at number 49 Woodland Road, a laborer at 57, a painter at 65, a poultryman at 95, a sweep and a postman at 96, a clerk and an upholsterer at 102, a grocer at 118, a gardener at 146, a postman at 148, and a painter at 156. In 1910 twelve of fifty-six baptisms at St. Peter's, Leigham Court Road, came from working-class Wellfield Road, and eight of the twelve families were semi-skilled or unskilled[22] The vicar of St. Mary-the-Less described himself, very reasonably, as "a grandfather to the parish." Congregational and Wesleyan chapels attracted a few parents who wished to have their children baptized (the Baptists, of course, did not), but even so it was the Church of England which drew the unskilled and semi-skilled—laborers, carmen, porters, and gardeners.[23] And it was to the parish church

20. A. S. Jaspers, *A Hoxton Childhood*, p. 73.

21. Ted Child, *Mt. Ararat South-west Nine* (1964), p. 24.

22. From the baptismal registers of respective parishes.

23. West Norwood churches, percentages of baptisms in the various social classes as defined by registrar general (see Table 18). From the baptismal registers of the respective churches. Those of the West Norwood Congregational Church are deposited at St. Aubyn's Congregational Church, Upper Norwood. Column 1 = social class (I and II = upper- and middle-class, pro-

that working-class mothers regularly went for churching, a sort of blessing given by the reluctant vicar who usually disapproved of the mother's confident expectation that the ceremony would prevent a future miscarriage.[24]

In 1880, 88 percent of Lambeth's marriages were solemnized in the Church of England. The percentage has fallen dramatically each decade over the last century and the percentage of marriages at the Registry Office grown correspondingly, although the church remained more popular than the Registry Office until the mid-twentieth century. The Registry Office was the only alternative for many divorced individuals who wished to remarry, but I have no further direct evidence about the meaning of a Registry Office wedding. Civil marriage has been cited as evidence of secularization and even of de-Christianization, although the choice of a religious ceremony has rarely been admitted as evidence of the vitality of religious faith. In some English and Welsh counties civil marriage was more popular in the mid-nineteenth century than it is today. Victorian London, on the other hand, combined the nation's lowest levels of church attendance with the greatest incidence of Anglican marriages.[25] In

fessional, IIIa = clerks, IIIb = shopkeepers, IIIc = skilled artisans, IV = semi-skilled, V = unskilled). Column 2 = Christ Church, Gipsy Hill, 1895–96, N = 121. Column 3 = St. Luke's West Norwood, 1900, N = 160. Column 4 = West Norwood Congregational 1897–1906, N = 31. Column 5 = St. Peter's, Leigham Ct. Rd. 1910, N = 50.

1	2	3	4	5
I and II	16.5	12.5	16.2	16.7
IIIa	5.0	11.9	16.1	13.0
IIIb	19.8	15.6	25.8	11.1
IIIc	35.5	22.5	29.0	27.8
IIIa, b, c	60.3	50.0	70.9	51.9
IV, V	22.0	36.9	12.9	31.4
IIIc, IV, V	57.9	59.4	41.9	59.2

Only 8 of 31 infants baptized at West Norwood Congregational Chapel, 1897–1906, were children of regular members, although some were probably children of regular attenders or pewholders.

24. B-274, p. 83, on churching at St. Mary, Lambeth; B-274, p. 125, at St. Phillip's, Kennington.

25. Olive Anderson, "The Incidence of Civil Marriage in Victorian England and Wales," *Past & Present*, 69, Nov. 1975, pp. 52, 55.

the generation before World War I, civil marriage spread most rapidly among the upper classes in Lambeth. At the lower end of the social scale, the daughters of semi-skilled and unskilled workers continued to prefer the Church of England. The percentage of all Anglican marriages from the Registrar General's classes IV and V (semi-skilled and unskilled) ranged from 23.9 to 26.4 for four sample years of 1880, 1890, 1900, and 1910, slightly above the average for all Lambeth marriages. Comparable figures for the Registry Office ranged from 13.3 to 19.8 percent. Of approximately 510 daughters of semi-skilled and unskilled Protestant workers married in Lambeth in 1910, over 400 chose an Anglican church and fewer than 70 the Registry Office. Slum churches were often crowded on Christmas Day when clergymen conducted several marriages at once.[26] (See Graph 1, p. 191.)

Churches and chapels also maintained links with the non-churchgoing population through the network of clubs and philanthropies discussed in the previous chapter, although what these organizations meant to the participants is extremely difficult to discover. Clergymen claimed that the enormous number of "Christian workers" involved in religious philanthropy had helped to erase the misrepresentation of religion which had prevailed earlier in the century. A Bible Christian minister thought that "things had improved because Christian workers are willing to go and show practical sympathy with people—the church is now stronger than for many years."[27] A Kennington clergyman claimed "greater friendliness than in the past. The Church is in touch with more people than years ago."[28] A C.O.S. worker thought that the parish of St. John the Divine "left no one untouched," and that the workers at St. Mark's, Kennington, another huge parish, "know everyone in every house."[29] A Unitarian minister on Stamford Street complained that "the poorer class will not come. We have a considerable number connected with us in other ways, but we can't get them on Sundays. It is a

26. Conclusions extrapolated from a 10 percent systematic sample of all Lambeth marriages in 1880, 1890, 1900, and 1910, from registers deposited in the Lambeth Registry Office. The clusters of weddings on Christmas Day render my systematic sample more than usually unreliable.

27. B-270, p. 39.

28. B-272, p. 39.

29. B-277, p. 177.

very singular thing, but they *won't* come on Sundays. . . . They crowd the Saturday night concerts in winter; they use the clubs, the banks, in large numbers but on Sunday you see nothing of them."[30]

In some cases charity deteriorated into bribery, which discredited the churches. "No one can go to church from a poor street without being a mark for gibes and sneers and remarks as to going for what they can get,"[31] the vicar of Emmanuel, Kennington, complained and others agreed that the mixture of church and charity kept people away. "A front row of cadgers is fatal to any mission," W. S. Caine observed, "and most of them have it."[32] But some working-class men and women regarded the mothers' meeting as nothing more than a perfectly respectable local social club, and the thrift society as a useful neighborhood institution. At St. Andrew's, Stockwell, "the yearly treat to the mothers' meeting is a very trying day for the clergy. The men, though not invited, escort the party through the streets in their coster carts and make a day of it too."[33]

Philanthropy provided a network of links between the churches and diffusive Christianity, but did little to promote definite Christian belief. Few clergymen imposed a positive religious test as a condition for participation, although some insisted upon very occasional corporate churchgoing. They hoped to use the parochial auxiliaries as a means of luring people into regular churchgoing and other parochial activities, and in some cases they succeeded. But philanthropic auxiliaries were not designed to produce regular churchgoers or propagate orthodox Christian views, and clergymen generally consoled themselves with the thought that the church's activities "turned them to higher things."[34] Ideologically, the philanthropic auxiliaries were more important to clergymen, patrons, and ordinary churchgoers than to participants, for good works supplied a major rationale for the church's existence.

In addition to the schools, the sacraments, and philanthropy

30. B-270, p. 111.
31. B-272, p. 37.
32. B-271, p. 13.
33. B-305, p. 57.
34. B-272, p. 41.

there was churchgoing, and the assumption that the working
classes never attended church requires some qualification. The
fifty thousand churchgoers counted on one Sunday in 1902 represent only a fraction of the people who found themselves in a
church service upon occasion. A certain amount of involuntary
churchgoing was unavoidable for those associated with other
church-related institutions such as the Anglican schools, which
conducted regular daily worship services. At St. Peter's, Vauxhall, "those who attend Sunday School are swept into church
for a celebration, and so brought to worship God in the only
way they can understand."[35] At Emmanuel, Kennington, the
mothers' meeting attended church once a month, and members
of any church auxiliary in any parish—especially the Church
Lads' Brigade and other uniformed organizations—might be expected to attend church parade regularly. Morning attendance at
St. Mary's, Lambeth, was distorted during the 1886 census of
church attendance by about four hundred volunteers of the
West Surrey Regiment; St. Stephen's, Clapham, by special services on behalf of the London and South Western Railway Servants' Orphanage.[36] In 1900 St. Matthew's, Brixton, held a special
service with patriotic hymns for the City Imperial Volunteers,
and in 1909 three hundred Norwood postmen and telegraph
messengers turned out for the third annual St. Luke's, West Norwood, Church Parade and heard a sermon by the bishop of
Southwark.[37]

Christmas Day was one of four festival days during the year
which attracted the occasional voluntary Anglican churchgoer. But
there were two sets of occasional churchgoers. The first—a sort of
penumbra to the hard core of regular and irregular weekly
churchgoers—attended the Christmas or Easter worship services
(or, if Nonconformist, the chapel or Sunday School anniversary).
The second—concentrated in but not limited to working-class
neighborhoods—ignored the ancient pattern of the church year
and, to the disgust of the stricter clergy, filled the churches only
during the Autumn Harvest Festival service when the church
was decorated with fruits and vegetables and during the New

35. Booth, *Life and Labour*, ser. 3, vol. 4, p. 43.
36. *British Weekly*, 12 Nov. 1886, p. 2.
37. BFP, 2 Nov. 1900; 21 May 1909.

Year's Eve watchnight service, which was thought to bring luck during the coming year. If attracted to church on Christmas Day it was by a wedding, not a celebration of Christ's birth. In its attitude toward the churching of women, harvest festivals, and watch night services, the Church of England was at war with the popular religion of "luck." That any working-class churchgoers might be found at all in a church which had excluded the poor as a matter of policy for centuries (pew rents were less important than the attitudes they reflected) and had struggled to eradicate rather than incorporate popular religious practices is more cause for wonder than the alienation of the workers from religion. But working-class men and women insisted upon appropriating the national church for their own festivals, and not all clergymen despised these services as mere superstition. Bands of youths from riverside Christian Endeavour Societies made the rounds of local public houses near Waterloo Station on New Year's Eve in an attempt to steer the inebriated crowds of potential watch-night churchgoers into chapel instead of church.[38] Scott Holland—a defender of "diffusive Christianity"—gently ridiculed his fellow clergymen who objected to having a well-attended church at Harvest Festival:

Why should all the great epochs of the Christian Year be overshadowed by the Feast of St. Pumpkin? So we wailed. We had broken our hearts over the meagre group of worshippers whom, by strenuous efforts, we got into church for Good Friday. As for Ascension Day, we almost despaired. Yet, lo and behold, we have only to wave a potato round our head and the church is packed from end to end. Why should people be so thrilled to see us wade through vegetables to the lectern? or emerge in the leafy pulpit like Jack in the Green? . . . There are all the loafers from the public house, their faces hardly distinguishable, in color and expression, from the tomatoes glistening near them. Is it not an irony, that only on this one night of the year can the whole parish unite in brotherly companionship and shake hands, and sing hymns, and recognize its common life?[39]

This working-class insistence upon remaking certain church services into popular festivals is worth stressing as a partial antidote to generalizations, handed down from generation to gen-

38. B-270, p. 25.
39. Henry Scott Holland, *A Bundle of Memories* (1915), p. 250.

eration since the 1851 religious census, about the working classes falling away from the churches. These generalizations are based entirely upon the absence of regular Sunday attendance in working-class neighborhoods, and assume unreasonably high levels of popular church attendance in the seventeenth and eighteenth centuries and before. Although they did not attend regular Sunday services, the working classes were not "out of touch" with the institutional church in 1900; although they were in a sense "indifferent to the claims of organized religion," they were not irreligious as a class. Although religion may not have been very important for most individuals, it is a fallacy to conclude that it was therefore an unimportant element of English society. Inner Lambeth was far from the churchgoing belt of suburban and agricultural England, and should have been among the most secular and indifferent parts of the country. But descriptive evidence of a general if passive acquiescence to semi-Christian doctrine, positive evidence of a general addiction to Anglican rites of passage, the obtrusive presence of ecclesiastical philanthropy, the universality of Sunday Schools, the spread of professional religious education in the Board Schools after 1870, and the popularity of occasionally attending popular festivals—when taken together—amount to a very impressive religious presence in Lambeth's pagan slums. The churches were an obtrusive part of the social landscape even in the poorest neighborhoods, where "diffusive Christianity" was shallow and positive Christian devotion rare.

This emphasis upon "diffusive Christianity" is not meant to obscure the virtual absence of regular, male Anglican churchgoing in poor and working-class neighborhoods. "People will do anything for you but come to church," the veteran incumbent of St. Anne's observed. "They don't see where this comes in. They are stunned at the idea."[40] The vicar of St. Mary-the-Less claimed that working-class adolescents would leave home or enlist rather than accompany their mothers to church.[41] "The people don't go," agreed a London City Missionary with a mission hall on a working-class street in suburban Lambeth. "The men lay abed on Sunday morning, mend their rabbit hutches

40. B-272, p. 174.
41. B-272, p. 105.

and pigeon lofts in the afternoon, and go for a walk in the evening. They have a stronger objection than ever to church."[42] Clergymen generally recognized that this had "always been so," and used different explanations when discussing working-class non-churchgoing and the decline of middle-class churchgoing. The working classes were rarely blamed (with significant exceptions)—it was the "harshness of their lives," or the "misrepresentation of religion," or "generations of neglect." Upper- and middle-class families had long regarded Anglican churches as their own property and insisted that services be conducted for their own benefit and convenience. The working classes accepted that view, and a few decades of missionary work could hardly overcome it. "Working men don't go to church for the same reason I don't go to race meetings," the rural dean of Kennington declared. "They know no more of the Bishop of Rochester than I know of Dan Leno."[43]

2. The Churchgoing Nation

Although there were working-class churchgoers, regular weekly Sunday churchgoing was disproportionately middle-class. But it would be a mistake to assume that middle-class churchgoers were therefore less materialistic, and had their minds fixed firmly upon the next world rather than this one. The records of Lambeth's churches and chapels reflect a thoroughly "this-worldly" attitude among churchgoers. The typical sermon contained ethical and moral advice. The minutes of deacons' meetings and parochial church councils record the minutiae of ecclesiastical administration. Even the autobiographies of doubters and dissenters frequently concentrate upon the political and social failings of the churches rather than upon intellectual doubts. Extended speculation about the nature of the Trinity, the meaning of the Atonement, or the precise workings of the Holy Spirit were simply not the common currency of ordinary churchgoers in Lambeth. Even the most devout and other-worldly factions, the Anglo-Catholics and evangelicals, often presented their arguments in a this-worldly context. Using the language of a

42. B-315, p. 69.
43. B-272, p. 57. Dan Leno was a famous music hall comedian.

legal brief, Anglo-Catholics propagated their own view of English ecclesiastical history rather than a supernatural cosmology, and evangelicals often (but by no means always) portrayed the conversion experience as a psychological technique which would transform a person's behavior and perhaps even improve his prospects in life. But to conclude that Lambeth's this-worldly churchgoing was "not really religious," or "social rather than religious," would betray a misunderstanding of both Christianity and Protestantism. The standards of Christian belief and behavior proclaimed in the New Testament are very exacting, and we have yet to see an entire society of any size giving away all of its possessions and collectively and individually turning the other cheek. Every variety of Christianity has fallen short of the ideals of the Sermon on the Mount. Catholicism has dealt with this dilemma with monasticism on the one hand and a combination of sacerdotalism and tolerance of popular syncretism on the other. The Protestant approach has been sectarianism of varying degrees of intensity on the one hand, and this-worldly asceticism with a strong ethical emphasis on the other. Some people in Lambeth rejected all of these solutions and took the New Testament literally, and the newspapers regularly reported cases of insanity and psychosis which took a religious form. But a very moderate sectarianism struggled with a kind of this-worldly ethical gospel for the allegiance of most Lambeth churchgoers, with the latter generally prevailing even among some groups which thought of themselves as withdrawn from the world.

It is sometimes assumed that religion is primarily a response to fundamental existential questions of pain, suffering, and death, and that the extension of man's rational control over his environment has reduced the importance of religious answers to those questions. Lambeth's churchgoing piety, however this-worldly, was not wholly this-worldly, and incorporated various means of dealing with these questions. But it is important to remember that the most affluent and most comfortable families, with the lowest death and unemployment rates, attended church in the greatest numbers. They were hardly immune to the anguish of death and suffering, but patterns of church attendance make it difficult to argue that the extension of scientific control over the environment through medical advances and economic planning has made religion irrelevant and therefore "caused" a decline of churchgoing. Stereotypes of Victorian deathbed scenes are an uncertain guide to the content of Lambeth's Edwardian sermons, which contain ethical advice upon everyday matters much more often than comforting words about the Christian's triumph over death.[44] Even a devout and recalcitrant evangelical Baptist like Archibald Brown concentrated, not upon death and the world to come, but upon God's help for and recognition of the socially insignificant Christian, ignored by his peers and superiors in this life.[45] Historians sometimes claim that a declining belief in Hell, or a general waning of supernaturalism, accounts for the decline in church attendance around the turn of the century.[46] But it is not at all clear that the Victorian churches had ever been able to exploit a fund of popular supernaturalist churchgoing piety. English popular Christianity had long before jettisoned the notion that regular churchgoing was essential for a Christian. The churches could not count upon popular religion to supply them with churchgoers; they had to compete in a free market in religion. They had to explain why the churches were important, and supernatural explanations alone would not do.

Churchgoing was often dismissed as little more than a form of suburban respectability, and it is true that the desire to maintain

44. The *Brixton Free Press* and *Norwood Press* carried weekly accounts of sermons at Lambeth's best-attended churches and chapels between 1900 and 1930. Sermon summaries appeared in parish magazines and sometimes in chapel commemorative histories and memoirs or biographies. Lambeth clergymen and ministers with published sermons (1870–1930) include A. J. Waldron (middle-of-the-road Anglican), Charles Edward Brooke (Anglo-Catholic), S. A. Tipple (very liberal Baptist), Arthur Mursell (liberal Baptist), Archibald G. Brown (evangelical Baptist), W. Fuller Gooch (independent evangelical), Christopher Newman Hall (Congregationalist), F. B. Meyer (Baptist/Congregationalist), James Baldwin Brown (liberal Congregationalist), Bernard Snell (liberal Congregationalist), Thomas Tiplady and Hugh Price Hughes (Wesleyans), and three bishops of Southwark: E. S. Talbot, Hubert Murray Burge, and Cyril Foster Garbett. Theological liberals are overrepresented in this sample, and smaller chapels of every persuasion underrepresented.

45. Archibald G. Brown, *Six Sermons Preached at Chatsworth Road Baptist Church, 1899–1902* (n.d.); *God's Full Orbed Gospel: Sermons Preached at the Metropolitan Tabernacle with a biographical sketch by the Rev. James J. Ellis* (1911).

46. Hugh McLeod, *Class and Religion,* ch. 8.

the good opinion of one's neighbors was prominent among the numerous motives for churchgoing. But "respectability" is a complicated matter which should not be reduced to petty suburban snobbery. Suburbanites had an impressive array of symbols of respectability at their disposal, and merely occasional churchgoing had long been perfectly acceptable. People defined churchgoing as respectable because they thought it was important, just as they defined cleanliness as respectable because they thought it was important. Regular churchgoers went above and beyond the call of duty because they thought the churches were particularly important. The churches were important, they thought, because they were a means of promoting and nurturing and inculcating civilized behavior and social harmony. This conviction was shared by liberals, evangelicals, and Anglo-Catholics, by Methodists and Baptists and Unitarians, by virtually every Lambeth sect. It was particularly important for the young to be exposed to church teaching, and they were sent off to Sunday School by parents of all classes who never attended an ordinary Sunday service, but it was important for everyone. The greater a person's stake in civilized behavior and social harmony, the greater the likelihood of his regular attendance at church; that is why church attendance is so closely correlated with social status everywhere in Victorian England. In Lambeth, those Anglican parishes with the most elaborate philanthropic activities attracted the most worshippers, and resisted the decline of churchgoing with the most success (see Chapter 2). The notion that the churches encouraged social harmony is easy to ridicule, along with the fussy middle-class anxiety about "social control," but civilized behavior and self-discipline are serious issues in a free society and it is not easy to discern their origins or prevent their decay. There were many ways to be respectable, but only one obvious and immediately accessible way to love one's neighbor, provide moral training for one's children, and contribute to the greatest happiness for the greatest number in English society simultaneously.

The Christian churches are not consciously designed primarily to maintain the health and stability of society, and the Edwardian social functions of the churches were an unintended consequence of the philanthropic activities of the Victorian churches. Many clergymen and ministers with an interest in theology proper or in the liturgy performed their social welfare functions reluctantly; Percy Dearmer, a new curate in St. Anne's, South Lambeth, wrote that "The first feeling of the unfledged parson, as he alights upon his future parish, is one of surprise that he should be called upon to assume the functions of a relieving officer."[47] But most clergymen and ministers embraced the social welfare activities of the churches with more enthusiasm, and the literature of churches and chapels of all varieties quite openly described their work as a "civilizing mission." The vicar of Holy Trinity, Lambeth, characterized his task as "upholding the tone, manners, and morals of the district"; the policy of the Lambeth Ragged School was to "squeeze out the bad by squeezing in the good."[48] According to the pastor of Gipsy Road Baptist Church, "The genius of the gospel was to make bad men good, and whilst it made strong the spiritual constitution it was not without effects on the physical. It made perfect citizens as well as Christians."[49] The minister of Christ Church, Westminster Bridge Road, described the "aim of religious education" as "the introduction of control into conduct to the end of social efficiency," and a Wesleyan mission hall director prophesied that "If we did not keep them [the young men] within our gates, the prison gates would close behind some of them . . . the choice for them was between Christ and Crime."[50] A report on citizenship prepared by the Diocese of Southwark declared that "organized Christianity is essential to the complete and harmonious development of the human being. . . . Churchmen and others may fairly claim that they are carrying out the intention of the State when they seek to lead a lad or girl onward from the club or institute to the confirmation class and the communicants guild."[51] The Duke of Devonshire asked supporters of the South London Church Fund:

Can you imagine for one moment what England would have been like today without those churches and all that those churches mean? . . .

47. Nancy Dearmer, *The Life of Percy Dearmer* (1940), p. 68.
48. B-272, p. 93; B-273, p. 97.
49. BFP, 10 June 1910.
50. BFP, 1 Dec. 1922; Thomas Tiplady, *Spiritual Adventure* (1935), p. 28.
51. Southwark Diocesan Conference, *The Church's Work for "Citizens in Training"* (1919), p. 12.

Certainly it would not have been safe to walk the streets. All respect, decency, all those things which tend to make modern civilization what it is would not have been in existence. You can imagine what we should have had to pay for our police, for lunatic asylums, for criminal asylums. . . . The charges would have been increased hundredfold if it had not been for the work the church has done and is doing today.[52]

Local constables and magistrates, among others, believed him and depended upon the churches. When Lambeth's chief constable appealed to the Rev. F. B. Meyer to help control disorderly youths in his neighborhood, confessing that "something more than force" was needed, Meyer organized the Christ Church Boys' Club.[53] Until the 1920s juvenile probation responsibilities were entirely in the hands of the Church of England Police Court Mission. Missionaries reporting on successful cases to the magistrates would observe that "he is in the church choir and a regular communicant" (one claimed to have cured a girl in his care of "restlessness, a most stubborn complaint").[54] Between the wars it was the opinion of the magistrates at the Lambeth Town Hall Juvenile Courts that "the majority of cases are due to the lack of any kind of home discipline or religious influence."[55]

Even more important were a group of "leading citizens" of South London who set an example not only by attending church but by funding the church's philanthropic work. Their motives were not necessarily the same as those of suburban housewives or London City Missionaries, but they are unlikely to be wholly dissimilar and are interesting in their own right. These men, or rather these families, paid little attention to borough or parish boundaries, and my account will necessarily encompass other parts of South London. Some of these patrons made their fortunes elsewhere and moved to South London in the mid-nineteenth century, while others prospered upon the profits of various riverside works, then moved away from the river and finally away from South London altogether. But even

52. BFP, 23 May 1913.

53. *The Christ Church Jubilee Souvenir Book* (1926), p. 29.

54. BFP, 18 Feb. 1916; J. Haslock Potter, *Inasmuch: The Story of the Police Court Mission 1876–1926* (1927), pp. 30, 49.

55. Lady Margaret Hall, *Social Services in North Lambeth and Kennington* (1939), p. 112.

after their business interests had outgrown South London, they retained a lively interest in local affairs. Sir Henry Doulton's enthusiasm for South London "became in the process of time a whimsical sort of patriotism, and nothing would induce him to take up any other allegiance. All through his long life he was proud to be a citizen of Lambeth."[56] Mark Beaufoy remained in his home amid the slums near his vinegar works in South Lambeth until the 1880s, when the complaints of his family became unbearable, but the other patrons lived on the more pleasant commons and hills which remained islands of respectability and, to other local inhabitants, splendor in the midst of general social deterioration. In the 1880s William and Alexander McArthur, Wesleyan patrons, both lived on Brixton Hill near William Higgs, the patron, designer, and builder of Baptist churches in South London and Surrey. On Clapham Common the Barclays, Quaker brewers, bankers and mission hall patrons, were neighbors of W. S. Caine, a Liberal M.P. and temperance advocate who maintained two mission halls in Lambeth. Henry Doulton, an Anglican benefactor, lived near Tooting Common until 1885, and on nearby Streatham Common lived the Unitarian patrons Sir Henry Tate and Frederic Nettlefold. The mansions of C. E. Tritton, heir of a banking fortune and patron of temperance organizations in Lambeth's Anglican churches, and Evan Spicer, Congregationalist politician and patron, stood at Upper Norwood and Dulwich respectively.

The sort of direct paternalism of the factory town in the North of England, where nineteenth-century millowners dominated the local church or chapel which stood near the mill, never flourished in Lambeth. The largest single employer, the London and South Western Railway, was organized on a regional scale. The building and printing trades were fragmented into hundreds of large and small firms, and the large builders such as Higgs of Brixton had employees scattered about dozens of worksites. In the local works with concentrated employment such as Doulton's potteries or Beaufoy's vinegar works, only the unskilled employees actually lived near the works in the eighties and nineties. Both families sent members to parliament in the middle or

56. Edmund Gosse, *Sir Henry Doulton: the Man of Business as a Man of Imagination*, Desmond Eyles, ed. (1970), p. 1.

late nineteenth century, but their neighborhood influence was diluted by the formless enormity of South London. Even in the absence of the more direct and obvious forms of patronage, however, Lambeth's churches and chapels were in one very important sense the creation of nineteenth-century industrial and commercial capitalism. This sample of patrons was chosen because the names appeared regularly among church and chapel records, but the list of the companies they owned, managed, or directed (and their successor companies) reads like a catalog of Britain's current economic giants: Guest, Keen and Nettlefold; Courtauld's; Tate and Lyle; Higgs and Hill; Barclay's Bank; Courage breweries; the Doulton potteries. As the scale of industrial organization grew, a more general conception of social responsibility replaced the impulse to build a chapel for one's employees. The main goal of the patrons' beneficence in Lambeth was not primarily the regimentation of their own employees, although they attempted that upon occasion, but the creation of a sober and industrious nation. Instead of the local church or chapel, they supported churches and chapels and mission halls in general.

Denominational allegiance remained important, although it coexisted with the general notion that all of the (Protestant) churches were doing valuable work. Seven of these ten families were Nonconformist, and three of the seven Unitarian or Quaker. Each of the three Anglican patrons was the son or grandson of a Nonconformist, and various members of the other families were in transit from chapel to church (which probably explains the intense hostility to the church displayed by some of the more devoted Dissenters). But all of these patrons displayed a this-worldly enthusiasm for the churches as social institutions.

Both the Doultons and the Barclays sponsored religious work among their own employees. Henry Doulton (1820–1897) abandoned Congregational Nonconformity and Liberalism for the Church of England and the Conservative Party in the 1860s, and thereafter supported Lambeth's parishes and cooperated with a local clergyman in establishing an artistic school for potters near his Lambeth works—the Lambeth School of Art.[57] Both Doulton

57. *The Royal Doulton Potteries: A Brief Summary* (1924), p. 15; Desmond Eyles, *Royal Doulton, 1815–1965* (1965), pp. 64ff.; Edmund Gosse, *A Critical Essay on the Life and Works of George Tinworth* (1883).

and the Quaker brewery owners, the Barclays, supported London City Missionaries who served as primitive industrial psychologists in their riverside works. George Goodman, known as the "Bishop of Lambeth Walk," maintained a "Potters' Temperance Society" along with the benevolent society, maternity society and cricket club at his Lambeth Walk Mission Hall, and directed his attention in particular to the kilnburners, "a very rough sort." His leaflets proclaimed: "We are all striving as members of the Lambeth Walk Mission to WIN men and women for Jesus; to make them SOBER, INDUSTRIOUS and HAPPY," and promised immediate benefits both to the individual and to the district.[58] Doulton and the Barclays contributed to the London City Mission on Friar Street, Southwark, and the Barclay and Perkins brewery in Southwark had a mission hall right on the premises with a paid missionary entrusted with the delicate task of promoting temperance among brewery employees. The missionary, according to Booth's interviewer, acted as "a kind of censor, who is ready to report to the authorities when any question of conduct, or it may be of home conditions, comes up."[59] Despite the fact that only one hundred fifty of the approximately seven hundred brewery employees lived near the brewery by 1900, Mr. Edwyn Barclay of the firm claimed that the mission "answers very well even from a business point of view; we know all about our men."[60] The firm also donated £400 a year to the Anglican Evangelical Oxford Medical Mission and began offering employees 30 shillings a week in pay instead of the customary 24 shillings and a ration of beer. The Barclays themselves were abstainers.[61]

Two prominent Anglican patrons also emerged, like Henry Doulton, from Nonconformist families which had helped to establish many of Lambeth's chapels. Although a banker with world-wide interests, C. E. Tritton (1845–1918) positively haunted Lambeth's Anglican churches. Firmly evangelical—a vice president of the British and Foreign Bible Society and the Church Missionary Society, vice chairman of the London Mis-

58. B-271, p. 25 and leaflet insert.
59. B-278, p. 107.
60. *Ibid.*
61. B-270, p. 71.

sionary Society—Tritton was one of a few Tory M.P.s popular with ardent Nonconformists in his constituency, for his Nonconformist heritage was evident in his enthusiasm for temperance, free trade, and nondenominational religious education. He was a "welcome and frequent speaker" at the parochial hall of every evangelical and middle-of-the-road parish in Lambeth for meetings of Church of England Temperance Society branches. As one of a group of four trustees for three of Lambeth's thirty-three parishes, he controlled as much of Lambeth's patronage as the Bishop of Southwark and contributed to the borough's reputation as an evangelical island in a relatively "high" diocese.[62] Another Anglican patron and M.P., Mark Beaufoy (1854–1922) was heir to a firm of vinegar distillers which had been in Lambeth since 1756 and was still one of the borough's largest single employers in the late nineteenth century. Once Quaker, the family was Anglican although still Liberal in the late nineteenth century. Mark Beaufoy's uncle, Henry Beaufoy, endowed the Lambeth Ragged School in 1851, and the Church of England Waifs and Strays Society was founded at the Beaufoy's South Lambeth home in 1881, an outgrowth of the extensive work of the local parish, St. Anne's.[63] For both of these men, Lambeth's parishes provided an institutional structure through which they worked to create a temperate and industrious British people.

The McArthur and Caine families settled in South London in the sixties and seventies and played equally prominent roles in the philanthropic and religious life of Lambeth. William (1809–1887) and Alexander (1814–1909) McArthur were Ulster Methodists who transformed a wholesale drapery business in Londonderry into a thriving Australian and colonial trade. In 1863 Alexander settled at Raleigh Hall, Brixton Rise, and in 1866 William also retired from business and moved to Brixton in order to devote the rest of his life to religion, philanthropy, and politics. William was a man of enormous energy who served as Lambeth's M.P., Lord Mayor of London, and mainstay

62. See BFP, 3 Jan. 1919 (obituary); J. B. Wilson, *The Story of Norwood*, prepared by H. A. Wilson (1973), p. 42; SLP, 28 Jan. 1905 and 11 Feb. 1905; Christ Church, Gipsy Hill, *Parish Magazine*, 1 Jan. 1899.

63. *Survey of London*, vol. 23 (1951), pp. 26, 142; vol. 26 (1956), p. 30; Barbara Kerr, *The Dispossessed: An Aspect of Victorian Social History*, chaps. 4, 5; Gwendolyn Beaufoy, *Leaves from a Beech Tree* (1930), passim.

of a typical list of religious societies: British and Foreign Bible Society, London City Mission, Evangelical Alliance, and Aborigines' Protection Society (he took a particular interest in the annexation of the Fiji Islands, in hopes of increasing the Methodist population of the Empire). His Brixton library contained a "large drawer with a multitude of small divisions, each labeled with the name of some particular philanthropy; in these he deposited the applications which he received relating to several institutions towards which he subscribed until he attended to them."[64] Both were the leading laymen not only of Wesleyan Methodism in general but of the Brixton Hill and Mostyn Road Circuits, which encompassed most of Lambeth Wesleyanism in the seventies and eighties. They collaborated with Hugh Price Hughes, minister at Brixton Hill in the eighties, in designing the Wesleyan Forward Movement, essentially a program to build large central mission halls throughout inner London.

W. S. Caine, the son of a Liverpool merchant, retired to Clapham Common in 1878 and turned his attention to mission halls. Much given to conversions, he had become obsessed with temperance upon reading, over a glass of sherry, a tract entitled "Haste to the rescue. An appeal to the educated classes to save the masses from their worst vice."[65] He founded the Anglo-Indian Temperance Society and served as president of the Baptist Total Abstinence Society, the Congregational Temperance Society, the British Temperance League, and the National Temperance Federation. Temperance fit into a wide-ranging program of social reform, for Caine supported trade unions, employers' liability, land reform, disestablishment, compulsory secular education, and the seating of Bradlaugh. He freely criticized evangelicals for their other-worldiness and supported all Sunday-opening legislation, but left the Liberal Party for a while over Home Rule only to return in disgust with Unionist attitudes toward temperance. Politics was one focus of his life, building mission halls in Lambeth the other. Converted to the mission hall cause upon reading Mearns's *The Bitter Cry of Outcast London* in 1883, he persuaded his own chapel, Stockwell Baptist, to sponsor Wheatsheaf Hall in 1884. It was an enormous success,

64. Thomas McCullagh, *Sir William McArthur: A Biography* (1891), p. 392.
65. John Newton, *W. S. Caine, M.P.* (1907), p. 25.

grew from seventeen to two hundred fifty members in ten years, and drifted for some reason into the Congregational Union even though "very few of our members had any more interest in Congregationalism than they had in Mormonism."[66] According to a jealous clergyman, Caine succeeded by saying "Come to my church. You may spit on the floor if you like."[67] His second attempt to establish a mission hall failed when the citizens of Pascal Street compelled his mission workers to retreat by "pelting the workers with ordure and refuse of all kinds."[68] But another successful mission eventually flourished on the slightly more respectable Vauxhall Street. Both the McArthurs and Caine looked upon chapels and mission halls as agencies of social reform. After publicly confusing the Metropolitan Chapel Building Society with the Metropolitan Board of Works, McArthur argued that "I may have made a mistake, but after all I am not far wrong."[69] Caine explained that:

From the beginning of the work in Wheatsheaf Hall we have placed in the very forefront the need of personal conversion to God as the one foundation of success; but we have also recognized the duty of using every means in our power to prepare men for the acceptance of general influences, by adding to our work anything that will make the dismal and squalid life of London brighter and better, everything that brings joy to the hard life, instruction to the ignorant, encouragement to thrift and temperance, or that gives innocent enjoyment to young and old.[70]

Two Nonconformist families, the Spicers and the Higgs, had enormous influence within Lambeth's Congregational and Baptist chapels respectively. Both Albert (1847–1934) and Evan Spicer (1848–1937) were born in Brixton into a Congregational, Liberal family of wholesale stationers. Evan Spicer settled in Dulwich and served as a leader of the Progressive party on the London County Council, vice chairman of the London County Council, and justice of the peace. Living adjacent to Norwood, he was local patron of the Norwood Liberal Association, and regularly opened his home for events in support of the quixotic

66. William Kent, *Testament of a Victorian Youth* (1938), p. 103.

67. B-272, p. 63.

68. B-271, p. 5.

69. McCullagh, *McArthur,* p. 285.

70. B-271, pamphlet inserted.

Liberal and Nonconformist candidates for this constituency.
When the lower Norwood Working Men's Institute, a private
foundation with Nonconformist backing, was in danger of falling into the hands of the Church of England, he used his position on the L.C.C. to secure council funding, and not only
helped to found Streatham Hill Congregational Church but
liberally supported other chapels, especially Browning Hall in
Walworth. Although Evan's instincts were more radical than
his brother's (he later became a Labour supporter), both men
seem to have been mainly interested in furthering the Nonconformist cause, for their parliamentary campaigns were ostenta-
tiously Nonconformist even when it was not to their advantage.[71]

William Higgs (1824–1883) was the entrepreneur of a family
which had throughout the nineteenth century supported and
maintained a variety of Lambeth's Nonconformist causes—Congregationalist, Baptist, and Wesleyan. His interests did not run
to religion of any sort—in fact "a love of buying and getting
gain was undoubtedly a marked feature of his character even in
boyhood."[72]—but the family's pastor, C. H. Spurgeon, was a
shrewd judge of character and enlisted him in the aspect of
church work which did interest him: building. Higgs was astonished to receive a letter from Spurgeon in 1856 informing him of
his appointment to a committee "to confer on the best course of
action for providing increased accommodation for the congregation who assemble with us."[73] As the Higgs building firm
prospered with contracts for the guards barracks in Chelsea, the
Royal Marine Infirmary in Woolwich, and St. Thomas's Hospital, a portion of the profits went toward the construction of
Baptist chapels in South London. When Higgs sold Kenyon
House, Brixton, and purchased the Gwydr House, Brixton Hill,
from Sir William McArthur, new houses were built on the old
estate and Kenyon Baptist Chapel arose on the site of the old
house. William Higgs and his brothers erected Lewin Road
Baptist Chapel in Streatham as a memorial to their father, and
William was a founder of Spurgeon's Orphanage in Stockwell

71. BFP, 4 March 1921; B-315, p. 143; B-277, p. 155; *Albert Spicer, 1847–1934:
A Man of His Time*, by One of His Family (1938), passim.
72. W. M. Higgs, *A History of the Higgs or Higges Family* (n.d.), p. 137.
73. *Ibid.*, p. 142.

where he was depicted in stained glass in the board room. After his death in 1883 (he left £250,000), two of his twelve daughters remained in the Brixton home and pursued "work among the poor" with the Kenyon Baptist Chapel and two other daughters went into foreign mission work.[74]

Unitarianism stood apart from the other denominations of South London despite the fact that liberals in each of the three major denominations had virtually "caught up" with the Unitarians theologically. Brixton's Unitarian minister complained that the liberals were even more aloof than the others, "perhaps because having gone some distance in the direction of a more liberal theology, they are more afraid of being tarnished with the brush of a still complete heterodoxy."[75] The head of one of the families associated with the Brixton chapel was Frederic Nettlefold (1835–1913), related to Joseph Chamberlain and chairman until the 1890s of Nettlefold's, Ltd., the screw manufacturing and engineering firm. He had married into the Courtaulds and after 1890 his major interest was textile manufacturing; two of his daughters met and married sons of another notable family attending the Brixton Unitarian Church, the Martineaus.[76] It must have been particularly galling to the chapel's minister when he failed to attract South London's most prominent Unitarian layman, Sir Henry Tate (1819–1899). The son of a Unitarian minister, he became wealthy by inventing the sugar cube, settled in Streatham late in the century, and attended Brixton Independent Church. He was known to admire fine preaching, and Brixton Independent's minister, the Rev. Bernard Snell, was not only one of London's leading preachers but extremely liberal in his theology.[77] Through the influence of Tate's second wife, who had long been a member of that congregation, Unitarian money began to flow into Congregational

74. *Ibid.*, p. 150; *Kenyon Baptist Church, Brixton, Jubilee Story 1884–1934* (1934).

75. B-303, p. 119.

76. See A. C. Crofton, *The Nettlefolds* (1962); R. K. Spedding, *Resurgam!* (1941).

77. *Brixton Independent Yearbooks*, 1904, 1909; Brixton Free Press, *Brixton's Churches* (1904); Tate once donated £5000 to the Unitarian Mansfield College "to promote and encourage the theory and art of preaching." Tom Jones, *Henry Tate 1819–1899* (1960), p. 29.

philanthropy, particularly after Tate's death. She endowed a third nurse for Brixton Independent Church in 1902 "for the sick poor of Brixton," and in 1909 spoke at the opening of new premises for the Moffat Institute, one of Brixton Independent's mission halls. "I believe strongly in the gospel of cleanliness," she noted, "and I think it must be at the base of every social reform among the masses; but it is of no use preaching unless an example is shown in a place like this, and I hope this Institute will be known as the cleanest, brightest, most helpful spot in Lambeth."[78]

These South London patrons exerted their strongest influence between 1860 and 1900 (by 1924 only one of them was still alive). They used their commercial and industrial wealth to build many of Lambeth's chapels, maintain its parish churches, and create a network of philanthropic auxiliaries and mission halls in cooperation with the clergy and an anxious middle-class public. Shrewd businessmen, they believed the churches' claims to social utility. William Higgs went to hear Spurgeon because he was "the only minister who keeps bricks and mortar out of my head during public worship."[79] Henry Doulton took an interest in South London churches although it was said that "the profession of religion never took a prominent part in his life."[80] W. S. Caine experienced a boyhood evangelical conversion but was obsessed with temperance reform, and Albert Spicer "urged that it was the business of religious organizations to work for the betterment of the condition of the people. Social reform was not to be taboo, but should be a first interest."[81] Churchgoing and social improvement were linked in their minds as two dimensions of one institution, and both fit into a general concept of civic responsibility in which the churches played a key role as a wholesome and civilizing influence.

It was difficult to explain precisely how the churches exerted their civilizing influence, and people of different social classes had different conceptions of what that civilizing influence meant and how it affected individuals. Patrons sent money to philan-

78. *Brixton Independent Yearbook,* 1909, p. 32.
79. Higgs, *History of the Higgs,* p. 139.
80. Gosse, *Sir Henry Doulton,* p. 26.
81. *Albert Spicer,* p. 21.

thropies and the local churches. Working-class mothers—and other mothers—hoped that Sunday School would improve the character of their children. Middle-class suburban families set a good example to the world by performing their collective duty of Sunday church attendance. Richard Church's parents— a postal sorter and an L.C.C. school teacher living on a street of skilled artisans, minor government employees, and clerks in Battersea—were non-churchgoers. But when Richard began questioning his mother about the Bible she became alarmed, "telling me that I ought to be thinking what the Bible was about, and not of the way it was written. . . . This made me so remorseful that I gratefully accompanied her, Father, and Jack to the Congregational Chapel, almost opposite my school. . . . My wrong approach to the Bible had started a new family habit."[82] His father had some Nonconformist ancestors somewhere in his family history. Everyone knew that morality depended upon religion, and when his son began to show signs of religious confusion it was quite natural that he should choose to attend a convenient, flourishing chapel. They expected to see direct benefits to their son's character, but others of a more altruistic temper attended simply in order to do their duty and support an institution which instilled discipline in English society. In either event, churchgoing was not simply suburban snobbery, although encompassing it; it was a public ritual of positive assent to a system of communal controls.

Middle-class churchgoers received the additional benefits of hearing their character praised. The minister of Wynne Road Baptist Church described the homeowners on Stockwell Park Road as "moral policemen," and claimed that "a good businessman is well fitted to be a good Christian man."[83] The vicar of St. Matthew's, Brixton, urged his parishioners to "remember the patron saint of your parish church, the ideal man for the model Christian in a business neighborhood. St. Matthew was diligent in his office work . . . a very ideal of business capacity, sanctified by the influence of gospel work."[84] There are numerous examples in Lambeth alone of this sort of flattery of the middle

82. Richard Church, *Over the Bridge* (1955), p. 82.
83. B-303, p. 133; BFP, *Brixton's Churches* (1904), p. 35.
84. *Brixton's Churches*, p. 14.

classes along with even more outrageous assertions about Christianity being good for trade, etc., and too much could be made of them. Churchgoers cannot have been too comfortable with their own activities and occupations if they listened with any care to what some of the most popular preachers were saying about the evils of competition. But churchgoing was clearly designed to legitimize the everyday as well as the Sunday activities of the congregation—to make them feel good.

Concern over communal controls and the satisfaction of doing their duty characterized both Anglican and Nonconformist churchgoers. The chapel as well as the church was regarded as a powerful civilizing influence, and it is clear that many Nonconformist churchgoers were unaware of the significance of the Dissenting tradition and found themselves in the chapel because it was convenient or featured a well-known preacher. But it seems likely that the Church of England benefited the most from the religion of civic duty, particularly three of the four parish churches built in the 1820s: St. John's, Waterloo Road; St. Mark's, Kennington; St. Matthew's, Brixton; and St. Luke's West Norwood. Built in the first of the new parishes created in Lambeth during the wave of parochial subdivision in the nineteenth century, they each had a commanding site at an important junction and an imposing classical style of architecture. (According to a recent historian, the Brixton parish church has "breathtaking 'Infinity' in its galleries focused on an awesome pair of Doric columns behind the altar; beneath are Egyptian porches to the vaults, fore-shadowing in their 'Terror' the circular catacombs by Bunning at the Highgate Cemetery.")[85] These four churches accounted for 15 percent of all Anglican church attendance in 1902 (excluding missions), and St. Mark's and St. Matthew's together accounted for more than 10 percent.

St. John's was stranded in a slum described as "worse than St. Giles." Its day schools were full to overflowing and its Vicar baptized over 400 infants in 1898, but only 61 churchgoers attended morning services in 1902, 156 in the evening. In the next district of Kennington, however, St. Mark's sat amid a neighborhood described as "poor but not necessitous—with much

85. Nicholas Taylor, "The Awful Sublimity of the Victorian City," in H. J. Dyos and Michael Wolff, eds., *The Victorian City* (1973); comments following page 448.

shabby gentility, clerks, shopkeepers, theatrical people, many lodgers, and a great many doctors."[86] In 1902, 408 attended in the morning and 982 in the evening and pew rents provided a substantial portion of the Vicar's salary. St. Matthew's Brixton, attracted over 500 to each service, and the Vicar expressed complacent satisfaction with his parish: "When I hear that London does not go to church I am amazed. My brother clergy in South Lambeth come here and say, 'How are you so successful?' "[87] St. Luke's, West Norwood, drew over 400 to each service in 1902, but that was considered unsatisfactory for a suburban parish. It was recovering from some sort of clerical scandal in the late nineties. The 1920s, however, was to be its best decade ever, and in 1920 the vicar was describing his parish as the "most powerful in South London."[88]

These and other Anglican parishes did not shun the upper-class connections which reinforced the example set by local notables. The Archbishop of Canterbury was Lambeth's most distinguished churchgoer. The Duchy of Cornwall (the estate of the Prince of Wales) was a substantial landlord in Lambeth and consequently an ecclesiastical donor, and the Prince of Wales laid the foundation stone for the new Church of St. Anselm in 1914 which was built in part with prominent donations from the Crown.[89] The vicar of St. John's, "an excellent specimen of the rich university man who I imagine drifted into the church because his parents wished it," directed his parish's annual report exclusively to potential donors, and in 1899 Lady Sybil Smith organized a concert at Grosvenor House in support of his parochial organizations.[90] The vicar of St. Mark's was the nephew of the dean of Westminster; the vicar of St. Matthew's, Denmark Hill, was personally chosen by the parochial patroness, Lady de Crespigny.[91]

The Anglican churches could draw upon nationalistic senti-

86. B-272, p. 119.

87. B-305, p. 131.

88. B-312, p. 211; St. Luke's, West Norwood, Parochial Church Council Minutes, December 1920. GLRO P/85/LUK.

89. *Survey of London,* vol. 23, p. 136.

90. B-269, p. 22.

91. B-271, p. 193; B-308, p. 103.

ment during such public celebrations as the two Royal Jubilees as well as during wartime. The vicar of Christ Church, Gipsy Hill, delivered a Jubilee sermon in 1887 equating the "hearty expression of loyalty and love to our lady sovereign" with "a grand tribute to God." "We see in her," he continued, "the chosen instrument of God for shaping and guiding the destinies of our country."[92] During the Boer War St. Matthew's, Brixton, played host to a patriotic concert which featured militaristic songs and odes by Kipling (during World War I its prayer books were recovered in khaki). Major General Sir W. Gatacre opened the new headquarters of the St. John the Divine, Kennington, Church Lads' Brigade in 1900, and the vicar pronounced the Brigade "a great influence in the parish in training up Christians, and he should not be sorry if it trained up good soldiers too."[93]

All of these attractions made Anglican churchgoing seem a natural and normal expression of civic duty for a middle-class family. And the clergy, for all of their genuine concern about the alienation of the working classes, did not abandon their role as chaplains to the influential. The vicar of St. Matthew's Brixton, "spends every afternoon in paying calls on the upper stratum of his people."[94] In a public protest against the transformation of the Brixton Theatre into the "Brixton Hippodrome" in 1906, his successor claimed the role of spokesman for "the influential classes who want 'high class' entertainment, not cheap, vulgar music halls."[95] The mission hall movement was itself a formal recognition of the middle-class character of ordinary Sunday churchgoing. The vicar of St. Peter's, Leigham Court Road, justified their new mission hall in 1892: "While the state of society remains as it is, such a church as ours will never satisfy the wants of both of the two very distinct sections of the parish, either as regards corporate or personal religion."[96] The sermons preached to these middle-class Anglican congregations

92. R. A. Allen, *God's Hand Over the Nation* (1887), printed sermon, GLRO P85/CTC1/40/7.

93. SLP, 3 Feb. 1900; 15 Sept. 1900.

94. B-305, p. 137.

95. BFP, 21 Sept. 1906.

96. St. Peter's, Streatham, *Annual Report,* 1892.

were notorious for their lack of content. An outsider stepped into a South London service between the wars and described a sermon which could have been delivered at any time in the late nineteenth or early twentieth century: "I can imagine no body of decent human beings, from Athenian ladies listening to an Epicurean philosopher in a rose garden to a Leaguer of the Guises hotly engaged in exterminating the local Huguenots, who might not have listened to it without offense."[97] These sermons contained some church doctrine (a great deal of it in Anglo-Catholic churches) and some general comments on ethics and good character along with praise of the church for all of its good works. Exhortations to be good were mingled with praise for doing good. "Congregations are judged very much these days," the vicar of St. Matthew's observed, "not only by what they teach about God, but what they do *for* God. All philanthropic work, and all social work, ought to be religious work."[98] His successor enjoyed baiting secularists for casting out the lower orders, for lacking "a mission for the lowest, the poor, the degraded."[99] St. Matthew's, Brixton, sponsored dozens of philanthropic organizations, which were the outward and visible sign of God's work in Lambeth. God's work was furthered by God's people, who were sitting in the pews, and to be reminded of that fact was a pleasant experience. The church's philanthropy supplied the ideological cement which bound together clergyman, patron, and ordinary churchgoer in a scientific age.

The dignity and beauty of the worship services added another dimension to Anglican churchgoing. Uniformed processions supplied a restrained spectacle, even if it was only the Church Lads' Brigade, and the dignified phrases of the Book of Common Prayer did not seem entirely out of place even in suburban brick Victorian Gothic churches. I have no autobiographical description of middle-of-the-road Anglican churchgoing in Lambeth, but Charles Booth's wife, Mary, wrote to her husband of her own churchgoing in a passage which describes the satisfactions of an Anglican service very well:

97. O. M. Hueffer, *Some of the English* (1930), p. 84. The church is not identified but resembles St. Matthew's, Brixton, or St. Mark's, Kennington.

98. St. Matthew's, Brixton, *Yearbook* (1899), p. 14.

99. A. J. Waldron, *Problems of Life* (1914), p. 67; sermons delivered as vicar of St. Matthew's, Brixton, 1906–1914.

I don't think you would have seriously disliked our religious observance yesterday. We went to the garrison Church, Tom, Dodo and I, and
saw the soldiers troop in to the sound of fife and drum. Then Prince
Edward of Saxe-Weimar, the Commandant here, with his staff amidst
galaxies of under-officers and men stationed to keep order. Then we,
with others following, had to find seats where we could. I looked round
at the soldiers and the little brasses let in everywhere so thickly under
the painted windows: "To the memory of Captain D . . . killed at A . . . ,
the Officers of the 44th, etc., etc." Above was hung the old, worn Col-
ours that had seen many fights, suspended now, tattered and faded,
from the capitals of the pillars. I liked it all and to be in the midst of
it, and to kneel and stand and hear the dear words of our Church
Service. Oh, I do love it very much! To have ever left it as much as I
have once seems strange to me, a sort of treason, rebellion, certainly
ingratitude.[100]

Churchgoing and "diffusive Christianity" were not wholly exclusive by any means, and the most prominent motive for
churchgoing—a sense of civic duty combined with the notion
that religious teaching was in some way good for individuals
as well as for society—coexisted with a variety of other motives
within denominations, congregations, families, and individuals.
It would be unfair to the churches to claim that churchgoing
was "not really religious" simply because it was not other-
worldly and failed to resemble the rather frantic supernaturalism of nineteenth century Roman Catholicism. Churchgoing was
intertwined with and inseparable from the social conditions of
late Victorian Lambeth, and the churches reinterpreted Christianity and their own denominational traditions in the light of
those conditions. Every Christian group has done precisely the
same thing for nearly two thousand years.

The churches were by no means passive, however, for they
stimulated religious practice and encouraged a consciously
Christian response to the collective ethical questions of South
London churchgoers. Furthermore, the other-worldly dimensions of piety were not absent. They are an essential element of
all religion, although their prominence within any particular

100. Cited in Belinda Norman Butler, *Victorian Aspirations: The Life and
Labour of Charles and Mary Booth* (1972), p. 57.

form of religion varies enormously. Lambeth's churchgoers were more likely than non-churchgoers to focus their attention upon the person of Jesus Christ. It is true that, even for churchgoers, Jesus was remarkably this-worldly. Evangelicals concentrated, not upon death and the life to come, but upon Jesus as a companion in life's daily struggles. Liberals regarded His life as the greatest of all ethical models. But this emphasis upon the person of Jesus Christ distinguished churchgoing piety from the largely Christ-less "diffusive Christianity." And however this-worldly churchgoing piety may have been, Jesus remained, even for the liberals, something "more than a man."

The reason why some churchgoers regarded Christ as a kind of personal companion and others did not is a mystery. This form of piety did not follow automatically upon regular church attendance. We know that some regular churchgoers thought very little about other-worldly matters, and furthermore, religious ideas and even religious faith were widespread outside the churches, although they often owed their existence to the promulgation of religious ideas by the churches in indirect ways. But a certain intensity of devotion to Christ was one unmeasurable consequence of churchgoing, and may well have been more widespread than the records indicate. "Accepting Christ" was the central element of the evangelical conversion experience, and the figure of Jesus the personal friend, the loving Good Shepherd, was pressed upon children even in liberal churches where adults regarded Jesus as little more than an excellent model for ethical behavior. The churches appear to have been the primary source of Christ-oriented but this-worldly piety, for it was not taught in the schools nor was it an element of popular religious culture. After Richard Church's parents began to attend the Congregational chapel, a "more attentive reading of the Bible and the Book of Common Prayer put my imagination to work in another direction than grammatical. The character, the very physical person, of Jesus began to loom up as a constant acquaintance. He became a companion of my long days at home and we walked together as freely as though he were a member of the small family."[101]

The image of Jesus exercised the adult imagination as well.

101. Church, *Over the Bridge*, p. 129.

As Charlie Chaplin's mother descended into poverty after a deteriorating voice left her unable to perform in the music hall, she began attending Christ Church, Westminster Bridge Road, and he has left his account of a child's response to their liturgical services:

Every Sunday I was made to sit through Bach's organ music and to listen with aching impatience to the Rev. F. B. Meyer's fervent and dramatic voice echoing down the nave like shuffling feet. His orations must have been appealing, for occasionally I would catch mother quietly wiping away a tear, which slightly embarrassed me. . . . Well do I remember Holy Communion on one hot summer day, and the cool silver cup containing delicious grape juice that passed along the pew . . . and mother's gentle restraining hand when I drank too much of it. And how relieved I was when they closed the Bible for it meant that the sermons would soon end and they could start prayers and the final hymn. Since mother joined the church she seldom saw her theatrical friends. That world had evaporated, had become only a memory.[102]

Christ Church alternated first with the theatrical world, then with the workhouse, then with the lunatic asylum, and it is clear that churchgoing, for this woman, was part of an attempt to save herself in a very secular sense. She was able to earn a few shillings dressmaking for the members of the church before going into the workhouse. After leaving it for the first time she "rented a room at the house of Mrs. Taylor, a friend of mother's, a church member, and devoted Christian. . . . She had an emphatic manner and abundant energy. She had taken mother under her Christian wing, and rented her a front room at a very reasonable rent, on the second floor of her large house."[103] This help failed to keep her out of the workhouse and sane. But Chaplin has left a striking if dramatized account of how one Lambeth churchgoer attempted to transmit her piety to her son:

I remember an evening in our one room in the basement at Oakley Street. I lay in bed recovering from fever. Sydney had gone out to night school and mother and I were alone. It was late afternoon and she sat with her back to the window reading, acting, and explaining in her inimitable way the New Testament and Christ's love and pity for the poor and for little children. Perhaps her emotion was due to my illness,

102. Charles Chaplin, *My Autobiography* (1964), p. 22.
103. *Ibid.* p. 57.

but she gave me the most luminous and appealing interpretation of Christ that I have ever heard or seen; of the woman who had sinned and was to be stoned by the mob, and of his words to them: "He that is without sin among you, let him cast the first stone at her."

She read into the dark, stopping only to light the lamp, then told of the faith that Jesus inspired in the sick, that they had only to touch the hem of his garment to be healed. . . .

As she continued, tears welled up in her eyes. She told of Simon helping to carry Christ's cross and the appealing look of gratitude Jesus gave him; she told of the repentant thief dying with him on a cross and asking forgiveness, and of Jesus saying "Today thou shalt be with me in Paradise." And from the cross, looking down at his mother, saying "woman, behold thy son." And in his last dying agony crying out, "My God, why hast thou forsaken me?" And we both wept.

"Don't you see," said mother, "how human he was; like all of us, he too suffered doubt."

Mother had so carried me away that I wanted to die that very night and meet Jesus. But mother was not so enthusiastic. "Jesus wants you to live first and fulfill your destiny here," she said. In that dark room in the basement at Oakley Street, mother illuminated to me the kindliest light this world has ever known, which has endowed literature and the theatre with their greatest and richest themes: love, pity, and humanity.[104]

She was no doubt exceptional in her particular expression of piety, although quite typical in her focus upon this world rather than the next. Many of the themes of Lambeth churchgoing come together in her story: the purpose of religious philanthropy, the churches as improving institutions, the adoration of Jesus. The source of her piety was the institutional church. The churchgoing which nurtured her piety—the churchgoing of Mrs. Taylor and the Rev. F. B. Meyer, of civic duty and social responsibility—was declining in the 1890s and that decline accelerated after 1900. Before discussing that decline, however, there is one other important dimension of Lambeth churchgoing which should be examined. Mrs. Chaplin was apparently unaware that Christ Church, Westminister Bridge Road, was a "Congregationalist" church, but many Nonconformist churchgoers and virtually all Nonconformist ministers were still very much aware of the stigma of Dissent in 1900.

104. *Ibid.*, pp. 24–25.

5

The Stigma of Dissent

Slightly more than one-half of Lambeth's Edwardian churchgoers attended a Nonconformist chapel rather than a parish church. Some chapelgoers were unaware of the significance of Nonconformity, and attended the local chapel because it was convenient or featured an attractive preacher. Furthermore, even the committed Nonconformists who were fully conscious of their distinctive religious tradition did not live in a religious ghetto. They were English men and women as well as Methodists or Dissenters, and most of what I have said about churchgoing in general applies to Nonconformists as well as to Anglicans. Backsliding Nonconformists lapsed into "diffusive Christianity." Nonconformists as well as Anglicans believed that churchgoing was a civic duty closely related to social order and social progress. Nonconformists embraced religious philanthropy with the same enthusiasm as Anglicans. But Nonconformists ordinarily went about their activities in a different way and drew upon different ideas to justify them. The most committed of them brought a different perspective to everything they did. For them, Nonconformity was a different way of being English, an alternative cultural tradition which was very much alive in the early years of the twentieth century.

It is no longer alive, and historians in search of the roots of the decline and decay of Nonconformity have strongly emphasized the moral and spiritual emptiness of the late Victorian chapel. The "apparent" growth of Nonconformist membership is said to mask a "real" decline, and public enthusiasm to mask an inner desolation and decay or even an outright betrayal of an admirable cultural tradition.[1] I agree in part with these assessments, but it is important that they not obscure the social importance of this tradition in the early twentieth century. In many ways Nonconformity was more important in England between the years 1870 and 1914 than in any other period since the seventeenth century, and its influence extended far beyond the walls of the chapel. Nonconformists dominated many of Lambeth's most important social institutions, and they brought with them into those institutions a distinctively Nonconformist way of looking at the world. The legal disabilities which had once created a sort of Nonconformist caste had all but disappeared by the turn of the century. But the cultural contrast between a suburban, middle-class Anglican parish church and a neighboring suburban, middle-class Nonconformist chapel could hardly have been more striking.

Lambeth Nonconformists conformed more or less to the usual stereotypes about the social composition of Dissent: they were shopkeepers and merchants, manufacturers and minor professionals, clerks and the "better sort" of artisan. Semi-skilled and unskilled workers, and paupers,[2] were definitely underrepresented (see Table 18). This social structure created an insoluble problem of self-definition and self-image. In a country where social groups identified themselves within a more or less agreed upon hierarchy of social class or status, Nonconformity was left out, for the

1. See Alan D. Gilbert, *Religion and Society in Industrial England: Church, Chapel, and Social Change, 1740–1914* (1976), chaps. 2, 7, 8; Donald Davie, *A Gathered Church: The Literature of the English Dissenting Interest, 1700–1930* (1978), lectures 5, 6.

2. Of all Lambeth marriages in 1900, 7.5 percent were Nonconformist, but only 2 percent of the inmates of Lambeth's Poor Law institutions in 1899 (54 of 2760; who were the two Unitarians in the Renfrew Rd. Workhouse?) B-271, p. 47.

various Nonconformist denominations and chapels usually sprawled uncomfortably across significant class barriers.

In the early nineteenth century an ill-defined class of "artisans" dominated Nonconformity, and Alan Gilbert has suggested that the decline in Nonconformist recruitment in the nineteenth century reflected the disappearance of capitalist out-workers as distinct from factory operatives.[3] The prominence of shopkeepers and clerks in the Edwardian chapel suggests, however, that Nonconformity encompassed occupational groups which were expanding rather than disappearing in a mature industrial economy. At the top of the Dissenting hierarchy, wealthy patrons— merchants and industrialists—dominated many chapels. But Nonconformity was not in general the ideology of bosses and employers. Nonconformist preachers found their presence mildly embarrassing, and encountered serious difficulties in explaining how these men made it through the eye of the needle and into the local chapel. (The moderator of the Kent and Sussex Baptist Association, in his annual address to the delegates assembled at Folkestone in 1903, declared that "The Church of Jesus Christ is not much the better for all the millionaires in the world (except our treasurer).")[4] Denunciations of selfish employers who "grind their workpeople," although not so common as exhortations to the drunken poor, appear frequently in sermons, and wealthy "Christian employers" were thought to be an exceptional group.

As the Nonconformist minister lowered his gaze to other portions of the social hierarchy, his confusion became even worse, and this leads us to the conclusion that the socially significant fact about a Nonconformist was his indeterminate social status. A substantial proportion of the English people hovered near the boundary between middle class and working class, where "shiny-arsed clerks" faced the scorn of warehouse workmen as well as their social superiors. A wealthy shopkeeper might be stigmatized by the very word describing his occupation. Working-class Nonconformists associated with middle-class neighbors in chapel, a fraternity which could hardly strengthen and might dilute their

3. Gilbert, *Religion and Society*, pp. 63, 146.
4. *Kent and Sussex Baptist Association Annual Report*, 1903, p. 2.

own sense of social class. A Nonconformist might be aggressively class-conscious, but *as a Nonconformist* he conformed only obliquely to the English class structure. Clare Davies's father, a bankrupt Wesleyan tailor about to embark on a successful career as a commercial traveler in Lincolnshire, huffily denied that class distinctions applied to him at all,[5] and one gets the definite impression that he would have been happier in Indiana, where social classes are invisible.

All of this ambiguity about the Nonconformist position in society may be found in the sermons of one of Lambeth's influential Edwardian ministers, the Rev. Archibald G. Brown, minister of Chatsworth Road Baptist Church, West Norwood. His previous pastorate had been in the East End; even there his congregation had contained "no black eyes, shabby waterproofs or battered bonnets," but respectable "traders, mechanics, managers, foremen, overlookers and skilled mechanics, the very bone and sinew of the land." And he could be the spokesmen for these people against those below them: "the right of respectable people to go to sleep is apparently nothing compared with the right of drunken blackguards to keep them awake. . . . This is English liberty, the liberty of the debauched to make life intolerable for the sober and quiet."[6]

But he also spoke bitterly of the oppression of the poor: "I have heard the cry of oppression in England; I have heard it in the sweating dens; I have heard it from the women who work seventeen hours a day for 1s7d."[7] He expressed sympathy with the men during the 1889 dock strike, opposed free economic competition because it hurt the working classes, and advocated state directed trade education and emigration programs in the early nineties. Fifteen years later he preached a sermon at the Metropolitan Tabernacle on the crying need for hospitals for the poor, on the injustice of superior medical care for the rich.[8] Insisting

5. "There was a strong sense of class in my family despite my father who would snort 'rubbish' at any manifestation of it," C. S. Davies, *North Country Bred* (1963), p. 63.

6. G. H. Pike, *The Life and Work of Archibald G. Brown* (1892), pp. 29, 97, 115.

7. Archibald G. Brown, *God's Full Orbed Gospel: Sermons Preached at the Metropolitan Tabernacle* (1911), p. 104.

8. *Ibid.*, p. 15.

upon the poverty of his middle-class congregation, he frequently railed against the misdeeds of the wealthy.[9]

At the far end of the theological spectrum from Archibald Brown, John Clifford was the most influential Baptist leader at the turn of the century. Writing in 1906, Clifford divided British society into four social classes:

In the first class are the rich and well-to-do, the merchants, capitalists, the children of fortune. The second is made up of the ghastly procession of the criminal and vicious. In the third are the artisans, the mechanics, the labouring myriads. The fourth, bringing up the rear, are the poor and needy.[10]

Not surprisingly, he closely identified the work of Christ with the third class, "who fill the air with their denunciations and compel emperors and statesmen, philosophers and capitalists, to listen to their demands."[11] But where, in the sermons of either man, were ordinary middle-class inhabitants of villadom, neither wealthy, nor vicious, nor poor and not of the labouring myriads? The best a Nonconformist could do in describing himself socially was "neither pauper, prisoner, nor peer."[12]

This uncertainty provides a clue to the social functions of the chapel. The Nonconformist cultural tradition itself supplied a category of social definition which allowed a man, whether Durham coal miner or suburban clerk, to despise his betters. Eric Bligh, the son of a doctor in Tooting, recalls that "as a child I always thought that we, so middle class, were the only really aristocratic people in the place. In those days many rich people remained in the neighborhood, but I was entirely unmoved by their possessions. We were Dissenters, and went to chapel with the grocers and small tradespeople, but I was sure we could do all this with grace, and not become social delinquents. My father explained to me that most of the rich people went to church just to be seen there."[13] Kingsley Martin realized when

9. Archibald G. Brown, *Six Sermons Preached at Chatsworth Road Baptist Church, 1899–1902*, n.d., p. 11.

10. "The sphere of the church in the coming social regime," in C. Ensor Walters, ed., *The Social Mission of the Church* (1906), p. 51.

11. *Ibid.*, p. 50.

12. *Baptist Handbook*, 1908, p. 248.

13. Eric Bligh, *Tooting Corner* (1946), p. 117.

quite young that "Nonconformists had the compensation that God was on their side. This had made Puritans regard themselves as in some way superior persons. Nonconformists belonged to the army of the good; ultimately they must conquer."[14]

Whether born into Nonconformity, or converted in an evangelical revival, or attracted by the friendliness and philanthropy of the local chapel, a Nonconformist found himself within a subculture which reproduced itself, for the peculiarities of Nonconformists, often quite minor, set them apart from their neighbors and were handed on to their children. "I was taught never to mix with common children who might teach me naughty words," H. G. Wells wrote of his childhood in Bromley. "The Hoptons, the greengrocers family over the way, were 'rough' . . . the Mundays next door were Methodists who sang hymns out of Church which is almost as bad as singing songs in it."[15] V. S. Pritchett claimed that "Nonconformists often affected small changes of consonant, 'p' becoming 'b' and an 's' becoming a 'z.' "[16] These peculiarities, combined with a sense of superiority, naturally engendered a certain amount of mild hostility which in turn heightened the need for the consolations of Nonconformity. Louis Heren was taught to consider the Nonconformists a race apart in the East End of the 1920s: "the mutual antipathies of the Catholics and Protestants were constant, and the Nonconformists hardly ever spoke to anyone. They were a kind of Christian Jews in that they assumed an unspoken superiority over others. They also separated themselves. They went to chapel and not to the church. They were supposed not to smoke or drink, and they were said to be mean. A man could be dying outside their chapel, our mother used to say, and they would not give him the smell of an oil rag."[17]

Popular hostility to Nonconformity does not appear to have

14. Kingsley Martin, *Father Figures* (1966), p. 22.

15. H. G. Wells, *Experiment in Autobiography* (New York, 1934), p. 51.

16. V. S. Pritchett, *A Cab at the Door* (1971 ed.), p. 39; Sir Henry Fowler claimed to be able to detect Methodists from their pronunciation of the word "Wesley"; Edith Fowler, *Life of Henry Hartley Fowler, First Viscount Wolverhampton* (1912), p. 526; cf. Kenneth Lindley, *Chapels and Meeting Houses* (1969), p. 33: "Churches have a smell like old bookshops and damp rocks; chapels have a smell of pine, varnish, and wax polish."

17. Louis Heren, *Growing Up Poor in London* (1973), pp. 10–11.

been very intense except among the immediate targets of puritanicalism, such as pub-owners, and a kind of amused contempt or a light dismissal was more common than outright bitterness. Hostility was most intense among literary people, and popular hostility was reinforced by unflattering literary portrayals. Nonconformist laymen—as depicted in Robert Browning's "Christmas Eve" or Orwell's *The Clergyman's Daughter*—and Nonconformist ministers—in *The Pickwick Papers* and *Bleak House* or Winifred Holtby's *South Riding* (a best seller of the 1930s)—appear as ranting, canting, physically repulsive, narrow-souled hypocrites. Writers and critics from Matthew Arnold to E. P. Thompson have been unable to contain their indignation when considering Nonconformity, and their unbalanced assaults are reminiscent of unreasoning anti-Semitism. The literary popular front against Nonconformity has often wounded and bewildered Nonconformists and their children, who were on the whole gentle and mild-mannered people whose greatest sin was to assume that they were as good as anybody else. Hostility of this sort continued long after the end of formal legal disabilities, and helped to drive the Wesleyans into the arms of the other Nonconformist denominations by the last two decades of the nineteenth century.

All but a handful of Lambeth's Nonconformists were either Baptist, Congregationalist, Wesleyan, or other Methodist, and their common sense of "Nonconformist" identity was stronger between 1880 and 1914 than at any other time in history. But there were important social distinctions within Nonconformity which only partially coincide with denominational boundaries, and which help to explain the social functions of the chapel and the progressive obsolescence of Nonconformity in the twentieth century. Total Nonconformist chapel attendance in Lambeth, as a percentage of the population, fell about 13 percent between 1886 and 1902, but Baptist attendance fell by only 6 percent and Free and Primitive Methodist attendance grew by over 60 percent. The Congregationalists and Wesleyans accounted for most of the decline with real decreases of 22 and 31 percent respectively (see Table 16). Speaking very generally, the wealthier denominations declined most rapidly. Of Congregational, Wesleyan, and Presbyterian marriages in my Lambeth sample, 26 percent were from families in the registrar general's classes I and II; only 16 percent of Baptist, Free Methodist, and other Non-

conformist marriages were. Of the former group 12.3 percent
were from the families of unskilled and semi-skilled workers
(classes IV and V); 17.7 percent of the latter group (see Table 19).
Taken alone, these contrasts in patterns of decline and social
status would mean very little, but I am persuaded from an examination of more subjective evidence that denominational
boundaries partially illuminate and partially obscure the existence of two distinct but not entirely exclusive types of Nonconformity: the plebeian and the genteel. In ideology, attitude, and
tone, plebeian Nonconformity more clearly reflected the sense of
marginality found among those near the boundary line between
lower middle class and working class. Genteel or liberal Nonconformity reflected the ideals of a relatively affluent group of Nonconformist laymen who were attracted to liturgical services,
liberal preaching, "New Liberal" politics, and philanthropy.

1. Plebeian Nonconformity

Plebeian chapels were scattered about the borough, but they
were concentrated in Kennington, the only one of Lambeth's
four districts where Nonconformity increased its overall church
attendance as a percentage of the population between 1886 and
1902. Three Free Methodist, one Primitive Methodist, one Baptist,
and one plebeian Congregational chapel each grew dramatically,
and a new Primitive Methodist and a new plebeian Congregational chapel opened their doors for the first time in the nineties.
The members of these chapels came from both sides of the
middle-class/working-class social boundary: "respectable working
people and a few tradesmen," "nearly all railwaymen," "artisans,
mechanics, lower middle class, and some unskilled," "working
class, chiefly mechanics," "railway and post office men, clerks,
etc., able to keep themselves respectable on Sunday," "comfortable working people . . . the wealthiest being a glass manufacturer."[18]

Their expansive optimism puzzled outside observers, for it

18. Descriptions by ministers of: York Road Congregational Chapel, B-270,
p. 57; Railway Mission Hall, B-271, p. 211; Stockwell, Southville, and Miles
St. United Methodist Free Churches, B-271, p. 157; Old Baptist Union, B-304,
p. 123; Dugdale St. Baptist Chapel, B-303, p. 11; Reheboth Strict Baptist
Chapel, B-303, p. 127.

stood in sharp contrast to their unobtrusive demeanor and shabby houses of worship. The Railway Mission Hall was built into the garden of a house and reached through a narrow entry, and the Kennington Park Primitive Methodist Chapel was structurally overshadowed by the Anglo-Catholic Church of St. Agnes, heightening its sense of papal persecution.[19] The Plymouth Brethren in West Norwood worshipped in a room above a "dingy unattractive little shop where Mr. Putley dealt in tops, whistles, bleaching, and bundles of wood and coal in frugal portions for the poorer people."[20]

These chapels functioned as psychological mutual aid societies for the "little people" of Lambeth. The minister of the Lothian Road Congregational Chapel explained that "we are a feeble lot but we manage to exist."[21] Arthur George Golding, a carpenter and a pillar of the Gresham Road Baptist Church from 1888 to 1922, was described as "conscientious, honest, unobtrusive, and never known to say a cross word."[22] William Kent recalled one member of Wheatsheaf Hall, a basically illiterate railway guard mainly grateful that "the Lord had saved his soul"; the secretary of one of his Sunday Schools was a semi-literate stonemason who read only the Bible and the *Daily News*.[23] Richard Church's Congregational parents, "like most people at that time and in that walk of life, were grateful for small assurances: a safe job, a respectable anonymity, a local esteem. Outside that limit lay a dangerous unknown which included crime, genius, fame, notoriety, and exalted rank. All the people who came to our house (few and infrequent) were of this persuasion, unanimous in their social and moral quietism. Behind my own parents' acquiescence in this lay an element of mystery, revealed only occasionally by remarks and references, and by my father's perverse attitude toward the aristocracy and to all manifestations of ambition, or of pursuits larger than he could comprehend."[24]

The pastor of Chatsworth Road Baptist Chapel (like many

19. B-271, pp. 207, 197.
20. J. B. Wilson, *The Story of Norwood* (1973), p. 34.
21. B-303, p. 3.
22. BFP, 18 Aug. 1922.
23. William Kent, *Testament of a Victorian Youth* (1938), p. 31.
24. Richard Church, *Over the Bridge* (1955), pp. 135–36.

graduates of Spurgeon's College, an excellent preacher) articulated these feelings of powerlessness and insignificance in his sermons. Consider the objects of God's concern, he urged. "There is nothing particularly attractive about them. They possess no sparkling gifts. Somehow, they never attract attention. It is so with them all through life. In their school days, if there is a cricket match, there are eleven picked for this side, and eleven for that, but he is always left out. . . . He has opinions of his own, but nobody ever asks what they are. If he does speak nobody listens to him."[25] Comfort was the underlying theme of his sermons—God's help in times of trouble. God recognized the powerless.

Other Nonconformists recognized them as well. William Kent identified two types of chapel worker in South London: those who volunteered from a sense of duty and those who could earn no distinction elsewhere.[26] The chief worker at the South London Mission in Southwark was identified by Charles Booth's interviewer as a "grill cook in the City by present occupation (he began as a barman and has fought his way through a good many personal and industrial difficulties)."[27] He met his wife at the mission, and the two of them spent all of their spare time there. The mission hall was compensation for anonymity. William Kent described the consolations of Nonconformity in his family: "It was a common feeling among Nonconformist parents . . . that any child that had elected to proceed from the land of the unborn into their family had made the wisest choice possible, and was fortunate indeed. It was due to religious obsession, sectarian astigmatism, rather than a priggish pride in their own virtue. If there was a real danger of damnation it was obviously a cause for real gratitude to be born into such a family."[28]

This assurance was remedy for a sense of marginality or exclusion which could exist on either side of the middle-class/working-class boundary. The Chatsworth Road Chapel was comfortable by the standards of most plebeian chapels, dominated by middle-class managers, merchants in the city, etc. Their pastor

25. A. G. Brown, *Six Sermons*, p. 3.
26. Kent, *Testament*, pp. 31ff.
27. B-270, p. 207.
28. Kent, *Testament*, p. 27.

drew his illustrations from the world of commerce. Imagine a catastrophe, he suggested, "the trouble that strikes at the foundation of everything. . . . It is the sort of amazement a man would have if he heard that the doors of the Bank of England were shut because there was such a run on it. It is the style of stupefaction that there would be if when dividend day came around it was announced that there was no dividend to be paid on the consols this year . . . mountains carried into the sea. The impossible coming to pass."[29] At Wheatsheaf Hall or the Railway Mission Hall, where chapel members were frequently maimed or killed during their work on the London and South Western Railway, his illustrations would hardly have struck home. But a sense of marginality was no simple reflection of occupation; the middle-class Baptists of the Chatsworth Road and Kenyon chapels were very much aware of the higher status of their neighbors, and of neighboring churches and chapels. Chatsworth Road did not attract the wealthy. Kenyon Baptist Church had "City men, commercial travellers, and clerks," its pastor claimed, "but we scarcely touch Brixton Hill," a neighborhood still wealthy in 1899.[30] A deacon of the Gipsy Road Baptist Church ran into a storm of criticism from church members when he proposed the purchase of a large manse which would "raise our status and encourage the settlement of a pastor who would attract more wealthy members."[31] The membership argued that wealthy members would ruin the church, and the deacon was forced to argue for recruitment on evangelistic grounds: the wealthy were in particular need of grace.

The Spurgeonite Baptists, along with a handful of Plymouth Brethren, Strict Baptists, and independent Evangelicals, emphasized the crucial importance of a "rational" adherence to theological orthodoxy, and were hostile to overt political activity except in extraordinary circumstances. The Primitive and Free Methodists, plebeian Congregationalists, and non-Spurgeonite Baptists also emphasized individual conversion, but not ideological conformity. Their theology was a non-dogmatic come-to-Jesus

29. A. G. Brown, *Six Sermons*, p. 8.

30. B-304, p. 3.

31. Gipsy Road Baptist Church, West Norwood. Minutes of the Church Meeting, March 1928.

sort, their tone that of the older, slightly anti-intellectual "ecumenical evangelicalism" of the early nineteenth century, combined in some cases with an old-fashioned political radicalism focused on temperance and education.

But all of the plebeian chapels shared a contempt for certain forms of middle-class respectability, an almost compulsive informality, and an insistence upon the need for conversion. W. S. Caine, the patron of Wheatsheaf Hall, complained of dogmatic evangelicalism: "The curse of the Evangelicals is that they preach the blood of Christ and forget the Sermon on the Mount."[32] But in striking contrast to the more liberal Congregationalists, he insisted that "we have placed in the very forefront the need for personal conversion to God as the one foundation of success."[33] This concern for conversion contributed to the steady if unspectacular growth of the plebeian chapels.[34] Ministers complained that their emphasis upon conversion would have produced even more chapel growth if it had not contained the seeds of its own destruction. "Our success contributes to our failure," the minister of Upton Chapel claimed. "As our people are brought in and become thrifty they move away toward Clapham."[35] Ernest Aves, Booth's interviewer, checked the membership lists of the chapel, which contained the year of entry, for corroboration, and found that "the earlier names on the list were remoter addresses. It showed clearly that the new recruits were gained from the district, the outer move subsequent. . . . They lose a good-sized church every year and have to make it up."[36]

In fact, plebeian Nonconformity inculcated a kind of respectability which subsequently threatened the life of the chapel in more than one way. "When they are converted they give up drink," W. S. Caine asserted. "This adds 5/- to their wages and soon makes a difference in their appearance. Indeed it is a distinct

32. B-271, p. 17.

33. *Ibid.*

34. Claylands Congregational Chapel added 33 members in 1898 for a net gain of 8 (25 transferred out or died); Gresham Baptist Chapel baptized 20 in 1897, added 8 by profession of faith, and received 9 transfers for a net gain of 8 members (29 transferred out or died). B-303, p. 211; B-271, p. 125.

35. B-271, p. 9.

36. B-271, p. 27.

hindrance now that our people look such decent folk."[37] Respectability not only set the chapel folk off from their neighbors; if carried too far it threatened the life of the chapel itself as people began to "outgrow" the friendly informality of the life of the plebeian chapel. A Baptist minister—new to then suburban Brixton—complained that he "can't get people during the week. . . . In [inner] Lambeth people almost made the chapel their home but here the homes are comfortable and there is not the same necessity."[38] Neither the public house nor the chapel was necessary in the suburbs. After moving from the East End to West Norwood, Archibald Brown complained of the dull respectability of villadom: "What I miss is the working class—no artisans. Nothing between villadom and dirty poverty."[39] Brown responded to this problem with typical Spurgeonite ingenuity, and enforced a kind of compulsory informality with a strong dogmatic basis upon his respectable, middle-class congregation. Upon his arrival, he received anonymous letters warning him that "the methods of the East End" would not work in West Norwood, particularly week-night prayer meetings. But conversion-oriented preaching and doctrinaire informality worked—the chapel added five hundred members in three years. "People get respectable and lose their standing," Brown observed. "You never lose members through stress of poverty and hard work."[40] W. S. Caine, the political Nonconformist who complained of the evangelicals, agreed with the anti-political evangelical Brown on the dangers of suburban respectability. "The poor are much nearer religion than the rich," he wrote. "When the poor man wants to lead a new life he wants a new slate. He thinks that he is going to Hell. If you persuade him that he is forgiven, you have the clean slate and he can start afresh. Then he must have something to do."[41] Brown's middle-class Chatsworth Road Chapel and Caine's working-class Wheatsheaf Hall were both noted for friendliness and informality. A journalist visiting the

37. B-270, pp. 1, 7.
38. B-303, p. 147.
39. B-313, p. 5.
40. *Ibid.*
41. B-271, pp. 16–17.

former was struck with "the reception one meets with on entrance to the service as a stranger and finally on departure."[42] It was W. S. Caine, the reader may recall, who offended some Anglican neighbors when he urged the people of Kennington to come to his church, and "spit on the floor there if you like."[43]

2. Liberal Nonconformity

Anglicans were not the only ones offended by the friendly informality of the plebeian chapels. Many Nonconformists were as well. When William Kent moved from Wheatsheaf Hall to Brixton Independent Church in 1904, he left plebeian Nonconformity for another world. For eight years he worshipped at Brixton Independent, but hardly exchanged a word with anyone at the church except the pastor: "Sometimes I faltered when faced with the alternative of a good sermon and no handshake at Brixton Independent Church and a bad sermon and a handshake at Wheatsheaf Hall."[44] According to the Rev. Bernard Snell, Brixton Independent's pastor, "The shopkeeper class is scarcely touched; the people are rather civil servants, journalists, and theatrical people."[45] The church was described as "a gathering placed for educated people," "an accumulation of intellectual and cultured people," "intelligent and right-minded men and women."[46] Brixton Independent was the most distinguished of the wealthier Nonconformist chapels in Lambeth, mostly Congregationalist and Wesleyan: Roupell Park Wesleyan Church ("the members keep one or two servants, a few keep three"); Trinity Congregational Chapel (with a servant-keeping congregation earning £200 to £350 a year, some more); Brixton Hill Wesleyan Church ("most church members keep servants, many more than one"); Christ Church, Westminster Bridge Road; and Central Hills Baptist Church.[47] These chapels were solidly comfortable rather than wealthy, although each contained a few

42. BFP, 15 Nov. 1907.

43. B-272, p. 63.

44. Kent, *Testament*, p. 220.

45. B-303, p. 69.

46. Brixton Free Press, *Brixton's Churches* (1904), p. 216.

47. Comments of their respective ministers, B-313, p. 29; B-303, p. 57; B-304, p. 103.

wealthy members. What distinguished them from other chapels was their attitude toward prosperity, for they were of the "Congregational type" described by Charles Booth:

> With them prosperity and religion go hand in hand. This they readily recognize, thanking God for his good gifts, and praying that they may use them rightly for their own advantage and that of others. There is no trace of sourness or severity in their theories of life. Pleasure is not tabooed. The young are trusted and encouraged. Happiness is directly aimed at but is associated with the performance of duty: duty to themselves, and to each other, and in various ways to the world around. Their pastors preach this ideal and boldly act up to it. They use their churches without hesitation for any purpose which is not actually irreligious.[48]

Liberal Nonconformity seems the reverse image of plebeian Nonconformity: liturgical services, a reserved formality, education rather than conversion, practical ethics rather than salvation by faith. Why?

John Ruskin attended a South London chapel much earlier in the nineteenth century, and his response, although an extreme case, throws some light on the subsequent development of South London Nonconformity:

> Dr. Andrews's was the Londonian chapel in its perfect type, definable as accurately as a Roman Basilica—an oblong, flat ceiled barn, lighted by windows with semi-circular heads, brick arched, filled by small-paned glass held by iron bars, like fine-threaded halves of cobwebs; galleries propped on iron pipes, up both sides; pews, well shut in, each of them, by partition of plain deal, and neatly brass latched deal doors, filling the barn floor, all but its two lateral straw-matted passages; pulpit, sublimely isolated, central from sides and clear of altar rails at end; a stout, four-legged box of well-groined wainscot; high as the level of front galleries, and decorated with a cushion of crimson velvet, padded six inches thick, with gold tassels at the corners. . . . Imagine the change between one Sunday and the next—from morning service in this building, attended by the families of small shopkeepers of the Walworth Road, in their Sunday trimmings (our plumber's wife, fat, good, sensible Mrs. Good, sat in the next pew in front of us sternly sensitive to the interruption of her devotion by our late arrival), fancy the change from this, to high mass in Rouen Cathedral, its nave filled by the white-capped peasantry of half Normandy.[49]

48. Booth, *Life and Labour,* ser. 3, vol. 1, pp. 121–22.

49. John Ruskin, *Praeterita* (1949 ed.), p. 121.

As Nonconformists became wealthier and more thoroughly integrated into English society in the nineteenth century, many of them went through a similar, although milder and attenuated, response to the "Londonian chapel." When the trustees of Surrey Chapel began to lay plans for a new chapel in Lambeth in the 1870s, their minister wrote to Ruskin and asked his advice about a suitable design. Ruskin only berated him for wishing to build a church at all (Nonconformity's critics were hard to please), but an enormous neo-Gothic structure was completed in 1876 despite that advice.[50] Charles Booth described it as "a great and successful attempt to adapt Gothic architecture to the Congregational ideal,"[51] and it boasted the third largest Congregationalist attendance in all of London in 1902 with 752 worshippers at the morning service and 1294 in the evening. Their services would not have been mistaken for those of Rouen Cathedral (the congregation's radicalism was evident in prayers offered for the American president as well as for the Queen, and in the masonry of the spire which was "relieved by two groups of inwrought red stone bands interspersed with rows of stars symbolic of the American stars and stripes.")[52] But the service was thoroughly liturgical, with chanted kyrie and psalms and, in the evening, a sung magnificat and nunc dimittis (from the Book of Common Prayer).[53] Other liberal chapels followed suit. Brixton Hill Wesleyan Chapel used the Book of Common Prayer in the morning service, and Trinity Congregational Chapel used the King's Weigh House liturgy of Thomas Hunter in 1900 with a paid choir and chanted psalms.[54] Central Hills Baptist Church used its own hymnal and prayer book with five orders of morning service which included sung responses, chants, and collects.[55]

Some chapels had always used liturgical forms, even in the early nineteenth century, but they became more common in the last two decades of the century and it was generally agreed that a formal liturgy was for the prosperous. "When Lambeth

50. Christopher Newman Hall, *Autobiography* (1898), pp. 316–18.

51. Booth, *Life and Labour*, ser. 3, vol. 4, p. 32.

52. A-47, p. 2; *Survey of London*, vol. 23, (1951), p. 73.

53. B-271, p. 83.

54. B-304, p. 103; B-303, p. 55.

55. *Upper Norwood Central Hills Baptist Church Hymnal* (1899).

[Wesleyan Chapel] was prosperous there had been a liturgical
service in the morning, but when it became poor the church became a mission and this service was abandoned."[56] Roupell Park
Wesleyan Chapel, in the suburbs, attracted Anglicans who objected to the doctrine of the local Anglo-Catholic parish of All
Saints, Rosendale Road, but still wished to attend liturgical
services; others "who do not find Roupell Park lively enough"
were sent off to the mission hall on Dulwich Road.[57] F. B. Meyer
catered to both sorts of Nonconformist at Christ Church, Westminster Bridge Road, in 1900. In the regular morning liturgical
services, "he was the ecclesiastic, growing each year more ethereal
and refined until he bore a curious resemblance to Cardinal
Manning." At the Pleasant Sunday Afternoon service, he was "the
bluff and cheerful 'skipper' " who expected the congregation, each
of them called "brother," to repair to one of two corners of the
room—the "teetotal corner" if he wished to sign the pledge or
the "consecration corner" if he wished to become a Christian.[58]

Meyer confined these activities to the afternoon service in order
to avoid offending the morning congregation, for liberal Nonconformists, like their Anglican neighbors, found the process of
conversion distasteful and the tactics of the conversionists vulgar.
This was related, in turn, to their preference for a theological
liberalism with its emphasis upon a gradual process of socialization rather than conversion, and its rejection of any kind of
radical dichotomy between the natural and the supernatural or
between this world and the next. Lambeth was an early center
of Victorian theological liberalism. The Doulton family persuaded Baldwin Brown to become minister of Claylands Congregational Chapel in 1845; both minister and congregation
migrated to the new Brixton Independent Church in 1870. This
new church, designed as a preaching center for Brown, was packed
for special sermons such as "The Doctrine of Annihilation" which
elucidated his rather timid universalism.[59] Another Brixton
minister, Arthur Mursell of Stockwell Baptist Chapel, partici-

56. Thomas Tiplady, *Spiritual Adventure: The Story of the "Ideal" Film
Service* (1935), p. 36.

57. B-313, pp. 29–31.

58. W. Y. Fullerton, *F. B. Meyer: A Biography* (n.d.), p. 111; B-271, p. 81.

59. Elizabeth B. Brown, *In Memoriam: James Baldwin Brown, Minister of
Brixton Independent Church* (1884), p. 20.

pated in a conference on "conditional immortality" at the Connor Street Hotel in 1876 and declared that the doctrine of Hell was a weapon in the hands of secularists.[60]

When Hell was abolished, conversion became less urgent. But the doctrine of Hell, although causing a great deal of psychological anguish among a certain number of individuals, does not seem to have played a large role in the emergence of liberal Nonconformity (it does not appear to have been a very popular doctrine with conservative or evangelical congregations either; it was, on the whole, ignored). The most important debate concerned the character of God's work in the world. In a symposium in *The Nineteenth Century* in 1877, Brown asserted that the life of the future was of the same character as life in the present—continuous with the growth of Christian society.[61] He consistently identified the growth of the Kingdom of God with the growing prevalence of Christian ethics. Furthermore, the laws of God were revealed to man through the use of his rational faculties, not through supernatural revelation. Brown urged his readers to "let the light of reason play upon Revelation . . . to find the true harmony of the written word with the laws of man's nature, with the constitution of society, with the order of creation, and with the testimony of history."[62] The Christian life was reduced to a life of ethical rationalism; a reasonable man could align himself with God's laws through the study of scripture, society, nature, and history. Consequently, everyday behavior was far more important than any kind of conversion experience. S. A. Tipple, the minister of Central Hills Baptist Church, supplied an intelligent summary of his own liberalism to Ernest Aves in 1900:

> Over the last fifty years the abstruse in theology has been largely displaced by the welfare of man . . . questions of education, benevolence, reform, liberty, labour, home life, had arisen, and had consigned to obscurity the comparatively useless themes and speculations of our forefathers. . . . The conviction in the past was that the great essential to salvation was correct belief, which tended in a large measure to con-

60. Geoffrey Rowell, *Hell and the Victorians* (1974), pp. 203–4.

61. *The Nineteenth Century,* vol. 2, pp. 511–17 (Oct. 1877); Rowell, *Hell,* p. 137.

62. E. B. Brown, *In Memoriam*, p. 24.

duct being deemed of less importance than it was in the present time. They ocupied themselves less today in talking of other people's correctness of belief, and they were [now] more capable of appreciating and esteeming those whom they considered sadly in error. Their charity was greater. If that meant, as some might suggest, somewhat less sureness, he would rather have the greater charity and somewhat less sureness, for he believed that in loving was the whole law fulfilled.[63]

There is a good deal to pity in his complacency, and a good deal to object to in his smugness. One of the least attractive aspects of late nineteenth-century Nonconformist liberalism is its condescension toward its own Nonconformist intellectual heritage, and to neighboring chapels which had the misfortune to be less "advanced." It is quite obvious that one of the psychological components of theological liberalism was the comfortable suburbanite's dislike of being called sinful. When the Torrey-Alexander revivalistic crusade came to Brixton in 1905, Bernard Snell of Brixton Independent Church wrote to the local press:

I think it was an entirely gratuitous piece of impertinence to bring such played out fallacies into an intelligent district like Brixton. Brixton has manifested considerable intelligence in not being vastly perturbed by the intrusion of well meaning but ill-equipped proselytism. Surely our neighborhood has done nothing to deserve the arrogant strictures of splenetic guests who misinterpret the hospitality that was extended to them.[64]

Torrey's message of conversion, he declared, "belonged to the Dark Ages that produced it, and not to this enlightened age . . . it was incompatible with the Sermon on the Mount."[65] There are many excellent objections to simplistic popular revivalism, and Snell touched upon some of them. Although the same cannot be said of all of their followers, most late nineteenth-century popular evangelists lacked a social conscience, and their version of Christianity was defective in other ways as well. But the tone of Snell's argument is unmistakable: the good citizens of Brixton, he believed, had made excellent progress toward meeting the standards of behavior outlined in the Sermon on the Mount through the sheer exercise of their superior intelligence. In his way, Snell was

63. B-315, p. 117.
64. SLP, 10 June 1905.
65. BFP, 9 June 1905.

as blind to the meaning of the Christian doctrine of sin as the popular revivalists who so offended him.

This said, it is necessary to offer an explanation of liberal Nonconformist attitudes which is also, in its way, a defense of them. Nonconformists themselves have taken the lead, since the "Genevan revival" of the 1930s, in charging late Victorian Dissenters and even Methodists of betraying their own religious heritage.[66] But liberal Nonconformity was more than a mere legitimation of suburban smugness; it was more than sentimentalism; it was more than political belligerence. Nonconformity was most threatened, as the plebeian Nonconformists realized, among the middle and upper-middle classes where "pleasure is not tabooed [and] happiness directly aimed at." Liberal Nonconformists paid little attention to the problems of recruitment, and most of them appear to have been born into the chapel. In their liturgical services and theological liberalism, these men and women were struggling to make sense of their parents' beliefs and make a version of them comprehensible for their own children. Plebeian Nonconformity was too vulgar, and the practical alternatives to liberal Nonconformity were the Church of England, outright secularism, a sort of high-minded Deism, and complete religious apathy.

Furthermore, the liberal Nonconformists were in at least two respects squarely within the "High Dissenting" tradition so admired by the dwindling band of twentieth-century Dissenting scholars: their staunchly intellectual sermons and their advocacy of political and social reform. Hostility to traditional theology and to what we now call "fundamentalism" did not reflect anti-intellectualism. Having outgrown Wheatsheaf Hall, William Kent found the "Christian agnosticism" of Brixton Independent's Bernard Snell "a new revelation."[67] (Snell often told the story of

66. See John Webster Grant, *Free Churchmanship in England 1870–1940* (1955); Nathaniel Micklem, *The Box and the Puppets 1888–1953* (1957); Micklem's obituary in *The Times,* 29 Dec. 1976; Davie, *A Gathered Church.* Neither Grant nor Davie understands the close relationship between theological liberalism and liturgical worship in turn-of-the-century Dissent; cf. John Kent, "Hugh Price Hughes and the Nonconformist Conscience," in G. V. Bennett and J. D. Walsh, eds., *Essays in Modern English Church History* (1966).

67. Kent, *Testament,* p. 212.

a man who prayed at a revival meeting: "Oh, Lord, save us from the evils of modern thought—yea, Lord, save us from all thought.")[68] Havelock Ellis, born into an Anglican family in Wandsworth, attended Brixton Independent in the 1870s and regarded himself as a disciple of Baldwin Brown, Snell's predecessor, and both Brown and Snell were generally thought to be in the vanguard of modern Progressive thought with their ethical reinterpretations of Christianity.[69]

S. A. Tipple preached at Central Hills Baptist Church for over half a century. "I believe," Eric Bligh wrote, "that he had a reputation as select, if not so widespread, as that of any of the great preachers in that second great age of the English sermon, for if you went to hear Liddon, you also went, if you were untrammeled enough to enter a chapel, to hear Mr. Tipple. Decade upon decade this frail and altogether charming man held forth in the little chapel which had been built for a hotter gospel, and people would make long journeys to yield themselves to his silvery spell."[70] William Kent was also impressed:

A short, lithe patriarchal figure with white beard, standing out strongly contrasted against the dark curtain behind, will never be forgotten by us. The small quiet church, the creepers with which its exterior were covered, topping gently against the windows, and allowing the light with difficulty to pierce through, all helped to make the time spent there precious and sacred. He was not afraid of silence, there was no irreverent hurry, there was always a pause of two or three minutes before he rose to invoke the divine blessing or sermon which, though disconcerting to a newcomer, was soon appreciated.[71]

According to Ernest Aves, "The sole question to which Mr. Tipple had devoted himself all these years was—What is truth?— and what he had seen and found he had declared unto them without fear."[72]

These ministers marked Lambeth's political as well as its intellectual vanguard. Christ Church, Westminster Bridge Road,

68. Kent, *Testament*, p. 216.

69. Havelock Ellis, *My Life* (1940), pp. 63ff.

70. Bligh, *Tooting Corner*, p. 54.

71. Kent, *Testament*, p. 211.

72. B-315, p. 117; see S. A. Tipple, *Sunday Mornings at Norwood: Prayers and Sermons* (1895).

was a center of radicalism in the late Victorian decades under Newman Hall, and Brixton Independent Church was the central institution of Lambeth's Edwardian Progressivism.[73] On "Citizen Sunday" in 1900, when the neighboring parish church of St. Matthew was decorated with flags in honor of the City Imperial Volunteers, churchgoers at Brixton Independent heard the Rev. Bernard Snell explain the identity of religion and politics, denounce those who exploit the London housing market, and demand the establishment of a Fair Rent Court in Lambeth.[74] In 1905 the mayor and councillors of Lambeth worshipped at Brixton Independent, and Snell took the opportunity to explain to them that unemployment was the inevitable result of a society where goods were produced for profit rather than the good of the community, that this situation should be changed, and that in the meantime the unemployed must be assisted without the stigma of pauperism.[75]

The achievements of liberal Nonconformity were no more appreciated in their day than they have been since. It is difficult to imagine a stronger contrast than that of S. A. Tipple or Baldwin Brown (both of whom began preaching in the 1840s) with Chadband and Stiggins. Yet the popular image of a Nonconformist minister remained that of a ranting, canting hypocrite, and Nonconformists have yet to recover from the unbalanced portrayals by the major Victorian literary figures. Even after Nonconformist civil disabilities had been largely eliminated, the liberal Nonconformists' resentment of the Church of England and the upper classes was nurtured by an intense desire to be recognized for what they were. Born into Nonconformity, they had remade it in their own image. Were their chapels not, in every way, as desirable and attractive as the neighboring parish churches? "Are they Christians?" the Rev. F. B. Meyer asked. "So are we. Are they Churchmen? So are we. Are they ministers of Christ? So are we—in labours as abundant; in prisons more frequent; in weariness and painfulness; in watchings often; in hunger and in thirst. We are members one of another. Without

73. See J. C. Carlile, *My Life's Little Day,* p. 16, on the political influence of Newman Hall.

74. BFP, 2 Nov. 1900.

75. BFP, 20 Oct. 1905.

us the Established Church cannot be made perfect."[76] In 1917 Bernard Snell was invited to address Brixton's Anglican Brotherhood, where he declared himself a "non-conforming member of the Church of England" and complained that in his twenty-seven years as minister in Brixton this was his first invitation to speak at any event connected with the parish church.[77] This resentment had become more intense as Nonconformists freed themselves of civil disabilities and achieved a greater degree of affluence. After the turn of the century, it fueled the flames of the Edwardian Liberal revival.

3. Nonconformity and the New Liberalism

Nonconformists of all varieties were deeply involved in politics, and it is difficult to understand Nonconformity without some understanding of the significance of that involvement. They had traditionally been involved in commercial and industrial pursuits. But as Victorian Nonconformity grew in both wealth and culture, even plebeian Nonconformists found themselves engaged in a wider range of activities beyond the chapel walls: philanthropy, education, local government, and politics among others. Some of these activities were of a quasi-religious nature, and required the construction of institutions more suited to specific tasks than the chapel or meeting house or local society.

Specialized interdenominational philanthropic and educational societies proliferated throughout the nineteenth century. Unlike those under the control of the clergyman, which usually respected parish boundaries and the authority of the incumbent, at least in principle, these institutions usually ignored the local chapel. The mission hall movement itself, for instance, and its associated network of philanthropies, was only partially under the control of the local chapel, which shared responsibility with organizations like the London City Mission. In 1910 the Free Church Yearbook published an ambitious but revealing list of one hundred eighty-eight societies (exclusive of purely denominational societies) which they thought deserving of Nonconformist support. This list was designed to provide opportunities for every

76. Fullerton, *F. B. Meyer*, p. 88.
77. BFP, 30 Nov. 1917.

variety of Nonconformist from the sabbatarian to the socialist, and classified these voluntary societies into seventeen categories: children (26), temperance (23), "social services and science" (15), land and allotments (11), native races (10), social purity (9), education (8), housing (6), peace and arbitration (6), Sunday observance (5), prisons and crime (5), health (5), emigration (3), "charity" (2), local government (2), and two miscellaneous categories which included, among others, women's rights, anti-vivisectionist, and evangelistic societies.[78]

The various denominational bureaucracies were, in their way, merely another variety of organization created to meet specific needs. By the 1790s the Wesleyans had equipped themselves with a very efficient national denominational structure, and the Baptists and Congregationalists followed suit in the early and middle nineteenth century. But these bureaucracies were never very effective vehicles for anything other than the specific tasks for which they were established: ecclesiastical housekeeping and the maintenance of ministerial standards, stipends, and morale. In the late nineteenth century numerous Nonconformists dreamed of creating another organization which would allow Nonconformists to be a "force in the land" in some undefined way. In 1892 the Quaker cocoa magnate George Cadbury, enamored of the ideal of "free church unity," helped to organize the Birmingham Free Church Council, which was composed of 154 "free church parishes," i.e., neighborhood associations of Nonconformist congregations from every denomination. He was so enthusiastic about the prospects of creating a national, united, Nonconformist "counter-church," of voluntarily cooperating but autonomous congregations and local councils, that he paid for the preparation of one hundred maps of Free Church parishes in other towns and cities, and became a tireless campaigner for "the parish ideal." These local Free Church Councils were loosely related to the National Free Church Council founded in 1896. But what were they to do?

By the turn of the century the Central South London Free Church Council was one of six hundred local councils in England and Wales. Before their complete politicization during the struggle to repeal the 1902 Education Act, the emphasis in the

78. *Free Church Yearbook*, 1910, pp. 292–97.

local councils varied greatly. Some focused on politics from the first (to Cadbury's dismay), others on evangelism, others on philanthropy, others on social reform. In Lambeth and Southwark, the Central South London Free Church Council specialized in the persecution of publicans and prostitutes.

In some of Lambeth's liberal chapels, where pleasure was not tabooed, Dissenting puritanicalism was regarded with some embarrassment. If pleasure had ever been taboo among Nonconformists, the prohibition had withered by the turn of the century when the chapels provided dozens of cricket clubs for the public. But puritanicalism (an ugly but unavoidable word) was very much a part of the Nonconformist cultural tradition, and liberal Nonconformists continued to be sympathetic to, or at least mute in the face of, assaults upon sabbath violators, brothel-keepers, and the drink trade. The outsiders who reduced the Nonconformist Conscience to a narrow-minded puritanicalism may be excused for their error, for Nonconformity was at its most aggressive between 1890 and 1910. Sometimes instead of merely persuading their neighbors, they bullied them.

On New Year's Day, 1898, the citizens of North Lambeth found at their doors a pamphlet entitled *New Year's Greetings to the Working Men and Women of South London*. This "greeting" from the fifteen ministers of the largely plebeian Central South London Free Church Council (their pictures printed prominently inside) was in fact an exhortation and, to some, a threat:

> Why not start the New Year with a resolution not to enter a public house or send for drink? Why not determine that no bad language shall pass your lips? Why not make up your minds that the betting tout shall get none of your money? . . . Let us rebuke bad language when we hear it. Let us tell the newspaper shops that we will not deal with them if they display indecent prints or sell our boys penny dreadfuls. Let us remonstrate with publicans when we see them selling liquor to those who are already drunk. Let us make it hot for houses of ill-fame, watching them and informing the police.[79]

Nonconformists had formerly been persecuted by the magistrates, but now they were employing them against their own enemies.

79. *New Year's Greetings to the Working Men and Women of South London* (1898), p. 5.

This council employed a full-time agent and spent over £500 a year to employ additional "watchers and witnesses" who supplied evidence against keepers of disorderly houses and publicans. By October of 1899 they claimed 143 prosecutions and 123 convictions, and had been sued for damages by a woman falsely arrested after a case of mistaken identity by one of their "watchers."[80] The hostility engendered on selected slum streets may well be imagined.

To many people, this was the "Nonconformist Conscience" of the late nineteenth century. But it is more complicated than that, for there were other dimensions to the Nonconformist Conscience which were equally important. The Nonconformist Conscience compelled chapel people to help the poor by thousands of individual acts of charity. The guiding light of the Central South London Free Church Council was F. B. Meyer, minister of Christ Church, Westminster Bridge Road, where Charles Chaplin's mother found refuge in her struggles with poverty and insanity. The Nonconformist Conscience compelled some chapel people to go beyond "mere philanthropy" to what they called social reform, to insist upon a regeneration of British society through positive voluntary and legislative action which would guarantee fairness and justice for everyone in England, rich or poor. They resorted, not to mere persuasion to achieve their goals, but to politics, and they set the terms of the political debate in Lambeth between 1890 and 1910.

The role of Nonconformity in late nineteenth- and early twentieth-century radicalism has been misunderstood in part because Nonconformists have been the victims of a convenient historiographical convention: the distinction between the "Old Liberalism" and the "New Liberalism." Until recently, Nonconformists were portrayed as doomed members of a Liberal tradition which was essentially Gladstonian.[81] According to the revisionist views of P. F. Clarke, H. V. Emy, Michael Freeden, and others, a "new" radicalism emerged in the 1890s and after; its theorists—J. H. Hobson, L. T. Hobhouse, C. F. G. Masterman,

80. B-273, pp. 111–13; B-270, pp. 35–37.

81. See Paul Thompson, *Socialists, Liberals and Labour: The Struggle for London* (1967); various books by H. Pelling.

W. H. Beveridge—concentrated upon economic issues and social reform rather than the "status" issues of the "old" radicalism such as civil equality, land, temperance, and education. These New Liberal thinkers looked upon Nonconformists as an obsolete but noisy Old Liberal status group, struggling for the redress of barely visible grievances, diverting the Liberal Party from its mission of "regenerative" social reform. Historians have agreed with them, and interpreted Nonconformist political activity as primarily a matter of sectarian self-assertion.[82] The one historian to deal with those Nonconformists who advocated social reform concluded that they were under the sway of "outside influences."[83]

The Old Liberal/New Liberal distinction, although useful for some purposes, contributes little to our understanding of the social importance of South London Nonconformity between 1885 and 1914. The furor over the 1902 Education Act confuses the issue, for this classically "old" status issue temporarily united every variety of Nonconformist behind the Liberal Party. But within Nonconformity itself there was a tradition of social radicalism which dated from the 1840s if not earlier, and which did more than anything else to shape the Progressive coalition in Lambeth politics in the years before World War I. This social radicalism became more prominent within Nonconformity after 1880, and it is related to the changing character of the activities of Nonconformist laymen beyond the walls of the chapel and

82. See P. F. Clarke, *Lancashire and the New Liberalism* (Cambridge, 1971); "The Progressive Movement in England," *Transactions of the Royal Historical Society*, 5th ser., vol. 24, 1974, pp. 159–82; *Liberals and Social Democrats* (1978); E. V. Emy, *Liberals, Radicals, and Social Politics, 1892–1914* (1973); Nonconformity is generally identified with the "old" radicalism in the articles in Anthony A. J. Morris, ed., *Edwardian Radicalism 1900–1914* (1974), and Kenneth D. Brown, *Essays in Anti-Labour History: Responses to the Rise of the Labour Movement in England* (1974). Michael Freeden, in *The New Liberalism* (1978), pp. 15–16, confuses what he calls "Nonconformism" with Evangelicalism, and denies that it was of any relevance to the "New Liberalism." Stephen Koss, in *Nonconformity in Modern British Politics* (1975), has elegantly demonstrated that many prominent Nonconformists were active in national politics, but makes no distinction between those who were collectivist social radicals and those who were merely Nonconformist "interest group" politicians.

83. K. S. Inglis, *Churches and the Working Classes in Victorian England* (1963), pp. 306–7.

outside the religious or quasi-religious interdenominational societies, denominational bureaucracies, and Free Church Councils.

Nonconformist laymen thought of themselves as, in some sense, God's agents in the world. They were doing God's work. But where did God's work begin, and where did it end? Never very happy with the distinction between the sacred and the secular, Dissenters and Methodists had for long applied the notion of a "calling" to their secular occupations—their vocations. (English examples documented by Weber provided much of the evidence for his "Protestant Ethic" thesis.) But in the late nineteenth century, Lambeth Nonconformists engaged in much more than "work" or "trade": local education with its associated politics after 1870; parliamentary politics and its associated constituency organizations after the redrawing of constituency boundaries in 1885; the London County Council after 1890; the newly reconstituted Borough of Lambeth after 1900. Some Nonconformists even found their way into the magistracy under Liberal governments. More Nonconformists were involved in politics and local government than ever before, and more and more of them discovered a "calling" in politics rather than in trade.

Lambeth was a solidly Liberal parliamentary constituency before the redistribution of seats in 1885, and Nonconformist or Nonconformist-supported patrons generally felt confident of effortless election and reelection. When Fredric Doulton retired in 1868 his seat was taken by Sir William McArthur, who subsequently received the active support of Lambeth's prominent ministers such as Newman Hall, Baldwin Brown, and James Guiness Rogers. But this situation changed dramatically in 1885, when the Conservatives swept all four of the newly created parliamentary seats within the boundaries of the parish (later the Borough) of Lambeth, a triumph which was repeated in 1886. Although the Liberals regained much lost ground, the suburban Norwood constituency returned a Conservative M.P. at every general election until 1945. In Lambeth, as in urban England generally, the Conservative Party became the natural political party of suburban householders. In the suburbs, Nonconformists appear to have been the only outspoken Liberal electors, and even chapel folk were not immune to the Tory trend. In the working-class wards of Kennington and Lambeth, however, and the mixed neighborhoods of Brixton, working-class electors voted for Nonconformist Progressive politicians in both local and national contests. Politics was becoming, to all appearances, class-based, and the political rhetoric of the Conservatives became a scarcely disguised appeal to middle-class anxieties.[84]

The class-based politics of the twentieth century is often thought to have displaced a status-based nineteenth-century politics of religion and ethnicity. But the emergence of class-based political conflict in Lambeth, which was intensified even more by the polarization of the London County Council into Progressive and Moderate parties in the 1890s, had the paradoxical effect of magnifying the importance of Lambeth's churches and chapels. Both church and chapel were, in theory, above partisan politics. But the traditional, informal link between the Conservative Party and the church not only survived the transition to a more popular form of largely class-based politics, it was reinforced. Most Anglican churchgoers were in the natural Tory constituency of middle-class ratepayers, and Tory politicians thought that they could win votes by defending the church against the intemperate attacks of Nonconformists, who were thought to be mostly Liberal anyway. However, because the church was officially neutral—it was after all a National Church —Anglicans cheerfully tolerated and even publicized prominent exceptions to the informal alignment of religion and politics. The public enjoyed reading about "radical parsons" or "socialist parsons" such as the Rev. W. A. Morris of St. Anne's, South Lambeth, who was known as the "gasworkers' parson" because of his advocacy of the strikers' cause at the gasworks in his parish.[85] The Rev. A. J. Waldron, vicar of St. Matthew's, Brixton, from 1906 to 1914, strenuously advocated the radical and Progressive cause in local politics without alienating his upper middle-class parishioners. The secret, he claimed, was to keep politics out of the pulpit. "Not a single layman of my church is a Liberal, and they all say I have never alienated anyone by the

84. These changes are discussed in more detail in my dissertation, "The Social Origins of the Decline of Religion in England, 1880–1930," Harvard Univ., 1978, pp. 445–79.
85. B-272, p. 155.

preaching of party politics."[86] Some had left, he admitted, because of his campaigning outside the church, but most simply smiled and claimed that he was "too idealistic."

These exceptions were classified under the heading of "clerical eccentricity." A parish church without a single Liberal layman was unlikely to produce very many active, Liberal local politicians. It is not surprising to find that Brixton's Moderate (i.e., Conservative) candidates for the Lambeth Borough Council in 1900 were John James Chapman, solicitor and a churchwarden at St. John the Divine, Kennington; James Edward Clark, tradesman and churchwarden of St. John's, Clapham; and J. N. Wyeth, churchwarden of St. John's, Angell Town.[87] Neither is it surprising to find that the Moderate Party used the parochial hall of St. John the Divine, Kennington, and the mission hall of St. Paul's, West Brixton, for election meetings that year.[88] W. H. Kidson, a chartered accountant who was Conservative agent for Brixton from 1885 to 1900, also served as a churchwarden of St. John the Divine, Kennington. At his funeral in 1900 wreaths were sent from the Lambeth Carlton Club, the Primrose League, and the Avondale Lodge Freemasons.[89] The first two, and possibly the third, were part of an informal network of institutions assumed to be Conservative which also included the South London Licensed Victuallers and Beersellers Trade Protection Association, church schools, Anglican philanthropic institutions, and a number of working-class Unionist drinking clubs which seemed to spring up after 1900 in response to the Socialist threat.[90] Most Conservative local politicians belonged to the Lambeth Carlton Bowling Club, and the Carlton Club sent tickets for its annual Christmas dinner for the poor to local clergymen.[91] The Lambeth Savings Bank, an Anglican institu-

86. BFP, 21 April 1911. By 1914 he had left the Liberal Party over Welsh disestablishment and Irish home rule.

87. BFP, 26 Oct. 1900.

88. BFP, 20 and 26 Feb. 1904. Lord Salisbury addressed a rally at St. John the Divine parochial hall which featured an attack upon the Baptist leaders John Clifford and T. H. Spurgeon by a local Moderate L.C.C. candidate.

89. SLP, 31 March 1900.

90. BFP, 5 April 1907, 4 May 1908.

91. SLP, 29 Dec. 1900.

tion, had two Conservative M.P.s as trustees as well as the rector of Lambeth.[92]

The church connection caused some problems for the Conservatives (or Moderates, as they were known in local politics). The Church of England Temperance Society was unusually well organized in Lambeth largely because of the tireless efforts of C. E. Tritton, an Anglican patron and Conservative M.P. for Norwood. But the interests of the CETS occasionally clashed with those of the South London Licensed Victuallers and Beersellers Trade Protection Association and some of its clerical admirers, who thought in terms of a sentimental alliance between "village pub and village church" (a minority view among Lambeth clergymen, and one that was adopted, I suspect, largely in order to irritate Dissenters).[93] Furthermore, squabbling among Anglicans over the spread of ritualism may have led to a Liberal victory in Brixton in the 1906 general election.[94] But the Moderates contended with fewer fratricidal conflicts and schisms than the Liberals largely because their program was straightforwardly reactionary. They did not propose to do anything except defend the British Empire overseas and resist the demands of a motley crew of lunatics at home: "faddist" temperance fanatics who promoted "old-womanish interference with the rights of amusement caterers and such like";[95] Progressive borough councillors who were barely disguised socialists; softhearted humanitarians on the Board of Guardians and London County Council who wanted to extend out-relief to the poor and put working-class housing in respectable Brixton; the "scurrilous, psalm-singing, canting hypocrites," in the words of one Moderate candidate, who attack the Church of England.[96] Sir Robert Mowbray thanked the electors of Brixton for returning him to Parliament unopposed in 1900 and reassured them that "he did not believe in

92. SLP, 11 April 1903.

93. See Cox, "Social Origins," pp. 453–55, on disagreement among South London clergymen over the proper attitude to take toward publicans.

94. See Cox, "Social Origins," pp. 456–57.

95. BFP, 21 Sept. 1900, editorial.

96. BFP, 1 March 1907, reference to Walter Hobbs, minister of Gipsy Rd. Baptist Tabernacle, West Norwood.

great political changes."[97] In 1901 Brixton's Moderate candidate for the London County Council announced that he saw "no burning question in Brixton for the L.C.C. to deal with—no housing question, no street improvement question, no dock question."[98]

Lambeth's Progressives (as they were called from the mid-nineties) struggled against the fissiparous tendencies of an extremely diverse political coalition of overlapping groups of Nonconformists (themselves divided on many issues), temperance advocates (Nonconformist, Anglican, and secular varieties), Gladstonian Liberal patrons, secularist radicals, a few reformers with no interest in religion at all, and Labour (represented by the Lambeth and Brixton Trades Councils). This coalition had been a fragile one from the beginning, for it was not based on a permanent identity of interests. But that is true of any political coalition, and unity was encouraged by the inability of any one group to succeed alone. Independent temperance candidates, or independent Labour candidates, met with certain defeat. The rise of permanently independent Labour politics after 1900 was a serious threat to the Progressive coalition, but it was by no means certain before 1910 that it would destroy it. Politics remained largely a question of Moderates versus Progressives until 1914.

Until the late 1880s and 1890s the patrons of South London religion in general, and often of South London's chapels in particular (see Chapter 4), were men with national and world-wide business interests even if their original source of wealth lay in South London. These wealthy cosmopolitan patrons took an interest in both church and chapel in part because of family tradition, which was often Dissenting, but also because they hoped that church and chapel would transcend class barriers and in some way civilize the poor. Their conception of politics was essentially paternalistic. After 1880, as these patrons drifted into the Church of England (Higgs), finally left South London for the country or West End (McArthur, Beaufoy, Doulton), retreated from the unfamiliar difficulties of the new politics (Beaufoy, Tritton, McArthur), or died (Tate, Caine), an aggressively democratic group of Nonconformist local politicians assumed the role

97. SLP, 24 March 1900.
98. BFP, 1 Feb. 1901.

of public representative of the Nonconformist interest within the Progressive coalition. In Norwood, this group included Walter Hobbs, minister of Gipsy Road Baptist Tabernacle and self-proclaimed champion of the poor on the Lambeth Board of Guardians; "Alderman" Nathanael Hubbard, Free Methodist coal merchant, first "advanced Liberal" on the old Lambeth vestry, member of the London County Council, a teetotaler since 1886 and advocate of old-age pensions since 1889, and Liberal parliamentary candidate for Norwood; George Shrubsall, insurance co-director, member of the Roupell Park Wesleyan Chapel, London County Council member for Norwood, parliamentary candidate for Norwood, and president of the South London Local Option League; F. D. Lapthorne, tea merchant, governor of the Mill Hill School, honorary treasurer of the National Brotherhood Movement, and six-time unsuccessful Liberal parliamentary candidate; in Brixton, Frank Adkins, lecturer for the United Kingdom Band of Hope Union, volunteer worker at Brixton Independent's Moffat Institute, and president of the Brixton Liberal Association; Caleb Hutchison, developer of a series of ham and beef shops in South London, member of Brixton Independent Church, supporter of the Moffat Institute and Beaufoy Institute, and Lambeth Guardian; Dr. Henry Walter Verdon, M.D., F.R.C.S., and barrister, Liberal parliamentary candidate for Norwood, and medical officer of health for Lambeth (his enthusiasm for reform led him to convert from Anglicanism to Congregationalism); Benjamin Crook, undertaker and builder, austere Baptist, borough councillor, and Liberal of the old school.

In the working-class districts of Kennington and North Lambeth a similar group met with more success: George Howlett, temperance reformer and coke merchant who began by helping his father provide "Saturday Night Popular Entertainments" in the slums and served twenty-nine years on the Lambeth Board of Guardians; George Prichard, school attendance officer, member of Lambeth Wesleyan Chapel, treasurer of the South London Free Church Council, sponsor of the South London Working Man's Exhibition, Lambeth borough councillor, and Guardian; W. J. Hosking, Sunday School teacher at Lambeth Wesleyan Chapel and long-time advocate of old-age pensions, Lambeth vestryman and councillor; William Wightman, schoolmaster, member of Claylands Congregational Chapel, London County

Councillor, and parliamentary candidate; George Brittain, builder, steward of South West London Wesleyan Mission, local preacher, borough councillor, and mayor of Lambeth; Frank Briant, superintendent of the Nonconformist settlement known as "Alford House Institute for Men and Lads," Lambeth Guardian for twenty-seven years, borough councillor for nineteen years, member of the L.C.C. for thirteen years, and M.P. for North Lambeth from 1918 to 1929 and 1931 to 34.

These men stand out for their deep involvement in both Lambeth Nonconformity and Lambeth public life. Unlike the older group of patrons, the economic interests of these men were more strictly local: four merchants or shopkeepers, three school or local government employees, a Nonconformist minister, a professional temperance lecturer, an undertaker, a local builder, an insurance co-director, and one "gentleman" who lived on the wealth accumulated by a family of solicitors and builders (Briant). With one or two exceptions they were associated with the Liberal Nonconformist chapels and denominations: five Congregationalists, four Wesleyans, two Baptists, and one Free Methodist, as well as two who can be identified only as Nonconformist. Four of the five Congregationalists were closely associated with Brixton Independent Church, three of the four Wesleyans with Lambeth Wesleyan Chapel and its successor, the South West London Mission (a creation of the Wesleyan "Forward Movement" initiated by Hugh Price Hughes in the eighties). These local politicians looked upon Lambeth's chapels as bases from which they struggled to promote social and political reform, to coordinate voluntary and government activity for the improvement of the condition of God's suffering poor, and to create a more just and Godly society in England.[99]

99. This information was obtained from references in the *Brixton Free Press, South London Press,* and *Norwood Press,* especially the following obituaries and description of political candidates: Hobbs, BFP, 20 March 1914; Hubbard, SLP, 16 Dec. 1905; Shrubsall, BFP, 21 May 1909; Lapthorne, NP, 21 June 1929; Adkins, BFP, 27 June 1923; Hutchison, SLP, 18 Aug. 1900; Verdon, BFP, 7 March 1924; Crook, BFP, 25 March 1910, 7 June 1929; Howlett, BFP, 2 Jan. 1914; Prichard, BFP, 29 June 1906; Hosking, BFP, 2 Nov. 1923; Wightman, SLP, 19 May 1900, 16 Dec. 1905. Howlett may have begun attending Anglican services at some time, for his funeral was in a church, but the clergyman was a fellow Progressive Guardian. Briant has an entry in *Who Was Who.*

How did they get elected? Nonconformists were far from constituting a majority of the electorate, but they maintained their influence within the Progressive coalition by the straightforward methods of dominating the local constituency associations and supplying the most energetic and articulate candidates for public office.[100] Although a minority, Nonconformists were potentially a very significant minority of the electorate, especially in the working-class wards where turnout was low, and these men stood unabashedly for the interests of Nonconformity, which they preferred to think of in terms of civil equality and democracy. One of the last acts of the old Lambeth civil vestry in 1900 was the election of two churchwardens for the ancient parish of St. Mary's, Lambeth, and two Dissenters including George Prichard were chosen after a bitter fight.[101] Controversies of this sort continued on the new Borough Council over the designation of a "municipal church" for the new council. The politics of status resentment extended to a wide variety of issues which were often opportunities for symbolic aggression by Nonconformists, notably sabbatarianism and temperance. Outsiders often reduced Nonconformity to meddling puritanicalism with some justification, although sabbatarianism and temperance were in fact very complex issues. "One of the most exciting evenings spent by the Lambeth vestry in many a day"[102] occurred in 1900 when a proposal to allow Sunday concerts at the public baths was rejected by the vestry baths committee. Although most Nonconformist Progressives appear to have supported the baths committee and opposed Sunday concerts, opposition to Sabbath-breaking had traditionally been strongest within the evangelical party of the Church of England. Both church and chapel had vigorous anti-sabbatarian minorities, and the Progressives and Moderates were both divided in their opinions after receiving anti-concert resolutions from seventeen South London Anglican clergymen as well as the Central South London Free Church Council. Nonconformist Progressive Alderman Hubbard, self-styled father of Lambeth's baths, responded to these memorials by denouncing "sabbatarianism in its most hateful form," and the Anglican Rev.

100. On constituency parties see Cox, "Social Origins," pp. 461–62.
101. SLP, 21 April 1900.
102. SLP, 7 July 1900.

W. A. Morris described Sunday as a "day open for any elevating influence." Liberal and Radical Associations in the working-class areas supported the Sunday concerts, and an amendment allowing them passed 42–39.[103]

Temperance, like sabbatarianism, was partly but not entirely a matter of symbolic Nonconformist status-group politics. But civil equality for Nonconformists, sabbatarianism, and temperance were not the elements of an electoral majority in Lambeth or anywhere else. The Moderates monopolized the economic interests of Lambeth householders interested only in keeping the rates down. Many Nonconformists were no doubt interested in keeping the rates down as well, and it is reasonable to assume that some of them quietly voted Moderate. But the Progressives had lost the retrenchment issue, if they ever had it. In fact, many Nonconformists, notably schoolteachers and school officials and borough council employees and committee members, not to mention local politicians, benefited from the expansion of local government. Three of the fourteen prominent Nonconformist local politicians mentioned above were either school or local government employees. The largest occupational category among Moderate candidates for the Lambeth Borough Council in 1900 was licensed victualler, but an equal number of Progressive candidates were schoolmasters or school attendance officers (seven of fifty-one, a number matched by the builders). Not one Moderate candidate was associated with education in any way.[104]

Government growth had a wide appeal to many who did not benefit from it directly in the late nineteenth century, and Lambeth's Progressives took advantage of that attitude. They stood, not for retrenchment and not merely for limitations upon the property rights of publicans and Sunday-trading shopkeepers, but for the positive expansion of local and even of national government through the creation of improving civic institutions. These institutions, they argued, benefited everyone. Unlike the Moderates, the Progressives did not indulge in overtly class-based political rhetoric, although it was generally understood that the measures they advocated were intended to benefit working people disproportionately. Wealthier Lambethans, for instance, could

103. *Ibid.*
104. SLP, 3 Nov. 1900; cf. Cox, "Social Origins," pp. 489–93.

purchase their own books, and in the 1870s the lines of conflict had been drawn over the adoption of a penny rate to support public libraries. At a public meeting in 1875 the feeling against libraries was so strong that every speaker in favor of them was howled down.[105] In 1886 a circular complained of "lazy, idle people in Lambeth reading themselves blind, silly, and round shouldered and bringing on chest disease and consumption at the hard working ratepayer's expense."[106] but the act was adopted locally that year. The first library donors were Lambeth's wealthy Nonconformist patrons, the first library simply an extension of the free library already open at W. S. Caine's Wheatsheaf Hall. The chief librarian of the parish, who supervised all construction as well, was T. F. Burgoyne, an author of books on libraries and Shakespeare, deacon of the Brixton Independent Church, and volunteer at the Moffat Institute.[107]

For the next thirty years the Moderates stood for retrenchment and ritualistically denounced the Progressives for bankrupting the ratepayers. The Progressives, dominated by Nonconformist local notables, stood for the Civic Gospel. Nathanael Hubbard was first elected to the Lambeth Vestry in 1886. He later served on the L.C.C., where Beatrice Webb described him as an Old Liberal, a "rough and ready temperance member" of the council as well as the "only nonentity" among the new aldermen in 1895.[108] But Beatrice Webb misunderstood Hubbard if she thought him interested only in temperance, for his proudest achievement was his successful campaign to have the Lambeth vestry establish public bath houses for the working classes.[109] He claimed that "a deep religious belief has caused me to make it my life's business to sacrifice my time and often my health to try to benefit the people by whom I am surrounded."[110] He was in demand at local chapels for his popular lecture, "No Mean City," on the biblical significance of the city.[111]

105. *Survey of London,* vol. 26, p. 16.

106. According to a historical account in BFP, 24 Oct. 1913.

107. *Ibid.*

108. Beatrice Webb, *Our Partnership* (1975 ed.), p. 71.

109. Norwood Press, 7 April 1929.

110. BFP, 5 Jan. 1906.

111. BFP, 15 Feb. 1901.

Progressives were involved in housing reform as well as the promotion of civic libraries and baths. Lambeth's medical officer of health after 1883 was Dr. Henry Walter Verdon, a son of the rector of Pendlebury who had come to St. Thomas's Hospital in Lambeth after attending Manchester Grammar School. In 1888 he submitted a report to the vestry proposing actions which would end housing problems, he argued, through the taxation of land values, leasehold enfranchisement, and improved technical education. In order to promote housing reform he stood unsuccessfully as Liberal candidate for Norwood in 1892. Although born an Anglican, he was naturally drawn into the world of Nonconformity because of his Progressive views. At his death the Brixton Free Press commented that "His association with Brixton Independent Church indicated his all-round Progressivism."[112] After the L.C.C. began the outright construction of working-class housing, the Progressives became even more thoroughly identified with government intervention in the area of housing.

Early and middle Victorian Dissenters were so closely identified with antistatist attitudes that it is difficult to envisage them as proponents of more, and more expensive, government. But their enthusiasm for local government and democratic education led to a partial but important transformation of Nonconformist attitudes toward government in general. Although generally united in their enthusiasm for improving civic institutions, late Victorian Nonconformists interpreted these institutions in different ways. The electors of the working-class Stockwell ward, for instance, repeatedly elected a puritanical Strict and Particular Baptist undertaker who claimed in his election manifesto that he would "represent progress and social reform by removing the existing moral and social evils around us and conducting the business of the parish on the highest moral principles of justice and equity."[113] This was an older, almost Painite, view of the state as a "remover of impediments" to the natural goodness of mankind (although Councillor Crook would not have thought of it in those terms, since he did not believe in the natural goodness of mankind). And this view persisted within the Progressive coali-

112. BFP, 7 March 1924.
113. BFP, 26 Oct. 1900.

tion throughout the New Liberal years. But most Nonconformist Progressives took a more enthusiastic view of the state as a positive good—indeed as potentially God's agent in the world—and this view of government was related in turn to Nonconformist attitudes toward poverty.

Lambeth's political Nonconformists stood for the poor. This is perhaps as surprising as their advocacy of government, for Nonconformity had been associated, at least in the minds of many of its literary critics, with a harsh, individualistic attitude toward the poor. Lambeth's poor were still likely to regard Nonconformity as a threat upon some occasions in the late nineteenth century. When Progressive Guardians attempted to "combat cohabitation" in the Pascal Street district, local residents responded with physical violence against mission hall workers.[114] The litigious aggression of the South London Free Church Council appears to have been equally unwelcome in the streets around Waterloo Station. But a two-sentence news item in the South London Press reflects a more important side of Nonconformist attitudes toward the poor at the turn of the century: "The case of a poor woman named Esland, who was prosecuted for pawning some articles left with her to make, reveals very vividly the miseries of underpaid labour in London. The costs of the defence in this case were defrayed by the South London Free Church Council."[115] The expansion of Nonconformist philanthropy had transformed Nonconformist ministers and lay philanthropists into advocates of the poor and experts on the problems of poverty. And in the late nineteenth century their philanthropic concerns became intertwined with Progressive politics. Anglican philanthropy was more extensive, but the church was associated for better or for worse with the Moderates who spoke for the ratepayer. Whether for that reason or others, clergymen and active Anglican laymen were less willing than Nonconformists to interpret their philanthropic activities in a political light.

Brixton Independent Church was an important ideological center for Lambeth Progressivism. That church's minister re-

114. B-271, p. 5.

115. SLP, 14 April 1900. There are some interesting comments on attitudes toward poverty within late Victorian and Edwardian Nonconformity in Edward Thompson's novel, *John Arnison* (1939).

garded the creation of missions, institutes, and settlements for the poor as the appropriate response to the Sermon on the Mount in modern circumstances, and one of his Congregationalist families took his exhortations quite literally. W. B. Briant, a builder, was patron of the Moffat Institute in North Lambeth, the site of an endless variety of free dinners and uniformed organization meetings for neighborhood children.[116] T. J. Briant, a city solicitor, ran the Lambeth Ragged School after 1870, provided porridge breakfasts for neighborhood children, and attempted to inculcate a love of music and good books with Dickens-reading parties and mandolin classes for local girls.[117] Frank Briant opened the "Alford House Institute for Men and Lads" on Lambeth Walk in 1882, a "center of comradeship and sport where a standard of manhood was maintained."[118] He used this philanthropic institution to build a political base in the slums of North Lambeth, and won at least twenty-one elections for the board of guardians, borough council, county council, and parliament. His major interest was the board of guardians; a fellow Progressive politician claimed that "no man has done more to humanize the poor law."[119] In 1900 he began a campaign to have the Guardians raise the coal allowance for the poor.[120]

He was joined in this campaign by another Brixton Independent member and Guardian, Caleb Hutchison, who was "particularly anxious to prevent the breaking up of the homes of the poor, if that could be prevented, by the allowance of out-relief. His strenuous advocacy of this plank in his platform brought him into conflict with some other members, and he has been chided for his too liberal-mindedness."[121] In 1911 Briant joined Lambeth's Socialists and advanced Liberals in a public campaign to create support for the minority report of the Poor Law Commission—in effect to abolish the poor law.[122] He listed his major achieve-

116. *The Wandering Polyzoon: A Story of the Moffat Institute* (1896), pamphlet.
117. B-273, pp. 47–57.
118. BFP, 30 Nov. 1922.
119. BFP, 30 March 1922 (George Brittain).
120. SLP, 10 Feb. 1900.
121. SLP, 18 Aug. 1900.
122. BFP, 11 Oct. 1911.

ments on the guardians as: 1. the humane reclassification of the poor; 2. the construction of special homes at Norwood for the aged poor; 3. the establishment of medical and nursing care for the poor in their own homes.[123]

The other tribune of the poor on the Lambeth Guardians was Walter Hobbs, Baptist minister of Norwood. He used Gipsy Road Baptist Chapel and (after a schism) Gipsy Road Tabernacle as a political base and cited his experience in providing free breakfasts for neighborhood children as a qualification for office.[124] He worked to insure a "Christlike interpretation of the citizens' duty to State children" by the Guardians, and claimed responsibility for requiring workhouse children to attend regular elementary schools, removing the workhouse badge, establishing an ambulance system for transporting Lambeth's aged to the workhouse infirmary, and teaching Sunday School to the workhouse children.[125] George Howlett, George Prichard, and George Brittain also served as Guardians, Howlett for twenty-nine years, and in 1904 the thirty-member Board of Guardians included six Nonconformist ministers and one London City Missionary, but only one Anglican clergyman.[126]

It is very difficult to distinguish the philanthropic activities of Progressive Nonconformists from those of the more evangelical Spurgeonite Baptists or those of the Anglicans. But the same old philanthropy took on a new significance for the Progressives. In the 1880s Scott Lidgett established a Wesleyan settlement house in Bermondsey, as part of the Forward Movement, because "he could not be content with appeals that sought rather to palliate existing evils by charitable help rather than radically to reconstruct the existing organization of society on the basis of righteousness and the comradeship of brotherly love."[127] Philanthropy became in his mind "radical reconstruction," and the Progressives labelled their efforts "preventive philanthropy" or "constructive philanthropy" to distinguish them from the old

123. BFP, 30 Nov. 1922.
124. John Stuart, *Pastor and Guardian: Walter Hobbs of West Norwood* (n.d.; *c.* 1912), p. 98.
125. *Ibid.*, p. 92; BFP, 20 Mar. 1914.
126. BFP, 1 April 1904.
127. Scott Lidgett, *My Guided Life* (1936), p. 59.

"merely remedial" philanthropy. This concept of "positive philanthropy" fit in with the liberal Nonconformist notion that God
did not work exclusively through supernatural intervention, but
also through the ordinary structures of politics and philanthropy.
As Hugh Price Hughes gradually began "to see the Jesus of
Nazareth in history and to view more clearly the nature of the
ideals and principles he had inculcated, he became increasingly
anxious to be found on their side."[128] Spiritual values are not a
"miraculous injection into nature," Scott Lidgett observed, for
God worked through the "natural" to spiritual ends.[129] Both men
were Wesleyans, and Lidgett was one of the most prominent
Progressive members of the London County Council. Their views
were shared by more obscure men, like W. J. Hosking, George
Prichard, and George Brittain of Lambeth's South West London
Mission.

By the Edwardian decade, Nonconformist Progressives had advanced from an advocacy of local government intervention to an
advocacy of national government intervention in the areas of
housing, pensions, and unemployment. In the 1904 L.C.C. election
the Progressive councillors who supported the construction of
"workmen's dwellings" in Brixton were abused by the Moderates
for "taking great care of his highness the British workman, and
intending to build a great palace for him at Brixton Hill."[130]
The Progressive majority on the Board of Guardians publicly
called for positive rather than merely remedial steps to deal with
unemployment in 1904, and urged the government to introduce
land and forestry reclamation schemes. Late in the same year
they convened a conference of representatives from all of the
South London Guardians which urged government action on unemployment.[131]

The nationwide campaign to introduce old-age pensions was
conducted from a Congregationalist settlement house in Walworth (adjacent to Lambeth). The York Street Congregational
Chapel was transformed into Browning Hall in 1894, and with
the financial support of the nation's leading liberal Congrega-

128. Dorothea Price Hughes, *Life of Hugh Price Hughes* (4th ed., 1905), p. 33.
129. Lidgett, *My Guided Life,* p. 152.
130. SLP, 20 Feb. 104.
131. SLP, 2 July 1904; 1 Oct. 1904.

tionalists it became a center of South London Progressivism. Its warden, F. H. Stead, was inspired by a vision of introducing the Kingdom of God through practical social reform, and published a handbook for like-minded enthusiasts entitled *The Kingdom of God, A Plan of Study*. In the late nineties seven men from Browning Hall's Pleasant Sunday Afternoon organization served on the local (Southwark) vestry, its sub-warden was a member of the Board of Guardians and had persuaded them to abolish the category of "pauper," and prayers for Progressive victories in L.C.C. elections were heard in its worship services. Their men's adult class studied Mazzini, Carlyle, and Ruskin, and plotted against the drink trade. In 1898 Stead invited Labour leaders from all over the country to hear Charles Booth at a conference on old-age pensions which met at Browning Hall and initiated the National Committee on Old Age Pensions.[132]

Stead directed this committee until old-age pensions were introduced. He was a thoroughgoing "New Liberal" who had no interest whatsoever in Nonconformist status issues such as disestablishment or religious education. But he looked upon the campaign for old-age pensions as a religious crusade and its passage as a miracle of divine intervention. God had turned the hearts of Britain toward an act of repentence for the sins of imperialism, he argued. "Was not the salvation of the aged from want and shame, and the immeasurable sequel of social redemption, sufficient for 'a God to mingle in the game.' The power of his redemptive intervention flowed into the life of the nation through the channels of prayer."[133]

Housing, unemployment, old age pensions—these coexisted with temperance, land, and education in Progressive rhetoric. Some Nonconformist politicians such as Benjamin Crook and William Wightman stressed the old radical issues and slighted the new. Others like Stead shared the New Liberal theoreticians' distaste for any issue which smelled of the Liberation Society or the United Kingdom Alliance. But the old and the new were jumbled together in the minds and utterances of many Noncon-

132. B-277, pp. 159–63; F. H. Stead, *How Old Age Pensions Came To Be* (1909); K. S. Inglis, *Churches and the Working Classes in Victorian England* (1963), p. 165; Belinda Norman-Butler, *Victorian Aspirations: The Life and Labour of Charles and Mary Booth* (1972), p. 126.

133. Stead, *Old Age Pensions*, pp. 300–301.

formist Progressives, especially Hubbard and Briant. There was
a certain amount of opportunism involved in the advocacy of
the New Liberal issues, for Labour was a prominent part of the
Progressive coalition and activists in the Brixton and Lambeth
Trades Councils had to be appeased in order to prevent independent Labour candidacies. It is difficult to measure the
appeal of the new issues to ordinary chapelgoers. There is some
scattered evidence of a Conservative drift among chapel members
late in the century. The minister of Surrey Tabernacle, Walworth
(Strict Baptist) believed that the majority of his congregation was
Conservative, although he was himself a strong Liberal and admitted to occasionally asking a member in a private conversation
"how any Strict Baptist can be otherwise."[134] There is even more
direct evidence of stresses and strains in the Edwardian chapel
following the introduction of New Liberal issues. A delegate to
the Liberation Society and prominent member of the West
Norwood Congregational Chapel resigned from the congregation
in 1907 after the Men's Brotherhood, a working-class Progressive
political organization with Nonconformist links, was allowed to
use the church hall for regular meetings (he objected to their
playing cards on the premises).[135] Wheatsheaf Hall was divided
over the propriety of sending their printing to a non-union firm,
a dispute complicated by the fact that the founder of this chapel,
W. S. Caine, had been a firm supporter of trade unions.[136]

But if anti-trade-unionists or even outright Tories were crowd-
ing into Edwardian chapel pews, they were forced to listen
cheerfully or at least passively to a great deal of Progressive
rhetoric in which the differences between the Old and the New
Liberalism were ignored. In the political excitement surrounding
the 1902 Education Act and the general elections of 1906 and
1910, the barriers between politics and the pulpit crumbled altogether. In 1902 the pastor of the Railton Road Methodist Free
Church wrote in the chapel newsletter that "My own sympathies
lie with the Progressive Party . . . its main idea has been to make

134. B-277, p. 135.
135. West Norwood Congregational Chapel, Minutes of the Church meeting,
1886–1911.
136. Kent, *Testament*, p. 188.

the strong help the weak, the mansion look after the cottage, the rich bear the burdens of the poor."[137] During the 1907 L.C.C. elections the Gipsy Road Baptist Church Messenger supplied a sociological analysis of support for the two parties: "The Progressives draw support from all followers of Jesus Christ—the Moderates from company promoters, slum landlords, drinksellers, bookmakers, and brothelkeepers."[138]

Radical utterances of this sort are often dismissed as a rag-bag of unrelated ideas with no coherent vision of society behind it. But they are no more incoherent than the popular Toryism or popular socialism of the day. Furthermore, the more prominent and intelligent Nonconformist ministers of the 1890s and 1900s were articulating a coherent general vision of society which, given the importance of Nonconformity in the Progressive coalition, was more important in some ways than the "organic individualism" of secularist New Liberal thinkers such as Hobson.[139] For a minority—but a prominent and popular and influential minority—of Edwardian Nonconformist leaders of every denomination, God's work was literally identified with the work of a virtually deified State. John Clifford's idiosyncratic brand of individualistic socialism, with its evocation of human brotherhood and contempt for economic competition, repeatedly found a warm welcome at meetings of the Baptist Union. In his New Year's Message to his London congregation in 1895 he declared the state "more sacred than any church, Anglican or Baptist, Romanist or Greek; for the State stands for the whole people in their manifold collective life, and any church is but a fragment of that life . . . citizenship rightly interpreted is more than churchmanship; to be a good citizen is more and not less than to be a good 'churchman.' "[140] R. J. Campbell, the popular pastor of the City Temple, spoke in similar terms in an address published in 1906: "I do not see why the whole problem of poverty in Great Britain could not be solved in twelve months. It is a question for the Christian conscience of the community.

137. SLP, 10 Oct. 1903.
138. BFP, 21 Feb. 1907.
139. See Freeden, *New Liberalism,* pp. 94–116
140. F. W. Byrt, *John Clifford* (1947), p. 128.

The State ought to become as a Church—a family, if you like."[141] The Congregational Union in 1910 heard from C. S. Horne, the first Nonconformist minister to sit in the House of Commons since the seventeenth century, that "In modern times the church has done something in relief of social distress and despair by Labour yards, Bureaus of Unemployment, cheap or free lodging houses, shelters, etc. In a few years time at the longest, I take it, all these forms of social effort will be done, and ought to be done, by the State in fulfillment of the sacred charge of the well being of all her citizens."[142] "There is no church meeting held in this country," he argued, "that is more constantly and practically concerned with living religious problems than the House of Commons."[143]

No longer sectarians on the fringes of society, Nonconformists found that sectarian theories of society no longer made sense. They were no longer withdrawn from the world, but participants in the world. Their political activities took on a religious significance, society became a kind of church, government became an agency of God's work in the world. Only by understanding this, can we understand some of the more extremist political comments of Edwardian Nonconformist ministers, for their mental world has wholly disappeared. "Democracy," C. S. Horne claimed, "was Theocracy. . . . Christianity tends more and more to express itself in free and democratic institutions. The Most High ruleth through the most low; and theocracy will come through democracy, the Will of God through the common people."[144] For Lambeth's own F. B. Meyer, the construction of L.C.C. tram lines across Westminster Bridge, over the objections of the House of Lords, took on a revolutionary and millenarian significance. Progressivism and social reform were merely the local manifestations of a world-wide, divinely inspired, advance for democracy and freedom, he argued in 1905. "The Revolution in Russia is symbolic of a world-wide movement which is destined to have a profound effect on the lives of obscure dwellers in our slums.

141. "Spiritual Socialism," in C. Ensor Walters, ed., *The Social Mission of the Church,* p. 199.

142. *Congregational Yearbook,* 1911, p. 6.

143. W. B. Selbie, *Life of C. S. Horne* (1920), pp. 217–18.

144. C. S. Horne, "Theocracy through Democracy," in Walters, ed., *Social Mission,* p. 122.

It is not without significance that Westminster Bridge is being seamed with tram lines for working girls."[145]

Were these comments intelligible to ordinary laymen? It is impossible to say, although it is significant that Clifford and Meyer were among the most popular speakers and authors in the world of Edwardian Nonconformity. Ministers in every denomination were saying similar things, and this kind of rhetoric, although most popular with ministers, also found its way into Lambeth's Progressive political circles. But it was largely unintelligible to New Liberal (or Fabian) theorists with no interest in or sympathy for Nonconformity. Masterman was a High Anglican in the Christian socialist tradition, A. G. Gardiner a nominal Anglican, Hobson a member of the secularist London Ethical Society.[146] Beveridge always denied that his interest in social reform was prompted in any way by Christian belief, despite his association with Toynbee Hall.[147] The most prominent New Liberal theorist with strong Nonconformist ties was Percy Alden, but his most influential writings were cast in secular language.[148] Most of his associates looked upon people like Clifford and Meyer with a mixture of contempt and despair. Any mention of not strictly economic issues like land, temperance, or education branded a person an Old Liberal in the minds of the New Liberals. But many Nonconformist Progressives did not see it that way. For Nonconformist social radicals, the new radicalism grew naturally out of the old.

For the New Liberals, Nonconformity was irrelevant largely because all religion was, or soon would be, irrelevant in modern England. That view of the importance of religion has triumphed completely in twentieth-century Britain. C. F. G. Masterman,

145. "The Opportunities of the Church," address to the Baptist Union, 1906, reprinted in *Baptist Handbook,* 1907, p. 219.

146. Edward David, "The New Liberalism of C. F. G. Masterman, 1873–1927," in Kenneth D. Brown, ed., *Essays in Anti-Labour History,* pp. 18–19; Emy, *Liberals, Radicals and Social Politics,* p. 106; Stephen Koss, *Fleet Street Radical* (1973), p. 22; Emy, *Liberals,* p. 106.

147. Lord Beveridge, *Power and Influence* (1953), p. 321.

148. Inglis, *Churches and the Working Classes,* pp. 165–66; Percy Alden, *The Unemployed* (1905); *Democratic England* (1912); cf. the socio-religious views in his "The Problems of East London," and "The Ideal Church for East London" in Richard Mudie-Smith, ed., *The Religious Life of London* (1904), pp. 19–44.

himself a believer, wrote extensively and acutely, not merely about Edwardian "diffusive Christianity," but about the sociology of religion in South London. Where I see great vitality in the midst of declining church attendance, he saw only complacency, decay, and spiritual emptiness.[149] Perhaps he was right, but the important thing about his views is that they were representative. Matthew Arnold was right to predict, in 1877, that the English educated classes would soon adopt the views of the continental intelligentsia on the importance of religion.[150] Many Americans have entertained similar views about the future of religion, although it has been more difficult to ignore the obvious social importance of religious institutions in twentieth-century America. In Britain, religious institutions have withered away in the twentieth century roughly according to prediction, and this decline of religious institutions has been of decisive importance in confirming Masterman's view. The empty church is the single most important piece of evidence adduced in support of the generalization: "religion is no longer important in England." Although there is such a thing as a self-fulfilling prophecy, the existence of the prediction is not itself an adequate explanation for the subsequent decline, and we must now turn our attention to a more thorough examination of its causes.

149. See C. F. G. Masterman, "The Problem of South London", in Mudie-Smith, ed., *Religious Life,* pp. 187–218; also Masterman, *The Condition of England* (1909), especially ch. 11, "Religion and Progress."

150. Preface to *Last Essays on Church and Religion* (1877), in A. Dwight Culler, ed., *Poetry and Criticism of Matthew Arnold* (New York, 1961), p. 502.

6

The Disintegration
of the Civilizing Mission

The 1902 *Daily News* survey of London church attendance was the last of the great Victorian censuses of religious practice, each of them prompted by curiosity, among churchgoers and non-churchgoers alike, about the state of English religion. After 1902, non-churchgoers ceased to be curious and churchgoers became all too painfully aware of the facts. In 1911 the *Daily News* began another census of London attendance, but "the hostility of sections of the churches to the whole proceeding brought it to a standstill. It was clear that the figures would reveal a fall, perhaps a substantial fall, in church attendance, and it was insisted strongly that the vitality of the churches could not be assessed on a numerical basis."[1]

That is unfortunate for historians. At least in London, church attendance appears to have been holding its own between 1850 and the 1880s, and declining between the 1880s and the turn of the century. There is some scattered evidence indicating that the rate of decline accelerated after 1902, at least for Nonconform-

1. H. Wilson Harris, *Life So Far* (1954), p. 95. Harris was in charge of the census; after its abandonment he published an interesting account of the churches' social work in London: *The Churches and London* (c. 1913).

ists. In 1927 the *British Weekly* conducted a limited inquiry into church attendance in a "working-class district" and a "suburban area" in London (see Table 20). Between 1886 and 1902 Anglican and Nonconformist attendance in the working-class district fell absolutely by about 10 percent; between 1902 and 1927 both fell by over 70 percent. The real rate of decline was higher than 70 percent, for although the author supplies no population figures, he explains that the district lost three thousand persons between 1902 and 1927. In the suburban area (where population estimates are supplied), Anglican attendance fell by about 50 percent in real terms over both periods. In the first period, Nonconformist absolute attendance grew by nearly 30 percent, but after 1902 the absolute gain became an absolute loss, and the real loss was nearly 60 percent, higher than that of the Anglicans.

These are very rough and not altogether reliable figures, and it is misleading to calculate a "rate of change" from figures for periods of different length. But they are all we have for church attendance, as opposed to other sorts of church-related activity, until the first Gallup Polls of the very late 1930s. The Nonconformist attendance figures confirm the pattern found in statistics of Nonconformist denominational membership: absolute growth and real decline in the eighties and nineties; absolute and real decline from the 1900s. Anglican church attendance declined more rapidly than that of the Nonconformists in the late Victorian decades, at least in London, but the Anglican decline may have slowed in the early twentieth century at a time when other Anglican statistics, such as the number of Easter communicants, were actually improving.

Anglican churchgoing was preeminently the churchgoing of civic duty and social responsibility. In Lambeth the decline of Anglican churchgoing was not uniform, but most pronounced in those parishes which paid the least attention to parochial machinery, i.e., those which merely supplied their parishioners with opportunities for Sunday worship and little else. The healthiest parishes were those with highly motivated clergymen, normally activists in either the High or the Evangelical church party, who supplied a broad range of opportunities for philanthropic and religious service. In order to understand late Victorian religion, it is necessary to understand that certain things were related in the minds of late Victorian churchgoers—things which are not related in our minds: for instance, sponsoring a coal club, attending Sunday services, district visiting, taking children on a Saturday outing, teaching shorthand classes, attending a Bible class, and (for Nonconformists and Anglican Christian socialists) serving on the L.C.C. Other lists could be drawn up, and individuals naturally placed a greater emphasis on some activities than on others. In the 1890s Percy Dearmer came to St. Ann's, South Lambeth, from Oxford, where he had been attracted to the church by a vision of Christian socialism which "meant opening the kingdom of art and beauty to all."[2] He found ordinary parochial work a great burden, although a burden he accepted out of a sense of duty. In her novel *The Difficult Way,* his wife portrayed the following encounter between a man who is clearly her husband ("John Pilgrim") and a parish worker, Mrs. Stamp:

"I shall leave the parish," she said.

John Pilgrim looked down upon her sadly. She had announced her intention of leaving the parish at least four times during the year that he had worked at St. Martin's; he knew that she did not mean it, but the words always brought with them a certain soreness. Had he followed his inclination he would have shaken himself free of the greater part of his turbulent workers. Had he done so so he would have gained nothing—nothing but peace—and the work would have suffered.

"Mrs. Stamp", he said at length, "why do you spend all this time among the poor? Why do you have a Young Women's Social Evening?"

"Why? Because I have always done it of course. I was brought up to do a certain amount of church work."

After a quick flash of surprise at her answer, John Pilgrim could smile. He had expected her to reply that she, like himself, worked for the love of God, upon which he could have drawn the moral of love for one's neighbor.

But Mrs. Stamp was in no mood to be preached at. She gathered herself up to renewed effort.

"What is the use of my having a social evening for young women on purpose to keep them away from the perils of the street and such like, when there's a Young Men's Bible class in the next room?"[3]

2. Nan Dearmer, *Life of Percy Dearmer, by His Wife* (1940), p. 35.

3. Mabel Dearmer, *The Difficult Way* (1905), pp. 64–65. Mabel Dearmer was his first wife, and this novel is frankly autobiographical.

Because of his love of God and beauty, John Pilgrim was orchestrating the parochial machinery of a South London working-class parish, and staring uncomprehendingly at a woman who defined "church work" as keeping young girls from the perils of the street. Both of them wanted to improve life in South Lambeth, and found themselves side by side in a church, where work among the poor, Bible classes for young men, social evenings for young women, worship services, and the love of God were inextricably mingled.

Parochial machinery not only gave "church workers" something to do. It also gave church men and women something to say to outsiders other than the conventional admonitions to love God. On a June Sunday in 1907 the vicar of St. Matthew's, Brixton, faced Joseph McCabe of the South London Ethical Society in an open-air debate in Brockwell Park. The argument revolved around the central issue in the decades-old controversy between secularists and churchmen—the relationship between religion and ethics.[4] "My object," McCabe said, "is merely to plead that I and a few more people banded together in an ethical society are tolerably respectable people."[5] The young can be taught, he argued, that good behavior is rewarded in this life, and the promise of secular happiness is an adequate sanction. Furthermore, social conditions have been improving dramatically while interest in religion is waning and church attendance declining. The Japanese derived their good character from "agnostic Confucianism infused with Shinto nationalism," and the French crime rate had fallen since they "rejected theology and Catholicism."

The vicar agreed that social conditions were improving, but associated that change entirely with the reformation of religion: "One hundred years ago in my home county of Devon it was not at all unusual to see a cock-fight held in the church under the parson's approbation. Think what a life some of the clergy of the Church of England lived then! They attended wine suppers six nights in the week, as the best preparation for the Sunday sermon. . . . Turn now to London. My friend thinks religion is

4. A. J. Waldron and Joseph McCabe, *The Independence of Ethics: Full Report of a Debate in Brockwell Park on Sunday, June 23, 1907* (1907).

5. *Ibid.*, p. 3.

going back. I do not! Never in the history of London was religion so earnest, so pure, so deadly enthusiastic about moral evils as at the present time." Citing Dr. Barnardo, Spurgeon, the Salvation Army, the Church Army, the Christian Social Union, and the settlement movement, he argued that "All the best movements today in London to make it better, cleaner, happier, and healthier are carried on under the inspection of religion."[6]

After the secularist cited the French for their high moral character, the debate was more or less over, for the French were popularly associated with immorality. Ask people, the vicar urged, whether they would trust their daughter to the average Frenchman. But the serious aspects of the debate concerned the relationship of the churches to social improvement, and both speakers had strong points. Church attendance was irrefutably declining as social conditions improved. Yet there was no army of secularists visibly at work to make things better. Or was there? Who was in fact responsible for social improvement?

The very structure of Charles Booth's massive survey of social conditions in London reflects the late Victorian success of the churches' argument: first came the anatomy of poverty, then the causes of poverty, then an exhaustive account of the churches as the most important of the "influences" working to counteract poverty and suffering.[7] *Life and Labour* was published, in its final form, in 1902, but Booth's assumptions were already dated by then, and 1907 was one of the last years in which spectators at open-air debates would hear arguments like the vicar's. Booth's assistant Ernest Aves made these comments in the manuscript notebooks concerning the parish of St. John the Divine, Kennington: "Perhaps it is worth noting that, since the work of St. John the Divine began in quite early days in the whole of this area, the character of this particular district would appear to have been acquired in spite of all the energy of this centre of Anglo-Catholic churchmanship. Some local influences making for degradation were apparently too strong alike for Mr. Elsdale

---

6. *Ibid.*, p. 7.

7. Booth's *Life and Labour of the People of London*, series one (1892), examines poverty on a street-by-street basis; series two (1895) seeks the causes of poverty in the economy by examining wages and occupational structure; series three (1902) is an exhaustive but subjective account of religious and other "social influences" at work to improve the condition of the people.

and Mr. Brooke [successive clergymen]."[8] There was probably not a working-class parish in England with stronger parochial machinery, more funds, or more clergymen than St. John the Divine, and the church had begun its work when the district was first built over. Yet streets of desperate poverty remained. The churches had failed.

But even more important than the "failure" of the churches to abolish poverty and class divisions was the evident success of alternative institutions which emerged between 1870 and 1920. A growing awareness of alternatives first eroded and then destroyed the association between "church work" and civic duty. The nineteenth-century churches were very flexible in responding to demands for social services of all sorts, but their limited entrepreneurial success led them to assume far more responsibility than they could reasonably claim—for education, for supplemental poor relief, for entertainment, for individual character, for social cohesion. In the late nineteenth and the early twentieth century, many individuals decided that the churches were not up to the task, or what is more important, that their definition of the task had become irrelevant or nonsensical. In virtually every sphere of activity, the churches found that they were competing with a more specialized institution, and they were generally (with some exceptions) eager to hand over responsibility to a more effective body. Their public, manifest motive for providing any public service was not to maintain the social influence of the church, but to educate the poor, relieve suffering, lighten the burden of the oppressed, maintain social discipline, etc. If someone else—a trained professional perhaps—could do a better job, why not let him? The churches could then concentrate on more purely "religious" tasks.

Sociologists call this kind of change a "process of functional differentiation"—the evolution of specialized institutions to meet specific needs in an expanding society. This differentiation is normally treated as part of the general bureaucratic rationalization of modern society which is the major cause of the global process of secularization.[9] In a variation of that argument, Talcott Parsons has argued, perversely, that differentiation represents, not

8. B-305, p. 7.
9. Peter Berger, *The Sacred Canopy* (New York, 1969), p. 133.

a decline of religion, but a general infusion of religious values into the whole of society.[10] These global pronouncements ignore the possibility that the religious consequences of "functional differentiation" may vary according to historical circumstances. "Functional differentiation" first strengthened, then weakened, Lambeth's churches. In the nineteenth century the churches competed successfully with other specialized institutions, notably in the area of education, while the ancient Lambeth civil vestry was left behind, and even found itself stripped of one function after another in a long drawn out process of disentanglement from the church. In 1835 control of the workhouse was transferred to the new Lambeth Board of Guardians.[11] During the cholera epidemics of the forties and fifties, Lambeth citizens petitioned the Metropolitan Commissioner of Sewers for improved drainage, and after 1855 the Metropolitan Board of Works had primary responsibility for that sort of public service.[12] The vestry had no influence on the physical growth of Lambeth, unlike the ancient manors which still controlled the length and terms of leases. The vestry had the greatest difficulty even in purchasing a plot of land suitable for the vestry hall, and was unable to purchase park land until 1888.[13]

The decay of the vestry provided an opportunity for the Church of England to strike out on its own. The first churches in nineteenth-century Lambeth were joint ventures by the vestry and a local church building commission established to disburse funds appropriated by Act of Parliament in 1818 for new church construction. The parish contributed £23,154, and the Church Building Commissioners £22,036, toward the construction of three of the four "Waterloo churches": St. Mark's, Kennington; St. Matthew's, Brixton; and St. Luke's, West Norwood.[14] But the creation of these parishes in the 1820s marked the beginning of the subdivision of the old parish into smaller ecclesiastical parishes within a larger civil parish, and further church

10. See "Christianity in a Modern Industrial Society," in Edward A. Tiryakian, ed., *Sociological Theory, Values, and Change* (1963), pp. 38ff., 60–65.

11. *Survey of London,* vol. 26, p. 183.

12. Pamela and Harold Silver, *The Education of the Poor: The History of a National School, 1824–1974* (1974), p. 91.

13. *Survey of London,* vol. 26, p. 67.

14. *Ibid.,* pp. 32, 133, 174.

and church school construction came from privately raised funds.[15] The new churches of St. Mary the Less (1838), Holy Trinity (1841), All Saints, York St. (1846), and St. Andrew's, Coin St. (1856) were built by the new Ecclesiastical Commission, not the Lambeth Vestry. The abolition of church rates in 1868 apparently passed without incident in Lambeth (although the neighboring vestry of Southwark continued to levy a church rate imposed by private act until the 1880s, and a "semi-official but compulsory" ministers rate as late as 1904).[16]

The growth of numerous specialized public and private bureaucracies—functional differentiation—strengthened the Victorian churches, for Lambeth's parishes emerged as institutions of growing importance along with the Ecclesiastical Commissioners, the Board of Guardians, the Metropolitan Board of Works, the chapels, and private philanthropies. The nineteenth-century pattern of growing ecclesiastical influence, up to a point, is nowhere clearer than in the provision of education, where Lambeth's churches assumed important new social functions only to find themselves displaced in the long run by even more specialized agencies. In 1798 Joseph Lancaster developed his "monitorial plan" of teaching at a school meeting at his home on the Borough Road, Southwark. In 1808 the Royal Lancastrian Society was created in order to propagate his methods; renamed the British and Foreign School Society in 1814, its Nonconformist association became more pronounced after the creation of a rival, the Anglican National Society, in 1811. There were only two schools in Lambeth at the beginning of the nineteenth century: a parochial boys school near Lambeth Palace and Archbishop Tenison's School for Girls. But as soon as the war years were over, the Anglican National Society and the largely Nonconformist British Society began a vigorous competition for educational supremacy.

In 1815 a public meeting in Stockwell initiated a drive to build the Stockwell and Brixton Auxiliary Parochial School "on principles of the Church of England in union with the National Society." In 1816 Archbishop Tenison's School was rebuilt. In

15. Silver, *Education of the Poor*, pp. 22–23.

16. On the Southwark church rate controversy, see F. W. Soutter, *Recollections of a Labour Pioneer* (1923), pp. 56–61; SLP, 9 Jan. 1904.

1817 the British Society opened the Lambeth Association School, and in the 1820s Anglicans attempted to establish parish schools along with the four "Waterloo Churches."[17] In 1824 and 1825 the Kennington National School received donations from the Crown, the Archbishop of Canterbury, Lambeth's endowed parochial schools, the churchwardens, and the South London Water Works.[18] Annual sermons in benefit of the schools supplied a regular source of income, and by 1829 National Schools existed in Lambeth, Waterloo, Kennington, Stockwell, Brixton, and Norwood.[19] The organizational resources of the church gave the National Schools an early head start in the competition for the minds of Lambeth's schoolchildren.[20]

Discrimination against Dissenters continued in the National Schools at least until the 1860s, leading to the further construction of British, Wesleyan, and Congregational schools. The Wesleyan day school in Brixton was established because the National Schools required attendance at the Anglican Sunday School and, according to a Wesleyan circuit minute book, "in some instances they caned children who were at our Sunday Schools."[21] The Congregationalists vigorously supported the British schools associated with their West Norwood, Stockwell, and Brixton chapels.[22] The National Schools gradually began to cater to the children who could pay a small fee, thus excluding the poorest. The Kennington National Schools opened in 1824 as free schools for the poor, but after 1835 parents were required to pay a penny a week—partly in order to maintain the school, partly in order to distinguish the National Schools from Poor Law Schools.[23] It was argued that even a laborer could afford this fee if thrifty, but that was a vicious bourgeois illusion. In

17. Silver, *Education of the Poor*, p. 22; *Survey of London*, vol. 26, p. 95; vol. 23, p. 142.

18. Silver, *Education of the Poor*, p. 23.

19. *Ibid.*, p. 68.

20. *Ibid.* p. 13.

21. Cited in Brixton Free Press, *Brixton's Churches* (1904), p. 25. The West Norwood Wesleyan Day School was founded in 1860. *Survey of London*, vol. 26, p. 182.

22. Edward Cleal and T. G. Crippen, *The Story of Congregationalism in Surrey* (1908), pp. 79, 230–32.

23. Silver, *Education of the Poor*, p. 44.

the 1840s a Ragged School for the very poor was established in a railway arch near the Kennington Schools, and in 1851 one of Lambeth's patrons, Henry Beaufoy, built a large, new Ragged School as a memorial to his wife.[24] Lambeth had been outfitted with schools for Anglicans, schools for Dissenters, and schools for the poor.

The government first supplied building grants to the school societies in 1833, and established a state system of inspection in 1839, a program of teacher training in 1846, and a system of "payment by results," much hated by schoolteachers, in 1862. But the educational initiative clearly lay with the churches. When the London School Board was established in 1870, however, the government and local school boards began to absorb the work begun by the churches, a process illustrated in the following table:

Schools Transferred to London School Board, 1870–1900[25]

	1871–75	76–80	81–85	86–90	91–95	96–1900	Total
CE	17	24	9	3	1	—	54
CE Ragged	7	—	—	—	—	—	7
Ragged	23	—	—	—	—	—	23
British	24	6	5	2	3	1	41
Wesleyan	5	—	—	1	2	—	8
Cong'l	4	2	—	—	1	—	7
Other	12	1	1	1	—	—	15
TOTAL	92	33	15	7	7	1	155

Of the Nonconformist denominations, only the Wesleyans were interested in maintaining schools after 1870, and they were weak in London. For many Anglican clergymen, however, the schools were an essential part of their parochial work. Many parents who wished to spend a little extra money on their children's education favored the National Schools as well. But after 1870 the church schools simply lacked the resources to

24. *Survey of London*, vol. 23, p. 142.

25. L.C.C., *London Statistics*, 1899–1900, p. xxxiii. I do not have similar statistics for Lambeth alone. The Lambeth Ragged School ceased regular elementary education in 1870. The British Schools associated with the Brixton and Stockwell Congregational Chapels remained open until 1888. Cleal and Crippen, *Story of Congregationalism*, pp. 230–32.

compete with the school board, particularly since many potential donors assumed, unless they were particularly devout Anglicans, that the problem of education for the poor had been taken
care of by the state. The Board Schools supplied 60 percent of
school accommodation in Lambeth by the turn of the century,
and it was generally understood that the 1902 and 1903 education acts were in part a government rescue operation for the
Anglican schools. In 1904 an L.C.C. inspector reported that St.
Mark's schools were entirely unsatisfactory and not worth the
expenditure required to put them in order.[26] In 1908 the L.C.C.
education committee reported on the "non-provided" schools
which had been forced upon them in 1903: 79 had been closed
(including the Wesleyan day school at Brixton Hill), 300 up-
graded, 37 given extensions for further repairs, and 6 transferred directly to the council. Thirty-six awaited further action.[27]
After this further rationalization, increasing government grants
for construction slowed but did not reverse the relative decline
of church schools. L.C.C. schools still provided about 60 percent of school accommodation in North Lambeth and Kennington in 1938, but a social observer wrote during that year: "The
main difference between the council and the Church schools is
in the buildings . . . even the older council schools compare
favorably with the Church schools."[28]

The state schools assumed responsibility, not merely for education, but for religious education as well. There is some reason
to believe that compulsory religious education in the state
schools promoted the diffusion of religious knowledge and increased the number of persons to whom Christian symbols and
language were meaningful. There is every reason to believe that
the schools did a better job than the chaotic Victorian Sunday
Schools, and in that sense, Lambeth was more "Christian" in
1914 than in 1870. But the churches themselves suffered from the
introduction of state-sponsored "diffusive Christianity." The
evident success of the largely new educational system weakened
their claim to be the "great engine of civilization," particularly

26. Silver, *Education of the Poor,* p. 137.

27. SLP, 14 Feb. 1908.

28. Lady Margaret Hall, *Social Services in North Lambeth and Kennington*
(Oxford, 1939), pp. 76–77.

in the 1890s when the Board Schools were thought to be producing visible results at last. Here was a great army of secular professionals working for social improvement.

The headmaster of Lambeth's Webber Street Board School claimed in 1899 that the behavior of his students had been thoroughly transformed since 1882. Teachers were no longer stoned in the streets. Students were not only cleaner, but more docile and cheerful, less insolent and insubordinate. Parents no longer threatened teachers with violence: some were even friendly, and virtually all of them made some attempt to dress their children respectably. Students from the "criminal streets" had ceased to regard teachers as police informers.[29]

This man did not claim credit for these social improvements, but others assigned it to him anyway and talked about the schools in language formerly reserved for the churches. In 1899 the minister of Trinity Presbyterian Church, Clapham Road, was optimistic about the prospects for eliminating poverty through the work of the London School Board.[30] When the Paragon Road Board School in Southwark was opened over the protests of the local incumbent in 1900, the *South London Press* observed that "if certain public elementary schools might not be necessary for educational purposes, they are certainly required on the grounds of hygiene and sanitation."[31] The *History of the Lambeth Ragged School* summarized thirty years of change in 1895: "Here too, as elsewhere, the varied religious organizations have revived and *above all,* for over twenty years the powerful influence of the Board School teacher has been at work—not the teaching alone, but the influence of direct personal magnetism of right-minded, God-fearing men and women."[32] As a result, the author claimed, both crime and drunkenness were on the wane.

An Edwardian Anglican observer of South London admitted that the schools had already assumed the major responsibility for religious education.[33] Although praising the selfless devotion of

29. B-273, pp. 187ff., an extensive interview.
30. B-271, p. 149.
31. SLP, 14 April 1900.
32. B-273, pp. 97ff., printed pamphlet inserted. Emphasis mine.
33. Alexander Paterson, *Across the Bridges* (1911), pp. 78–79.

"And what is your religion?"
"Well, Miss, I'm Church and me 'usband's Chapel; but little Maudie's County Council."

Functional Differentiation. *Punch,* 4 May 1921.

clergymen, he clearly thought the elementary school teacher much more important as a model of behavior: "The teacher is indeed *in loco parentis;* the boys must find their school a veritable *alma mater.* . . . It is around the figure of the teacher that the development of a boy's character must centre."[34] The schoolteacher had replaced the clergyman, and the Education Committee replaced the church. "Charity and philanthropy and religious agencies may effect much," he wrote, "but they only deal with groups and sections. *Every* child must go to school. The whole nation is in the melting pot. . . . The parish priest or missioner sighs for a chance of influencing every life in his district, and if he were given each one for eleven years, how near would he hope to bring heaven and earth! To the Education Committee alone is given that trust."[35]

Another example of functional differentiation can be measured with more precision, although its meaning is not correspondingly clearer. Between 1900 and 1930 the percentage of secular Registry Office marriages grew from 20 to 40 (see graph on next page).

Registry Office marriages became popular first with the middle classes. Their increasing popularity represents a breakdown of resistance to secular marriages among semi-skilled and unskilled families. There is nothing religious about a Registry Office marriage, and the Church of England lost an important point of contact with ordinary people as church marriages ceased to be routine. But the popularity of Registry Office marriages appears to have been largely a matter of practical competitive advantage rather than any aversion to religion or the church. For a small informal marriage, the Registry Office was more appropriate than a cavernous Victorian church which dwarfed the small group of attenders. Furthermore, the Church of England was not in the business of accomodating divorced persons who wished to remarry. Religion maintained its hold on burial services entirely because the government provided no secular alternatives. Although this caused some irritation among committed secularists, there was no groundswell of popular demand for a secular burial service.[36]

Although eroding a link with the people which was an important element of "diffusive Christianity," the new popularity

34. *Ibid.*, p. 83.

35. *Ibid.*, p. 61.

36. See the complaints of Havelock Ellis in *My Life* (1940), p. 513.

Graph 1

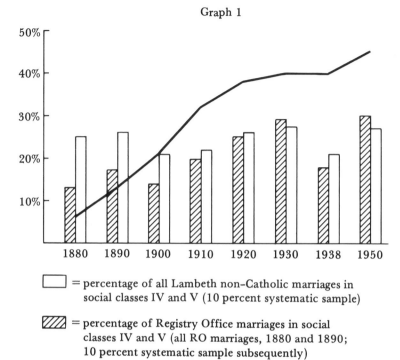

☐ = percentage of all Lambeth non–Catholic marriages in
social classes IV and V (10 percent systematic sample)

▨ = percentage of Registry Office marriages in social
classes IV and V (all RO marriages, 1880 and 1890;
10 percent systematic sample subsequently)

BLACK LINE = percentage of all Lambeth non-Catholic marriages
in the Registry Office (see Table 18)

of secular marriage ceremonies did not affect the basic *raison
d'etre* of the late Victorian churches in the same way that the
emergence of state education did. The achievements of the London School Board changed half-conscious assumptions about
which institutions were more important, and which were less
important (and when we say that religion has "declined" we
usually mean that it has become less important, and that it is
thought of as being less important). The School Board was only
a portent of other specialized bureaucracies—both public and
private—to come. By the end of the century the Lambeth Vestry,
the School Board, the London County Council, and the government were all expanding their activities, and it was difficult for
them to do anything at all—except paving, lighting, and sewer-

age—which did not encroach upon the churches. The churches were even involved peripherally in public health, with a parochial sanitary committee in Kennington and vigilant youth clubs in North Lambeth on the lookout for defective flushings and drains.[37]

The Lambeth Vestry tentatively began to move into three new areas—libraries, baths, and housing reform—after 1880 amid Nonconformist Progressive enthusiasm for the Civic Gospel. I have already discussed the first free library in Lambeth, which W. S. Caine opened in 1884 with one thousand volumes at the Wheatsheaf Mission Hall in South Lambeth. In 1885 he rented a separate house for the library on South Lambeth Road, and when Lambeth adopted the Free Libraries Act in 1886 it simply absorbed the Wheatsheaf Hall Library, which became the first public library in Lambeth.[38] Caine was appointed library commissioner, and Lambeth's two prominent Unitarian patrons, Frederic Nettlefold and Sir Henry Tate, cooperated with the vestry in the construction of five more in the next six years. In 1899 Caine was busily promoting the idea of a free picture library which would loan pictures to working men to hang in their homes for one month at a time.[39]

A deacon of Brixton Independent Church was Lambeth's chief librarian, and another was Lambeth's medical officer of health, responsible for regular and systematic housing inspection from the 1880s. The Progressive Free Methodist Alderman Hubbard, first elected to the vestry in 1886, was known as Father of the Parish Bath Houses. In the midst of the debate stirred up by prominent Anglican clergymen who declared South London "pagan" in 1900, the editor of the *South London Press* retorted that South London had less crime, fewer disorderly houses, more libraries, public baths, friendly societies, and cooperative societies than North London. "In view of all these circumstances is it not time to drop all this nonsense about South London and

37. B-305, pp. 16ff.; B-272, pp. 79ff.

38. B-271, p. 3; on the evolution of Lambeth's vestry see Janet Roebuck, *Urban Development in Nineteenth Century London: Lambeth, Battersea and Wandsworth, 1838–1888* (1979).

39. *Ibid.,* p. 19.

its wickedness?"[40] He did not claim that South London had more churches than North London. Public baths and libraries, promoted by Nonconformist civic patrons, were thought to be an antidote to paganism.

Lambeth's civil vestry retained the right to appoint two churchwardens of the ancient ecclesiastical parish of St. Mary's, Lambeth, until 1899, when the churchwardens were reconstituted as a body entirely independent of the civil vestry. At the same time, the vestry was finally reconstituted as a new Borough Council, given reasonable powers, and designated the primary unit of local administration.[41] But instead of finally settling the issue of church and state in Lambeth, this change precipitated a lengthy lawsuit between the churchwardens and Borough Council for control of two of Lambeth's most lucrative charitable bequests. It was only then—in the early twentieth century —that the successor of the old vestry found itself in open conflict with the churches, contending for control of the same funds, and claiming precedence in the provision of social services.

In 1899 the charity commissioners conducted an enquiry into Lambeth's charitable trusts and discovered that forty-six bequests were yielding a gross annual income of £14,306, a considerable sum.[42] Most of the smaller bequests were vested in trustees, individual Anglican parishes, or Nonconformist chapels, but the churchwardens and the Borough Council both claimed portions of the two oldest legacies, the "Pedlar's Acre" and the Walcot Charity. The name of the donor of the "Pedlar's Acre," now part of the site of London's County Hall, had already been forgotten in 1639, although it had long been in the churchwarden's accounts. An Act of Parliament in 1826 had placed control in the hands of the Lambeth Vestry, and another Act of 1900 confirmed the control of the new Borough Council, which sold the site to the London County Council in 1910 for £81,342. The rector and churchwardens of St. Mary's contested this act, demanding a portion of the revenues for ecclesiastical purposes. A church-

40. SLP, 21 April 1900.

41. *Survey of London,* vol. 26, p. 30.

42. B-271, p. 25; itemized in Lady Margaret Hall, *Social Services,* pp. 153ff.

warden named Hardy pursued an impressive antiquarian survey of the site's legal status, but in 1911 the courts awarded the sum entirely to the Borough Council, suggesting that the churchwardens recoup their losses by selling the results of Hardy's research.[43]

The churchwardens had more luck with the Walcot Charity, vested in "trustees for the parish" of St. Mary, Lambeth, in 1667 on behalf of the poor. Parliament confirmed the control of the ecclesiastical parish in 1828, but that arrangement was contested by both the Borough Council and the London County Council after 1900. In one of its first acts the new Borough Council declared its intention of diverting the funds of the Walcot and three other charities from voluntary schools to pensioners chosen by the Borough, to "transfer non-ecclesiastical charities from church to people."[44] The London County Council Education Committee subsequently proposed diverting a portion of the funds to technical education. In 1910 the courts left management in the hands of the rector and churchwardens who agreed to pay a yearly fixed sum for pensions and Anglican schools in Lambeth, and devote the residue to a new secondary school in North Lambeth and to "technical instruction" supervised jointly by the parish, the Lambeth Borough Council, and the London County Council.[45]

After 1889 the London County Council also encroached upon the churches. The Technical Institute Act empowered it and other local authorities to provide technical education, and the L.C.C. technical education committee's expenditure grew from £4,528 in 1893–94 to £207,746 in 1900–1901.[46] At the same time the number of students enrolled in evening schools sponsored by the London School Board, sometimes known as "evening continuation classes," grew dramatically.[47] Both bodies displaced the churches and chapels, which had been supplying adult education on an informal basis for decades. The Brixton

43. *Survey of London,* vol. 23, pp. 62–63; BFP, 15 Dec. 1911.

44. SLP, 10 Aug. 1900.

45. BFP, 6 Dec. 1907; 1 July 1910; Lady Margaret Hall, *Social Services,* p. 153.

46. L.C.C., *London Statistics,* 1902–1903, p. 101.

47. L.C.C., *London Statistics,* 1899–1900, p. xxiv; 5,563 students in 1883–84; 109,121 in 1898–99.

Unitarian Church and the West Norwood Congregational Chapel had opened educational institutes for working men as early as the 1850s.[48] After closing its day school in 1870, the Metropolitan Tabernacle continued evening classes in science, math, bookkeeping, and shorthand until 1899, and other congregations sponsored "adult schools" on the Quaker model.[49] The evening classes of the L.C.C. competed with the Pleasant Sunday Afternoon meetings and Men's Brotherhoods so popular with the chapels. In 1905 the Kennington Road Commercial Schools sponsored a "special L.C.C. class in citizenship," and other evening schools featured debating societies of the sort popular in the chapels and "popular lectures on winter evenings" which could hardly be distinguished from a Pleasant Sunday Afternoon gathering.[50]

Lambeth in the early twentieth century supported three separate specialized institutions devoted to adult and technical education, and each of the three—Morley College, the Beaufoy Institute, and Norwood Technical Institute—had a religious or quasi-religious origin. Morley Memorial College for Working Men grew out of the improving activities sponsored by Emma Cons at the Old Vic in the 1880s. In 1889 Samuel Morley, the Congregational patron, supplied the funds for a working man's college which had enrolled 640 students—all clerks and artisans— by 1892 (see Chapter 3). In the early nineties it had little formal competition, but by the turn of the century a college pamphlet noted that "the locality is now able to offer many more educational facilities than in the past, especially through the Borough Polytechnic and the Board Evening Continuation Classes."[51] The college responded to L.C.C. competition by attempting to arrange classes which did not require an extensive plant and which supplied something of a liberal education. But demand continued to run strongly for elementary science, elocution, and shorthand, and the college was absorbed into the L.C.C. adult

48. R. K. Spedding, *Resurgam!* (1941), p. 9; Cleal and Crippen, *Story of Congregationalism,* p. 79.

49. Eric Hayden, *A Centennial History of Spurgeon's Tabernacle* (1962), p. 77; William Kent, *Testament of a Victorian Youth* (1938), pp. 221ff.

50. BFP, 12 Feb. 1915; 19 Sept. 1919.

51. B-273, p. 153.

education program. In 1923 it left the dressing rooms of the Old
Vic for a new site on Westminster Bridge Road.[52]

The Beaufoy Institute emerged from the old Lambeth Ragged
School, built by the Anglican patron Henry Beaufoy in 1851.
After 1870 it was maintained by T. J. Briant, a Congregationalist
and member of Brixton Independent Church, along the lines of
an institutional church or mission with Sunday School, thrift
and youth clubs, sewing and mandolin classes.[53] In 1904 part
of the building was demolished to make way for a widening of
the London and South Western Railway, but new premises
were established on Prince's Road and in 1908 the school was
given to the L.C.C. which established a technical day school. By
the 1930s it was training 180 boys in engineering.[54]

The Norwood Technical Institute evolved from the Mechan-
ic's Institute at the Congregational Chapel in West Norwood. In
1858 Arthur Anderson, a member of that chapel and a director
of the P & O Steamship Line, established and endowed the
Lower Norwood Working Men's Institute. It was managed by
a committee of working men under the supervision of the Congregational minister and a nonsectarian board of trustees. The
Institute flourished for a couple of decades but it had come upon
hard times by the early nineties. The building had not been
modernized at all and, according to the Congregational minister,
the nonsectarian trust had been "collared by the clergy."[55] But
another Congregational patron came to the rescue. Evan Spicer
became interested in polytechnics while serving as L.C.C. member, and in 1895 arranged for a subsidy from the L.C.C. Technical Education Board and established Norwood Technical
Institute as a branch of the Borough Polytechnic in Southwark.[56]

By 1900 it enrolled 500 students. I have no account of its program, but it was run along the same lines as the larger parent

52. See Denis Richards, *Offspring of the Vic: A History of Morley College*
(1958).

53. B-273, pp. 53ff.

54. SLP, 7 Feb. 1908; Lady Margaret Hall, *Social Services*, p. 83.

55. B-315, p. 143.

56. *Ibid.*; J. B. Wilson, *The Story of Norwood* (1973), p. 36; J. Scott Lidgett,
My Guided Life (1936), p. 207.

institution, the Borough Polytechnic, which had two divisions: 1. educational classes for those aged sixteen to twenty-five, some of a trade and some of a general nature; 2. an "institute" which included Wednesday lectures, Saturday concerts, a men's club room, a Sunday social hour, thrift agencies, holiday clubs, an emigration bureau, a library and reading room, a gymnasium, an athletic field, and a literary society. Its resemblance to a large, well-financed, liberal Nonconformist mission hall or settlement house was reinforced by the Sunday afternoon religious meeting.[57] The L.C.C. Technical Education Committee was funding institutional churches in Southwark and Lambeth. In 1904 the Norwood Institute was reorganized as a separate, independent institution under the L.C.C. Education Committee.[58] After 1968, when the West Norwood Congregational Chapel finally closed its doors, the nearby Technical Institute used the chapel building for storage space. The chapel had been devoured by its offspring.

The Congregational patrons who first promoted adult and technical education in Lambeth also encouraged the voluntary provision of free meals for schoolchildren. In this they were joined by dozens of small-scale philanthropic entrepreneurs, for many children could be fed for very little money. The London Congregational Union claimed that Congregational churches supplied ten thousand free breakfasts a week to schoolchildren in 1891.[59] Four Lambeth Board Schools sent an average of 534 children per day to Brixton Independent's Moffatt Institute for penny dinners in 1903.[60] The Working Men's Mission on the New Cut entered into a contractual agreement to feed the schoolchildren at a neighboring Board School in 1899.[61] The Lambeth Teacher's Association cooperated with St. Peter's, Walworth, where they established a large food depot and supplied four thousand meals weekly in 1900.[62]

57. B-273, pp. 85ff.

58. Survey of London, vol. 26, p. 183.

59. John Taylor, The L.C.U. Story, 1873–1972 (1972), p. 18.

60. Brixton Independent Yearbook (1904).

61. B-270, pp. 245–47.

62. SLP, 24 Feb. 1900.

The Boer War stimulated a great deal of public concern about the unsatisfactory physical condition of the working class, which was attributed in part to the inadequate diet of schoolchildren. In a report which received national attention in 1904, the Medical Inspector for Schools in Lambeth, Dr. Eichholz, claimed that 90 percent of Lambeth's students were hindered in their studies by physical defects.[63] Private philanthropy obviously was not doing the job, and in the midst of the demands for social reform and national efficiency heard in Edwardian England it is not surprising to find that one of the first acts of the new Liberal government was the Education (Provision of Meals) Act of 1906. Feeding schoolchildren was visible, inexpensive, and simple, since they were already being fed in many schools, but this act was rightly described by its opponents as the first step in the destruction of the nineteenth-century poor law. By 1912 the L.C.C. Education Committee was supervising the feeding of forty thousand children a week.[64] Religious philanthropists folded their tents and returned to their churches and chapels. Brixton Independent Church reported that "the Penny Dinner season of 1909 was the shortest on record; the work could not be begun until the opening of a new building in February, by which time arrangements had already been made under the L.C.C. for feeding the necessitous schoolchildren of the neighborhood. . . . As a result of the L.C.C.'s arrangements, it became clear at the beginning of the present winter that the work of the Penny Dinners, as such, was *over*."[65]

District visitation soon went the way of penny dinners. The district visitors had for long been under attack by the charity organizers, and in the 1890s the C.O.S. initiated two programs in South London designed to supplant the amateurism of the district visitors: the systematic training of volunteer workers and formal training of professional social workers. The former was first proposed in a paper read to the C.O.S. in 1894 by Mrs. Rose Dunn Gardner, a lifelong C.O.S. worker in Lambeth and

63. N. J. Smith, *A Brief Guide to Social Legislation* (1972), p. 113.

64. Harry Jeffs and Herbert Evans, eds., *Social Workers Armoury* (New York, 1913), p. 83.

65. *Brixton Independent Yearbook*, 1909, p. 29. Emphasis theirs.

member of the Lambeth Board of Guardians for many years.[66] She admitted that it would be difficult to accomplish because of widespread resistance to the local C.O.S. committees, often amateurish themselves, which were to supervise such work. Settlement houses provided a more promising opportunity for regular training, and the Women's University Settlement, Blackfriars Rd., Southwark, offered England's first professional training in social work in the 1890s.[67]

Little came of the proposals to train amateurs systematically, but professional training expanded. In 1899 the settlement had nine residents in social work and six "student residents" in training.[68] The motive for the original development of professional work came directly from the ideology of the C.O.S., which regarded religious philanthropy as a primary cause of poverty. "Suffering and want," the acting head of the settlement claimed, "are very largely traceable to the weakening of character. . . . Contrary influences in the district, making for dependence and thus for the weakening of character, are strong and the most active are the religious agencies."[69] She specifically condemned two contrary influences, the Anglo-Catholic sisters of St. Alphege's parish and voluntary workers from Christ Church, Westminster Bridge Road. Southwark had for long been notorious for philanthropic abuses, and the mission of this settlement was to displace religious philanthropy. Its annual report for 1899 proudly announced that social workers from the settlement had taken over the responsibility for district visitation in the parish of St. Paul's, Westminster Bridge Road.[70] The training given at the Women's University Settlement evolved into the C.O.S.'s "School of Sociology" in 1903 which was eventually absorbed into a professional training program at the London School of Economics in 1912.

66. Mrs. Dunn Gardner, "The Training of Volunteers," reprinted in Marjorie J. Smith, *Professional Training for Social Work in Britain: An Historical Account* (1965 ed.), pp. 69–78; cf. Lord Beveridge, *Power and Influence* (1953), pp. 43–47.
67. Marjorie Smith, *Professional Training*, p. 16.
68. B-273, p. 159.
69. *Ibid.*, p. 171.
70. *Ibid.*, p. 163.

In the meantime the district visiting societies, which had played such an important role in Lambeth's religious life, began to disappear altogether. In 1911 the District Visiting Society of St. Michael's, Stockwell, invested £182 in 3 percent stock, but distributed only £9 in relief. The district visitors had been replaced by two professional visitors, a London City Missionary, and a "Bible Woman." By 1915 the District Visiting Society had ceased to appear in parochial records.[71] In 1913 the St. Aubyn's Congregational Church Annual Report announced that "The Visiting Society formed thirty years ago has ceased to exist," and 1915 was the last year that a list of district visitors appeared in the St. Andrew's, Stockwell, parish magazine.[72]

Although professional social workers displaced district visitors in some parishes, there were not enough of them to usurp the position of all of South London't voluntary district visitors. But even the attempts to supplement professional activity with voluntary effort were supplied, not by the churches, but by the London Education Authority. The Education (Administrative Provision) Act of 1907 followed up the Education (Provision of Meals) Act of 1906 by compelling local authorities to have each schoolchild medically examined three times during his or her school career.[73] The L.C.C. extended this medical supervision by establishing voluntary "Children's Care Committees." Mrs. Hillier Holt, the wife of Brixton's Progressive candidate for the L.C.C., delivered a speech to the Brixton Liberal Woman's Guild upon "Woman's Duty. Their Share in the Voluntary Work of Social Reform." She explained the two types of L.C.C. visitation work: 1. the Children's Care Committee followed up the medical examinations by visiting the homes of those requiring attention and, if necessary, seeing to the provision of meals, boots, clothing, and the prevention of cruelty; 2. the L.C.C. "After Care" Committee kept in touch with children after they left school at age fourteen, and tried in particular to encourage girls to enter the L.C.C. schools of domestic economy. The "After Care" committees were apparently never very active, and

71. St. Michael's, Stockwell, *66th Report of the Various Religious and Benevolent Institutions,* 1911; *Parish Magazine,* 1915.

72. St. Aubyn's Congregational Church, Upper Norwood, *Annual Report,* 1913, p. 30; St. Andrew's, Stockwell, *Parish Magazine,* 1915.

73. N. J. Smith, *Brief Guide,* p. 114.

there were complaints about the lack of volunteers for either committee. But it could not be denied that, as Mrs. Holt put it in 1913, "The L.C.C. had the care of the children of London."[74]

The disappearance of penny dinners and district visitors was only the most visible sign of a highly significant transformation of attitudes about the relationship between the churches and society which reached a crisis point between 1906 and 1914. Other institutions had been encroaching upon the churches for several decades. But during the Edwardian decade, the very definition of the social problem changed, and the churches simultaneously began to think of their own social role in a different way.

Early in our own century, people began to view "the social problem," not as one of undifferentiated "pauperism," but as one which had several components each susceptible of scientific analysis. Instead of "the poor," there was old age, unemployment, "sweating," and inadequate housing. The investigations of Booth and Rowntree contributed to this trend; although Booth was himself an old-fashioned moralizer, convinced that charity caused poverty, he did at last endorse old age pensions.[75] The social criticism of the Independent Labour Party and the Social Democratic Federation was important, and the New Liberals followed suit with their own condemnation of "mere palliatives," i.e., the very mission halls, settlements, relief tickets, and thrift clubs which had replaced another set of "mere palliatives" during an earlier wave of anxiety about the social problem in the 1880s. Although heavily involved in the provision of "mere palliatives" himself, Frank Briant began to demand that the Lambeth Borough Council and the Board of Guardians supply work for the unemployed. The churches' generalized "work among the poor," which mingled coal clubs with Holy Communion, had been thought of in the eighties and nineties as a promising approach to the social problem, or at least as the best approach available. But the churches never offered precise

74. BFP, 31 Jan. 1913; for a discussion of these committees from the church's point of view, see Southwark Diocesan Conference, *The Church's Work for "Citizens in Training"* (1919), pp. 16ff.

75. Cf. the very interesting article by E. P. Hennock, "Poverty and Social Theory in England: the Experience of the Eighteen-eighties," *Social History*, no. 1, Jan. 1976, pp. 67–91.

solutions to specific problems, only a general assault upon general problems of poverty, class division, and disorder.

In 1900 F. H. Stead of the Browning Settlement organized a special conference on "poverty and overcrowding" at the Borough Polytechnic in Southwark. The leading participants were Charles Booth, Lord Hugh Cecil, the Bishop of Rochester, the Roman Catholic Bishop of Southwark, the President of the Newington Free Church Council, and the President of the Central South London Free Church Council.[76] But these church people had little of value to say about overcrowding. After 1900 people ceased to assume that they would have something to say, since the solution, insofar as there was a solution, was thought to be state sponsored public housing. The L.C.C. built its first public housing in Lambeth in 1905, and the following table clearly shows the transition from private philanthropy to the state:

Working Class Housing in Lambeth, 1870–1930[77]

1875	Peabody Buildings, Stamford Street, 16 blocks, additions 1900, no baths.
1879	Surrey Lodge, South London Dwellings Co. (Miss Cons of the Old Vic), 158 units on Kennington Road, no baths or water in flats.
1894	Guinness Building, Vauxhall Walk, 303 units, "associated tenancies," two lavatories each landing.
1905	L.C.C. Housing, 45 units, additional units 1928, 1934, 1935, 1936, 1937, 1938, 3112 dwellings.
1914	Duchy of Cornwall, 48 units, additional units 1932–34, 1938.
1927	Lambeth Borough Council, additional units 1931, 1932, 1936, total of 352 dwellings.

In the 1930s the Ecclesiastical Commission and the church-sponsored Lambeth Housing Movement built ninety units, but mainly with government funds. The churches were regarded as minor partners of the state, and partners with suspect motives in this case, for the Ecclesiastical Commissioners were acting amid a storm of criticism of the conditions of existing housing on their Lambeth property.[78]

Neither the establishment of Labour Exchanges in 1908 nor the provision of Juvenile Labour Exchanges for school leavers

76. SLP, 28 April 1900.

77. From Lady Margaret Hall, *Social Services,* pp. 70–75.

78. BFP, 25 June 1920; 19 Aug. 1921.

much affected the churches, although some parishes had "industrial societies" to provide work for women, and servants' registries to help place domestic servants. The provision of old-age pensions in 1908 passed without much comment at the parochial level, although it was hailed in many chapels. Even though much of the churches' relief was directed to the elderly, this particular act neither drew away volunteer workers nor established a competing local bureaucracy. But the National Insurance Act of 1911 (or perhaps it was the cumulative impact of all of the Lloyd George reforms) had the unintended consequence of eliciting cries of protest from some of the churches over a collapse in financial support for their remaining charities. A few of the larger church-related societies actually benefitted from this act along with the well-established, registered Friendly Societies. The Christ Church, North Brixton, Slate and Loan Club formed an "approved society" under the act which flourished until 1954, and the "approved insurance branch" of the Bermondsey Settlement enrolled 3600 members in 1935.[79] But most of the church-related "insurance" societies were simply small slate clubs, often run by the district visitors. There had already been a movement afoot among the clergy to discourage slate clubs and promote permanent benefit societies, but the Insurance Act prompted clergymen to hand over their responsibilities to the Foresters and Oddfellows altogether.[80]

In 1912 St. Michael's, Stockwell, sponsored a social gathering for the parish relief fund. The vicar took the opportunity to announce that this would "probably be the last function in aid of the parish relief fund. They would probably not need it next year for they had heard of the benefits—the rare and refreshing fruit—which were to be gathered from the insurance act."[81] Other clergymen showed less enthusiasm. The vicar of Christ Church, North Brixton, complained that "it is a regrettable fact that people are not so charitable as in years gone by, and many hospitals had complained that they had lost many of their subscribers. What would be the ultimate effect of the Government

79. Christ Church, N. Brixton, Slate and Loan Club, notes by J. Avery, 30 Jan. 1963 deposited in GLRO, A/CBS/1–7; J. Scott Lidgett, *My Guided Life* (1935), p. 140.

80. See *Southwark Diocesan Directory*, 1908, p. 207; BFP, 19 Sept. 1913.

81. BFP, 13 Dec. 1912.

Insurance Bill he did not know but many persons who were in the habit of contributing toward hospitals and other charitable institutions had sent letters saying they could not continue to do so."[82] The *Brixton Free Press* reported in 1912 that local clergymen were generally upset by "those who are making the additional state burdens an excuse for cutting down subscriptions to charities. . . . It is to be feared that in some cases a withdrawal of charities, or a threat of withdrawal, is simply an expression of political feeling."[83]

It is difficult to know what to make of these comments. Perhaps some Anglicans expressed their displeasure with Lloyd George by withholding their support from the Church of England, although it is hard to believe that Lloyd George would have been greatly displeased. The parochial accounts which I have examined show no dramatic collapse in receipts, but there is such an enormous variation in what they included and how they were compiled that they cannot be considered very reliable. The Southwark Diocesan and South London Church Fund, which provided grants for additional personnel to parishes throughout South London, encountered greater difficulty in procuring grants from one group of reliable donors—the City Guilds—about the time of World War I. Sixteen guilds and the City Court of Common Council donated an average of £347 a year between 1878 and 1920, but only £179 a year in the twenties (£220 a year for the entire inter-war period; see Table 21).

Failing support from the churches intensified a festering financial crisis for the Brixton Dispensary and the Brixton Nursing Association, a crisis which was solved in a particularly humiliating way for the churches. In 1912 cinema owners in Lambeth proposed to devote their Sunday profits to these two institutions if they were allowed, in return, to open on the Sabbath.[84] The cinema had already put a great deal of pressure upon the popular entertainments offered by the churches, but clergymen and ministers generally approved of films as an effective antidote to the public house, which was suffering as well. A curate of St. Matthew's, Brixton, wrote commending the cinema: "We clergy

82. BFP, 28 July 1911.
83. BFP, 2 Feb. 1912.
84. BFP, 10 May 1912.

used to organize Saturday night temperance concerts. Now, the picture palaces have drawn away our audiences. More power to them! They can do the work better than we."[85]

But entertainment on Sunday was another matter, and five clergymen governors of the dispensary threatened to withdraw ecclesiastical funds if the cinema funds were accepted. To this the *Brixton Free Press* retorted that the churches supplied only £72 during the previous year while one cinema alone offered over £250, that support from the churches fell yearly, that the dispensary had been accepting funds from the National Sunday League Sunday concerts at the Empress Theatre, and that it would be a "beautiful and Christian form of revenge to obtain the profits of those Sunday pleasures for the purpose of extending the powers of healing among the sick and poor."[86] The clergy were unmoved, but Sunday cinema was licensed by the L.C.C. anyway and the profits given to other charities. In 1914–15 thirteen Lambeth cinemas (including one located in a railway arch, a traditional mission hall site) and one music hall donated £1535 to organizations such as the British Dental Hospital, the Camberwell Costers Benevolent Association, the Vehicle Workers' Benevolent Association, the Woman's Imperial Health Association, and the St. John's Ambulance Brigade.[87] The dispensary held out until 1917, when it solved its financial problems by accepting cinema funds, "realizing that either their prejudices or the dispensary must go."[88] Parishes and chapels which supplemented the dispensary with their own nurses gradually discontinued the practice upon the resignation or retirement of existing ones.[89]

In some areas the churches continued to innovate in the provision of some social services, but after 1900 they were almost immediately smothered in each instance by the Lambeth Borough Council or the L.C.C. or the government or some other agency. Infant Welfare Centers are a case in point. They were designed to combat infant mortality and, in the interests of

85. BFP, 14 June 1912.
86. BFP, 10 May 1912.
87. BFP, 23 July 1915.
88. BFP, 2 Feb. 1917.
89. St. Luke's, W. Norwood, P.C.C. minutes, April 1924; St. Aubyn's Congregational Church, Upper Norwood, *Annual Report,* 1927.

national efficiency, promote good nutritional habits among working-class women so that their children would grow into healthy adults. Nonconformists, with their usual flexibility, recognized the possibilities first. The Central South London Free Church Council (in cooperation with Christ Church, Westminster Bridge Road, which probably paid the bills) opened the Lambeth Creche and Mission at 95 Kennington Road in 1903 with one professional nurse and two honorary medical visitors.[90] Within two years the ubiquitous Briants of Brixton Independent Church established the Moffatt Institute Maternity and Child Welfare Center.[91] The chapels were partially superseded almost at once as St. Thomas Hospital established an infant welfare center in 1906.[92] Private voluntary associations then appeared with the specific purpose (unlike the missions) of raising funds for infant welfare centers, and in 1912 the Borough of Lambeth established a "municipal milk depot" (a step which the Progressives had advocated for several years) to supply free milk for small infants.[93] In 1916 the borough initiated the "Lambeth Maternity and Child Welfare Scheme" under the direction of its Medical Officer of Health, "incorporating the voluntary welfare centres which were springing up in Lambeth."[94]

Lambeth was advanced in the provision of social services, but in 1917 the medical officer of health of the Local Government Board reported that 51 county councils had provided for the visitation of women and children by health visitors, including all of the Metropolitan Boroughs except Camberwell, and that nationally 396 maternity welfare centers had been established by local authorities and 446 by voluntary societies.[95] By this time the initiative lay firmly with the council, although church- and chapel-related societies were still involved peripherally and the council itself favored mission halls—either functioning or abandoned—as sites for new centers. Voluntary organizations still administered them but the council supplied

90. SLP, 11 July 1903.
91. Retrospective account in BFP, 23 July 1920.
92. Lady Margaret Hall, *Social Services*, pp. 23–26.
93. *Ibid.*
94. *Ibid.*
95. Reported in BFP, 2 Nov. 1917.

the bulk of the funds (seven-eighths by 1938).[96] By 1922 Lambeth had twelve centers (including a new one in a disused pub which was known as the "Babies Pub").[97] Infant Welfare Centers received, rightly or wrongly, part of the credit for the dramatic fall in infant mortality rates between 1902 and 1922.[98]

The declining birth rate combined with increasing living standards and a mysterious improvement in public order helped to alter public perception of the social problem early in the century. There was no longer an enormous undermass of dirty poverty which the churches could combat with undifferentiated "church work." By the 1930s the birth rate had fallen so dramatically that Lambeth's schools could offer babies' rooms in an infant school "for any child of three whose parents wish it."[99]

Fewer children were easier to care for in an orderly manner, and less threatening in general. The inter-war press commented proudly not only upon the increase in material prosperity, but upon the visibly improving level of public order. There were fewer children to create disorder, for one thing, but the change was more general. Why should the English public become more orderly? The influence of an effective educational system no doubt contributed, for after the turn of the century school teachers could count on the cooperation of a generation of parents who had themselves been through school. Was the dramatic fall in alcohol consumption and in convictions for drunkenness during the twenties a cause or a symptom? As the social threat posed by drink waned, the temperance advocates became more isolated and irrelevant despite their notable victories during World War I. A census of men sleeping in the open air in 1929 found only three persons in Lambeth—a far cry from the Edwardian situation. Of what use were the temporary shelters of the Salvation Army and the Church Army? The poverty and disorder which loomed very large in the minds

96. Lady Margaret Hall, *Social Services*, p. 23.

97. BFP, 30 Nov. 1922.

98. Lady Margaret Hall, *Social Services*, pp. 12–16. Lambeth's infant mortality rate (deaths in the first year) fell from 122.7 per 1000 live births in 1902 to 56.3 per 1000 in 1922. This is in line with national trends, and with national and local trends in the crude death rate per 1000 persons. See A. H. Halsey, ed., *Trends in British Society Since 1900* (1972), pp. 335, 338.

99. Lady Margaret Hall, *Social Services*, p. 17.

Public Order in Brixton.
Brixton Free Press, 30 Nov. 1923.

of churchgoers in the eighties and nineties played a lesser role in the public debate about social conditions between the wars. A voluntary organization wishing to enroll private citizens of no great wealth could do very little about the housing shortage or unemployment in the North. Whatever the cause of social improvement, it was not the churches, and that, as C. F. G. Masterman wrote in 1909, was

the kernel of the whole matter. Ethical advance is accomplished (as it seems) by spiritual decline. . . . Growth of morality is coincident with a decline of religion. Violent controversialists still endeavour to demonstrate the opposite, exhibiting murders, thefts, and adulteries accompanying the introduction of secular education or the disestablishment of the Church. On a large survey the facts do not bear such an interpretation. The work of civilization steadily advances. The vision of a universe beyond or behind the material steadily fades.[100]

Between the wars the churches were no longer associated in the public mind with the social problem, and the impulse to help out in some way was largely diverted into the voluntary care committees of the Borough Council and the L.C.C. The L.C.C. voluntary school care committee carried public health demonstrations (such as a model of a child's teeth and mouth used to impress upon parents the evil effects of decay and inattention) into children's homes. The infant welfare centers also enrolled "health visitors" who went into homes in part to ensure that mothers were not simply after "free milk and other benefits." (Why else should they come to an infant welfare center?) The Lambeth Borough Council's "Infant Life Protection Visitors" kept an eye on all registered foster mothers.[101] A special L.C.C. "Aftercare Association for the Mentally Defective," with headquarters in the Welsh Chapel near Clapham Junction, tried to place boys in boot-making and girls in factory jobs, and supplied holidays for the mentally defective.[102] Even the old standby of the chapel Sunday School—a treat in the country—was superseded by a specialized (although private) organization. The "Children's Country Holiday Fund," with two branches in Lambeth, sent volunteer visitors to collect from parents beginning each January and raised enough to send four hundred fifty children for a fortnight's holiday in 1938.[103] The churches played only a marginal, supplementary role with their social

100. C. F. G. Masterman, *The Condition of England*, p. 226.
101. Lady Margaret Hall, *Social Services*, pp. 11, 33, 40.
102. *Ibid.*, p. 48.
103. *Ibid.*, *p.* 41.

services. Frank Briant supported a "poor man's lawyer" to help veterans and their wives after World War I. Lambeth Mission established an "invalid's kitchen." The Ecclesiastical Commission opened a play house for young children in a former pub near one of their estates. The Christ Church, Westminster Bridge Road, unemployed men's club heard lectures on boot and engine repair.[104]

It is not my intention to replace one inadequate generalization—Darwin killed off religion—with another equally inadequate and misleading one—the welfare state killed off religion. Nor do I wish to argue that the coal club was more important than holy communion, or that the "religious" aspects of Lambeth religion were so derivative or epiphenomenal or insubstantial that they could not exist at all without the "social" aspects. It is abundantly clear that religious ideas have their own autonomous and compelling power over individuals and over entire societies. Religious activists in Lambeth took the question of the nature and work of Jesus Christ very seriously, and many of them chatted with Him personally on a daily basis. But it is also clear that religious ideas and religious piety do not exist in some "pure" religious form—in a social vacuum. Religious ideas and sentiments, like other ideas and sentiments, only exist within a complicated network of institutional and social relationships. They only exist within the context of a unique set of historical circumstances. What was happening in the late nineteenth and the early twentieth century was the gradual disintegration of a complicated view of the world—a world in which the offhand distinctions which we now make between the "social" on the one hand and the "religious" on the other hand did not apply in the same way that they do now. As social and institutional relationships changed, assumptions about religion changed—including assumptions about the importance of religion. And that is the kernel of the matter. The Rev. C. E. Brooke of St. John the Divine, Kennington; W. S. Caine of Wheatsheaf Hall; Frank Briant of the Brixton Independent network of philanthropies— each of these men thought that religion *and* the churches *and* "church work" were all of the utmost importance. In some way, the coal club and Sunday School and a burial guild and public

104. *Ibid.*, pp. 57, 93, 106, 138, 144.

worship and individual conversion were related in their minds in a way in which they are not related in ours. And the effort which they invested in churches and chapels worked in a limited way. Volunteers staffed their parishes and chapels, and worshippers were attracted to public worship. Although much less than they had hoped for, it was a substantial achievement.

But their work did not regenerate British society, and after these men died, people ceased to assume that it would. It was not primarily a matter of conscious decision, of individuals who attended church deciding "Well, the churches are no longer useful or important institutions. I believe that I will begin to sleep in on Sunday." It was a matter of unconscious assumptions. Some individuals dropped out of the churches, but many more, without thinking about it, merely ceased to find their way into the churches. No one stepped forward to replace Lambeth's late Victorian religious activists, the men and women who worked the parochial machinery and urged both their friends and their clients to attend church. And it is not difficult to see why. The churches, having nothing to say to the general public, had lost their drawing power. People like Masterman, friends of the churches, were saying that the churches were unimportant and religious belief waning, and the clergy had no effective rebuttal. Many clergymen were saying the same thing.

It is interesting to compare two handbooks on parochial organization written by South London clergymen. The Rev. Charles Kemble's *Suggestive Hints on Parochial Machinery* (1859) urged the clergyman to "bring the gospel to bear on all dwellings within the bounds of his parish . . . diffuse Christian influence through all classes . . . present Christianity under its practical aspects . . . effect a moral improvement in society."[105] To this end he should establish a Sunday School, district visiting society, maternity society, provident club, communicants guild, and library. Political sociologists distinguish between two kinds of voting, instrumental and expressive. When casting an instrumental vote, the voters wish to effect or prevent some change or set of changes in government or society. When casting an expressive vote, they wish to express their membership in or solidarity with some group in society. Kemble's parish of St.

105. Charles Kemble, *Suggestive Hints on Parochial Machinery* (1859), p. 3.

Michael's, Stockwell, offered the potential late Victorian church-goer both instrumental and expressive forms of religious behavior. By participating in parochial activities, he or she could simultaneously "bring the gospel to bear" and "effect a moral improvement." And whether one participated directly in these activities or not, a Sunday churchgoer could express his solidarity with a group of highly respectable people who were carrying out these activities.

By the time the bishop of Woolwich wrote *The Parish Priest in his Parish* in 1933 the instrumental dimension had disappeared altogether and the expressive dimension was much less attractive. Unlike Kemble, he assumed that the Sunday morning congregation represented the devoted core of parishioners with very few occasional or less committed worshippers. The auxiliaries of his ideal parish—children's organizations, uniformed organizations, youth clubs, men's club, women's club—were directed toward the parish faithful. The only parish organizations which reached out to non-churchgoers, the uniformed organizations like the Boy Scouts, he mistrusted as a distraction from home life. By far the most important organization, he argued, was the adult woman's club led by the vicar's wife.

How was the parish to reach out beyond its active parishioners? He considered various evangelistic techniques—open air preaching, advertising, a parochial mission—but showed no enthusiasm for any of them. He regarded it as improper to use baptism, churching, or marriage as evangelistic opportunities, although it was appropriate to urge confirmation upon adolescents. "Steady persistent visiting," he concluded, "is the best evangelistic method we have."[106] But he regarded recruitment as a secondary goal of visitation. Elsewhere he described the object of visitation as "quite simply to know and be known (and perhaps sometimes to invite them to church)." The sick were given first priority for visitation, followed by the congregation; parents of the children in the uniformed organizations, Sunday Schools, and day schools; and "men." This last group was included primarily for the benefit of the clergyman: "We should constantly be coming across not only women but men. It is only too possible to get

106. The Right Rev. A. L. Preston, Bishop of Woolwich, *The Parish Priest in his Parish* (1933), p. 69.

Vicar's Wife. *"I hope you'll come soon to some of our 'Pleasant Hours,' Mrs. Pickles. There'll be tea, followed by a half-hour lecture by the Vicar on some interesting topic."*
Mrs. Pickles. *"I see, Mum—making an hour and a-half in all."*

In Touch with the People. *Punch,* 6 Aug. 1924.

so immersed in other things that we forget how to deal with men." He constantly reminded his readers that it was not rude for a clergyman to invite someone to church, but an obvious difficulty arose when a clergyman rarely saw anyone beyond his familiar parishioners: "I have been told that some parish priests shrink from visiting men and non-church folk generally because they do not know what to say."[107]

This is a picture of a church in retreat, with nothing to do and nothing to say. It is no wonder that no one attended church. Their one "growth area" of the inter-war years—the uniformed organizations such as the Boys' Brigade, Church Lads' Brigade, and Boy Scouts and their female equivalents— did the churches no good in terms either of recruitment or of their general social image. The emphasis upon uniformed orga-

107. *Ibid.,* pp. 12, 13, cf. pp. 58, 104.

nizations is an example of the churches' filling in the gaps in state provision of social services between the wars. The Church of England also expanded its "moral welfare" work among young women, catering to public anxiety about "social purity" which was related in some mysterious way to the falling birth rate, and the churches continued to function as partners with the state in juvenile probation work until the Home Office absorbed the work of the Police Court Mission in 1938.[108] The uniformed organizations along with other less expensive youth clubs in working-class areas were intended to prevent the need for both "moral welfare" and probation work. In 1938 North Lambeth and Kennington alone, one small corner of South London, sustained 257 youth clubs—uniformed and non-uniformed—for those between the ages of five and eighteen, far more than in 1900.[109]

Although loosely supervised by a Lambeth Juvenile Organizing Committee, virtually all of these clubs were sponsored by a church or chapel. The uniformed organizations—the Boy Scouts, the Boys' Brigade, the Church Lads' Brigade, the Boys' Life Brigade, the Girl Guides, the Girls' Life Brigade, the Girl Campaigners—reached their highest English membership levels between the wars despite the backlash against militarism, which led to endless internal controversy and outright schism.[110] They can be sorted out and classified in various ways, including their relationship with the various denominations and degree of militarism. But the point of each of them was more or less the same: to get young people away from the bad influences of the streets and encourage activities which build character. An advertisement for the Church Lads' Brigade in 1904 asked: "How shall we keep a

108. See C. S. Garbett, *In the Heart of South London* (1931), pp. 130, 141, 146; J. Haslock Potter, *Inasmuch* (1927); Lady Margaret Hall, *Social Services,* p. 118.

109. Lady Margaret Hall, *Social Services,* p. 96.

110. On membership figures, see A. H. Halsey, *Trends in British Society,* p. 568; also The Boys' Brigade, *The Report of the Haynes Committee on the Work and Future of the Boys' Brigade* (1964); Annual Reports of the Church Lads' Brigade and Scout Association; Austin A. Birch, *The Story of the Boys' Brigade* (2nd ed., 1965); H. J. Hanham, "Religion and Nationality in the Mid-Victorian Army," in M. R. W. Foot, ed., *War and Society: Essays in Honor of J. R. Western* (1973), pp. 159–80; J. O. Springhall, *Youth, Empire, and Society: British Youth Movements 1883–1940* (1977).

hold over our lads when they leave their day and Sunday schools? . . . Left to themselves in their leisure hours, they are apt to lounge and idle about the streets and this at an age when their wealthier brothers are enjoying the free and healthy life of a public school or college." For some, military drill was thought to build character. The Rev. Paul Bull of the Community of the Resurrection at Mirfield (Church of England) even saw religious benefits in drill: "To call the consecrated anarchy of the average Sunday School 'spiritual' and to call drill 'secular' is absurd. Good drill is one of the most spiritual exercises I know."[111] Richard Church's Congregationalist parents "were persuaded that my attacks of abdominal pain would be alleviated by my learning to form fours and handle a musket."[112]

The founders and leaders of the uniformed organizations intended for them to strengthen religion in general and the churches in particular. The Boys' Brigade and the Church Lads' Brigade were organized as auxiliaries for the Nonconformists and the Church of England respectively. The Boy Scouts was far more successful, largely because its founder Baden-Powell had a genius for creating activities which were fun (such as camping) rather than dreary (such as drill). But the Boy Scouts were equally zealous in establishing links with the various churches and in promoting church attendance. Between the wars the Scouts generally included more groups controlled by a church or chapel than "open" groups which required no church affiliation or connection. Their statement of religious policy adopted in 1910 (and still in effect in 1970) required adult Scout leaders ("Scouters") to put unattached Scouts in touch with some religious body. A later pamphlet went much further, and urged the leader even of an "open" group to "ask the parents to allow him to take their son to his own church."[113] Scouters were urged to discuss religion frankly at troop meetings and to encourage Bible reading and a close study of the life of Jesus (they were warned, however, that "in using the lives of the Saints, illustrations from those who are men of action, rather than those who were ascetics and mystics,

111. The Rev. Paul Bull, "Work Among Lads," *The Guardian,* 30 Dec. 1903, reprinted in St. Peter's, Streatham, *Annual Report,* for 1903.

112. Richard Church, *Over the Bridge* (1955), p. 137.

113. See the Boy Scout Association, *Scouting, Religion, and the Churches: An Interpretation of Scout Policy* (1957 ed.), p. 11; (1969 ed.), p. 13.

will be more helpful to the boy").[114] Baden-Powell described the Scout spirit as "simply the practical application to his everyday life of the essence of Christianity."[115]

There were two fundamental elements of the religious viewpoint propagated by the Boy Scouts, and one of them would have been very familiar to the late Victorian middle-of-the-road Anglican or liberal Nonconformist: a sense of duty. "Scoutcraft," Baden-Powell wrote, "is the means through which the veriest hooligan can be brought to higher thought and to the elements of faith in God; and coupled with the Scout's obligation to do a good turn every day, it gives the base of duty to God and duty to neighbor on which the parent or pastor can build with greater ease the form of belief that is desired."[116] The second element was more remote from the English religious tradition. Baden-Powell had a vivid imagination. ("Have you never seen the buffaloes roaming in Kensington Gardens? . . . And can't you see the smoke from the Sioux Lodges under the Albert Memorial? I have seen them there for these fifty years.")[117] He believed that boys could be led to a realization of God by rousing their sense of wonder at the glories of nature, and Scouters were instructed to make sure that their boys have such experiences. The Scout Association found it necessary to "let it be said, very emphatically, that *Scouting in no sense encourages nature worship*."[118]

The romantic religion promoted by the Boy Scouts, although far from orthodox evangelicalism, was no more unorthodox than that of many of the English churches and chapels. But far from solving the problems of the churches, the Boy Scouts contributed to them. Despite their warm approval of religious faith and positive encouragement of church attendance, the Boy Scouts were a separate and distinct organization. Like the state school system, the Boy Scouts were now responsible for what the churches had formerly attempted: building character in the young and even, like the schools, inculcating religious faith. Like the schools, the

114. *Scouting, Religion, and the Churches* (1957 ed), p. 12.

115. Boy Scout Association, *Annual Report,* 1918, p. 22.

116. *Ibid.,* p. 9.

117. *Ibid.,* p. 8.

118. *Scouting, Religion, and the Churches* (1957 ed.), p. 13 Emphasis theirs.

Boy Scouts stole from the churches, not merely "secular" activities, but the religious functions which the churches might be expected to monopolize. The *Brixton Free Press* welcomed the establishment of a new Scout troop in 1910 in language reminiscent of that formerly used about mission halls: "In days to come many a lad will have occasion to say, when he sees the prison van drive by, 'But for the Boy Scouts, there go I.' "[119] Four years later the paper asked: "What is being done to cope with the problem of the young? . . . There is greater leniency in the home, more liberty in the streets, and a greater license to indulge in the varied amusements which an ever advancing civilization has brought to our doors. An immense amount of good is being wrought by such organizations as the Boys Brigades and the Boy Scouts, while Lads' Clubs and Evening Continuation Classes are also achieving useful work."[120]

In 1921 an article appeared in the *Brixton Free Press* praising the Boy Scouts for guaranteeing a mature religious faith in adults by not forcing religion upon children. The supernatural, the author claimed, was naturally distasteful to boys, but the Scouts inculcated a love of nature which "in later years induces the simple but real religion of a God-fearing man."[121] Some churches, the author implied, promoted a "flabby, invertebrate philosophy" which might repulse a healthy boy. This elicited a letter from the Scoutmaster of the 24th Lambeth troop, who rightly smelled heresy: "No atheist can become a Scout and no Scoutmaster can admit an atheist (if there is such a freak as a child atheist) unless they are both liars."[122] The author of the article, in reply, did not deny the accusation of atheism outright. In the Scout oath, he claimed, the word "God" is used "in the sense understood by boys, i.e., living up to the highest ideals they are capable of imagining."[123]

The Boy Scouts at least tried to promote regular church attendance and did not, like the Sunday Schools, interfere with it by holding their meetings during worship services. This should

119. BFP, 13 May 1910.
120. BFP, 20 Feb. 1914.
121. BFP, 22 July 1921.
122. BFP, 29 July 1921.
123. BFP, 5 Aug. 1921.

have helped the services. Between the wars an observer of South London reported that "a stranger wandering through the streets of my borough, especially upon a Sunday, might have deduced a very active religious life from the processions of one kind or another which lent colour to the streets: little boys dressed as Scouts or soldiers, little girls dressed as decorously skirted sailors, bands—especially bands. There was one composed of very serious little boys and girls with a very little girl as a most energetic drum major, which caused me, at least, infinite joy upon occasion."[124] But the notion that boys would "graduate" from the Boy Scouts to regular church attendance was an illusion. Most Scout churchgoing, like that of the other uniformed organizations, consisted of involuntary participation in Sunday morning church parades. The most likely consequence of that was a strengthening of the notion that religion is something exclusively for children. By their close association with the churches, the Scouts merely strengthened the growing conviction that religion is not a serious matter. Already in 1911, shortly after the Boy Scouts were founded, the Scoutmaster at camp with his troop began to appear in humorous short films, and the fumbling Scoutmaster joined the well-meaning but naïve curate as an object of good-natured ridicule.[125]

The expansion of various kinds of youth work failed to solve the basic problem for the churches, which was the absence of anything of general social significance to say to outsiders and the consequent inability to recruit from outside of the dwindling band of the faithful. Parochial and congregational activities *for* church members took on an added importance as the churches experienced a sort of "retreat into the church." There was a new emphasis upon the appeal of belonging rather than the obligation to serve, but it was difficult to explain the precise appeal of belonging. A South London observer of the twenties

124. O. M. Hueffer, *Some of the English* (1930), p. 86.

125. See Denis Gifford, *The British Film Catalogue 1895–1970* (Newton Abbott, 1973, largely unpaged). Films about the Scouts in 1911 included two comedies, "Charley Smiles Joins the Boy Scouts" and "The Scoutmasters' Motto," and two chase films, "Run to Earth by Boy Scouts" and "Baden Powell Junior." Clerics were featured in three comedies, "The Parson's Wife," "The Parson Puts His Foot In," and "A Seaside Comedy."

reported: "Nor was there any lack of religious effort, the more evident as the churches and chapels had by that time taken a leaf from the book of commerce and advertised their advantages on the walls and in the local press at least as ardently as did the shopkeepers and in similar ways. Usually they dwelt rather upon the material than the moral comforts they offered, as in such appeals as 'A Warm Welcome,' 'Why Go Elsewhere?,' 'Church is a Place to Spend a Happy Evening.' "[126]

Parishes competed with each other in the provision of whist drives and dances; in 1923 the St. Andrew's, Stockwell, parochial church council spent an entire monthly meeting discussing the Saturday night whist drive and dance and "various suggestions were made by which to make them popular among the parishioners and to keep undesirables away."[127] Congregational activities of St. Andrew's Presbyterian Church, Upper Norwood, between the wars included the Brownies, tennis and badminton clubs, a dramatic society, a woman's meeting, and a discussion circle.[128] Both St. Luke's, West Norwood, and the West Norwood Congregational Church established very popular lawn tennis clubs in the twenties.[129] The parish magazine of Christ Church, Gipsy Hill, devoted much of its space to the fortunes of various parochial athletic teams as well as to the Scouts and Girl Guides, and the Mostyn Road Wesleyan Circuit choir festival received much more attention in the twenties than formerly.[130]

Church members sometimes worried about self-absorption and lack of outreach. In 1919 a member of West Norwood Congregational Church attended a monthly church meeting to complain "that all our meetings were occupied with the consideration of matters financial, and that no effort was made for the church to work outwardly. The church was too self-centered, with the result that it had no influence in the neighborhood and was not

126. Hueffer, *Some of the English,* p. 85.

127. St. Andrew, Stockwell, P.C.C. minutes, Sept. 1923.

128. J. McEwan, *The Touch: A Record of St. Andrew's Presbyterian Church, Upper Norwood, 1925–1949* (1949), p. 7.

129. St. Luke's West Norwood, *Parish Magazine;* West Norwood Congregational Church, minutes of the church meeting, 1911–1924.

130. Christ Church, Gipsy Hill, *Parish Magazine,* 1927–1930; Mostyn Rd. Circuit Quarterly Meeting, 1932–1941 (minutes).

in touch with the people. He urged the usefulness and desirability of having a visiting committee."[131] St. John's, Angell Town, initiated a new sports and social club in 1924, but the parochial church council devoted much time that year to discussions of a "lack of work of the church among the poor and sick."[132] The parochial church council of St. Luke's, West Norwood, upset about the exclusive attention given to social activities, insisted upon a new "religious page" in the parish magazine in 1929 so that reports of sermons would appear along with accounts of the Girl Guides. "Religion" was then given one page of the parish magazine, where formerly it had no place at all.[133]

The parochial church council itself, a creation of the Church of England Enabling Act of 1919, was of less interest to the general public than the old Easter vestry meeting. There was much grumbling when it was discovered that the councils had absolutely no power at all over the choice of a clergyman or the clergyman's legal right to conduct the worship service as he pleased, but the councils had a great deal of say in the organization of parochial activities. This strengthened the congregational aspects of the Anglican parish, and there was little that parish councillors could do to reverse the trend toward self-absorption. Many clergymen were worried about a lack of outreach as well, but many of them were inspired by an even more complex form of ecclesiastical self-absorption, the ecumenical movement. That brings us to the special problems faced by Nonconformists between 1880 and 1930, problems which are as important in explaining the collapse of the churches in the twentieth century as those which have been discussed in this chapter.

131. West Norwood Congregational Church, Minutes of the Church meeting, 1911–1924, July 1919.

132. St. John's, Angell Town, Brixton. P.C.C. minutes, 1913–34. GLRO.

133. St. Luke's, W. Norwood, *Parish Magazine*.

7

The Eclipse of Nonconformity: New Ideas and a New Generation

Lambeth's Nonconformists entered the twentieth century with the same hopeful confidence as Nonconformists throughout England and Wales. Even in the midst of the Boer War and a crushing defeat for the Liberal Party, Nonconformist ministers could look back upon a century or more of growth in both numbers and status, and look forward to a bright future for the "Free Churches." The future belongs to us, the minister of Brixton Independent Church told his Congregation in 1900, and particularly to our denomination, for "none of all the churches are more Catholic and Evangelical, more mobile and progressive, less provincial and 'Philistine,' than our Independent churches."[1] This attitude reached (sometimes literally) apocalyptic levels within Nonconformity in the months leading up to the general election of 1906. But immediately after their greatest triumph, Nonconformists experienced a crisis of confidence from which they have never recovered. Their common identity as part of an alternative English cultural tradition began to disintegrate rapidly, marking an important turning point in English history.

All of the churches experienced something of a crisis between

1. *Brixton Independent Yearbook,* 1900, minister's notes.

1906 and 1912 as they faced up to their cumulative loss of social responsibility, and the chapel experienced that crisis along with the neighboring parish church. But something else, over and above the general crisis of the churches, occurred within Non-conformity. Throughout the nineteenth century, Nonconformists had sustained themselves with an ideology of success. Growing numbers were a sign of God's favor, and rough numerical equality with the Church of England was evidence that Nonconformity met the religious needs of England at least as well as the national church. Were falling numbers, then, a sign of God's disfavor?

As early as 1907 delegates to the Home Counties Baptist Association listened to a sermon on "The Present Spiritual Drought."[2] But it was in 1908 and 1909 that something akin to panic set in. A speaker at the Primitive Methodist Conference in 1909 confessed his "deep sense of humiliation and shame over declining statistics. . . . When a soldier hears of reverses in every part of the field he knows that the situation is becoming critical. . . . Like a beleaguered city, the church is hemmed in on every side by the forces of evil."[3] In February 1909 the Rev. Stanley Parker addressed the Mostyn Road Wesleyan Pleasant Sunday Afternoon on the topic: "Is Christianity Doomed?" Never, he claimed, had ministers bewailed the fact of decreasing membership as they did today.[4] Two months later the Gresham Baptist Sunday School Anniversary gathering heard that declining numbers reflected an inadequate emphasis on the young, that the country was in danger because of the decline of the churches, and that "the legislation which Parliament had enacted for the benefit of children should urge them on as a Christian church to do their best."[5]

The following excerpts from the annual reports of a suburban Congregational chapel in South London demonstrate the Edwardian transition in Nonconformist morale:

[1906] Our work has gone quietly on in all its different departments, and though there is no rose coloured story of success to tell . . . [there are] many tokens of the Divine Blessing and Presence in our midst.

2. D. G. Fountain, *E. J. Poole-Connor* (1966), p. 106.

3. *Primitive Methodist Conference Minutes,* 1909, pp. 217–18.

4. BFP, 5 Feb. 1909.

5. BFP, 30 April 1909.

[1908] This has been a year of steady, patient work in the service of our divine head and of his church.

[1910] So far as external appearances go, honesty compels me to say that there is little progress to speak of, and in some respects there would seem to be a partial falling off, which is, as you can imagine, my friends, a great grief to me. And yet it would be a sad failure of faith if we, as the servants of One who has given us so many promises, were to altogether lose heart, and give way to despondency. The tide which ebbs, flows again in due time.[6]

The minister of Gresham Baptist Chapel in Brixton blamed the Baptist Union for destroying chapel morale by issuing pessimistic reports on the "arrested progress of the church." He, for one, saw in the signs of the times, not the ebb and flow of history, but the imminent end of history altogether with the second coming of Our Lord.[7] But many Baptists foresaw a future much less agreeable for Nonconformists.

"The Arrested Progress of the Church" was a report delivered to the spring assembly of the Baptist Union in 1908 by J. H. Shakespeare.[8] As secretary of the union for the past ten years, he had guided it through an unprecedented period of rationalization and expansion. The Union had raised £250,000 for their Twentieth Century Fund, opened a new Baptist Church House in London, acquired control of two Baptist newspapers and amalgamated them into *The Baptist Times and Freeman,* and initiated a new Young People's Union, touring club, insurance society, historical society, publications department, Women's League, and official Baptist hymnbook.[9] Where, then, was the arrested progress?

Although Nonconformists were very unhappy with the Liberal government over both the nature of its successive education proposals and its inability to succeed with any kind of education act, the magnitude of the political catastrophe awaiting Nonconformity under this government was not yet fully evident. By progress, Shakespeare meant growth. A natural pessimist, Shake-

6. St. Aubyn's Congregational Church, Upper Norwood, *Annual Reports.*

7. BFP, 22 Oct. 1909.

8. J. H. Shakespeare, *The Arrested Progress of the Church* (1908), printed address.

9. See Ernest A. Payne, *The Baptist Union: A Short History* (1964 ed.), pp. 156–168.

speare had been warning Baptists of real membership losses
since the early 1890s.[10] As long as absolute gains exceeded
absolute losses each year, no one paid any attention. But in 1908
Shakespeare made his complacent brethren sit up and take notice
with an announcement that "The Free Churches of this land
report a decrease of 18,000 members for last year, and this in
contrast to a large increase in population."[11] The Baptists alone
"lost" 5000 members that year, but the losses were shared by
every major Nonconformist denomination, confirming the sociological unity of Nonconformity despite its doctrinal and ec-
clesiological differences. Shakespeare acknowledged that Nonconformity had experienced periods of membership decline before
which were subsequently reversed, but he made it clear that he
did not really believe that the reversal would follow this time.
He sensed, along with thousands of Nonconformists, that English
Nonconformity had reached a historic watershed. "I have been
told by deacons in different parts of the country," he said, "that
a kind of settled gloom lies upon the church, and that they need
some heartening word. . . . It is as if our planet, by some slight
change on its axis, plunged these islands into a lower average
temperature of twenty degrees."[12]

In several painstaking studies of Nonconformist statistics,
Robert Currie and Alan Gilbert have demonstrated how Nonconformist growth or decline in any given year was the sum of a
complicated process of recruitment, deaths, transfers, and membership termination. Their research also supplies some evidence
that the single most important factor in Nonconformist growth
is recruitment.[13] In a pluralistic society, religious organizations

10. J. H. Shakespeare, *Baptist Church Extension in Large Towns* (1892),
printed address.

11. Shakespeare, *Arrested Progress,* pp. 4–5.

12. *Ibid.* pp. 7, 13.

13. See the statistics assembled by Robert Currie in *Methodism Divided: A
Study in the Sociology of Ecumenicalism* (1968), pp. 95–99. The Wesleyan
Methodist triennial "growth rate" between 1881 and 1931 is positively correlated with the recruitment rate at $R^2 = .5145$. There is no significant correlation between the overall growth rate and the "loss rate" (i.e., resignations)
or the "leakage rate" (i.e., transfers out who fail to transfer in to a new
chapel).

must recruit or die, and the decline of England's Protestant churches reflects a long-term failure to recruit. Far from accelerating, losses of all sorts have declined along with rates of recruitment.

In addition to carefully compiling ecclesiastical statistics from an impressive variety of sources, Currie and Gilbert have constructed a general theory of church growth and decline in Britain.[14] Like many models in historical sociology, this theory illuminates but also obscures. Things which are observed to have happened (e.g., high growth is associated with high loss) or reasonably suspected to have happened (e.g., a larger proportion of non-members' children is recruited during periods of high growth) are incorporated into a general theory. But then the model or theory takes on a life of its own, and absolves its creators from the obligation to think clearly. Statistical trends, once incorporated into the model, become largely self-propelling and wholly irresistible. They are in the model, and require little or no further analysis or explanation. Growth rates decline because of a "slackening of an earlier historical impetus to expansion."[15] Sunday School membership declines because of a decline in the "status-value" of Sunday School.[16] And the Edwardian transition in Nonconformist growth and morale occurred because, decades earlier, the Nonconformist churches began to experience a declining membership to population ratio (MPR) and, in Currie's words, "a falling MPR is pathological," i.e., it is a truly irresistible historical force which sustains itself and accelerates all by itself.[17]

Even if the planet did not tilt on its axis, something did happen to Edwardian Nonconformity. At the very least there was an acceleration in the rate of decline of recruitment which requires explanation. In part the "losses" were actual losses of new

14. Robert Currie, Alan Gilbert, and L. S. Horsley, *Churches and Church-goers* (1978), pp. 8–9, 69–74, and *passim;* also in an earlier form in Currie, *Methodism Divided,* and Gilbert's *Religion and Society in Industrial England* (1976).

15. Currie, Gilbert, and Horsley, *Churches,* p. 120.

16. *Ibid.,* p. 89.

17. Currie, *Methodism Divided,* p. 70; in this book (1968) Currie identifies the 1880s as the decade of transition; Gilbert places it firmly in the 1840s in his *Religion and Society* (1976), ch. 8.

members recruited during a wave of Nonconformist growth between 1902 and 1906. Periods of high growth apparently leave
Nonconformists with more than the usual numbers of members
with a tenuous commitment to the chapel community, perhaps
recruits from families with little or no chapel connection. Currie
and Gilbert employ the useful terms allogenous growth (the
recruitment of juveniles from non-chapel families) and autogenous growth (the recruitment of juveniles from families of the
chapel). There is a good deal of evidence, both statistical and
anecdotal, to support the theory that late nineteenth- and early
twentieth-century Nonconformist recruitment was heavily autogenous except in times of extraordinary growth.[18] It is perhaps
unwise to make too sharp a distinction between the two kinds of
growth, for if the churches and chapels became less attractive
and less useful to outsiders they were probably thought of as
less useful and less attractive by insiders as well. However, in
addition to the temporary losses following the Edwardian revivals,
Nonconformists probably experienced greater difficulties in recruiting and retaining their own children early in the twentieth
century for a number of reasons.

In the first place, there were fewer children to recruit. In 1901,
32.4 percent of the total population of England and Wales
were under fifteen, in 1931 23.8 percent. Although there were
over seven million more persons in England and Wales in 1931
than in 1901, there were a million fewer persons under fifteen.[19]
It is difficult to sort out the Welsh Sunday School statistics
(which are peculiar) from the English, but even when Great
Britain is taken as a whole it is clear that this change in age
structure affected Nonconformity. Between 1901 and 1931 British
Sunday School enrollments fell 11, 26, and 21 percent for the
Baptists, Congregationalists, and Wesleyans respectively (see
Table 22). Because of temporary growth in the 1920s (soon to be
reversed even in Wales), each denomination had roughly 10
percent more adult members in 1931 than in 1901 in Great
Britain. To many Nonconformists, the Sunday Schools appeared
to be disintegrating. But real rather than absolute membership

18. Currie, Gilbert, and Horsley, *Churches,* p. 81.
19. A. H. Halsey, ed., *Trends in British Society Since 1900* (1972), p. 33.

statistics tell a different story. Each denomination experienced a real membership decline (as a percentage of the population aged fifteen or older) of about 20 percent, while the Sunday Schools experienced a less severe real decline (as a percentage of the population fourteen and under): less than 1 percent for the Baptists, 18 percent for the Congregationalists, 13 percent for the Wesleyans.

Eliminating Welsh statistics and choosing slightly different dates produces an even more illuminating contrast. In 1936 English Congregationalists had 5 percent fewer adult members than in 1904, and 42 percent fewer Sunday Scholars (see Table 23). But their real membership decline (as a percentage of those over fifteen) amounted to 31 percent while their real decline in Sunday School enrollments (as percentage of those aged three to fourteen) was not much worse—35 percent. There were roughly the same number of adult English Baptists in 1936 as in 1904, but over one hundred thousand fewer Sunday Scholars. Yet their real membership decline amounted to 28 percent, their real decline in Sunday School enrollments only 18 percent.

The shrinking pool of potential recruits supplied an incentive for Nonconformists to tamper with the structure of the Sunday School in an attempt to improve their retention rate. A prominent Baptist demonstrated the ineffectiveness of the Sunday School with a few simple figures in an article in the *Baptist Times*:

Some will ask what justification there is for asserting that we lose our children to the world in such appalling numbers. . . . According to the *Baptist Handbook* we have in our Sunday Schools nearly 565,000 children, and taking that figure to begin with some things become speedily plain. . . . If in a school of 100 scholars only one were, by the united efforts of pastor, people, and teachers, persuaded to join the church this year, and that average—one in a hundred—were maintained throughout all of our schools, we should add to the church before the year is over nearly 6000 new members. And if instead of one we were able to get two, we should add over 11,000, three nearly 17,000, and so on. . . . 5 percent is surely not beyond us. . . . the result would be that on our present school figures *we should add more than 28,000 new members to the church a year*. And a regular addition of fewer than 28,000 would not only solve our present problem of decreasing members and half-empty churches, it would speedily present another which would be truly inspiring, viz., how to provide churches for the people who were pressing into them. And this in spite of annual natural loss by death, removal, etc.[20]

Part of the problem in fact lay with the organization of the chapel Sunday School, for Sunday School attendance did not lead structurally to chapel attendance. The child was placed in an infant class, ascended by stages to the senior class, and then graduated, as often as not, to nothing at all. There was no adult class (Sunday School was for children in London and most of England), and classes were often conducted during all or part of the morning worship service so that children never acquired the habit of church attendance. The largely Nonconformist Sunday School Union, convinced that falling Sunday School enrollments reflected "wholly antiquated methods," celebrated its centenary in 1903 by introducing the modern, "scientific," graded lessons which American Sunday School reformers developed in the late nineteenth century.[21] The Union also established a school to train Sunday School teachers at Selly Oak, Birmingham, and the Anglicans, not to be outdone, founded a similar institution in 1909: St. Christopher's College, Blackheath. After 1916 the Sunday School Union published standard graded courses for all ages and encouraged the formation of adult Sunday School classes.

Their goal was to break down the identification of Sunday School with children. Churchgoers of all ages would attend Sunday School on Sunday morning, then attend public worship. Sunday Scholars would graduate into an adult Sunday School class where many churchgoers would encourage them to attend worship. Afternoon Sunday School classes, at least as popular as morning classes at the turn of the century, were left in limbo along with the evening service, which was the major service of the day for many English chapels. This scientific scheme caught on in the American South and Midwest (in the face of considerable resistance), but not in Britain where the identification of Sunday

20. Donald Maclean, "The Problem of the Churches: The Outsiders, the Children, and the Great Gulf," *Baptist Times and Freeman,* 14 May 1915, cf. W. J. Townsend, H. B. Workman, and George Eayrs, *A New History of Methodism,* vol. 1 (1919), p. 474.

21. See D. P. Thompson, ed., *The Sunday School and the Modern World* (1924), p. 124.

School with children, and the corresponding adult resistance to attending Sunday School, remains stronger, to put it mildly.[22]

Despite all of their concern with structure, Nonconformists failed to improve their retention rate. They enrolled a smaller portion of a shrinking pool of potential recruits in the early twentieth century, and there is some evidence that it was becoming more and more difficult to recruit members of the most promising Nonconformist constituency: children of chapel members (not to be confused with Sunday School members). Outsiders as well as insiders might find that the appeal of Nonconformity was waning along with the waning social utility of all of the churches. But there were special problems within Nonconformity, problems which were not wholly new. From the very beginnings of Dissent in the seventeenth century, Nonconformist parents in prosperous families confronted children who were likely to defect. The pattern naturally varied from family to family and did not exist at all in some families with particularly strong Nonconformist traditions. But the severe difficulties involved in maintaining a Nonconformist family tradition over several generations were so common that they are taken for granted in the history and literature of Nonconformity. If Lambeth's late nineteenth-century Nonconformist patrons did not lose interest in the chapel, their children or their grandchildren did. Mark Beaufoy was an Anglican in a traditionally Nonconformist family (see Chapter 4). C. E. Tritton and Henry Doulton abandoned their parents' Dissent for the Church of England. Alexander McArthur's son became a clergyman. The Baptist patron William Higgs began attending Anglican services late in life. Frederic Nettlefold of Norwood (1835–1913) was known in the community for his prominent support of the Effra Road Unitarian Chapel. His son and heir, Frederic John Nettlefold (1867–1949), was also a prominent patron of an important South London social institution, the Crystal Palace Football Club.[23]

The reasons for this declension are not difficult to find. The

22. *Ibid.*, pp. 60, 196.

23. A. C. Crofton, *The Nettlefolds* (1962), *passim;* on these patrons see the references in Chapter 4.

Nonconformist cultural tradition made very little sense to children who were not only wealthy, but also not excluded in any significant way from sources of status in British society. C. E. Tritton became an Anglican at Charterhouse. Although W. S. Caine remained a Congregationalist until his death, one of his sons became a doctor and the other went to Balliol and became a barrister and then a novelist.[24] One daughter married an M.D., the other two M.P.s. It would be little short of astonishing to find that they all remained Congregationalist temperance advocates. Albert Spicer's daughter recalled that:

By the time father began his public career, Nonconformity had been freed from nearly all official disabilities, but there were still a certain number of secondary effects, notably social inferiority. As school children, we were conscious of this, and realized that, despite our father's public position there was, particularly amongst those of our friends who came from Conservative households, the feeling that we were not really "gentlefolk." The only thing was to invite them to tea, and watch their faces as the door was opened by a butler, followed by a footman with silver buttons. This raised our status.[25]

She also observed that "for nearly a century the Spicers have been one of the leading Congregationalist families in the country—the tradition is showing signs of decay."[26]

This problem was never one of mere prosperity, but a complicated matter of social class, institutional and legal status, and subjective social perceptions. The stigma of Dissent did not disappear at once with prosperity and the removal of legal disabilities. But as Nonconformists became more prosperous and more thoroughly integrated into Victorian society, especially through participation in new educational and administrative bureaucracies, the crisis of generations spread far beyond the families of distinguished patrons and industrialists. I have discovered ten autobiographies and biographies published between 1918 and 1972 with information about this crisis of generations

24. John Newton, *W. S. Caine, M.P.* (1907), p. 12.
25. *Albert Spicer: A Man of His Times, by one of his family* (1938), p. 22.
26. *Ibid.*, p. 15.

among South London Nonconformists of relatively humble circumstances.[27] Some contain only fragments of information, and others relate a tenuous or short-lived connection with a chapel or the story of a father who fell away from Nonconformity. Most of the autobiographers achieved some sort of distinction in life. But the experiences are similar to those of young Nonconformists in other parts of the country, notably those recorded in C. S. Davies's *North Country Bred* (Lancashire), Kingsley Martin's *Father Figures* (Hereford and Finchley), and Kathleen Raine's *Farewell Happy Fields* (Ilford) as well as Arnold Bennet's Clayhanger novels and Edward Thompson's neglected novels of Edwardian Nonconformity, *Introducing the Arnisons* and *John Arnison*.[28] In each case the son or daughter of a chapel family fails to see why he or she should continue within the Nonconformist tradition. Beyond that, the experiences vary enormously. Some merely fall away, as a matter of course, while others do battle with an oppressive inherited tradition which threatens their identity.

A minister's son, John Arnison, confronted a friend of his father's who

Plainly took it for granted that John was going to take up his father's work.

That settled it. What proved more than anything else that John, despite his upbringing, belonged to the new generation, was his revolt when anyone fiddled on his heart-strings or suggested that his spiritual and mental life must go on lines of consanguinity. "Your mother's devotion," "Your father's work"—by God! no! and never! and he was

27. 1. Kingsley Amis, *Whatever Became of James Austen? and Other Questions* (1970); 2. E. B. Bax, *Reminiscences and Reflexions of a Mid and Late Victorian* (1918); 3. Eric Bligh, *Tooting Corner* (1946); 4. Richard Church, *Over the Bridge* (1955); 5. Fenner Brockway, *Bermondsey Story: The Life of Alfred Salter* (1949); 6. Havelock Ellis, *My Life, The Autobiography of Havelock Ellis* (1940); 7. William Kent, *Testament of a Victorian Youth* (1938); 8. William Margrie, *My Eighty Years in Camberwell* (1957); 9. V. S. Pritchett, *A Cab at the Door* (1968); 10. Malcolm Muggeridge, *Chronicles of Wasted Time: Part I. The Green Stick* (1972).

28. C. S. Davies, *North Country Bred: A Working Class Family Chronicle* (1963); Kathleen Raine, *Farewell Happy Fields* (1973); Kingsley Martin, *Father Figures* (1966). I would include Gosse's *Father and Son* if the Plymouth Brethren were not so far from the Nonconformist mainstream.

not blaspheming. He was appealing, in strict literalness, to the truth within his own soul.[29]

The intellectual as well as the psychological forms of the revolt varied. E. B. Bax reacted with unequivocal hostility to all religion—the Victorians were "poisoned and warped by the foulness and follies of their creed."[30] Eric Bligh and William Kent both agonized over their relationship to Nonconformity and left it with great reluctance (although Kent eventually became an outright secularist). Both men came from families and chapels which emphasized conversion. Kent, William Margrie and Havelock Ellis (who came from an Anglican family and only attended chapel briefly) embraced some form of secularism. But if new ideas were seducing young Nonconformists, it seems as if almost any new idea would do the job. Eric Bligh and Richard Church were strongly attracted to the Church of England. V. S. Pritchett's father converted to Christian Science (and his cousin to Anglo-Catholicism). Others embraced socialism—Bax a materialistic Marxism, Davies the secularist Clarion Club, Salter a sort of Nonconformist Christian socialism, Martin and Muggeridge's father the orthodox left-wing Labourite position. Kathleen Raine rejected her father's Methodism (which she thought ugly) but could hardly embrace socialism as an alternative since her father was an ardent socialist as well. She was attracted by aestheticism and the literary life. Edward Thompson complained that "Nonconformity has given its children a dull world—dull, dull, unfathomably inexpressibly dull."[31] His John Arnison was challenged by socialism and Roman Catholicism, but enchanted with literature. As more young Nonconformists received secondary and university educations, more of them must have faced the dilemma of Donald Davie:

The "chapel" interest does indeed play a crucial and momentous part in the literary history of England; as the "enemy" or precisely that which, in each generation, English artists must do battle with, and circumvent the best they can. On this showing, you perceive, my situation all those years ago—as a young Baptist in love with English poetry,

29. Edward Thompson, *John Arnison* (1939), p. 297.

30. E. B. Bax, *Reminiscences*, p. 20. His parents lived in Hampstead, then Streatham.

31. Thompson, *John Arnison*, p. 66.

and determined to write poems himself—was quite simply anomalous—self contradictory.[32]

If not secularism, socialism, or aestheticism—then perhaps Anglicanism. Eric Bligh's father, a South London doctor, "received his particular attitude to sacred things from four generations of Nonconformity, and I do not think that in the process of handing down it had changed at all. . . . His ancestors had been of the small commercial world. To their faith, not won without mental strife, he had added the acquirements of an extremely skillful physician, and yet his medical training seems scarcely to have touched the inherited view of God, of life, and the world."[33] This view he attempted to inflict upon his children:

> In later years the gentle strength of his religious views was to create an atmosphere so permeating and miasmatic that he was to see his own children gradually separating themselves from him, and fleeing from the heavyweight influence of that grace and simple faith which were to him the mainspring of his life. How deeply he loved us; but nevertheless and all the more he applied to us those same methods of evangelisation with which he had earlier brought the glad news to the coolies.[34]

Eric read "with great pleasure the fun Mr. Arnold makes of Dissenters, and resolved that my own days should be devoted, not to Hebraism, but all to sweetness and light."[35] The elder Bligh "was never seen within a barge pole's length of the parish church . . . which history had taught him to mistrust." His son, even before he left home, was seduced by the local Anglican church, by the beauty of the Book of Common Prayer, by the piety, he claimed, as well as the beauty of the National Church.[36]

In the North London suburb of Ilford, Kathleen Raine confronted a father who was both Methodist and socialist. "His only cultural inheritance was the Methodist Christianity his father had inherited from his grandfather who had walked, so my

32. Donald Davie, "The Nonconformist Contribution to English Culture," *TLS*, 16 Nov. 1976, p. 1459. This essay was reprinted in his *A Gathered Church* (1978).

33. Eric Bligh, *Tooting Corner*, p. 69.

34. *Ibid.*, p. 65.

35. *Ibid.*, p. 315.

36. *Ibid.*, pp. 70, 253–54.

father would often tell us, twenty miles to hear John Wesley preach, and twenty miles back, to go down the pit on a Monday morning, strengthened in that darkness by his faith in another world than that cave where prisoners are chained."[37] Having advanced from pupil-teacher in a village school to a degree from Durham University to a position as schoolmaster in a London suburb, he remained loyal to the Methodism of his ancestors even though "the congregation of shopkeepers and commercial travellers were no more my father's kind than they were of my mother's. He missed the warmth of that Methodism Coleridge so well described as 'a stove' ('heat without light,' as he said); the revival meetings, the 'speaking with tongues,' the 'simple faith'; but this he would never admit, for he, too, was trying to keep faith with a vanished past, though one neither my mother nor myself could share with him."[38] Christian egalitarianism was part of his inheritance, for his own father "had always refused promotion, though a poor miner, even to the rank of foreman; for as a Christian he had felt it wrong to hold office over his fellows."[39] Her father refused to admit that he had risen in the world, and insisted that the brotherhood of man required the abolition of property. A Methodist local preacher, "he often spoke for the League of Nations Union, which he saw as a practical means of leading the world a little nearer to that heavenly city which was, he believed, already coming down from heaven as an earthly reality as the socialist cause grew in power and numbers."[40]

His daughter rejected this bundle of Methodism, egalitarianism, and socialism. Methodism was hostile to culture, she argued: "Ignorance then as now seeks in bewildered envy to destroy what it cannot possess; what it cannot even perceive. . . . Yet those sour world-hating Puritans my father reverenced as saints of his religion; those smashers of all the riches of English Gothic culture, of the images of the Virgin, Refuge of Sinners. . . . My father . . . was without curiosity because for him all was settled long ago, when on the verge of manhood he himself underwent conversion to what he himself called—and indeed

37. Kathleen Raine, *Farewell Happy Fields,* p. 64.

38. *Ibid.,* p. 111.

39. *Ibid.,* p. 104.

40. *Ibid.,* p. 111.

it was—'a living faith,' a life-long orientation which needed no confirmation from books, from which indeed too much reading would have been only a distraction."[41] No less than egalitarianism and socialism, her suburban neighbors threatened her individual creative genius. "Neighbors! my heart said, these are not *my* neighbors."[42] "I rejected socialism and the greatest good for the greatest number for those values which few can reach, in the belief that the high and the beautiful things are of value in themselves."[43] Christianity she rejected altogether, although "Had I learned Christianity from its art rather than in the psuedo-historical, psuedo-factual mode taught by Nonconformists, I might have understood many things of which I had no conception until much later."[44] Another young Methodist from her chapel, in a revolt more dramatic than hers, entered an Anglican monastery. "What more natural to a youth hurt, frustrated in his ambition to become a doctor, his texture of love dreams torn by the conflict of guilt, than to turn to that religion, more authoritative than parents, which can open even in the suburbs a door of escape from meanness of culture and narrowness of life into all the grandeur, beauty, dignity and wisdom of Christian civilization."[45]

Raine writes of the 1920s, Eric Bligh of the Edwardian decade. Just before World War I, Clara Davies faced a parting of the ways with her Methodist parents in Lancashire. Her father's tailor shop had gone bankrupt when she was very young:

After the sale my father gathered the family round him in the almost denuded house. There was no money and very little food. My father addressed his God, saying something, I gather, to the effect that he, my father, had done his best and that it was time He took over. This prayer was immediately answered by the arrival of a neighbour with a cooked meal and after this was eaten my father saw an advertisement for a traveller in wholesale men's and boy's clothing. . . . The firm who advertised were at Leicester; my father set out immediately and reached the firm's premises before any other applications had been received. The partners of the firm were Jews and they were so impressed by my father's

41. *Ibid.*, p. 75.
42. *Ibid.*, p. 110.
43. *Ibid.*, p. 130.
44. *Ibid.*, p. 119.
45. *Ibid.*, p. 148.

story of divine intervention, by his personality, and by the pertinacity with which he urged his claims (for he must have been desperate) that they engaged him on the spot.[46]

But worldly success took its toll. At age fourteen Clara was already refusing to attend the sacrament; at eighteen she was bicycling about the countryside distributing the anti-religious propaganda of the Clarion Club. "Our family were radicals and from my father's time we had been active in the cause of woman's suffrage. My relatives were reasonably progressive for the period, but socialism and irreligion they could not stand. We parted with strained civility."[47]

Arnold Bennett records a similar tale in *Clayhanger*. Darius Clayhanger, a young kiln-worker in the Five Towns, ends up in the workhouse with his parents, but is rescued by a kindly Primitive Methodist local preacher. He then prospers as a printer and converts to Wesleyan Methodism, but his son, Edwin, is as bored with his father's religion as he is (initially) with his father's profession. The son's attitude to religion closely resembles Bennett's own as an adolescent:

I myself never felt within me the operation of the religious instinct. Even as a schoolboy, in the late seventies of the last century, brought up as I was in a society which honestly deemed itself to be in continuous and close communion with God, I never felt anything but a cautious disdain for the impassioned beliefs surrounding me. Nor was I in the least degree aware of the great undermining controversies then so violently proceeding in the intellectual world above me. . . . I was interested in the manifestations of religion only to avoid and ignore them.[48]

Bennett's explanation of his own "loss of faith" follows the Victorian conventions:

The empire of Christianity is crumbling because it has been attacked at its weakest point . . . its sole weak point; the once universally accepted convention that the theory of the direct, divine inspiration of the Bible must not be questioned. . . . From the moment when geologists demonstrate that the earth could not have been made in six days or

46. Davies, *North Country Bred,* p. 57.

47. *Ibid.,* p. 82.

48. Arnold Bennett, *The Religious Interregnum* (1929), p. 7.

six years or six thousand years . . . from that moment the convention was doomed. It had to be. Nothing could maintain it. The breaches in it inevitably multiplied faster and faster until the thing lay in ruins.[49]

He also, quite wrongly, accuses the Victorian churches of exalting faith and giving conduct a secondary role in human affairs. But Bennett himself admits to having been wholly oblivious to the great Victorian debates over Genesis and geology. The Edwardian conflict of generations involved a greater variety of "new ideas," but the pattern is the same: upwardly mobile prosperous father and rebellious child bored with or threatened by the chapel.

It is difficult to measure ideological and intellectual changes like that with any precision. Were young Nonconformists merely experiencing the revolt against Victorianism of the early twentieth century, and finding the Nonconformist tradition a convenient target? Were there turning points in the history of Nonconformity proper (such as the Edwardian "New Theology" controversy) which marked a greater "quantity" of doubt and dissatisfaction? Some ministers argued that an old problem was becoming more troublesome late in the century. James Guiness Rogers, for instance, wrote of the problem in 1903 after a long and influential ministry at an affluent Congregational church in Clapham: "I am not insensible to the evils arising from the restlessness of the age and the passionate desire to adapt an old faith to a new century . . . there is in many minds a revolt against what they call the tyranny of the past, and the difficulty is to oppose so dangerous a tendency without at the same time trampling unduly on the liberty of individual thought. This has really been the most perplexing problem of the Christian minister, especially in London, during the last quarter of a century. I could extend that period to a much more distant date. It seems to me that I have never been free from that kind of controversy, and it is not easy to see how it is ever to cease."[50] The family of lapsed, middle-class Nonconformists became a recognizable social type in the late nineteenth and the early twentieth century. "Our next door neighbours," H. G. Wells wrote, "were a very pleasant couple named Popham, small rentiers with cultivated tastes who

49. *Ibid.*, p. 8.
50. James Guiness Rogers, *An Autobiography* (1903), pp. 137–38.

read well and thought of doing something to mend the world. They were the children of that serious Nonconformity which founded so many sound businesses in the mid-Victorian epoch, turned them into honest joint stock companies, and left its children just enough to travel, trifle with the arts, and supply the backbone of the new British intelligentsia."[51] But not of the new British Nonconformity.

It is possible to isolate some changes within Nonconformity—in addition to, although associated with, prosperity and upward mobility—which contributed to a generational revolt of peculiar intensity within those mainline Nonconformist denominations dependant upon "autogenous" growth. Victorian Nonconformists placed an inordinate emphasis upon education, politics, and, increasingly, public service as the spread of university and secondary education and the creation of a local administrative bureaucracy in 1870, 1888, 1894, and 1899 provided many opportunities for Nonconformists to achieve status outside of the chapel. James Baldwin Brown, a prominent liberal Congregationalist minister in Lambeth from 1845 to 1884, took special pride in his son's education: "He made considerable sacrifices to secure for him the utmost advantages that are open to a young Englishman through a public school and university training, and this, not merely to procure for him access to a learned profession, but for the sake of mental enlargement and general cultivation which are to be gained in the ancient seats of learnings."[52] R. F. Horton recalled the attractions of the establishment for a young Nonconformist at Oxford: "that atmosphere of culture, that centre of vivid interests, that open vista to the highest honours in church and state . . . the sunshine of social recognition."[53] Nonconformists fought throughout the nineteenth century to have the universities opened up, only to begin complaining in the 1880s of the consequences. According to Basil Martin, at Oxford in the early eighties "so many of the men from Nonconformist homes became Episcopalian that it sometimes appeared that, whilst the university had gained by opening its doors more

51. H. G. Wells, *Experiment in Autobiography* (1934), p. 509.

52. Elizabeth B. Brown, *In Memoriam: James Baldwin Brown of Brixton Independent Church* (1884), p. 91.

53. R. F. Horton, *My Autobiography* (1917), p. 60.

widely, the Nonconformist churches had suffered."[54] There is little question that the Anglican church benefited enormously.

The establishment of the Nonconformist colleges at Oxford—Mansfield, Manchester, and Regents Park in particular—was an attempt to stem the tide. In 1892 the president of the Baptist Union advocated a Baptist College at Oxford, because "the young warriors reared under the shadows of a 'Trinity' or a 'Balliol' . . . will be emasculated ere they fight. Like the Shechemites who submitted to circumcision in order to atone for the wrong that had been done, these men will fall easy victims to the sword of Jacob's crafty sons."[55] A Baptist chaplain at Oxford claimed in 1915 that over forty dons were "of Nonconformist origin," but few identified themselves as Nonconformist. (Middle twentieth-century studies of British academics have shown an inordinate number with Nonconformist family backgrounds.)[56] The problem extended to the public schools. The Executive Committee of the Congregational Union warned against sending children to secondary schools hostile to Nonconformists, and formed a committee to "keep a watchful eye . . . on the great public schools of the country, with a view to protect Nonconformist youth from sectarian influences."[57] In 1910 the *Methodist Recorder* complained that "for daughters especially of wealthy Methodists there are no really suitable Nonconformist schools; . . . in Church of England services they grow accustomed to liturgical services."[58]

Anxious about seduction or indoctrination, Nonconformists saw only part of the problem. The superior Anglican liturgy supplied the Church of England with a competitive advantage among the wealthy and well-educated, it is true. But the spread of university and secondary education among Nonconformists was only one aspect of a much more widespread integration of

54. Basil Martin, *An Impossible Parson* (1935), p. 42.

55. *Baptist Handbook,* 1892, p. 40.

56. *Baptist Times,* 30 April 1915, p. I; cf. A. H. Halsey and M. A. Trow, *The British Academics* (Cambridge, Mass., 1971), p. 416. Nearly 23 percent of their sample were from a Nonconformist family background, twice the percentage of Nonconformists in the general population. Under 5 percent of the sample were from Roman Catholic backgrounds.

57. *Congregational Yearbook,* 1891, p. 8.

58. *Methodist Recorder,* 6 Jan. 1910, p. 3.

Nonconformists into the life of the nation. The explanation for Edwin Clayhanger's boredom with the chapel (there is no mention of Anglican indoctrination or Darwinian doubt) may be found, arguably, in the very first pages of the novel: "Many people for many years had been engaged in providing Edwin with knowledge. He had received, in fact, 'a good education,' or even, as some said, 'a thoroughly sound education,' assuredly as complete an equipment of knowledge as could be obtained in the county."[59] The point is not that he learned something at Old-castle Middle School which made him reject Nonconformity, or that an educated person could not be a Nonconformist, or that he was lured away by an alien ideology, but that a "sound education" might remove one of the psychological pillars of Nonconformity, a sense of marginality and exclusion.

Around the turn of the century, if not before, Nonconformists began to complain of the "excessive demands" which the chapel made on their time, notably with the proliferation of weekday auxiliaries. But these same offices and organizations had been created in the middle and late Victorian chapel in response to lay demand for them. When John Clifford began his pastorate at the Praed Street Baptist Chapel in West London in the 1860s, "The Sunday Services were not enough, the people wanted somewhere to go during the week, there were no clubs or classes for young folk and no counter-attractions to the public house."[60] The other reason for the existence of chapel auxiliaries, much commented upon in the nineteenth century, was recognition. Clara Davies's uncle, a bricklayer who was "a little wanting," scandalized his Wesleyan relatives by joining the Salvation Army. "Blowing a bugle in the Salvation Army was the nearest that Uncle Bob came to achieving a sense of personal value. . . . [He] did not get much out of life, but had one of the most magnificent funerals that it is possible to imagine. The united Salvation Army communities of Manchester turned out to do him honour. After an impressive service at the citadel . . . a procession half a mile long, preceded by an assembly of brass bands, accompanied the cortege . . . no King had a more impressive farewell."[61]

59. Arnold Bennett, *Clayhanger* (New York, 1910), p. 11.

60. James Marchant, *Dr. John Clifford* (1924), p. 42.

61. Davies, *North Country Bred*, p. 37.

By the 1890s many of the chapel auxiliaries had evolved into something wholly separate from the chapel, and the remaining ones often seemed superfluous to mainstream Nonconformists if not to members of the Salvation Army. As chapel auxiliaries became absorbed in the work of the school boards or local government, the *Congregational Yearbook* complained that "Many of our churches are very busy at the present time in the formation of societies to supersede themselves."[62] The school system itself provided education for Nonconformist children, employment as schoolmasters for Nonconformist parents, recognition as school board members for Nonconformist notables, and eventually evening classes for potential members of the chapel debating societies. In 1892 the Kent and Sussex Baptist Association urged the passage of a parish councils bill and encouraged Nonconformists to participate in local government, but in 1909 the moderator of that association complained that "our laymen are neglecting church for work on town and county councils, education committees, and the various societies that exist for the public at large."[63] The Municipal Corporations Act of 1835 began the process, but only in the urban boroughs outside of London. Local government acts of 1888 and 1894 extended an effective local administration to the entire nation. By 1890 the new threat of "civil position" was added to the traditional Nonconformist warnings against the ancient enemy, "worldly success." In 1890 the president of the Wesleyan Conference, in his presidential address, claimed that "In the early days of Methodism influential laymen used to preach. . . . Amongst men of culture and social position the practice of preaching has declined. Such men prefer civic duties today, and when they occupy public position with dignity and honour, we rejoice with all our hearts; still we urge our educated young laymen to listen to the call of God."[64]

Nonconformists were caught in the cruel dilemma of promoting their own destruction, for they took enormous pride in the worldly positions so long denied them. The Primitive Methodists heard warnings against allowing "your business interests, your

---

62. *Congregational Yearbook,* 1891, p. 69.

63. Kent and Sussex Baptist Association, *Circular Letter,* 1894; *Annual Report,* 1909.

64. *Wesleyan Methodist Minutes of Conference,* 1890, p. 350.

keenness for civil position, your desire for commercial success, consume all of your time and energy."[65] But in 1907 the minutes of the Wesleyan Conference proudly noted that the conference included "two M.P.s, two mayors, a host of aldermen, JPs, councillors, guardians of the poor."[66] In 1913 the National Brotherhood Council, a central federation of the local brotherhoods which had evolved out of the Nonconformist Pleasant Sunday Afternoon meetings, published a "handbook for transforming society into the Kingdom of God."[67] Readers were urged to pursue that goal, not as chapel members, but as guardians of the poor and members of the parish council, rural or urban district council, borough council, county council, local education authority, education authority after-care and feeding committees, local housing committee, local sanitary committee, the trade union movement, the cooperative movement, and voluntary organizations chosen from a list of literally hundreds devoted to the elimination of every imaginable vice, evil, and flaw in English society. From Balliol to the local sanitary committee, alternatives threatened the life of the chapel. Arnold Bennett observed the dilemma of the struggling urban chapel in the 1920s, and speculated upon the members' motives: "Nor is the desire for office sufficient to account for the sacrifices; offices far more influential and carrying far more prestige than those connected with the organization, go a-begging in the vast parish or borough in which the organization struggles, from one year to the next."[68]

South London's local chapel notables (as opposed to the wealthy patrons with national stature) were typically prosperous shopkeepers or small entrepreneurs. But it is impossible to avoid noticing another sort in the eighties and nineties whose income or position in the community came from the educational or administrative bureaucracy: George Prichard, school attendance officer, member of Lambeth Chapel, treasurer of the South London Free Church Council, Guardian, churchwarden; Harry Alfred Ticehurst, assistant master of Stockwell Road L.C.C.

65. *Primitive Methodist Conference Minutes,* conference address, 1897, p. 194.

66. *Ibid.,* 1907, p. 219.

67. Harry Jeffs and Herbert Evans, eds., *Social Workers Armoury: What a Brotherhood Man Can Do* (1913).

68. Bennett, *Religious Interregnum,* p. 5.

school, then master of Tooting L.C.C. school, lifelong member of Brixton Hill Wesleyan Chapel "with a special interest in the choir"; Alderman N. W. Hubbard, a Free Methodist who served on every imaginable municipal body between 1886 and 1929; Thomas Gautrey, Liberal candidate in the boisterous Peckham by-election of 1908, a pupil teacher at a British school in Catenham, Cambridgeshire, then Queen's Scholar at Borough Road Teacher's College, assistant master of a school at Nunhead, then headmaster's assistant, member of the London School Board and London County Council.[69]

Walter Hobbs, pastor of Gipsy Road Baptist Chapel, became so involved with the Lambeth Board of Guardians that a faction of his church forced him to resign. He took his supporters with him and built a tin tabernacle across the road, and his biography is entitled *Pastor and Guardian*.[70] "One of the reasons why the churches are comparatively empty," a Brixton Wesleyan minister complained, "is that many men are finding so many spheres of social service outside the Christian Church."[71] But these men did not cease to think of themselves as Nonconformists merely because they were public servants as well. Hobbs flaunted his Nonconformity as a Guardian, as did many other local politicians and schoolteachers. Sometimes their influence was almost embarrassing. Nonconformists served as churchwardens. N. W. Hubbard and George Shrubsall, licensing justices, terrorized licensed victuallers from the bench. Passive resisters at the Lambeth Town Hall faced two magistrates who were themselves passive resisters. Prominent Nonconformists found themselves appointed managers of Church of England schools as a result of the hated 1902 Education Act, and the Strict Baptist undertaker and passive resister, Councillor Crook, was nominated school manager of the Roman Catholic school in Brixton.[72] The proliferation of these

69. BFP, 29 June 1906; 16 Feb. 1923; *Norwood Press*, 3 May 1929; SLP, 20 March 1908.

70. John Stuart, *Pastor and Guardian: A Sketch of the Life of the Rev. Walter Hobbs of West Norwood* (n.d.).

71. BFP, 12 Feb. 1909.

72. SLP, 7 Feb. 1908; BFP, 16 June 1905; 17 March 1905. Ernest Jones, deacon of Brixton Independent Church, was one of the magistrates. Frank Briant, H. G. Turner, and George Brittain were appointed school managers of CE schools. This position had ill-defined responsibilities.

positions in the late Victorian educational, political, and administrative bureaucracy provided an alternative to mere prosperity as a means of integrating Nonconformists into British society and eliminating the stigma of Dissent. Even if they devoted less time to the chapel, these men retained their Nonconformist identity. But would their children?

Theological liberalism, with its liturgical services, was the Nonconformist response to the twin challenges of prosperity and prominence, of worldly success and civil position. William Kent's father owned a printing shop on the Clapham Road which prospered in the 1890s. In 1902 the family moved to a much more respectable street in Clapham, and in 1903 his father won a by-election to the Wandsworth Borough Council.[73] William attended the plebeian Wheatsheaf Hall, although his parents were Wesleyans. (Young Nonconformists often chose their own chapel as a means of asserting their independence. The minister of Loughborough Park Chapel claimed to have a number of young married couples who chose that chapel in order to avoid their parents.)[74] The members of the Wheatsheaf Hall adult Bible class eagerly discussed Robert Blatchford and the theology of R. J. Campbell. Thomas Huxley's *Agnosticism* jolted Kent severely in 1902; in 1904 he resolved his religious quandary by joining Brixton Independent Church. He continued to attend Wheatsheaf Hall Literary Society, but also joined the Brixton Independent Literary Society (which discussed topics such as "Will Bernard Shaw Be Among the Immortals?") and began attending classes at the Kennington Road Evening School.

Disillusioned with Brixton Independent by 1913 (he called it the "slippery slope"), Kent became a rationalist, joined the South London Ethical Society, began teaching in their Sunday School, and made a volume of Gibbon into the family Bible.[75] This did not last, however, and he later dabbled in spiritualism—willing to try anything rather than give up some form of church. "What, however, assisted me back to the path of sobriety and reason," he wrote, "was not merely the utter inability of those persons to convince anybody except those who wanted no convincing, but

73. William Kent, *Testament of a Victorian Youth,* p. 162.

74. B-303, p. 30.

75. Kent, *Testament,* p. 255.

my own difficulties in making up my mind which brand of Christianity I was going to accept. One day I would feel evangelical and 'Sankey moodious'—another day semi-Unitarian."[76] He remained a member of the South London Ethical Society at least until 1934, and continued to deliver lectures to its dwindling congregation (326 members in 1918, 90 in 1936) as late as 1938.[77]

Kent finally pronounced religious liberalism a transparent form of wish-fulfillment. The Rev. Bernard Snell's "beliefs were simply other names for his wishes."[78] He criticized him for picking and choosing among verses of scripture, for using words to mean almost anything, and for calling almost everyone a Christian (Brixton Independent admitted an avowed agnostic to the diaconate during World War I).[79] He is perhaps applying rather strict standards, but he does point to a genuine problem of legitimacy. All religious groups reflect the ideals and prejudices of their members (or their clergymen), but that fact was more obvious for nineteenth-century Nonconformist liberalism. Like European theological liberalism in general, it was not anti-intellectual but it was often anti-theological. Cut loose from theological moorings, the liberal churches appeared to float aimlessly on the top of society, making them more vulnerable to the reductionistic critiques of those first discovering the social nature of all religion.

Furthermore, although theological liberalism is still with us and probably always will be, there is something to the notion that the particular form which liberalism took in late Victorian England made it unusually vulnerable to reappraisal during the years following 1914. The Rev. Bernard Snell thought so, and his Christmas message of 1914 was filled with despair:

Utter insanity . . . our civilization bankrupt, our hopes shattered, our consciences shocked. We are all caught in the grip of a great horror, impotent all of us. . . . The nightmare of international hatred and insensate bloodshed is pressing home the conviction that the only chance of enduring peace lies in the recognition of the fact that all

76. *Ibid.*, p. 260.
77. South London Ethical Society, *Annual Reports,* 1917–1938.
78. Kent, *Testament,* p. 250.
79. *Ibid.*

mankind is of the Holy Family of which the Father is the Holy God himself. . . . Our prayers are that out of this welter of woe may be born a new civilization.[80]

The nearby parish church of St. Matthew's recovered its prayer books with khaki and opened a rifle range in the crypt. Evangelical Baptists began comparing the Kaiser to Nimrod and Nebuchadnezzar and drawing analogies from the Books of Daniel and Revelation. Snell thrashed about helplessly during the war, sometimes condemning German culture as a sick threat to Christian civilization and calling for reprisals (to Kent's disgust), at other times risking the displeasure of the Tory press by warning against a "war against the German people."

The twenties proved little more hospitable to Snell, who remained minister of Brixton Independent until 1934. "I am far from being a detractor of the times," he claimed in 1921, "but all will admit that the shallow soil, the thorny ground, and the wayside of the parable were very much more in evidence today than the good ground." Although he had no desire to "be a Stiggins," he condemned recent risqué books which "had exposed England to contempt throughout Christendom, as if she were incapable of moral earnestness."[81] He continued to argue, however implausibly, that a reasonable man will draw religious conclusions: "We cannot rest our argument for immortality on the statement that 2,000 years ago God wrought a wonder in Palestine such as he will not or cannot do today . . . reason forbids that the noblest product of the universe—man—could be destroyed."[82] The ideology of liberal Nonconformity simply proved less adaptable to new circumstances than either evangelical Nonconformity, with its emphasis on transcendence and the doctrine of sin, or the Church of England, more firmly rooted in a group of historic institutions rather than in a particular way of looking at the world.

Before concentrating too much upon changing circumstances and new ideas, however, it is important to remember that liberal Nonconformity had for long confronted unique problems in sustaining church growth. The problem was lack of intensity.

80. BFP, 25 Dec. 1914.
81. BFP, 24 June 1921.
82. BFP, 1 April 1921.

Coleridge put it very well: "Socinianism, moonlight; Methodism, etc., a stove. O for some sun that shall unite light and warmth!"[83] Snell complained in 1909 that "many of the best people whom I know are making a serious mistake. They learn in our liberal churches to escape from 'the bondage of the letter.' They cheerfully throw overboard the crudities and incredulities of old uses and tradition. They thank God that they know too much to be any longer bound down to the narrow and impoverishing ways of those who were unhappily not as enfranchised as themselves; and then they turn their backs on the churches, to which they owe almost everything, and leave them to perish. That is neither reasonable nor generous."[84] The liberal Central Hills Baptist Church was noted for its lack of weeknight church life. The Rev. S. A. Tipple of Central Hills "used to be sent away for long holidays, and even at normal times the social work of the church was entirely discontinued. The minister would preach once on Sunday and then the chapel doors would be shut, and he would retire to his books, undisturbed by mid-week organizations."[85] As a liberal missionary in Soho, Basil Martin greatly envied the intensity of the evangelicals:

How I envied the Salvation Army! What would I not have given to be able to stand up in the street and say "I was a drunk and like some of you, I was destitute and degraded. I was a libertine, but Jesus Christ saved me, washed me clean, and filled my heart with joy." . . . But the message I had to give was useless in Soho. My words had no more effect than those of an unknown tongue. . . . The only thing likely to convince the people of Soho seemed to be a miracle, for when I was preaching in the street one evening a man demanded "ocular demonstration." . . . Yet these mission people were full of enthusiasm. It has been my trouble all through my life that so many of those who are doing the most practical work hold views which I cannot accept.[86]

One consequence of the waning intensity which accompanied the spread of liberalism was a lack of attention devoted to the religious beliefs of children. In addition to confronting greater

83. *The Notebooks of Samuel Taylor Coleridge,* ed. K. Coburn, vol. 1 (1957), p. 467.

84. *Brixton Independent Yearbook,* 1909, p. 7.

85. Bligh, *Tooting Corner,* p. 54.

86. Basil Martin, *An Impossible Parson,* pp. 55–56.

recalcitrance among a shrinking pool of potential recruits, a section of Nonconformist parents ceased even to make an effort at recruitment. The decline of Nonconformist membership can hardly be called mysterious in those circumstances. Liberal Nonconformists defined themselves, in part, by their attitude toward conversion, which they rejected as vulgar and old-fashioned. They shared with most Anglicans a belief in the gradual socialization of children. Unlike the Anglicans, however, they had no formal structure of socialization (guilds, confirmation classes, etc.), only the chaotic Sunday Schools. But it is not a question of structure or technique so much as a question of attitudes. Parents who encourage or expect or hope to see a conversion experience for their children are likely to communicate the importance of religious faith to the individual much more emphatically at a time when children are vulnerable to parental attitudes. This stance may produce a violent counter-reaction, but it is less likely to leave the child apathetic. It is no accident that the plebeian and evangelical denominations emphasizing conversion—Baptists, Primitive Methodists, Free Methodists—maintained their strength longer than the Congregationalists and Wesleyans.

In 1905 the minister of Camberwell Green Congregational Church edited a series of letters and essays on the religious status of children which demonstrates how thoroughly the doctrine of a "conversion experience" had been discarded by churchmen and leading Nonconformists alike.[87] The bishop of Durham, an evangelical, argued that conversion, while necessary, "may evidence itself by the gentlest growth of grace from babyhood."[88] The Hon. and Rev. J. G. Adderly, writing as "High Churchman," urged baptism as "the normal way in which each human life is taken into union with Christ."[89] The Presbyterian and Nonconformist contributors argued either that conversion was unnecessary (F. W. Stanley, a Brixton Unitarian, and R. J. Campbell, minister of the City Temple), or that it was a gradual and perhaps imperceptible process (Prof. James Orr, P. T. Forsyth, and J. Scott Lidgett among others). Only the single Baptist

87. Thomas Stephens, ed., *The Child and Religion* (1905).
88. *Ibid.,* p. 22.
89. *Ibid.,* p. 24.

professed himself "unable to see how anyone can be in the king-dom until he is old enough to exercise his own choice. . . . I believe this choice, which from the human side we call con-version . . . should be expected in very little children, who can often understand what sin is and what forgiveness means far better than many suppose, and should be regarded as the normal experience of child life in every household where the little ones are brought, not to any ceremony, but to the living Christ, in prayer and faith."[90] This contrast within Nonconformity was recapitulated in two longer essays. R. F. Horton, outlining the views of the Free Churches, denounced all dogmatic teaching of the young, argued strenuously for the necessity of conversion, and then explained away conversion as nothing more than a gradual process of socialization. A Baptist, on the other hand, argued that during adolescence "the critical period has come when the work of preceding years should find its consummation . . . this is the time when a personal religious decision is most commonly reached."[91]

In one sense the Congregationalists and Wesleyans were merely recognizing in theory what had been common practice all along in every Nonconformist denomination. Even the Baptists faced a chronic problem in deciding what to do with obviously religious children who never reached a religious crisis of any kind. The moderator of the Lancashire and Cheshire Baptist Association complained in 1907 of having occasion "to ask some young proba-tioners [i.e., ministers] to give an account of their conversion, and the answer in each case was that they had been brought up in Christian homes."[92] While holding to the need for a definite experience, Baptists sometimes described it as the awakening of a "keener sense of duty" or something of the sort rather than a supernatural warming of the heart. But the Baptists did hold to the theory of conversion, even many liberal Baptists such as John Clifford, while many Congregational and Wesleyan ministers had a sense of a dramatic change in attitude toward conversion in the late nineteenth century. Guiness Rogers, for instance, wrote in 1903: "A short time ago I undertook to preach at the

90. *Ibid.*, p. 30.
91. *Ibid.*, p. 302.
92. *Baptist Times,* 21 June 1907.

opening of a new Congregational chapel in a simple Scotch town in which no new place of worship had been opened during the last half century. . . . It was my pleasure to find that here was flourishing a very earnest type of what must be described as old-fashioned piety. . . . I found myself in the midst of men who believed in conversion and not only believed in it but ventured to talk of it. . . . This is a state of things to which all churches must return if they are to retain their true power."[93]

Prominent Edwardian Wesleyans attempted to end the system of basing membership upon the class meeting, which was designed for individual testimony about the conversion experience. R. W. Perks, a wealthy patron who supported this effort, always recalled with disgust the atmosphere of forced conversion at the Kingswood school of the 1860s. Young people of today, he argued, are "naturally affected by the prevalent modernism," and laxer membership requirements "make it possible for his own children and those of thousands of other families all over the country to enter conscientiously and freely into membership."[94] In 1910 the *Methodist Recorder* linked the abandonment of the class meeting with changing views of conversion. "The religious temper of today is not favorable to the view that weekly attendance at a class meeting . . . is essential to the well being of the spiritual life . . . the proving of the efficacy of saving grace in personal experience is no longer the peculiar mark of Methodism. . . . The diversity of human temperament and the necessary variety of Christian experience cannot be forgotten."[95] In 1921 a Methodist minister complained that "If I make an evangelistic appeal at an ordinary service people complain that I am taking unfair advantage. If I try to meet that criticism by announcing beforehand that I am going to hold an evangelistic service, they complain that such an announcement keeps many of our people away."[96] Victorian "spurts" of Nonconformist growth were associated with, although not necessarily a consequence of, waves

93. Rogers, *My Autobiography*, p. 135.

94. R. W. Perks, *Sir Robert William Perks, Bart.* (1936), p. 20; Denis Crane, *R. W. Perks* (1909), p. 132.

95. *Methodist Recorder*, 10 Feb. 1910, p. 13.

96. *Ibid.*, 6 Jan. 1921, p. 6.

of revivalism. The last of those waves of extraordinary growth
occurred between 1903 and 1906. Their disappearance may well
be explained, not so much by greater resistance among the
general public to revivalistic appeals, as by the greater reluctance
of Nonconformists of all sorts to resort to such techniques.

This attitude spread among plebeian Nonconformists as well,
notably in those chapels which were not shielded from the perils
of respectability by the theology of C. H. Spurgeon. William
Kent observed a growing reaction against vulgarity in Wheatsheaf Hall (which had been established in part as a protest against
respectability). It first surfaced in divergent attitudes toward the
ambiguity inherent in the blood imagery of evangelical hymns.
When the congregation sang the verse "Shall we be carried to
the skies/on flowing beds of ease/Whilst others fought to win the
prize/and sailed through bloody seas," they split into three
factions: a minority which sang bloody, the opposition which
sang "stormy," and "the neutrals [who] sang nothing or slurred
it over with some kind of joyful noise."[97] More significant, however, was the changing attitude toward children. In the 1890s,
during special Sunday services, children were coaxed into an
inquiry room at the rear of the church where they were encouraged to "decide for Jesus" while hymns were sung.[98] By 1904
the chapel was split into pro-conversion and anti-conversion factions, and charges of Unitarianism were levelled at some young
members, including Kent.[99]

The son of a printer, Kent was a civil servant with the L.C.C.,
and Lambeth's Nonconformists were apparently moving into
routine, clerical white-collar positions more rapidly than the
general population (see Tables 24 and 25). Even more significant
than this evidence of relative upward mobility is the disappearance of significant occupational differences between liberal and
plebeian Nonconformists in the early twentieth century. The
complete incorporation of Lambeth's Baptists into the middle
class is particularly striking, although they partially protected
themselves from the consequences by embracing a conservative

97. Kent, *Testament*, p. 25.
98. *Ibid.*, pp. 54–55.
99. *Ibid.*, pp. 180ff.

theology which emphasized conversion and recruitment. The other plebeian chapels had no such resources, and almost all of them are now closed.

I am not arguing that Nonconformity declined because Nonconformists abandoned conversion. It is possible to imagine circumstances in which gradual socialization would work very well. The important change was one of attitude, not technique. Prosperity and the construction of an educational and political bureaucracy which supplied functional alternatives to the chapel helped to produce a generation of Nonconformist parents who took a laissez faire attitude toward the religious attitudes of their children. Kingsley Amis's father, who grew up in the Denmark Place Chapel in Camberwell, "never put the slightest pressure on me to have anything to do with religion, explaining that he knew far too well what it felt like to be forced to attend chapel."[100] Richard Church's father tried to force him into the civil service, but he raised no objection at all, or at least no objection worthy of recording in an autobiography, to his son's confirmation in the Church of England in 1908.[101] Even those parents who felt strongly about religion sometimes ended by sanctioning their children's defection. Kent's father told him that he did not mind his joining the "slippery slope" of Brixton Independent Church, and Eric Bligh's father encouraged him to attend the Church of England which was better than no church at all.[102]

Set adrift, Nonconformist children fell prey to whatever movement or ideology seemed attractive. Many on the fringes of Nonconformity must have shared the dilemma of V. S. Pritchett. His grandfather was a Congregationalist minister, his father drifted from Congregationalism to Christian Science, and his confused mother, a nominal Anglican, sent him to Sunday Schools of various denominations: "I had scarcely ever been to church but had lived in a house filled with religious echoes and disputes. I had been brought up as a Christian without being taught very much of what Christianity was."[103] Kent drifted

100. Kingsley Amis, *Whatever Became of Jane Austen?* (1970), p. 193.

101. Richard Church, *Over the Bridge* (1955), pp. 210–12.

102. Kent, *Testament,* p. 217; Bligh, *Tooting Corner,* p. 254ff.

103. Pritchett, *A Cab at the Door* (1971 ed.), p. 167.

from church to church trying to find one which fit his mood, and the daughter of a Plymouth Brother, who writes fondly of her childhood, observed every child of the family leave the Brethren. All, however, remained in some church or another, and one "tried a process of elimination, working her way through all denominations from Plymouth Brethrenism to Roman Catholicism."[104]

Explanations of the decline of England's churches usually dwell upon "secularization" or "urbanization" or "industrialization" or the growth of "materialism" or "secularism" or something of the sort. But it is possible to be much more specific about what happened to Nonconformity in the late nineteenth and the early twentieth century. The chapels were hit all at once by the emergence of new philanthropic, administrative, and educational bureaucracies which destroyed their claims to social utility, by a changing age structure, and by a generational revolt which struck Nonconformity with particular intensity because of the waning of a "marginal" Nonconformist cultural tradition in the face of economic success and civil position. Insofar as liberal Nonconformity was a success for parents, it was a failure for children.

Most autobiographies record a defection from Nonconformity to some early twentieth-century form of secularism, socialism, or the literary life. It is at least possible, however, that in the quiet of the suburbs among those who do not write, the Church of England has been the great beneficiary of the crisis within Nonconformity. The Church of England was the traditional path out of Dissent for wealthy Nonconformists, and as affluence and social standing spread further down the social scale, the local parish church must have seemed a sensible choice for the young Nonconformist who wished only to attend an attractive service occasionally. Unfortunately evidence about this trend, if it was a trend, is scattered and unreliable. In 1900 the vicar of St. Saviour's, Herne Hill, claimed to be "astonished by the number of children who come to school and for confirmation who say that their parents are Nonconformists. He has remonstrated with Nonconformist parents in cases of confirmation and has been told

104. "Septima," *Peculiar People: An Account of the Religious Experiences of the C. Russell Hurditch Family, by one of his daughters* (1935), p. 141.

by them that they like their children to think for themselves and not to feel bound to join the chapel."[105] Between 1910 and 1929 the vicar of St. Andrew's, Stockwell, a working-class parish, confirmed twenty-one Nonconformists, although six were Presbyterian and may have been Scottish.[106] In 1927 the vicar of Christ Church, Gipsy Hill, a suburban parish, urged the young Nonconformists who attended services there to be confirmed, a step which implied "no belittling of their former church membership" but would allow them to receive holy communion as a right rather than as a courtesy.[107] Such scattered bits of information (although from one London borough) are difficult to evaluate, and the Church of England first tabulated "receptions into the CE" in 1954. In the three years 1954, 1955, and 1956 the Church of England received an average of 11,295 persons per year from non-Roman Catholic denominations.[108] They were presumably from the Church of Scotland and the Nonconformist denominations, or foreigners. In 1958 alone they received 6959. Assuming a rate of 5000 Nonconformists a year, the Church of England would have gained 50,000 from Nonconformity during the 1950s alone, which was nearly one-fourth of the total membership of the Congregational Union of England and Wales in 1956 (218,671; the Methodist Church, Baptist Union, and Congregational Union had together about 1.25 million members). It is impossible to say whether or not this was happening on a significant scale earlier in the century, although a minority of young Edwardian Nonconformists clearly found the forbidden delights of the Church of England almost irresistible. Young Anglicans who had the church inflicted upon them would have found that attitude mysterious indeed. Young Nonconformists were arguably more susceptible to the appeal of the National Church than any other Edwardian social group.

Political fragmentation seriously exacerbated the Nonconformist identity crisis. Social radicalism in the tradition of John Clifford did not disappear, but the Liberal Party did and with

105. B-305, p. 163.

106. Confirmation register at the church.

107. Christ Church, Gipsy Hill, *Parish Magazine*, Feb. 1927.

108. Church Information Office, *Facts and Figures about the Church of England* (1962), p. 52.

it the Progressives in Lambeth and L.C.C. politics. The remaining social radicals often balked at socialism and the Labour Party. Social radicals of the twenties such as the Rev. Thomas Tiplady of the Wesleyan Lambeth Mission and the personally popular Liberal M.P. Frank Briant took positions on the wickedness of capitalism and the necessity of some degree of nationalization which would place them on the "Marxist" fringe of the Labour Party of the 1980s, at least in the minds of Tory editorial writers.[109] Although some social radicals did find their way into the Labour Party, these men drew the line at outright socialism, not because of their Nonconformist individualism or their hostility to the state, but because of their horror of industrial strife and openly avowed class conflict. They could not accept the notion that social justice might come through class-based industrial strife rather than citizen-based political action. Compulsory arbitration, they argued, was just as appropriate to the coalfields as to the battlefields. Thoroughly demoralized before the end of the war, John Clifford wrote in his diary in 1917 that "We have lost the ethical and spiritual primacy, and it has passed to the Puritan Commonwealth of the U.S.A. With all its faults it has been more faithful to the Puritan ideals, and that fidelity gives them power and authority today. It has little of the oligarchical interests that we have here."[110] Too good a Baptist to join his liberal friends in their enthusiasm for the ecumenical movement, he launched his own campaign in 1922 to revive Nonconformity through personal evangelism.

Clifford's quandary is evidence of the eclipse of the Nonconformist tradition which had been meaningful to so many English men and women as recently as the Edwardian decade. Clifford was reaching back into his own past, and his denomination's past, to find a new direction for Dissent. But most Nonconformists responded to the decay of a distinctively "Nonconformist" cultural tradition by embracing either "fundamentalist" evangelicalism or the ecumenical movement. Both worked in turn to weaken further the Nonconformist tradition for they were simultaneously broader and narrower than Nonconformity. Nonconformist evangelicals reached out to evangelicals in the Church

109. See Thomas Tiplady, *Social Christianity in a New Era* (1919).
110. James Marchant, *Dr. John Clifford* (1924), p. 229.

of England and in the "independent" churches of no denomination, while the ecumenical movement was based upon the
premise that the existence of a separate cultural tradition was
itself a scandal. And by focusing upon apostasy and heresy and
slackness on the one hand, and the evils of schism and overlapping on the other, both movements diverted attention from the
fundamental dilemma of all of England's Protestant churches:
the lack of anything to say to someone who was not already
committed.

Evangelicals in each of the Nonconformist denominations reacted to the decay of Nonconformity and the decline of church
attendance by withdrawing even more firmly into a kind of
orthodox ghetto, and by rejecting that portion of their own
tradition which dictated a concern with social improvement as
well as individual conversion. The annual reports of the London
City Mission, which began to show an appreciation of the various
sorts of social problems between 1895 and 1910, lapsed after the
war into an incoherent obsession with the "Three Social Evils:
Intoxication, Gambling, and Immorality."[111] After the war puritanical attitudes appeared to be more prominent in Nonconformity in general because they existed in isolation from the
broader social concerns which had characterized pre-war philanthropy and social radicalism. This residue of puritanicalism
was not limited to the extreme evangelicals, and Nonconformists
became more accurately classified in the public mind as a group
of people unaccountably worried about restricting drinking,
prohibiting greyhound racing at the Crystal Palace, and forbid-
ding the Irish Sweepstakes. During the 1929 election the *Baptist
Times* seemed mainly concerned with whether or not a candidate
would campaign on Sunday, a far cry from the serious (though
highly partisan) discussion of the issues in 1906 and 1910.[112]

In the case of more extreme evangelicals, the unintelligibility
of puritanicalism to the general public was reinforced by a
revival of an equally unintelligible millenarianism. West Norwood's independent evangelical Lansdowne Hall flourished in
the 1920s under the direction of the Rev. Fuller Gooch, who was
active in the Prophecy Investigation Society and contributed to

111. London City Mission, *Annual Reports,* 1920–1932.
112. *Baptist Times,* 19 April, 25 April, 16 May 1929.

magazines such as *Silver Morn, Rainbow, Things to Come, Morning Star, Prophetic News,* and the *Advent Witness.*[113] For Gooch, the imminent second coming of Christ was indisputably foreshadowed by the restoration of Israel and the apostasy of the church, particularly its Nonconformist branch. In a tortuous exegesis of the Books of Daniel and Revelation he explained the precise meaning of the Roman Empire, the Turkish threat to Europe, the Reformation, and the future disposition of Turkey, Egypt, and Palestine, arguments all buttressed with citations from similar studies by Isaac Newton.[114] The effect of all of this speculation was to isolate further the independent evangelicals not merely from the Nonconformist denominations but from the British people as well. The *Norwood Press* carried weekly transcripts of the sermons in the major West Norwood chapels during the twenties. The puritanical statements of the Baptist minister were at least comprehensible, if not very attractive. But when Fuller Gooch preached on prophecy, as he often did, the persons responsible for transcribing his sermons inevitably lost track of his argument and allowed the newspaper account to become unintelligible gibberish.

The older evangelical emphasis upon conversion and growth was displaced by an emphasis upon combatting apostasy and heresy. Fuller Gooch had left the Baptist Union in the 1890s in the wake of C. H. Spurgeon's "Downgrade" charges. In the 1920s he was instrumental in the formation of a loosely structured new denomination, the Fellowship of Independent Evangelical Churches, committed to the maintenance of doctrinal purity and to strident attacks upon the apostasy of mainstream Nonconformity.[115] By the 1960s the FIEC had grown from a handful of churches to over 250.[116]

Mainstream Nonconformity moved toward the ecumenical movement in the 1920s, but had no more success than the evangelicals in discovering a new constituency or finding something to say to the people of England. In 1923 one of the last of the

113. H. M. Gooch, *William Fuller Gooch* (1929), p. 89.

114. William Fuller Gooch, *Reconstruction in Bible Light* (1919).

115. See D. C. Fountain, *E. J. Poole-Connor, 1872–1962* (1966), pp. 24–26, 32.

116. See Ernest W. Bacon, *Spurgeon: Heir of the Puritans* (1967), p. 144; E. J. Pool-Connor, *Evangelicalism in England* (1951), p. 261.

pre-war Nonconformist social radicals to hold onto his office after
the war, the Rev. Scott Lidgett, lost his L.C.C. seat to Labour.
In his memoirs, he complacently recorded the fact that he had
spent the previous day, not out campaigning, but "peacefully at
Lambeth Palace, discussing [church] reunion."[117] At the national
level, the leaders of the major Nonconformist denominations
devoted a larger and larger portion of their time to largely fruitless ecumenical consultation instead of politics, social reform,
and philanthropy. Toward the end of his autobiography (1943)
the Rev. P. Carnegie Simpson, a leading English Presbyterian,
apologetically noted that "From the topics which have occupied
the last considerable number of pages, it may seem not only that
my life had become again immersed into the vortex of ecclesiasticism but even that this was my main occupation. Any such impression is wide of the mark."[118] Such an impression is right on
the mark, as is his apologetic tone, for the ecumenical movement
left Nonconformist leaders even more isolated from ordinary
English people and even less equipped to answer the question:
"Why should I attend church?"

The ecumenical movement has been interpreted as a "response
to decline,"[119] although it would make just as much sense to
label it a means of avoiding any response to decline. But the
ecumenical movement was and is a world-wide phenomenon, with
a wide appeal in countries where the churches are not declining,
and with roots in the world-wide Protestant missionary movement,
in the development of nineteenth-century Protestant liberalism,
and in the genuine horror many Christians feel when they con-
front the apparently endless process of denominational and
sectarian fragmentation. The psychological precondition for
Nonconformist participation in the ecumenical movement was
some form of Anglican recognition of the existence of Nonconformist ministers at the local level. When Charles Booth surveyed
Lambeth's churches in 1899, the two sets of religious professionals

117. J. Scott Lidgett, My Guided Life (1935), p. 222.
118. P. Carnegie Simpson, Recollections (1943), p. 94; cf. A. E. Garvie, Memories and Meanings of My Life (1938); J. C. Carlile, My Life's Little Day
(1935); J. D. Jones, Three Score Years and Ten (1940); Sir Henry Simpson
Lunn, Nearing Harbour (1934); N. Micklem, The Box and the Puppets
(1957).
119. Currie, Methodism Divided, p. 316.

lived in entirely separate worlds, meeting only in the inter-denominational meetings of the more extreme evangelical phil-anthropic societies. The rural dean of Camberwell explained that he "nods at the Noncons but nothing more."[120] Many Anglican clergymen claimed to be ignorant of the very existence of some chapels within their own parishes, and almost all of them displayed an appalling ignorance of Nonconformist history and current activities. The first sign of a breakthrough in co-operation appeared, oddly enough, in the midst of the intensely bitter Edwardian educational and political controversies. Ordinary Anglican clergymen began appearing at ordinary Nonconformist Pleasant Sunday Afternoon and chapel anni-versary meetings in Lambeth, supplying what Nonconformist ministers wanted more than anything else: recognition.[121] Al-though progress was slow, and clergymen encountered criticism for fraternizing with the enemy, by 1914 it was generally recog-nized in the press that there was an admirable trend toward greater cooperation at the local level.[122] The real breakthrough was the war, which made controversies over educational funding and Welsh disestablishment seem petty. Joint "services of inter-cession" became the rule rather than the exception, and those led in turn to the formation of local Christian councils after the war in Brixton and Upper Norwood.[123]

These local "Christian councils" formed the basis for the inter-war ecumenical movement in Lambeth. On the denominational level, negotiations about church unity began in earnest after the Lambeth Conference of 1920 issued the "Appeal to All Christian People." The very existence of negotiations, however fruitless, was itself a form of recognition—enough to prevent Noncon-formist ministers from reviving the pre-war ideal of a Noncon-formist counter-church strong enough to challenge the Church of England. Instead they dreamed of a united Protestant church in England.

There were two distinct but inseparable aspects of the move-

120. B-305, p. 107.
121. See BFP, 27 Oct. 1905, 3 Nov. 1905, 29 June 1906.
122. See BFP, 10 April 1908, 23 April 1909; H. Wilson Harris, *The Churches and London* (1914), p. 76.
123. See BFP, 1 Feb. 1918; 3 Jan. 1919; St. Aubyn's Congregational Church, *Annual Report,* 1918, 1919.

ment for church union. On the one hand there was a desire to rationalize the structure of the churches in order to eliminate wasteful duplication, on the other hand a movement to unite all of the churches into one far more powerful body which would be a "force in the land." As a practical matter, the ecumenical movement has appealed in both of its dimensions to the clergy rather than the laity, for it primarily addresses the issue of clerical status even while claiming, inaccurately, to address the issue of growth and decline. The rationalization of overlapping chapels occurred most dramatically after the Methodist Union of 1932, which eventually resulted in the closure of hundreds of tiny chapels. Many Baptist and Congregationalist ministers looked on in envy, and abandoned their commitment to congregational democracy along with their commitment to social radicalism. What shepherd wants a tiny, ailing flock when he can have a large prosperous flock which will bring in an ample income? Tiny chapels repelled prospective worshippers as well as prospective ministers, it was argued, and when four tiny chapels with 40 members each are consolidated into one healthy chapel with 160 members, that chapel will grow. But the result has often been one chapel of 100 members achieved against the wishes of the laity who usually have deep feelings for the sacred space of their wasteful little chapels. Articles upon Methodist reunion monopolized the columns of the *Methodist Recorder* in the late 1920s, but the circuit minute books of the three Wesleyan circuits in Lambeth show no concern at all except when they were required to vote. The only excitement was created when the Brixton Hill Circuit refused to accept the Railton Road Free Methodist Church and Conference tried to place it in the Mostyn Road Circuit. The Mostyn Road circuit, suspicious of "congregational methods," refused them as well, and the chapel was placed, where it still remains, in a distant suburban circuit.[124]

Many Nonconformist ministers joined with Anglican clergymen in wishing, not merely to close chapels, eliminate waste, and avoid duplication, but to mold all of England's fragmented churches into one body. Their corporate energy could then be concentrated against the "enemy," rather than against each

124. Mostyn Road Circuit, minutes of the quarterly meeting, 1932–1941, Minet Library; cf. Brixton Hill Circuit, minutes, 1931–1941, Minet Library.

other, and the churches would (again) be a force in the land. But united for what? Their difficulty in answering that question lays bare the failure of the ecumenical movement. Everyone agreed, Churchmen and Dissenters, that all of the churches should struggle against "secularism" and "materialism." There was also considerable support for the notion that the churches, once united, could contribute to the solution of social problems, a conviction which inspired many participants in the Anglican Life and Liberty movement and all of the participants in the ecumenical Conference on Politics, Economics, and Citizenship (C.O.P.E.C.) in 1924. In 1922 the secretary of the Life and Liberty movement claimed that every single church was moribund, and that only a united church could destroy materialism, slums, and intemperance,[125] and in 1923 Dr. Garvie of the Congregationalist New College, Hampstead, predicted a day coming soon when "the church will be one society united in service of Jesus Christ and a force to settle social and economic questions."[126]

But this kind of argument took a very peculiar turn and involved an inaccurate view of English history which could not have helped the churches. Clergymen and ministers argued that the church was an irrelevant failure because it could not solve social problems, and church unity was proposed as a cure for the disease. The ecumenical social reformers (such as William Temple) often argued that the church not only was a failure, but had been for some time—since the industrial revolution, for instance. The argument that the churches were irrelevant to most people was true enough, but men such as Temple had no understanding of how many of the churches' social functions had disappeared since the 1890s. Dissenters and Churchmen alike lacked any understanding of the positive reforming role of late Victorian and Edwardian Nonconformists, who were written off as "political." As the late Victorian argument (the church is doing more for society than any other institution) was replaced by the inter-war argument (the church is a failure), it naturally became even more difficult to call upon the general support of the nation. In 1923 the Clapham parish church held a special Labour service with a church parade by local Labour organizations and

125. BFP, 14 April 1922.
126. BFP, 7 Dec. 1923.

a sermon by the rector apologizing, naturally, for the failure of the churches. At a conference at the rectory afterward a representative of the Independent Labour Party said that "the Church had been a failure in the past, and it was not their place to go to the assistance of a failure."[127]

The ecumenical social reformers were not entirely without influence in inter-war Lambeth. In Herne Hill, Streatham, Brixton Hill, and Norwood, local Christian councils endorsed the general sentiments of the C.O.P.E.C. conference, several parishes founded social unions or social service committees, and a Lambeth Christian Social Council pressed for social reform at the borough level. The parochial unions encountered great difficulty in deciding what to do, for they could hardly content themselves with passing resolutions in the manner of a national conference of dignitaries. Furthermore, they were committed to social action at a time when the churches had never been more isolated from society. At St. Peter's, Leigham Court Road, for instance, the clothing, coal, and blanket clubs were closed in 1906, the savings bank in 1907, and the vicar's discretionary (relief) fund in 1920. The parish social union was founded in 1923.[128] In 1922–23 the St. Andrew's, Stockwell, social service committee drew the attention of the authorities to such evils as "racing tipsters in Brixton and the dangers of crossing the Clapham Road at the Swan."[129] In 1926 the same committee decided to urge the prosecution of a landlady who crowded forty persons into eleven rooms at 317 Clapham Road.[130]

Despite these efforts, the people of Lambeth, and even the clergy, did not really look to the churches to solve social problems. In 1924 the rector of Lambeth, in a sermon to the borough council, had asked: "What was the real meaning of their work?" To further the Kingdom of God, he answered, by assuring the people of Lambeth a healthy environment. Inadequate housing, he claimed, lay behind non-churchgoing, and the borough council was responsible not only for furthering the Kingdom of

127. BFP, 14 Sept. 1923.

128. St. Peter's, Streatham, Parochial Accounts, 1906–1925.

129. St. Andrew's, Stockwell, *Annual Report of the P.C.C.* 1922–23, GLRO, P85/AnD1/18.

130. *Ibid*. 1926.

God but, apparently, for restoring church attendance.[131] The Norwood Labour Party heard a report on C.O.P.E.C. in 1924, and several members complained of its lack of concrete proposals: "An appeal to fine sentiment without seeking in a Christian spirit a solution to economic problems would not go far towards establishing a new social order"; "if the church would only help socialists to get the social system altered it would find that the task of getting Christianity put into practice would be immeasurably easier. The church leaders gave no clear lead whatsoever."[132]

The Lambeth Christian Social Council, in cooperation with a Lambeth Housing Committee, attempted to meet criticism with a more ambitious contribution to the solution of the housing shortage. The Housing Committee grew from a small committee established by the bishop of Southwark in 1916.[133] In the early twenties it achieved little because of constant controversy over the status of Lambeth housing owned by the Ecclesiastical Commission, for the Labour members of the borough council delighted in exposing the church as one of the borough's leading slumlords. The Lambeth Chrisitan Social Council seems to have been formed in 1923 or 1924. It was heavily influenced by C.O.P.E.C., more or less absorbed the activities of the Central South London Free Church Council, and adopted the Lambeth Housing Scheme as its major project. In 1926 the committee "threatened" (amid the ridicule of the Tory press) to build flats themselves if the council did not. By 1929 they had secured a £1000 option on a site from the Ecclesiastical Commission, hired a publicity expert, and embarked upon a program of raising money from the churches on a special "Housing Sunday." John Galsworthy delivered an Easter Sunday evening radio broadcast in benefit of this and other London housing societies (the scheme is similar to the one promoted by the Rev. Hilary Cherwell in *The Forsyte Saga*). In 1932 twenty-four self-contained units were completed.[134] But the borough council

131. BFP, 18 Jan. 1924.

132. *Norwood Press*, 19 Nov. 1924.

133. BFP, 3 Oct. 1919.

134. BFP, 29 March, 1929; *Norwood Press*, 2 August 1929; Lady Margaret Hall, *Social Services*, p. 75.

constructed 352 dwellings between 1927 and 1936, the L.C.C. 3112 in 1905, 1928, and 1934–38.[135] C.O.P.E.C. and its associated local groups seemed long on talk and short on action by comparison.

Although failing to reestablish the churches' credibility, the Lambeth Housing Movement did alert middle-class congregations to the housing problem in a very practical way. The resolutions of the ecumenical social reformers may have lacked content, but they did not lack significance for their real audience: churchgoers. William Temple, the presiding genius of C.O.P.E.C., is usually classified within the Anglican Christian socialist tradition, but it is impossible not to be struck with the similarity of his language to that of many Edwardian Nonconformist social radicals. Both John Clifford and William Temple were fond of demanding an end to social evils without considering the means; both identified English society as in some sense a Christian community, and called upon English men and women to live up to their ideals. It is as if, through the limitless energy of William Temple, some of the reforming zeal of Edwardian Progressivism had been injected into the Church of England. Both the Church of England and the Free Churches were composed of a laity which would normally be conservative rather than socialist in the political polarization of the twenties, with the exception of Primitive Methodists and some other Nonconformists in industrial areas and Wales. Yet when the general strike occurred the Anglican church in particular was a moderating influence, urging conciliation upon the government. And the clergy were, likewise, constantly bringing social problems to the attention of their congregations and urging them to think about reform rather than reaction. But they never developed an effective appeal to the marginal Christian or the concerned outsider, the kind of appeal which had sustained the Victorian churches. And their appeal to churchgoers rested upon the premise that the churches were a failure. Who but a churchgoer would want to "go to the assistance of a failure"?

135. Lady Margaret Hall, *Social Services*, pp. 70ff.

8

A New View
of the Decline of Religion

It is difficult to overstate the extent to which the very best historians of Victorian religion are addicted to the language of inevitable and irreversible decline, decay, and failure, and explain that historical change with references to an underlying "process" of secularization. They judge a Victorian religious movement by the standards of the movement itself, even though its goal was the conversion of an entire city or an entire social class or an entire nation, a goal which could be achieved only by force of arms. The Victorian churches, or evangelicalism, or the Victorian missionary enterprise, or the Salvation Army, or virtually any aspect of the Victorian religious experiment then can be described as a failure because it did not achieve its goal even at the time of its maximum influence.[1] And once a movement actually has begun to decline instead of growing, no explanation whatsoever is necessary because of the convenience of the theory of secularization. According to Geoffrey Best, late

1. For example, one of the very best books on any aspect of Victorian religion, John Kent's *Holding the Fort: Studies in Victorian Revivalism* (London, 1978).

nineteenth-century Christianity "had grown so big, been so successful, that in a world nevertheless imperfect and changing and irresistibly secularising it simply could not avoid some retrenchment, some decline."[2]

If not secularization, then what? Even though the concept of secularization obscures as much as it illuminates, intelligent men and women find it persuasive largely because of an absence of more persuasive alternatives. The demonstration of its inadequacy does not achieve its elimination. I should make it clear, once again, that I am not disputing the fact that our view of the world, our cosmology, has been transformed by scientific advances since the Reformation, a fact which poses new and unique problems for Christian thinkers.[3] Nor am I asserting that the advent of heavy industry, the polarization of society along class lines, the growth of cities, and geographical and social mobility do not, other things being equal, cause new problems for the churches which can, and often do, contribute to a decline of religious practice.[4] What I object to is the air of inevitability which results from wrapping all of these changes up into a package called "the process of secularization" and using that package as an explanation of social change in the modern world. My objection to that concept is based upon an examination of the facts. The social changes involved in secularization do not invariably and inevitably lead to the decay of religious ideas and institutions. Furthermore, an appeal to an underlying process of secularization obscures a very interesting and ongoing adaptation of religious forms to the modern world.

It should be possible to substitute a modest, useful metaphor for an ambitious, misleading one. Instead of thinking of religion as an inevitable casualty of the "transition to modernity," what-

2. Geoffrey Best, *Mid-Victorian Britain, 1851–1875* (New York, 1972), p. 170.

3. If the problems were literally insurmountable, there would now be no educated or intelligent Christian believers.

4. David Martin, *General Theory*, p. 3, does recognize that the effect of these components of secularization may be nullified by other events. But what if none of these things occurred, and the state (or whoever held political power) declared a "free market in religion" in a pre-modern society? Some religions and some churches would grow and others would decline; religion would be more important in some places than in others.

ever its form, we should think of religion as competing in a free market in ideas whose rules are set by the state. Those rules have changed dramatically since the Reformation. There has always been tension between the Christian churches and the "secular" world, a tension which was not eliminated by the adoption of Christianity as the state religion of the Roman Empire in the fourth century. For over a millenium the inevitable pluralism of a secular world left to its own devices was repressed by force of arms, and a false religious unanimity achieved through force and fraud. But the state-church solution was no solution at all. The truly devout within the church itself recognized the hollowness of compulsory Christianity, and many embraced monasticism. Even more important, schism and protest and irreligion continued to exist behind the façade of religious unanimity, and surfaced whenever strict control was relaxed for any period of time.

With the crumbling of state support for one church or for one religious orthodoxy, what had been suppressed came into the open. The churches, and religious thinkers, had to adapt to the fact of competition. (By pluralism, I mean no more than the possibility of open or tolerated or partially tolerated political and religious challenge to religious orthodoxy as defined by an established state church. The form of that challenge varied, and still varies, enormously.) It is in this context that the social changes beginning with the population explosion and the industrial revolution of the eighteenth century have caused chronic problems for the churches, just as earlier examples of massive social dislocation caused problems for the churches which were more successfully hidden or ignored. Steelmakers are not intrinsically resistant to Christianity because of their nearness to the heart of modern technology. But steelmaking does involve drastic changes in social relationships, and the voluntary nature of modern religion has greatly increased the chances that a particular church will find itself the victim of unanticipated social changes. In general the most flexible churches with the greatest internal emphasis upon growth have responded most successfully to industrialization and urbanization in those countries where they are allowed to respond. (E. P. Thompson complains of Methodism's "promiscuous opportunism" during the Industrial Revolution.)[5] The least flexible churches with the greatest dependence upon the state have responded with the least success. Thus we can probably expect continued decay in the Protestant state churches of northern and western Europe, and continued growth from the competitive Protestant denominations and sects of North and South America and Africa, with the Roman Catholic Church falling somewhere in between.

This view of religion in the modern world frees us to examine the Victorian religious experiment without assuming that its failure was either inevitable or easily explained by reference to inexorable global forces of social change. The British Protestant churches have in fact experienced something akin to a collapse in the twentieth century. Church membership rolls have dwindled and dwindled with no sign of reversal in sight. Church attendance has fallen in every decade of this century with the exception of a brief revival associated with the aging of the postwar babies in the 1950s. People outside the churches have been less and less inclined to take them seriously, and the response of people within the churches has been one of gloomy defeatism.

Religion was more important in late Victorian society than many contemporary observers would allow, and the unrealistic hopes and expectations, and inaccurate visions of a religious past, have obscured that importance. Hardly anyone escaped some kind of religion indoctrination in the Sunday Schools. The introduction of formal religious teaching by trained professionals promoted the diffusion of religious knowledge through the state school system, and it is at least possible that the schools rather than the churches were the primary source of the demystified, ethically oriented popular religion which social observers found when they went out inquiring into popular views. But it is certainly misleading to claim that the working classes were completely out of touch with organized religion when they were indoctrinated with a form of it in the schools. Working-class adults were also "in touch" with the churches and with organized religion through the sacramental rites of passage of

5. E. P. Thompson, *The Making of the English Working Class* (New York, 1963), p. 362.

the Church of England, although the British people remade these rites into popular ceremonies on their own terms, and in that sense were both in touch with organized religion and indifferent to the claims of organized religion.

A third way in which the churches stayed in touch with the people, in addition to the indirect agency of the schools and the direct though perverse agency of the sacraments, was philanthropy. The word philanthropy is not quite right, but I have not been able to think of a better one. The Victorians thought of it as "church work." Almost all of the activities of what we now call the welfare state were prefigured in some activity of some Lambeth church. Philanthropy appears to the outside observer to have been the primary activity of the churches, Nonconformist as well as Anglican. Its only possible rival was the construction and maintenance of church buildings, which cost more but took up less of the congregation's time. These philanthropic activities appear to have emerged, not from a tradition of rural paternalism, but from the response of the churches to urban social conditions in the middle and late nineteenth century.

What the poor and the working classes thought about philanthropy, about "church work," is difficult to say. There is some evidence of a quite natural resentment of the patronizing attitudes of churchgoers. There is some evidence that working-class and poor people took over some institutions and made them into something which they could consider their own. What is clear is that these philanthropic activities were very important, not only to clergymen, but to the more or less middle-class churchgoers who provided them.

This brings us to the question of more or less regular churchgoing, since it was churchgoers who were the source of religious philanthropy. It has often been said that churchgoing was disproportionately middle-class, and it was, but like all generalizations of that scale it requires some qualification. In addition to regular weekly churchgoers and intermittent weekly churchgoers there were two groups of yearly or twice yearly churchgoers. One group attended on Christmas or Easter, and appears to have resembled the regular weekly churchgoing group socially. Then there was another group of working-class churchgoers who attended the Autumn Harvest Festival and the New

Year's Eve services, irritating the clergy with their manifest lack of the approved forms of piety. Furthermore, there were some working-class parishes and chapels where the ordinary weekly churchgoers were working-class. When all the qualifications are made, however, we are left with a group of several million largely middle-class English churchgoers who attended church regularly and ran these philanthropic organizations. Why did they do it? Why did they stop?

Middle-class churchgoing is sometimes reduced to a question of suburban respectability, and that is part of the answer. But there were many ways to be respectable and churchgoing was only one of them. Regular churchgoing was not necessary (with some important exceptions) in order to maintain a minimum level of respectability. An occasional appearance would suffice if the children were sent to Sunday School. Others argue that churchgoers were churchgoers because they were devout Christian believers, and some of them were, although it is reasonably clear that at least some of them did not have their minds fixed firmly on the next world rather than on this one. But where did these devout religious people become religious? The answer is, generally, in church. The churches promoted a piety which was both important and very different from the kind of diffusive popular religion of non-churchgoers. Churchgoing piety placed a heavy emphasis upon Jesus, upon Christ as the personal friend and the loving good shepherd, and it was only taught in church and in the homes of churchgoers. It was not, with some exceptions, taught in the schools. The churches could not count on a fund of popular churchgoing piety to supply them with churchgoers, for English popular Christianity had long ago abandoned the notion that regular churchgoing was essential for a Christian. This is why purely theological or spiritual claims on behalf of the churches were relatively rare, and why the churches had to devise some appeal to outsiders in order to get people to church in the first place, and keep them there.

It is a mistake to define the motives for churchgoing and religious faith as strictly religious on the one hand or strictly social on the other. At the height of the Victorian age, John Stuart Mill cleanly distinguished the question of the utility of religion from the question of the truth of religion, and directed his arguments toward an audience which, he assumed, believed in the former but not in the latter.[6] He was right to identify, as a bulwark of the Victorian churches, the argument that religion is necessary "for social and moral purposes." But it was not so easy, at the congregational and parochial level, to separate the utility of religion from its truth. "Pure" religion does not exist, and religious faith is always embedded in concrete historical and social circumstances. But it is also demonstrably true that "religious" ideas were taken very seriously by many late Victorians. Once active in the churches, most churchgoers took religious teachings seriously, at least in principle, and outright hypocrisy was as rare as a "pure" theological commitment. Late Victorian piety was intertwined with anxiety about social conditions, and the theological link between the two was the Sermon on the Mount, in particular the parable of the Good Samaritan. Even the staunchest evangelical, after brandishing scripture for a bit, would very often proceed to another argument which was given even more prominence.

Victorian churchgoers believed that the churches were *important*. Society would fall apart without morality, morality was impossible without religion, and religion would disappear without the churches. It was, therefore, your civic duty to attend church and support the other work of the churches. The clergymen, ministers, and prominent laymen in every sort of Lambeth church, rich or poor, Anglican or Nonconformist, liberal or evangelical, made these arguments over and over again. And you were not expected to take this theory of the relationship between churchgoing and social stability on faith alone. The churches brought forth tangible evidence to support their assertion that Christianity was important, and it was invariably the same: they cited the past and present work of the religious philanthropic societies, and the ordinary parochial and congregational work of Lambeth's churches and chapels. Religious faith and "church work," i.e., philanthropy, were inseparable dimensions of one religious commitment in the minds of Lambeth churchgoers. Churchgoing and work among the poor were two ways of expressing a more fundamental concern with social stability and

6. John Stuart Mill, *Autobiography*, ed. Jack Stillinger (Boston, 1969), p. 44.

social improvement. Consequently, church attendance in Lambeth, as elsewhere, varied very roughly with social status. The greater a person's stake in social cohesion and social stability, the greater the appeal of the argument: society will collapse without the churches.

This is not a reductionistic argument. It is an argument about the context in which the church operated, and the meaning of religious language in the minds of churchgoers. Victorian piety cannot be reduced to a material base of Victorian philanthropy, nor can it be said that the coal club was more important than holy communion to Lambeth's churchgoers. But religious faith and "church work," holy communion and the coal club, were related in the minds of many of Lambeth's Christians. As circumstances changed that relationship ceased to be intelligible.

Within this general framework of religion, morality, and churchgoing, each denomination had its own special appeal both to outsiders and to those who were born into the denomination. The "most snobbish church in Christendom,"[7] the Church of England benefited in particular from the association of churchgoing with high social status. But roughly half of Lambeth's churchgoers were Nonconformists. One group of liberal Nonconformists, which included some Baptists, almost all Congregationalists, all Presbyterians, and Wesleyan Methodists, appear to have been Nonconformists largely because they had been born Nonconformists. They wanted to worship with people who did not despise them, and they were attracted to liturgical worship services, liberal theology, liberal politics, and philanthropy. A second group of plebeian Nonconformists included many Baptists, the Free Methodists, the Primitive Methodists, the Bible Christians, the Brethren, and various other groups. Many of their chapels seem to have functioned largely as psychological mutual aid societies, and their sermons, their hymns, and their chapel offices offered recognition to the insignificant and future rewards to the despised.

The real decline of churchgoing and its associated piety appears to have begun in the 1880s. The churches were growing until about 1850, and may have been holding their own until

7. Daniel Jenkins, *The British: Their Identity and Their Religion* (1975), p. 81.

the 1880s, although that is an informed guess. In the 1880s a
decline of churchgoing and a decline in real but not absolute
levels of church membership began. Just after the turn of the
century the decline in churchgoing accelerated, and in 1906, 1907,
and 1908 every single Nonconformist denomination began to
shrink. The general decline of England's Protestant churches
has continued throughout the century.

In the early twentieth century the churches experienced a
crisis in morale. By 1900 they had accustomed themselves to
what had always been a fact: regular churchgoing was a minority affair. But ordinary parochial clergymen and ministers generally regarded the churches as important social institutions. A
century of intellectual disarray had been accompanied by the
growth of liberal theology and by a massive institutional revival.
But the 1920s were different. On the most obvious level, clergymen of that decade claimed that the churches were irrelevant to
the "real" needs of society. They no longer said that society
would collapse without the churches. Instead, they constantly
berated their bewildered congregations for their remoteness
from the struggle for social reform, for their remoteness from
the English people. They did this without offering any suggestions as to how those faults might be remedied, although some
suggested that the ecumenical movement might be the answer.

This was not merely one of those mysterious shifts in the
climate of opinion which occasionally occur within institutions.
The churches had in fact become irrelevant. The philanthropic
apparatus which I described in Chapter 3 had disappeared or
was in the process of being dismantled by the early 1920s. The
government, the London County Council, the relatively new
Lambeth Borough Council, and private but professional philanthropic societies had begun to provide social services in a
systematic fashion. Even more important, it was *assumed* that
they had responsibility for such things, even if they did not. The
churches were left with little to do and even less to say, since
"church work" had been a central justification for their existence. In sociological jargon, it was a process of functional differentiation, but it is important to remember that this change
was not a global transformation which reduced the importance
of all religions everywhere in the world. It was a particularly
British transformation which reduced the importance of Lam-

beth's churches only because they had chosen to invest so heavily in philanthropy as they competed for influence in Victorian
society. In a different context, "functional differentiation"
might even strengthen the churches.

The Nonconformists faced additional problems which were
equally important, and it was the convergence of several problems with changes in the climate of opinion which accounts for
the severity of the decline of religion in twentieth-century England. Nonconformists who prospered had always been tempted
to shed the stigma of Dissent through a simple act of apostasy.
In the late nineteenth century, a second threat was added to
prosperity: civil position. The development of a comprehensive
educational system after 1870, the establishment of the London
County Council in 1890, the creation of the Lambeth Borough
Council in 1900, the evolution of local political party and
trade union organizations, all provided bureaucratic opportunities for many middle- and lower middle-class men and
women to gain a modest degree of self-esteem from their peers
as schoolteacher, schoolmaster, school attendance officer, school
board member, borough councillor or alderman, voluntary member of various municipal committees on education, health, and
housing, voluntary school manager, or school health visitor.
This problem affected both liberal and plebeian chapels, but
liberal chapels faced additional problems because, allergic to
revivalism and others forms of aggressive recruitment, they depended heavily upon their own children to replenish chapel
membership. This became more difficult around the turn of the
century for two reasons. In the first place, there were fewer children. The birth rate was falling and families were shrinking,
especially in the middle-class families of the liberal chapels.
With a smaller pool of potential recruits they had to persuade a
larger and larger percentage of their children to remain Nonconformists simply in order to maintain their growth rate.

But it became *more* rather than *less* difficult to communicate
the importance of religion in general and the Nonconformist
tradition in particular to their children. This generation of
liberal Nonconformist parents, unlike their ancestors, was well
integrated into English society. Nonconformity was a habit for
many of them. As a result, they took a laissez faire attitude
toward the religious socialization of their children, an attitude

which was nurtured by the prevalence of liberal theology with its emphasis upon ethics rather than conversion. Set adrift, Nonconformist children fell prey, not to any *particular* set of new ideas, but to any set of new ideas which came their way: secularism, socialism, the literary life, Christian Science, spiritualism, Anglo-Catholicism, nominal middle-of-the-road Anglicanism.

This is where the importance of new ideas comes in, the importance of the climate of opinion. External changes in the way educated people viewed religion exacerbated the internal problems generated within Nonconformity as well as the broader problems which all churches faced. The new respectability of agnosticism, and the cultural reaction against Victorianism which went under the label of the "new hedonism," left many young people with an uneasy feeling that Christianity had been "disproved" and that the churches were stuffy and old-fashioned. Nonconformists faced special problems because of the severity of the crisis of generations within Nonconformity, but clergymen and ministers of all denominations were faced, repeatedly, with the task of persuading late Victorian and Edwardian young people that the churches were not old-fashioned social institutions, and that Christianity had not become irrelevant. As long as the churches were demonstrably important social institutions, they could appeal to a combined sense of altruism and piety and civic duty, and they did, with some success. How many drunkards have the Darwinians reclaimed? How many children are being fed by secular intellectuals? The answer was: not very many.

But from the 1880s on, these arguments became gradually less plausible until, by the 1920s, they became impossible and were rarely heard. It became impossible to refute the assertion that the churches were irrelevant because it was true. The clergy were saying so themselves. Who wants to associate with an irrelevant institution? What is the point of attending church? Why should anyone come to the aid of a failure?

This is, of course, a story of unintended consequences. The churches eagerly participated in the dismantling of their own philanthropy because they realized that other bodies could do the job better. Although aware of the dangers of prosperity, Nonconformists were also proud of the economic and civil prominence which destroyed them. Many people would have believed that Christianity was irrelevant even if the churches had been thriving; many Americans, especially intellectuals, are astonished to discover the facts about the pervasiveness of the churches and the Christian faith in America. But in England it was the actual collapse of the churches which allowed the complete triumph of the argument that religion is something which belongs to another age. The empty church is the single most important piece of evidence brought forth by people who argue that religion has become unimportant. They are right, but not for the reasons they think.

Religion received important support from the state in the twentieth century with the advent of devotional broadcasting on the BBC, and the passage of the education acts of 1902 and 1944 which salvaged the Church of England schools and required every school to have a daily worship service as well as scripture teaching. The combination of religious broadcasting, which receives a wide audience, and religious teaching in the schools serves as a substitute for active church participation, and sustains a form of "diffusive Christianity" in England even as the churches wither away.

But passive "diffusive Christianity" has always existed as a kind of penumbra to active church-oriented Christianity. As the churches lost members, fewer active Christians were available to participate in the supply of official religion. It became more and more difficult to recruit devout scripture teachers for the schools, and religious teaching drifted even farther away from the active Christ-centered piety of the churches. The religion of the BBC became more diluted and pluralistic. Fewer members and fewer resources prevented the churches from competing effectively with other institutions in the supply of popular rites of passage. Many couples found a Registry Office marriage more convenient than a church marriage early in the century, and by mid-century capitalist popular culture was supplying alternatives to confirmation as an adolescent rite of passage. The churches have simply lacked the resources to respond, and have turned inward instead, preoccupied with denominational structure and church union . . . but that is another story.

Tables

Table 1   Church Attendance in Lambeth, 1851, 1886/88, 1902

% = percentage of total population (rounded off)
CE = parish churches
NC = Nonconformist chapels
Msn = mission halls

	Morn	%	Even	%	Total	%
1851. Estimated population, 139,325						
CE	16,274	11.7	11,495	8.3	27,769	20.0
NC	7,743	5.6	7,282	5.2	15,025	10.8
Total	24,017	17.2	18,777	13.5	42,794	30.7
1886. Estimated population, 267,391 (msn figures 1888)						
CE	16,603	6.2	18,394	6.9	34,997	13.1
CE msn	811	0.3	1,736	0.7	2,547	1.0
Total	17,414	6.5	20,130	7.5	37,544	14.1
NC	12,764	4.8	14,184	5.3	26,948	10.1
NC msn	958	0.4	4,104	1.5	5,062	1.9
Total	13,722	5.1	18,288	6.8	32,010	12.0
NC + CE	29,367	11.0	32,578	12.2	61,945	23.2
NC msn + CE msn	1,769	0.7	5,840	2.2	7,609	2.8
Total	31,136	11.7	38,418	14.4	69,554	26.0

Table 1, *continued*

	Morn	%	Even	%	Total	%
1902. Estimated population, 303,738					
CE	11,383	3.7	12,603	4.2	23,986	7.9
CE msn	772	0.3	1,654	0.5	2,426	0.8
Total	12,155	4.0	14,257	4.7	26,412	8.7
NC	10,515	3.5	12,947	4.3	23,462	7.7
NC msn	2,218	0.7	5,905	1.9	8,123	2.7
Total	12,733	4.2	18,852	6.2	31,585	10.4
NC + CE	21,898	7.2	25,550	8.4	47,448	15.6
NC msn + CE msn	2,990	1.0	7,559	2.5	10,549	3.5
Other[1]	1,487	0.5	441	0.2	1,928	0.6
Total	26,375	8.7	33,550	11.1	59,925	19.7

These statistics have been re-worked. For instance, Spurgeon's Metropolitan Tabernacle was included in the Lambeth returns for 1886 and in the Southwark returns for 1902. It is in Southwark. My population figures for 1851 are based on the Registrar General's registration districts, for 1886 on the sum of the estimated population of each ecclesiastical parish, and for 1902 on the sum of the population of each ecclesiastical parish in 1901. The nondenominational missions (e.g., of the London City Mission) were assigned to the Nonconformists rather than the Anglicans largely because I found that, at least in Lambeth, Nonconformists sponsored most of them. Afternoon attendance is excluded. The Roman Catholic figures returned for Lambeth in 1886 were excluded because they were not, in fact, taken from Lambeth churches.

Sources: Census of Great Britain, 1851: religious worship, England and Wales: reports and tables. (1690) H.C. (1852–53). 89, 1; *British Weekly*, 5 Nov. and 17 Dec. 1886, 13 Jan. 1888; R. Mudie-Smith, ed., *The Religious Life of London* (1904).

1. Roman Catholics, along with a handful of Christadelphians and Swedenborgians.

Table 2   "Twicers," Inner and Greater London, 1902–3

IL = Inner London, GL = Greater London
Column 1 = morning attendance
Column 2 = morning worshippers who returned for the evening service
Column 3 = column 2 divided by column 1 as percentage
Column 4 = number of parishes or chapels

		1	2	3	4
Bapt	IL	4,107	1,956	47.6	14
	GL	2,571	884	34.4	6
	Total	6,678	2,840	42.5	20
Cong	IL	2,507	875	35.0	9
	GL	1,008	325	32.2	4
	Total	3,515	1,200	34.1	13
Wes	IL	2,549	987	38.7	9
	GL	314	150	47.7	2
	Total	2,863	1,137	39.7	11
Other NC	IL	367	114	31.0	3
	GL	647	284	43.9	5
	Total	1,014	398	39.2	8
All NC	IL	9,530	3,936	41.3	35
	GL	4,540	1,643	36.2	17
	Total	14,070	5,579	39.7	52
CE	IL	3,783	923	24.4	13
	GL	1,484	330	22.2	4
	Total	5,267	1,253	23.8	17
TOTAL	IL	13,313	4,859	36.5	48
	GL	6,024	1,973	32.8	21
	Total	19,337	6,832	35.3	69

Source: Mudie-Smith, *Religious Life of London,* pp. 449–50. Census takers counted the number of morning worshippers who returned for the evening service in 69 parishes and chapels.

Table 2A "Twicers" in Lambeth, 1902-3

Table 2, column 3, gives the percentage of the morning congregation which should be subtracted from total morning and evening attendance (All NC, CE, and TOTAL above) to produce an estimate of the number of worshippers in any set of statistics from the 1902-3 census. In the following table, t = total attendance, morning and evening, in Lambeth; m = adjusted morning attendance; and w = estimated number of worshippers.

	t	m	w	% of pop
CE	$26{,}412 - (.24 \times 12{,}155) =$		$23{,}495$	7.74
NC	$31{,}585 - (.40 \times 12{,}733) =$		$26{,}491$	8.72
Total	$59{,}925 - (.35 \times 26{,}375) =$		$50{,}693$	16.70

In the sample in Table 2, Nonconformists attracted more "twicers" than Anglicans. But even when Lambeth's figures are adjusted to account for an estimate of "twicers," Nonconformists continue to outnumber Anglicans.

Table 3   Age Structure and Sexual Composition of Lambeth Denominations, Ranked According to Percentage of Children in the Congregation, 1902

Column 1 = percentage of overall (morning and evening) attendance accounted for by mission halls
CE = parish churches   NC = chapels only
CE-T = parish churches + Anglican mission halls
NC-T = Nonconformist chapels + Nonconformist mission halls
m = percentage of congregation male aged 15 or over
f = percentage of congregation female aged 15 or over
c = percentage of congregation children under 15

		Morn				Even	
	1	m	f	c	m	f	c
CE		24.6	42.6	32.8	26.8	54.1	19.1
NC		30.6	36.2	33.4	31.7	50.1	18.2
CE-T	9.2	23.9	40.7	35.5	25.5	52.4	22.1
Bapt	9.4	27.0	35.2	37.8	28.8	51.6	19.6
NC-T	25.8	28.6	32.9	38.6	29.5	46.8	23.7
Cong	11.4	27.5	30.1	42.4	31.0	47.6	21.5
Wes	41.6	27.3	30.4	42.3	28.5	43.8	27.7
Other Meth	29.4	27.2	25.8	47.0	29.2	44.0	26.8
All msn		19.1	17.4	63.0	24.8	40.0	35.6

	ratio f to m	
	Morn	Even
CE	1.73	2.02
NC	1.18	1.58
CE-T	1.70	2.05
Bapt	1.30	1.79
NC-T	1.15	1.59
Cong	1.09	1.54
Wes	1.11	1.54
Other Meth	0.95	1.51
All msn	0.91	1.61

Table 4 Sex Ratio and Church Party, Lambeth, 1902 (adults)

"High" parishes	
1. St. Peter, Vauxhall	2.22
2. St. John the Divine, Kennington	1.38
3. St. John, Angell Town	1.92
4. St. Peter, Leigham Court Road	1.96
Mean	1.87
"Evangelical" parishes	
1. St. Andrew, Coin St.	1.29
2. Christ Church, N. Brixton	1.86
3. St. Jude, East Brixton	2.97
4. Christ Church, Gypsy Hill	2.86
Mean	2.25

Ratio of women to men, both Sunday services, mission halls excluded. Each "high" parish is matched by number with an "evangelical" parish of similar social composition.

Table 5 Social Status of Lambeth Districts

Column 1 = population 1901
Column 2 = area in acres
Column 3 = persons per acre
Column 4 = families or separate occupiers
Column 5 = inhabited houses
Column 6 = families or separate occupiers per inhabited house

	1	2	3	4	5	6
N. Lambeth	85,681	515.3	166.3	20,429	9,120	2.24
Kennington	96,094	1,018.9	94.3	22,864	12,931	1.77
Brixton	84,232	1,349.7	62.4	19,914	12,926	1.54
Norwood	35,888	1,196.5	30.0	7,680	6,091	1.26

Note: These census districts overlap, but do not coincide precisely with, the four parliamentary divisions with the same names created in 1885. All but three or four of Lambeth's ecclesiastical parishes may be placed in one of the census registration districts. Unless otherwise noted, all subsequent "districts" are based upon the ecclesiastical parishes arranged as nearly as possible into the four registration districts. Calling the innermost district North Lambeth avoids confusion; it was known locally simply as "Lambeth."

Table 6 Church Attendance and Social Status in Lambeth, 1886/88 and 1902

m = morning attendance as percentage of district population
e = evening attendance as percentage of district population
t = total attendance as percentage of district population
( ) = persons per acre

		1886/88			1902		
		m	e	t	m	e	t
N. Lambeth	CE	3.3	4.5	7.8	2.3	2.7	5.0
District	NC	3.3	5.7	9.0	2.4	5.8	8.2
(166)	TOTAL	6.6	10.2	16.8	4.7	8.5	13.2
Kennington	CE	7.4	9.0	16.4	3.7	5.3	9.0
District	NC	3.9	3.5	7.4	3.8	5.3	9.1
(94)	Other	—	—	—	0.8	0.1	0.9
	TOTAL	11.3	12.5	23.8	8.3	10.7	19.0
Brixton	CE	8.1	8.5	16.6	4.2	5.0	9.2
District	NC	6.7	10.1	16.8	4.6	6.0	10.7
(62)	Other	—	—	—	0.7	0.3	1.0
	TOTAL	14.8	18.6	33.4	9.5	11.3	20.9
Norwood	CE	11.1	10.5	21.6	8.0	7.0	15.0
District	NC	11.8	13.7	25.4	8.2	9.8	18.0
(30)	TOTAL	22.9	24.2	47.0	16.2	16.8	33.0

Percentage change, 1886/88 and 1902[1]

		m	e	t
N. Lambeth	CE	−30.3	−40.0	−35.8
	NC	−27.3	+ 1.8	− 8.9
	TOTAL	−28.8	−16.7	−21.4
Kennington	CE	−50.0	−41.1	−45.1
	NC	− 2.6	+51.4	+23.0
	TOTAL	−26.5	−14.4	−20.2
Brixton	CE	−48.1	−41.2	−44.6
	NC	−31.3	−40.6	−36.4
	TOTAL	−35.8	−39.2	−37.4
Norwood	CE	−27.9	−33.3	−30.6
	NC	−30.5	−28.6	−29.4
	TOTAL	−29.3	−30.6	−29.8

[1] *See* Tables 5 (note), 12, 12A, and 16.

Table 7 The Deployment of the Clergy in Lambeth, 1902[1]

Column 1 = parochial population 1901
Column 2 = number of clergymen, including curates[2]
Column 3 = number of persons per clergyman
Column 4 = total (morning and evening) attendance as a percentage of parochial population

	1	2	3	4
North Lambeth				
Emmanuel	7,355	3	2,452	4.0
Holy Trinity	5,718	4	1,430	5.3
St. John the Evangelist	10,024	3	3,341	2.2
St. Mary, Lambeth	11,000	3	3,667	6.0
St. Andrew	7,635	3	2,545	6.9
St. Mary Less (and St. Anselm)	12,738	3	4,246	4.1
St. Peter, Vauxhall	10,354	4	2,589	7.3
St. Phillip, Kennington	11,299	3	3,766	4.1
St. Thomas	8,235	2	4,118	5.9
Kennington				
All Saints, S. Lambeth	11,392	4	2,848	7.1
Christ Church, N. Brixton	6,797	2	3,399	27.5
St. Anne, Vauxhall	10,140	4	2,535	5.5
St. Barnabas	9,782	2	4,891	5.7
St. James, Camberwell	6,584	1	6,584	6.5
St. James, Kennington	6,044	1	6,044	1.7
St. John Divine, Kennington	15,288	10	1,528	11.8
St. Mark, Kennington	15,988	3	5,329	10.0
St. Michael, Stockwell	6,909	1	6,909	6.6
St. Stephen, S. Lambeth	6,459	2	3,230	5.1
Brixton				
Holy Trinity, Tulse Hill	4,176	2	2,088	22.6
St. Andrew, Stockwell (with Epiphany Msn)	19,369	4	4,842	6.8
St. John, Angell Town (with St. Catherine)	11,030	1	11,030	6.1
St. Jude, E. Brixton	7,192	1	7,192	9.6
St. Matthew, Brixton	12,092	2	6,046	11.2
St. Matthias, Upper Tulse Hill	5,415	2	2,708	8.7
St. Paul, W. Brixton	10,798	1	10,798	9.4
St. Saviour, Brixton Hill	9,350	2	4,675	11.0
St. Saviour, Herne Hill	7,179	2	3,590	6.8

[1] See Tables 5 (note) and 13.

[2] Source: Crockford's Clerical Directory, Southwark Diocesan Directory (1906), parish records.

Table 7, *continued*

	1	2	3	4
Norwood				
Christ Church, Gipsy Hill	5,338	2	2,669	28.0
All Saints, Rosendale Road	3,665	1	3,665	37.3
Emmanuel	7,433	3	2,478	11.3
St. Peter, Leigham Ct. Rd.	4,780	3	1,593	19.5
St. Luke, W. Norwood	16,180	1	16,180	6.0

Statistical Relationship Between Variations in Column 1
(Parochial Population) and Variations in Column 4 (Total Parochial
Church Attendance)

	R	R^2
North Lambeth	−.2077	.0431
Kennington	+.0699	.0048
Brixton	−.4939	.2439
Norwood	−.7983	.6372
Lambeth	−.3954	.1563

Statistical Relationship Between Variations in Column 3
(Persons per Clergyman) and Variations in Column 4 (Total Parochial
Church Attendance)

	R	R^2
North Lambeth	−.2414	.0583
Kennington	−.3079	.0948
Brixton	−.4441	.1972
Norwood	−.5689	.3236
Lambeth	−.2039	.0416

For explanation see R. Floud, *An Introduction to Quantitative Methods for Historians,* p. 138. Churchmen hoped to see an R^2 of 1, i.e., a perfect relationship between smaller parishes and fewer persons per clergyman on the one hand and higher church attendance on the other. Although not equivalent to the number of individual churchgoers, total Sunday attendance is a fair measure of clerical "productivity." An R^2 of .5 or more is significant for historical data.

Table 8 Parochial Size and Clerical Deployment in Lambeth

Column 1 = mean parochial population, 1886[1]
Column 2 = mean parochial population, 1902
Column 3 = mean number of persons per clergyman, 1886
Column 4 = mean number of persons per clergyman, 1902

	1	2	3	4
North Lambeth	9,836	9,373	4,054	3,128
Kennington	8,463	9,538	3,378	4,330
Brixton	7,901	9,622	3,759	5,885
Norwood	5,781	7,479	1,927	5,317
Lambeth	8,356	9,204	2,938	4,576

1. See also Tables 5 (note) and 13.

Table 9 The Deployment of the Clergy in Lambeth, 1886[1] and 1902

Column 1 = mean parochial population
Column 2 = mean parochial persons per clergyman
Column 3 = mean parochial attendance per clergyman
Column 4 = mean parochial total attendance as a percentage of parochial population

1886	1	2	3	4
North Lambeth	9,836	4,054	228	7.6
Kennington	8,463	3,378	605	17.1
Brixton	7,901	3,759	620	17.8
Norwood	5,781	1,927	499	27.0
1902	1	2	3	4
North Lambeth	9,373	3,128	156	5.0
Kennington	9,538	4,330	342	9.0
Brixton	9,622	5,885	540	9.2
Norwood	7,479	5,317	737	15.0

1. See also Tables 5 (note) and 13.

Table 10   Age Structure and Sexual Composition of Lambeth Congregations in 1902, by District[1]

Morn = morning congregation
Even = evening congregation
m = percentage of congregation male aged 15 or more
f = percentage of congregation female aged 15 or more
c = percentage of congregation children under 15
CE = parish churches
NC = chapels
Msn = mission halls
T = total

	Morn			Even			Ratio F/M	
	m	f	c	m	f	c	Morn	Even
N. Lambeth								
CE	19.2	27.9	52.9	23.6	48.7	27.7	1.45	2.06
CE msn	14.5	5.4	80.1	11.4	27.4	61.0	0.37	2.40
T-CE	18.8	26.0	55.2	22.2	46.2	31.6	1.38	2.08
NC	34.0	35.4	30.6	30.9	48.8	20.0	1.04	1.58
NC msn	13.8	8.9	77.0	26.1	37.4	36.5	0.64	1.43
T-NC	26.7	25.9	47.4	28.6	43.3	28.1	0.97	1.51
CE + NC								
+ Msn[2]	22.3	26.3	51.4	26.4	43.9	29.7	1.17	1.66
Kennington								
CE	28.1	43.3	28.6	30.7	54.0	15.3	1.54	1.75
CE msn	16.0	13.3	70.7	15.4	34.7	49.8	0.83	2.25
T-CE	26.8	40.1	33.0	29.0	51.9	19.0	1.49	1.78
NC	29.7	35.1	35.0	33.4	47.7	18.9	1.18	1.42
NC msn	17.7	17.9	64.0	26.4	40.8	32.9	1.01	1.54
T-NC	27.2	31.4	41.4	30.9	45.3	23.8	1.15	1.46
CE + NC								
+ Msn[2]	27.7	35.6	36.6	29.9	48.6	21.4	1.29	1.62

Table 10, *continued*

	Morn			Even			Ratio F/M	
	m	f	c	m	f	c	Morn	Even
Brixton								
CE	23.2	43.2	33.6	25.3	51.8	22.8	1.86	2.05
CE Msn	3.0	2.4	95.0	17.9	52.9	29.2	0.80	2.96
T-CE	22.3	41.4	36.3	24.6	51.9	23.5	1.85	2.11
NC	30.4	35.1	34.5	31.2	51.0	17.8	1.15	1.63
NC msn	26.0	26.5	47.5	21.1	41.4	37.5	1.02	1.96
T-NC	29.7	33.6	36.6	28.6	48.6	22.8	1.13	1.70
CE + NC								
+ Msn[2]	26.1	37.8	36.0	26.9	50.0	23.1	1.45	1.86
Norwood								
CE	25.8	50.1	24.1	24.6	63.2	12.2	1.94	2.57
CE msn	20.3	43.2	36.5	12.7	38.2	49.1	2.13	3.01
T-CE	25.7	49.9	24.3	22.8	59.5	17.7	1.94	2.61
NC	30.3	38.9	30.8	31.1	52.2	16.7	1.30	1.68
NC msn	26.0	18.8	55.0	21.6	42.0	36.0	0.72	1.94
T-NC	30.2	38.5	31.3	30.1	51.2	18.7	1.27	1.70
CE + NC								
+ Msn[2]	27.9	44.0	28.1	27.0	54.7	18.3	1.58	2.03

1. See Table 5 (note).
2. Includes Roman Catholic statistics.

Table 11 Age Structure and Sexual Composition of Church Attendance in 13 London Boroughs and Urban Districts in 1902

m = male church attendance as a percentage of all men aged 15 and over
f = female church attendance as a percentage of all women aged 15 and over
c = children's church attendance as a percentage of all children under 15

		Morning			Evening		
		m	f	c	m	f	c
1. Hampstead	CE	5.8	7.6	12.4	5.2	6.8	7.1
	NC	5.0	3.8	6.6	6.4	5.6	3.8
	Total	10.8	11.4	19.0	11.6	12.4	10.9
2. Kensington	CE	6.3	10.0	13.0	4.9	6.9	7.9
	NC	2.3	1.9	4.4	2.9	3.2	3.4
	Total	8.6	11.9	17.4	7.8	10.1	11.3
3. Westminster	CE	6.9	9.3	20.1	4.9	8.8	11.4
	NC	2.0	2.0	3.8	4.1	5.2	4.5
	Total	8.9	11.3	23.9	9.0	14.0	15.9
4. Richmond	CE	7.4	12.2	17.4	6.5	10.4	9.3
	NC	4.3	3.5	9.9	4.6	5.4	4.9
	Total	11.7	15.7	27.3	11.1	15.8	14.2
5. Ealing	CE	15.2	19.0	26.5	12.2	16.4	14.3
	NC	9.2	7.8	11.8	9.8	10.7	7.6
	Total	24.4	26.8	38.3	22.0	27.1	21.9
6. Bromley	CE	8.6	10.2	19.8	10.2	13.6	8.0
	NC	6.9	7.2	11.9	7.9	10.2	6.2
	Total	15.5	17.4	31.7	18.1	23.8	14.2
7. Lambeth[1]	CE	3.1	4.6	8.1	3.9	6.9	5.7
	NC	3.9	3.8	8.9	5.6	7.7	7.6
	Total	7.0	8.4	17.0	9.5	14.6	13.3
8. Poplar	CE	1.5	1.9	8.7	2.3	5.0	6.2
	NC	2.4	2.1	6.7	3.6	5.5	8.5
	Total	3.9	4.0	15.4	5.9	10.5	14.7
9. Southwark	CE	1.6	1.9	8.9	2.3	3.8	4.7
	NC	2.5	2.5	7.8	4.2	6.7	13.4
	Total	4.1	4.4	16.7	6.5	10.5	18.1
10. East Ham	CE	2.0	2.2	5.6	3.7	6.7	6.0
	NC	4.3	3.1	9.3	7.6	12.0	12.0
	Total	6.3	5.3	14.9	11.3	18.7	18.0
11. Bermondsey	CE	1.6	2.0	10.1	2.5	4.6	6.9
	NC	2.3	1.9	6.9	4.7	6.0	12.9
	Total	3.9	3.9	17.0	7.2	10.6	19.8
12. Shoreditch	CE	1.4	2.1	3.7	1.9	4.2	5.6
	NC	1.8	1.6	4.2	3.0	4.9	9.7
	Total	3.2	3.7	7.9	4.9	9.1	15.3
13. Bethnal Green	CE	1.2	1.5	6.1	3.2	4.7	6.2
	NC	2.1	2.2	6.1	3.5	5.7	10.9
	Total	3.3	3.7	12.2	6.7	10.4	17.1

1. The Lambeth statistics are based exclusively on summaries in Mudie-Smith, *Religious Life of London,* and population figures for the Borough of Lambeth from the census which differ slightly from the statistics for Lambeth used in my other tables. See the explanation in Table 5.

Table 11A Age Structure and Sexual Composition of Church Attendance in 13 London Boroughs and Urban Districts in 1902, Arranged According to Social Status

Dom = ratio of female domestic indoor servants to families or separate occupiers, 1901 census

Prof = male and female professionals per 1000 persons, 1901 census, inner London boroughs only

f ÷ m = ratio of adult women to adult men as proportion of adult women and adult men in the general population, i.e., the ratio which would be produced at a worship service if the population were 50 percent adult female and 50 percent adult male

$\dfrac{(f + m)}{c}$ = ratio of adults at worship as a percentage of all adults to children at worship as a percentage of all children

				Ratio f ÷ m		Ratio $\dfrac{(f + m)}{c}$	
	Dom	Prof		Morn	Even	Morn	Even
1. Hampstead	.798	52.5	CE	1.3	1.3	1.1	1.7
			NC	0.8	0.9	1.3	3.2
			Total	1.1	1.1	1.2	2.2
2. Kensington	.749	39.2	CE	1.6	1.4	1.3	1.5
			NC	0.8	1.1	0.95	1.8
			Total	1.4	1.3	1.2	1.6
3. Westminster	.533	36.0	CE	1.3	1.8	0.8	1.2
			NC	1.0	1.3	1.1	2.1
			Total	1.3	1.6	0.85	1.4
4. Richmond	.498		CE	1.6	1.6	1.1	1.8
			NC	0.8	1.2	0.8	2.0
			Total	1.3	1.4	1.0	1.9
5. Ealing	.686		CE	1.3	1.3	1.3	2.0
			NC	0.84	1.1	1.4	2.7
			Total	1.1	1.2	1.3	2.2
6. Bromley	.478		CE	1.2	1.3	0.95	3.0
			NC	1.04	1.3	1.2	2.9
			Total	1.1	1.3	1.0	3.0
7. Lambeth	.176	32.5	CE	1.5	1.8	0.95	1.9
			NC	0.97	1.4	0.87	1.8
			Total	1.2	1.5	0.9	1.8
8. Poplar	.080	10.5	CE	1.3	2.2	0.4	1.2
			NC	0.88	1.5	0.7	1.1
			Total	1.0	1.8	0.5	1.1
9. Southwark	.074	11.23	CE	1.2	1.6	0.4	1.3
			NC	1.0	1.6	0.64	0.81
			Total	1.1	1.6	0.5	0.94
10. East Ham	.084		CE	1.1	1.8	0.75	1.7
			NC	0.7	1.6	0.8	1.6
			Total	0.84	1.7	0.78	1.7

Table 11A, *continued*

	Dom	Prof		Ratio f ÷ m		Ratio (f + m) c	
				Morn	Even	Morn	Even
11. Bermondsey	.065	8.6	CE	1.3	1.8	0.35	1.0
			NC	0.8	1.3	0.6	0.8
			Total	1.0	1.5	0.5	0.9
12. Shoreditch	.055	7.3	CE	1.5	2.2	0.95	1.1
			NC	0.9	1.6	0.8	0.8
			Total	1.2	1.9	0.9	0.9
13. Bethnal Green	.056	6.9	CE	1.3	1.5	0.44	1.3
			NC	1.1	1.6	0.7	0.84
			Total	1.1	1.5	0.6	1.0

Summary of Table 11A

	Boroughs	Mean f ÷ m		Mean c		Mean (f + m) c	
		Morn	Even	Morn	Even	Morn	Even
CE	1–3 (wealthy)	1.4	1.5	15.2	8.8	1.1	1.5
	4–6 (suburbs)	1.4	1.4	21.2	10.5	1.1	2.3
	Lambeth only	1.5	1.8	8.1	5.7	0.95	1.9
	8–13 (poor)	1.3	1.9	7.2	5.9	0.55	1.3
NC	1–3 (wealthy)	0.86	1.1	4.9	3.9	1.1	2.4
	4–6 (suburbs)	0.9	1.2	11.2	6.2	1.1	2.5
	Lambeth only	0.97	1.4	8.9	7.6	0.87	1.8
	8–13 (poor)	0.89	1.5	6.8	11.2	0.7	1.0
Total	1–3 (wealthy)	1.3	1.3	20.1	12.7	1.1	1.7
	4–6 (suburbs)	1.2	1.3	32.4	16.8	1.1	2.4
	Lambeth only	1.2	1.5	17.0	13.3	0.9	1.8
	8–13 (poor)	1.0	1.7	14.0	17.2	0.6	1.1

Table 12 Percentage Change in Real Church Attendance in Lambeth, 1886/88–1902

CE = parish churches
NC = nonconformist chapels
Msn = mission halls
Total includes minor sects

	Morn	Even	Total
CE	−39.8	−39.7	−39.7
CE msn	−16.7	−16.0	−16.2
Total	−38.6	−37.7	−38.1
NC	−27.5	−19.6	−23.4
NC msn	+103.0	+27.0	+41.3
Total	−18.3	− 9.4	−13.1
NC + CE	−34.3	−31.0	−32.6
NC msn + CE msn	+48.0	+14.0	+22.0
Total	−25.5	−23.1	−24.1

Table 12A Attendance in Lambeth in 1886/88 As a Percentage of Population Compared with Attendance in Lambeth and Croydon Combined in 1902

	Morning	Evening	Total
Lambeth 1886/88	11.7	14.4	26.0
Lambeth + Croydon 1902	11.7	14.2	25.9

Table 13   The Deployment of the Clergy in Lambeth, 1886

Column 1 = parochial population, 1886 estimate
Column 2 = number of clergymen, including curates (Source: Crockford's and parish records)
Column 3 = number of persons per clergyman
Column 4 = total (morning and evening) attendance as a percentage of parochial population (It is impossible to estimate the number of worshippers at this level)

	1	2	3	4
North Lambeth				
Emmanuel	7,656	2	3,828	6.6
Holy Trinity	7,157	5	1,431	5.9
St. Andrew	8,517	3	2,839	5.6
St. John the Evangelist	12,731	2	6,366	7.1
St. Mary, Lambeth	12,542	3	4,181	12.3
St. Mary the Less	10,840	5	2,168	8.3
St. Peter, Vauxhall	10,003	4	2,501	8.0
St. Phillip, Kennington	10,219	1	10,219	3.4
St. Thomas	8,863	3	2,954	11.2
Kennington				
All Saints, S. Lambeth	9,700	2	4,850	19.1
Christ Church, North Brixton	6,838	2	3,419	27.0
St. Anne, Vauxhall	7,922	2	3,961	11.6
St. Barnabas	9,890	3	3,297	11.0
St. James, Camberwell	5,211	1	5,211	27.2
St. James, Kennington	6,384	2	3,192	6.1
St. John the Divine, Kennington	12,100	9	1,344	12.0
St. Mark, Kennington	15,455	4	3,864	17.4
St. Michael, Stockwell	5,534	3	1,845	19.5
St. Stephen, S. Lambeth	5,604	2	2,802	20.5
Brixton				
Holy Trinity, Tulse Hill	6,302	3	2,101	23.2
St. Andrew, Stockwell	14,024	3	4,675	9.1
St. Catherine	5,368	1	5,368	6.6
St. John, Angell Town	5,470	3	1,823	16.4
St. Jude, East Brixton	6,627	2	3,314	30.5
St. Matthew, Brixton	13,924	3	4,641	12.4
St. Paul, West Brixton	6,899	2	3,450	29.0
St. Saviour, Brixton Hill	6,053	3	2,018	15.4
St. Saviour, Herne Hill	6,444	1	6,444	17.3
Norwood				
Christ Church, Gipsy Hill	4,668	3	1,556	33.3
Emmanuel	5,190	2	2,595	25.6
St. Peter, Leigham Court Rd.	2,889	3	963	39.9
St. Luke, West Norwood	10,377	4	2,594	9.1

Table 13, *continued*

Statistical Relationship between Variations in Column 1 (Parochial Population) and Variations in Column 4 (Total Parochial Church Attendance)[1]

	R	R²
North Lambeth	+.3704	.1372
Kennington	−.2991	.0894
Brixton	−.3665	.1343
Norwood	−.9814	.9631
Lambeth	−.5314	.2824

Statistical Relationship between Variations in Column 3 (Persons/Clergyman) and Variations in Column 4 (Total Parochial Church Attendance)

	R	R²
North Lambeth	−.4192	.1757
Kennington	+.3469	.1204
Brixton	−.3989	.1591
Norwood	−.8595	.7387
Lambeth	−.3272	.1070

1. *See* Table 5 (note) on districts and *see* Table 7 for explanation of R and R².

Table 14   Lambeth "High Church" Attendance, 1886/88–1902

21 of 84 Lambeth clergymen were identified as "High" by the *Clerical Ritualist's Who's Who* (1908), an Evangelical publication, but the only evidence of Catholic tendencies for eleven of these men was their signature on the "Russel-Wakefield Declaration of 1903 for the toleration of the first prayer book of Edward VI." Only 13 of 84 clergymen were members of either the English Church Union or the Confraternity of the Blessed Sacrament, representing only six of 32 parishes. Five of those six parishes were definitely "High" in 1886 as well as 1902: Holy Trinity, Lambeth; St. Peter's, Vauxhall; St. John the Divine, Kennington; St. Andrew's, Stockwell; St. Peter's, Leigham Court Road. All Saints', Rosendale Road, was definitely "High", but founded in 1899. Another reputedly "High" parish, St. John's, Angell Town, was in constant turmoil over liturgical issues. The following table summarizes attendance figures for the five parishes which were distinctly "High" in both 1886/88 and 1902.

Percentage "Real" Change

	Morn	Even	Total
5 "High" parishes	+ 4.7	−30.9	−17.1
All Lambeth parishes	−38.6	−37.7	−38.0

Table 15 Rank List—Percentage Decline in Real Anglican Church
Attendance in Each Lambeth Parish, 1886/88–1902

Number 1 = least severe decline in parochial church attendance as a percentage of parochial population

Number 29 = most severe decline in parochial church attendance as a percentage of parochial population

1. St. Andrew's, N. Lambeth. Energetic evangelical clergymen holding their own in an entirely working-class parish.
2. St. Phillip's, Kennington. Working-class, evangelical; day schools.
3. Christ Church, N. Brixton. An evangelical preaching center.
4. St. John the Divine, Kennington. Very high, well financed, working class parish with mixed congregation.
5. St. Peter's, Vauxhall. Very high, working class. Harvest festival 1886 service.
6. St. Matthew's, Brixton. Parochial, fashionable, very mildly evangelical.
7. Holy Trinity, Lambeth. High, working class parish with declining population.
8. Christ Church, Gipsy Hill. Evangelical, activist, suburban, wealthy.
9. St. Andrew's, Stockwell with Epiphany Mission. High, enormous effort.
10. St. Saviour, Brixton Hill. Evangelical, "low."
11. St. Luke's, W. Norwood. Parochial, middle of the road.
12. St. Mark's, Kennington. Parochial, low.
13. St. John's, Angell Town with St. Catherine. Troubled by liturgical turmoil and an incompetent clergyman.
14. St. Thomas's, Westminster Bridge Road. Evangelical.
15. St. Barnabas.
16. St. Mary the Less, with St. Anselm, Kennington Road.
17. St. Peter's, Leigham Court Road. Suburban and very high.
18. St. Mary's, Lambeth. The ancient parish church. Surrey Regiment at services in 1886.
19. St. Anne's, Vauxhall.
20. Emmanuel, W. Dulwich. Harvest festival, 1886.
21. St. Saviour, Herne Hill. Mildly evangelical and low.
22. All Saints', South Lambeth. Low and dry, but unusually activist.
23. St. Michael's, Stockwell. Low and dry, no effort.
24. St. Paul's, W. Brixton. Low, evangelical and old fashioned.
25. St. Jude's, E. Brixton. Low and evangelical. Closed one mission.
26. St. John the Evangelist, Waterloo Road. Mildly high, closed one mission.
27. St. James's, Kennington.
28. St. Stephen's, S. Lambeth. Feeble "low evangelical" parish with incompetent clergyman.
29. St. James's, Camberwell. Low and dry, no effort. Harvest Festival, 1886.

Note: Holy Trinity, Tulse Hill, was subdivided between 1886 and 1902 into three parishes, two evangelical and one high. The area of the old parish would rank very high if included on the list, largely because of continued suburban growth within its boundaries, but I was unable to reconstruct the boundaries.

Table 16   Real Percentage Change in Nonconformist Church Attendance in Lambeth by Denomination, 1886/88–1902

Chap = chapel attendance only
Msn = mission attendance only
T = attendance at chapels and mission halls
All NC includes Presbyterians, Unitarians, Brethren etc.
PM = Primitive Methodists
+ alone = no attendance 1886/88 only
− alone = no attendance either year

		Morn	Even	Total
Free Methodist and PM	Chap	−13.2	+41.0	+12.8
	Msn	−	+	+
	T	−13.2	+136.0	+60.3
Baptists	Chap	−14.3	−12.8	−13.1
	Msn	+	+140.0	+380.0
	T	− 4.2	− 7.2	− 5.9
All NC	Chap	−27.5	−19.6	−23.4
	Msn	+103.0	+27.0	+41.3
	T	−18.3	− 9.4	−13.1
Congregationalists	Chap	−24.5	−21.0	−22.6
	Msn	+ 8.3	−25.0	−16.7
	T	−22.1	−21.9	−22.0
Wesleyans	Chap	−54.3	−53.1	−54.0
	Msn	+133.3	+121.5	+125.0
	T	−38.8	−25.1	−31.2

Table 17   Church and Chapel Auxiliaries in Lambeth, 1899–1900

This is a listing of parochial and chapel auxiliaries taken from the personal interviews of Lambeth clergymen and ministers used in the preparation of Charles Booth's *Life and Labour of the People of London* and deposited at the library of the London School of Economics. The manuscript interviews were conducted by Booth's assistants and were quite straightforward; they included facts and figures, extensive direct quotations from the clergyman or minister, and the interviewer's concluding subjective estimate of the man and his work. They appear to be reliable despite Booth's highly subjective and arbitrary use of them in the preparation of the published volumes. In some cases I have supplemented them with information from parochial and chapel records, but *only* if they indicate an auxiliary active during 1899 or 1900, the years of the interviews. For some parishes, notably Christ Church, North Brixton, and Christ Church, Gipsy Hill, the information which can be gleaned from both sources is inadequate, and the numbers would have been even larger if parochial records from another year between 1890 and 1910 had been used. The survey covered virtually every Anglican parish but only the larger Nonconformist chapels, and Nonconformist philanthropy is further understated by their dependence upon interdenominational societies.

Key to Columns

1. clergyman or minister's estimate of yearly direct relief in pounds
2. mothers' meetings
3. maternity societies
4. professional nurses, ( ) = *shared*
5. slate clubs, friendly societies, and thrift societies
6. membership of slate clubs, friendly societies, and thrift societies (*incomplete figures*)
7. boot, coal, clothing, or blanket clubs
8. savings banks or children's penny banks
9. young men's clubs, literary societies, debating societies
10. girls' or young women's clubs
11. women's clubs, excluding mothers' meetings
12. men's clubs
13. gymnasium or recreation classes
14. adult temperance societies
15. children's temperance societies
16. uniformed organizations (Boys' Brigades, Church Lads' Brigades, etc.)
17. Christian Endeavor Societies
18. regular (weekly or monthly) concerts or public entertainments
19. vocational education classes
20. Bible classes
21. sports clubs (mainly cricket)

Table 17, *continued*

CHURCH OF ENGLAND	1	2	3	4	5	6	7
North Lambeth							
Emmanuel	125	1		1	1	63	1
Holy Trinity	100	1					1
St. Andrew	149	1	1				
St. John Evangelist	218	1		1	3		
St. Mary, Lambeth	100	1			2		
St. Mary-the-Less (with St. Anselm)	100	1			1		
St. Peter, Vauxhall	200	6		(1)	1		1
St. Phillip, Kennington	50						
St. Thomas	172	1	1		1		1
Kennington							
All Saints, S. Lambeth	100	3					
Christ Church, N. Brixton	190				1	45	
St. Anne, Vauxhall	100				1		
St. Barnabas	60	1			1		
St. James, Camberwell	8						
St. John the Divine	323			1	3		
St. Mark	61	1		1	3	193	
St. Michael, Stockwell	516	1	1		1		
St. Stephen, S. Lambeth	30	1			2		1
Brixton							
Holy Trinity, Tulse Hill	60						
St. Andrew, Stockwell (with Epiphany)	176	2		1	4	70	
St. John, Angell Town (with St. Catherine)	44	2	1				2
St. Jude, E. Brixton	70	2			2	300	
St. Matthew	242	1	1		1	36	1
St. Matthias, Tulse Hill							
St. Paul, W. Brixton	60+	2					
St. Saviour, Brixton Hill	135	1	1		2		
St. Saviour, Herne Hill	?	1			1		1
Norwood							
Christ Church, Gipsy Hill	400				2		
All Saints, Rosendale Rd.	70	1			1		
Emmanuel, W. Dulwich	130	1			1	885	2
St. Peter, Leigham Ct. Rd.	99		1				3
St. Luke, W. Norwood	?	1					3
TOTAL C of E	4088	34	7	6	35	—	17
NONCONFORMIST ( ) = *no. of chapels*							
Baptist (15)	(5) 93	4	1		1	500	1
Congregational (12)	(7) 452	6		2	13	1865	
Wesleyan (9)	(3) 90	8			4	804	
Other Methodist (6)	(6) 140	2	1		2	350	
Other (13)	(4) 75	3	1	8	3	640	3
TOTAL NONCONFORMIST	850	23	3	10	23	4159	4
GRAND TOTAL	4938	57	10	16	58	—	21

8	9	10	11	12	13	14	15	16	17	18	19	20	21
1		1			1	1	1					1	
1		1		1			1	1					
		1	1										
1	1	2				1	1	1		1	1		
1	2	1		2	1		1			1	1		1
1	2	2	1	1		1						2	3
	1					1							
1						1							
	1					1	1	1					
1	1		1	1									
1	1	1		1				1					
1+	1	1	1	1+		1	1			1			
1	2	2				1	1	1					
1													
1								1					
						1							
1	1	3	1	2		1	2	1		1	1	1	1
							1						
						1		1				1	
	1	2				1	1	1				1	1
							1						
1				1								2	
		1						1					
								1					
	1			1	1	1	1						
	1	1		1		1	1	1				2	
	1				1								1
1		1			1		1						
15	17	20	5	12	5	14	15	12		4	3	10	7
	3	2				1	5		6		2	7	
5	5	2	1	1	2	3	7	2	8	2	2	6	10
3	4	1	2				3	2		3	3	2	3
1	1						4	1	5				3
1	6	2			3	1	2		5	4	3	2	2
10	19	7	3	1	5	5	21	5	24	9	10	17	18
25	36	27	8	13	10	19	36	17	24	13	13	27	25

Table 18 Occupational Structure of Fathers of the Bride in Lambeth, by Denomination, 1880, 1890, 1900, 1910

Source: Marriage registers in the Lambeth Registry Office, by the kind permission of the Registrar General. The local registry offices have no facilities for historical research; consequently a more complete sample was impossible. Roman Catholic marriages are excluded.

Classification: Adapted from General Register Office. *Classification of Occupations, 1950* (1951). My modifications are based upon those of W. A. Armstrong, "The Use of Information about Occupation," in E. A. Wrigley, ed., *Nineteenth Century Society* (Cambridge, 1972). Unfortunately the information about occupation in the marriage registers is even more unsatisfactory than that of the census enumerators' books, and many shopkeepers who should be classified in Class II have been put into Class III for lack of information about the number of their employees. Changes in occupational structure cause distortion as well. For instance, Class III grows and Class IV shrinks as vehicles are motorized. The marriage registers appear to be the only records where some evidence of a person's religious preference is written down beside some evidence of his occupation. The occupation of the bride's father is probably the best evidence of the occupational composition of the various denominations since weddings were normally held at the church or chapel of the family of the bride. Sons of Nonconformist families marrying Anglican brides would be more likely to marry in the parish church than in the chapel.

Admonition: A marriage in a Nonconformist chapel is good evidence of some type of commitment to Nonconformity. An Anglican marriage on the other hand may be entered into by people with the widest variety of attitudes to the Church of England, including some Nonconformists. A Nonconformist marriage, however, by no means implies regular chapel attendance, and may reflect a purely ancestral commitment.

Sample: A ten percent systematic sample of all marriages in Lambeth for each year; a ten percent systematic sample of all Anglican marriages for each year; a ten percent systematic sample of Registry Office (secular) marriages for 1900 and 1910. The number of Registry Office marriages in 1880 and 1890, and the number of Nonconformist marriages for each of the four years, was too small in each case to allow me to take a reliable scientific sample. Consequently I enumerated every Nonconformist marriage in each of the four years, and every Registry Office marriage in 1880 and 1890. The choice of years was arbitrary, and too much weight should not be placed on the results from any one year.

Table 18, *continued*

Classification (examples)

Class I: professional, clergy, company director, company secretary
Class II: manager, manufacturer, lower managerial and professional (head clerk, police superintendent, supervisor, teacher, Nonconformist minister), independent means, wealthier shopkeeper, bookkeeper, journalist (shopkeepers so designated were normally placed in IIIb in the absence of additional positive evidence of their status)
Class IIIa: routine clerical
Class IIIb: small shopkeeper, shop assistant, dealer, dairyman, milkman, butcher, baker, hairdresser, optician, pawnbroker, commercial traveller, insurance agent, rent or money collector
Class IIIc: skilled operative, motorized driver, cook, market gardener, builder, decorator, tailor, nurseryman, performing artist, waiter
Class IV: semi-skilled, gardener, carman, thatcher, lighterman, waterman, ticket collector, tram conductor
Class V: unskilled, porter, labourer, messenger, docker
Class VI: other, unknown

Abbreviations

N = number of marriages recorded in Lambeth, excluding Roman Catholics
N 10% = 10 percent systematic sample of all marriages
CE 10% = 10 percent systematic sample of all Anglican marriages
RG = all marriages in the registry office
RG 10% = 10 percent systematic sample of RG
NC = all Nonconformist marriages in Lambeth

Number and Percentage of Marriages in Each Category

	1880			1890	
N	2,342		N	2,026	
CE	2,089	89.2	CE	1,653	81.6
RG	143	6.1	RG	265	13.1
NC	110	4.7	NC	108	5.3
	1900			1910	
N	2,483		N	2,473	
CE	1,780	71.7	CE	1,530	61.9
RG	515	20.7	RG	810	32.8
NC	187	7.5	NC	133	5.4

Table 18, *continued*

	I	II	IIIa	IIIb	IIIc	IV	V	VI
	\multicolumn{8}{c}{Percentage in Each Occupational Classification by Denomination}							

	I	II	IIIa	IIIb	IIIc	IV	V	VI
1880								
N 10%	6.4	7.7	3.4	14.5	36.8	12.4	12.8	6.1
CE 10%	5.3	8.6	3.3	12.9	37.3	12.0	13.9	6.7
RG	14.0	16.1	3.5	15.4	37.1	7.0	6.3	—
NC	9.0	16.2	2.7	26.1	29.7	9.9	4.5	2.0
1890								
N 10%	3.4	9.9	2.0	11.8	41.9	13.9	11.8	5.4
CE 10%	2.4	7.8	2.4	12.6	41.9	13.2	13.2	6.4
RG	6.0	17.4	1.5	17.0	40.8	7.2	9.8	—
NC	2.8	23.1	0.9	19.4	35.2	9.3	8.3	—
1900								
N 10%	5.7	8.6	2.9	15.1	40.4	14.3	6.9	6.0
CE 10%	6.3	7.4	3.4	13.6	36.9	15.9	8.0	7.5
RG 10%	5.9	11.8	2.0	17.6	49.0	9.8	3.9	—
NC	—	19.8	2.1	18.2	46.5	8.0	4.3	—
1910								
N 10%	2.8	10.5	4.0	15.0	38.9	15.0	7.3	6.3
CE 10%	2.0	9.8	3.9	11.1	37.3	17.0	8.5	9.9
RG 10%	4.9	11.1	2.5	21.0	40.7	13.6	6.2	—
NC	3.0	17.3	5.3	16.5	39.1	6.0	8.3	4.5

Table 19   Percentage of Lambeth Nonconformist Marriages by Denominational Group, Sum of 1880, 1890, 1900, and 1910

Column 1 = Baptist, Free Methodist, Primitive Methodist, and Other (N = 198)
Column 2 = All Nonconformists (sum of 1 and 3, N = 539)
Column 3 = Congregationalist, Wesleyan, Presbyterian (N = 341)

	Occupation	1	2	3
I	higher prof	2.5	3.2	3.5
II	lower prof	13.6	19.1	22.3
IIIa	clerk	2.5	2.8	2.3
IIIb	shopkeeper	22.8	19.7	19.4
IIIc	skilled artisan	39.9	39.0	38.4
IV	semi-skilled	9.6	8.2	7.3
V	unskilled	8.1	6.1	5.0
VI	other	1.0	2.0	1.8

Table 20 Changes in London Church Attendance, 1886–1902–1927

In 1927 the *British Weekly* conducted an inquiry into levels of church attendance in two London neighborhoods in order to measure changes since the censuses of 1886 and 1902. For his "working-class district," the author chose a parliamentary subdivision of inner London with about 80,000 people, thirty-six churches, chapels, and mission halls, and a declining population. His "suburban area" was an ancient village engulfed by London in the nineteenth century with one Roman Catholic, six Anglican, five Nonconformist, and five "various" churches in 1927. I can identify neither district with any confidence, although the working-class district sounds as if it might be in Southwark, Bermondsey, or Camberwell. Both were within the L.C.C. (1886 church attendance figures were available), and the suburban area had a relatively low attendance in 1902 when compared with other suburban areas, suggesting a peculiar definition of "suburban" by the author. It is not clear whether he used the 1888 census of mission hall attendance or not, and the decline from 1886 to 1902 would be substantially underestimated if he did not. (It is consistent with the rate of decline in other areas of London.) His categories of Anglican and Free Church included missions of both. Independent and non-denominational Nonconformist churches were classified as "other" along with Christadelphians, Swedenborgians, and Roman Catholics.

Source: *British Weekly*, 23 Feb. 1928 and 1 March 1928; reprinted in Arthur Black, ed., *London Church and Mission Attendance* (1928), copy at the Baptist Library, London.

		Attendance			Absolute change (percent)		
		Morn	Even	Total	Morn	Even	Total
		Working-Class District					
CE	1886	2,038	2,975	5,013			
	1902	1,830	2,688	4,518	−10.0	− 9.6	− 9.9
	1927	640	720	1,360	−65.0	−73.0	−70.0
NC	1886	2,667	3,337	6,004			
	1902	1,960	3,467	5,427	−26.5	+ 4.0	− 9.6
	1927	360	1,010	1,370	−81.6	−70.9	−74.8
Other	1886	543	1,446	1,989			
	1902	341	604	945	−37.0	−58.0	−53.0
	1927	330	840	1,170	− 3.2	+39.0	+24.0
		Suburban District					
CE	1886	1,788	1,221	3,009			
	1902	1,522	866	2,388	−15.0	−29.0	−21.0
	1927	857	673	1,530	−44.0	−22.0	−36.0
NC	1886	838	757	1,595			
	1902	1,139	917	2,056	+36.0	+21.0	+29.0
	1927	570	575	1,145	−50.0	−37.0	−44.0

Table 20, *continued*

		Attendance			Absolute change (percent)		
		Morn	Even	Total	Morn	Even	Total
Other	1886	91	110	201			
	1902	—	198	198	—	+80.0	− 1.5
	1927	178	247	425	—	+25.0	+115.0

Suburban churchgoers ÷ population (percent)[1]

		Attendance			Real change (percent)[2]		
		Morn	Even	Total	Morn	Even	Total
CE	1886	11.9	8.1	20.1			
	1902	6.3	3.6	10.0	−47.0	−56.0	−50.0
	1927	2.6	2.1	4.8	−59.0	−42.0	−52.0
NC	1886	5.6	5.2	10.6			
	1902	4.7	3.8	8.6	−16.0	−27.0	−19.0
	1927	1.8	1.8	3.6	−62.0	−53.0	−58.0
Other	1886	0.6	0.7	1.3			
	1902	—	0.8	0.8	—	+14.0	−39.0
	1927	0.6	0.8	1.3	—	—	+63.0

1. Population estimates supplied for suburban district only; 1886: 15,000; 1902: 24,000; 1927: 32,000.
2. Rounded off to whole figures.

Table 21   City Guild Donations to South London Church Fund, 1878–1929

	1878–1920 £	1921–1929 £
Court of Common Council	105	
armourers		11
clothworkers	700	
fishmongers	353	
girdlers	11	
goldsmiths	1,350	500
grocers	6,305	600
haberdashers	21	53
innholders		5
ironmongers	63	
leathersellers	226	16
mercers	4,844	300
merchant taylors	315	123
salters	294	
skinners	301	
tylers and bricklayers		5
vintners	21	
TOTAL	14,909	1,613
(Average per year)	(347)	(179)

Source: Southwark Diocesan and South London Church Fund *Annual Report,* 1920 and subsequent reports.

Table 22   Sunday School Enrollment and Church Membership, Percentage Change in Great Britain, 1901–1931

	Sunday School		Membership	
	absolute	real	absolute	real
Baptist	−10.5	− 0.5	+ 8.7	−20.3
Cong	−26.3	−18.0	+11.0	−18.8
Wesleyan	−21.3	−12.5	+ 9.9	−19.2

The absolute change is merely a comparison of overall membership or enrollment levels for 1901 and 1931. The real change measures membership as a percentage of the population aged 15 and over, and Sunday School enrollment as a percentage of the population under 15. The figures are taken from Currie, Gilbert, and Horsley, *Churches and Churchgoers,* and A. H. Halsey, ed., *Trends in British Society Since 1900.* The growth in absolute membership reflects temporary gains of the 1920s, and is not evident in the statistics for England alone (see the following table).

Table 23   Sunday School Enrollment and Church Membership,
Percentage Change in England, 1904–1936

	Sunday School		Membership	
	absolute	real	absolute	real
Baptist	−27.8	−17.8	−0.6	−28.2
Cong	−42.4	−34.6	−4.7	−31.3

In this table the real change measures membership as a percentage of the
population aged 15 and over, and Sunday School enrollments as a percentage
of the population aged 3–14, rather than 1–14 as in the previous table. Population figures were taken from estimates made in *Facts and Figures about the
Church of England* (1962 ed.), p. 63; Sunday School and membership figures
from the *Congregational Yearbook* and *Baptist Handbook*.

Table 24   Percentage of Lambeth Nonconformists in Routine Clerical
Occupations (Class IIIa)

All = all marriages = 10 percent systematic sample of all non-Catholic marriages in Lambeth
NC = all Nonconformist marriages

Mean percentage of marriages in		Groom	Both fathers	Bride's father
Class IIIa in the four sample years	All	8.6	3.1	3.1
1880, 1890, 1900, and 1910	NC	18.9	3.0	3.0
Mean percentage of marriages in				
Classs IIIa in the four sample years	All	7.5	2.5	2.6
1920, 1930, 1938, and 1950	NC	21.3	4.7	5.5

For further explanations see Tables 18 and 19. This table indicates that
daughters from Nonconformist families in Lambeth married a disproportion-
ate number of clerks in the years before World War I even though the percentage of Nonconformist parents in routine clerical occupations approximated
the percentage in the total population. After World War I, however, Nonconformist parents were disproportionately clerical as well.

Table 25 Percentage of Lambeth Nonconformist Marriages by Denominational Group, 1920–1950

Column 1 = Baptists, Free Methodists, Primitive Methodists, other (after 1930, former Free and Primitive Methodist chapels)

Column 2 = All Nonconformists

Column 3 = Congregationalists, Wesleyans, Presbyterians (after 1930, formerly Wesleyan chapels)

Occupation		1	2	3
I	higher prof	0.7	2.1	2.9
II	lower prof, mfg	16.3	14.7	13.7
IIIa	clerk	6.1	5.9	5.8
IIIb	shopkeeper	15.0	13.1	12.9
IIIc	skilled artisan	40.8	41.0	41.1
IV	semi-skilled	6.8	8.5	11.2
V	unskilled	6.1	8.2	9.5
VI	other	8.2	6.4	2.9

Sample: Sum of all Nonconformist marriages in sample years 1920, 1930, 1938, 1950.

Comment: In Table 19, which tabulated Nonconformist marriages between 1880 and 1910, the Congregationalists, Wesleyans, and Presbyterians included more individuals from Classes I and II and fewer from Classes IV and V, than other Nonconformists. After the war the numbers from Classes I and II were about the same for both groups. The Congregationalists, Wesleyans, and Presbyterian chapels actually drew more heavily upon semi-skilled and unskilled occupations, but that is a deceptive statistic: three chapels, West Norwood Congregational, Christ Church Westminster Bridge Road, and the Wesleyan Springfield Hall, included in their statistics a number of marriages from members of their associated Brotherhood organization, a working class auxiliary distinct from the ordinary membership.

BIBLIOGRAPHICAL NOTE

The most useful manuscript collections have been the Booth Collection at the British Library of Economic and Political Science (see Table 17) and the Surrey Collection at the Minet Library of the Borough of Lambeth. Church attendance statistics were taken from Richard Mudie-Smith, ed., *The Religious Life of London* (1904); the *British Weekly,* 5 and 17 December 1886, 13 January 1888; and the Census of Great Britain 1851, *Religious Worship: Report and Tables* (1853), P.P. 1852–53, vol. 89. Information about occupational structure was derived from the marriage registers at the Lambeth Registry Office, by the kind permission of the Registrar General. The *Brixton Free Press, South London Press,* and *Norwood Press* reprinted many sermons (cf. Chapter 4, note 44).

The notebooks in the Booth Collection, when supplemented with a variety of parish and chapel minutebooks, parish magazines, printed parish and chapel histories, biographies, and autobiographies, provided information about more than 150 South London churches, chapels, and other similar institutions. A search for parish and chapel records which have not been deposited in a library or record office turned out to be disappointing in one sense. Although minute books and parish magazines existed in great quantities, the information which could be obtained from them was so fragmentary that it could not be used in a systematic or orderly way except as a supplement to the interviews in the Booth manuscripts. But I did find it much easier to reconstruct mentally the inner life of a Lambeth church or chapel after exploring Lambeth's surviving Victorian churches and chapels, and reading parish magazines or congregational yearbooks on the spot. William Kent's *Testament of a Victorian Youth* (1938) was the most useful autobiography (see Chapter 7, note 27). Readers interested in a detailed list of sources should see the bibliography in my dissertation, "The Social Origins of the Decline of Religion in Modern England, 1880–1930," Harvard, 1978.

I was very much influenced by the works of other historians, and particularly influenced by four recent local studies of religion in England: James Obelkevich, *Religion and Rural Society: South Lindsey 1825–1875* (1976); Hugh McLeod, *Class and Religion in the Late Victorian City* (1974); Robert Moore, *Pitmen, Preachers and Politics: The Effects of Methodism in a Durham Mining Community* (1974); and Stephen Yeo, *Religion and Voluntary Organizations in Crisis* (1976). The statistical work of Robert Currie, Alan Gilbert, and Lee Horsley was indispensable, especially in Robert Currie, Alan Gilbert, and Lee Horsley, *Churches and Churchgoers: Patterns of Church Growth in the British Isles Since 1700* (1977); Robert Currie, *Methodism Divided: A Study in the Sociology of Ecumenicalism* (1968); and Alan Gilbert, *Religion and Society in Industrial England: Church, Chapel and Social Change 1740–1914* (1976). There are a great variety of books about this or that aspect of Victorian religion, including four which I found particularly useful: G. S. R. Kitson Clark, *Churchmen and the Condition of England, 1832–1886* (1973); K. S. Inglis, *Churches and the Working Classes in Victorian England* (1963); John Kent's *The Age of Disunity* (1966), and his more recent *Holding the Fort: Studies in Victorian Revivalism* (1978).

The theory of secularization provided an intellectual starting point for this book, especially as found in Brian Wilson's *Religion in a Secular Society* (1966), and his *Contemporary Transformations of Religion* (1976); in David Martin's *The Religious and the Secular: Studies in Secularization* (1969) and *A General Theory of Secularization* (1978); in Thomas Luckmann, *The Invisible Religion: The Problem of Religion in a Modern Society* (1967); and in Peter Berger, *The Sacred Canopy: Elements of a Sociological Theory of Religion* (1967).

INDEX

314 INDEX

Browning Hall, 170–71, 202
Buddhism, 80

Caine, W. S., 44–45, 47, 111, 115–16,
140–42, 160, 165, 172, 192, 210–11,
230
Camberwell, 252
Campbell, R. J., 173–74, 244
Censuses of church attendance:
(1851), 5, 22, 35; (1886/88), 22, 35,
57; (1902), 22, 35, 177; (1927), 178
Central Hills Baptist Church, 142,
144, 145–47, 149, 247
Central South London Free Church
Council, 161; and puritanicalism,
152–54; and sabbatarianism, 163;
and the poor, 167; end of, 262–64;
infant welfare center at, 206
Chaplin, Charles, 127–28
charitable bequests, 193–94; Pedlar's
Acre, 193; Walcot Charity, 194
Charity Commission, 87
Charity Organization Society, 65–70,
198–99
Chatsworth Road Baptist Chapel, 45,
85–86, 132, 137–39, 141
children, 205–7; socialization of, —
and conversion of, 248–53, —and
liberal theology, 247–52
children's dinners, 67, 169, 197–98;
state, 198
Christ Church, Gipsy Hill, 41, 219,
254
Christ Church, North Brixton, and
National Insurance, 203–4;
parochial management of, 41; Slate
and Loan Club, 74. 203 and n
Christ Church, Southwark, 73
Christ Church, Westminster Bridge
Road (Congregationalist), 154; and
philanthropy, 69, 199; and
unemployment, 210; Benefit Club
of, 74; infant welfare center at,
206; social class of, 142; Sunday
Schools at, 81; worship at, 127–28,
145
Church, Richard, 137, 252
church attendance: and age structure,
34–35; and Boy Scouts, 215–18; and
chapel size, 46–47; and civic duty,
121, 182; and ethics, 180–82; and
morality, 109–10, 180–82, 270–71;
and nationalism, 122–23; and

parochial organization, 42–43; and
philanthropy, 108; and religious
belief, 91–92, 106–7, 126–28, 270–
71; and respectability, 107–8, 123,
270; and social control, 108–10;
and social improvement, 116, 119–
21, 180–82; and social status,
31–33, 34, 38, 272; and the young,
108; children's, 27; Christmas, 102;
Easter, 102; evening, 22, 32, 36–37;
family, 27; harvest festival, 102–3;
involuntary, 102; meaning of, 107–
10, 116, 119–21, 123, 209; middle-
class, 120, 123, 269–70; morning,
22, 32, 36–37; motives for, 270; New
Year's Eve, 102–3; occasional, 102–
3, 269–70; pattern of decline in,
7, 22, 35–47, 177–78, 272–73, —
and recruitment, 224–26, —and
social status, 36–37, —
Nonconformist, 36–37, 43, —of
twicers, 22, 35–36; sexual ratios in,
25–26, 27, 34–35; turning point in,
7, 177–78; upper-class, 122;
working-class, 93, 103–5; see
also religious behavior; decline of
religion, pattern of
churches: and entertainment, 219;
and ethics, 209; and housing, 262–
64; and middle class, 62–63, 269–
70; and morality, 109, 209; and
philanthropy, 100–101, 269; and
progress, 209; and public order,
207–9; and social control, 109–10,
113, 207–9; and social progress, 116,
119–20, 180–82, 201–2, 207–9; and
social status, 61–64; and sports,
219; and the poor, 62–73, 269; and
the working class, 269; and the
young, 218; failure of, 261–62,
264; growth of, 268; image of, 218,
264, 275; importance of, 5–7, 21–25,
48–50, 107–10, 180–82, 261–62, 264,
270–72, 275; irrelevance of, 180–82,
210–13, 272–73, 275; lack of appeal
in the 1920s of, 218–19; self-
absorption in 1920s of, 219–20;
turning point for, 7–8, 177–78,
207–9, 211–13; see also Church of
England; Nonconformity; decline
of religion; church attendance
Church of England, 4–6, 27, 48; and
Conservative Party, 157–60; and

247–52; and church unity, 152, 257–64; and civil position, 241–44, 274–75; and Conservative Party, 172; and cricket, 85–86; and ecumenical movement, 257–64; and education, 79–80, 185–86, 238–40; and entertainment, 85–86; and government growth, 164–67, 170, 173–74; and growth, 222–29; and housing reform, 166; and Liberalism, 154–55 (*see also* Progressivism; radicalism); and literature, 134–35, 235; and liturgy, 144–45; and marginality, 138, 239, 272; and middle class, 131; and militarism, 82; and new ideas, 236–38, 244, 274–75; and old age pensions, 170–71; and philanthropy, 53–58, 59–61, 67–69, 169–70; and politics, 35, 149–50, 154–55, 160–76, 254–55; and Progressivism, 149–50 (*see also* Nonconformity and social radicalism); and prosperity, 229–30, 274–75; and puritanicalism, 85–86, 153–54; and recognition, —by Church of England, 258–59, —by peers, 240–41; and recruitment, 147–49, 224–26, 274–75; and resentment of Church of England, 150–51, 258–59; and respectability, 140–41, 251–52; and sabbatarianism, 85–86, 163–64; and self-absorption, 258; and social class, 43, 130–33, 136–37; and socialism, 236; and social radicalism, 56–57, 61, 149–50, 155–57, 162, —in 1920s, 254–55; and social reform, 53–58, 89, 132, 151–52, 154–55, 162; and social status, 136–37, 229–30; and the city, 165; and theological liberalism, 244–45; and the poor, 167–69; and the state, 173–75; and the young, 83–85, 253–54, 274–75; and uniformed organizations, 82; and upward mobility, 140–41, 229–30, 236, 238–40, 251–52, 274–75; and wealth, 131; and working class, 131; and World War I, 245–46; appeal of, 272; at Oxford University, 239; causes of decline of, 130–31, 224–29, 231–37, 253, 274–75; chapel

auxiliaries of, —functional alternatives to, 240–41, —function of, 240–41; chapel size in, 46–47; corporate activism of, 55–56; crisis of generations in, 231–37; disabilities of, 48, 150–51, 185, 229–30, 258–59; evangelical, 92, — and puritanicalism, 256, —in the 1920s, 255–57; functional alternatives to, —Board of Guardians, 243–44, —local government, 241–44, —magistracy, 243–44, —school board, 241–44, —school managers, 243–44; integration of into society, 239–40; leakage of to Church of England, 112, 229–30, 233, 235, 252, 253–54; morale in, 221–23; patrons of, 112, 160; pattern of decline in, 43, 135, 224–29; significance of, 129–36, 153–54; Sunday Schools and decline of, 226–29; turning point in, 177–78, 221–23; *see also* names of chapels; Free Church Councils

North Lambeth, 28

Norwood, 30–31, 32, 44–45, 60, 132, 141

Norwood Technical Institute, 196–97

nursing, *see* medical care

old age pensions, 170–71, 203

Old Vic, 86–88, 195–96

Orwell, George, 135

Oxford, Nonconformist colleges at, 239

Parsons, Talcott, 9n, 182–84

paternalism, 111–12

Paul Report, 33, 43n

pensions, and the churches, 203

Perks, R. W., 57n, 250

philanthropy, 58–59, 100–101; and bribery, 67, 72–73, 81, 101, 199; ' and children, 114; and church attendance, 100; and the state, 203–4; and women, 64–66; meaning of, 59–61, 101, 169–70, 203–4, 269; motives for, 66–67, 88–89; professionalization of, 198–201; social functions of, 51

pluralism, 13, 18, 48, 50, 267

political parties, 23

politics, 35, 43, 149–50, 156–76; and social class, 157